FUNDAMENTALS OF
SPEECH
COMMUNICATION

FUNDAMENTALS OF
SPEECH
COMMUNICATION

The Credibility of Ideas

Bert E. Bradley
Auburn University

 Wm. C. Brown Publishers

Book Team

Editor *Stan Stoga*
Developmental Editor *Jane F. Lambert*
Production Editor *Debra DeBord*
Art Editor *Jess Schaal*
Photo Editor *Michelle Oberhoffer*
Visuals Processor *Kenneth E. Ley*

 Wm. C. Brown Publishers

President *G. Franklin Lewis*
Vice President, Publisher *George Wm. Bergquist*
Vice President, Publisher *Thomas E. Doran*
Vice President, Operations and Production *Beverly Kolz*
National Sales Manager *Virginia S. Moffat*
Advertising Manager *Ann M. Knepper*
Marketing Manager *Kathleen Nietzke*
Managing Editor, Production *Colleen A. Yonda*
Production Editorial Manager *Julie A. Kennedy*
Production Editorial Manager *Ann Fuerste*
Publishing Services Manager *Karen J. Slaght*
Manager of Visuals and Design *Faye M. Schilling*

Cover photos by: **top left** James Shaffer, **top middle** © Mike Douglas/The Image Works; **top right, bottom (both)** © James Shaffer

Cover design by Carol V. Hall

The credits section for this book begins on page 392 and is considered an extension of the copyright page.

Library of Congress Catalog Card Number: 90–80272

ISBN 0–697–08591–0

Printed in the United States of America by Wm. C. Brown Publishers, 2460 Kerper Boulevard, Dubuque, IA 52001

10 9 8 7 6 5 4 3 2

To my wife Jeanne
and my grandchildren Michael, Amanda, and Andrew

Brief Contents

Contents

Part 2 PREPARATION

Part 3 THE SPEECH

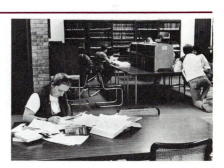

Part 4 FORMS OF COMMUNICATION

20 Evocative Speaking *331*

Preface

Fundamentals of Speech Communication: The Credibility of Ideas is written for college students enrolled in an introductory public speaking course. This book, first published in 1974, is written with a solid grounding in theoretical principles yet is balanced with suggestions for practical application. After many years of teaching public speaking, I believe that it is just as important, if not more so, to explain *why* something is done as it is to state simply that it *should* be done.

The field of speech communication is the heir of time-proven principles discovered through scholarly study by many people separated by time, geography, and culture. As in the first five editions, this classic heritage lives on, yet, where possible and appropriate in the sixth edition, a great deal of contemporary experimental research from the fields of speech, psychology, and sociology has been used to develop and support theories presented throughout the book. Why are numerous empirical studies cited and discussed? Because they are critical to help students understand that research is important in achieving credibility in their own public speaking roles. This research orientation has proven successful over the years, evidenced not only by the book's continuing popularity, but also by the numerous books that have appeared on the market taking the same approach.

Organization of the Book

Fundamentals of Speech Communication is structured to accommodate myriad course outlines. Many professors enjoy using the book as it is currently arranged, but others like to shuffle the chapters around. Each chapter is designed to stand alone so that an instructor can change the chapter sequencing without loss of continuity or clarity. The book is organized into four parts and twenty chapters.

Part 1, "Basic Considerations," discusses the fundamental principles in the speech-making process, explains what students can expect from their first public speaking experience, and provides insight into performance apprehension. Also in this first part, students are asked to consider the ethical dimensions of speech making and to learn how to become effective listeners.

Part 2, "Preparation," discusses how to approach speech making. Students are shown how to create ethos, how to understand audience attitude, how to select the subject and purpose of a speech, and how to present a speech.

Part 3, "The Speech," gets into the nuts and bolts of speech making. In this part, students learn how to structure a speech and how to begin and end it. Nonverbal and reasoning skills are also discussed. Students learn how to develop content and create meaning in their speeches.

Part 4, "Forms of Communication," presents various types of speeches, including those to inform, to persuade, and for special occasions.

Learning Aids

Each chapter begins with an *outline* to acquaint students with the material and to help them structure their study of the chapter. At the end of each chapter, a *summary* briefly reiterates the main concepts presented in the chapter, and numerous *exercises* ask students to apply what they have learned. This active participation is intended to help students better retain the material they've just read. Finally, the *notes* provide students with a plethora of research sources.

At the end of the book, students will find two invaluable *appendices*. Appendix A discusses the criticism of speeches. Appendix B contains seven sample speeches, three of which were written by experienced students. Four are speeches written by professional people. All seven should serve as models for students as they write and present their own speeches throughout the term.

Finally, this edition contains a *glossary,* which defines the most important terms from the book that students should know.

New to This Edition

Throughout the fifteen years the book has been on the market, readers have made numerous suggestions about the information they would like to see in the book. Ongoing efforts to accommodate them have resulted in material that is clear, current, and as credible as possible. The sixth edition includes the following.

1. A new chapter (chapter 10) on research. This chapter helps students, many of whom are freshmen and sophomores, locate library materials that will support and develop the ideas in their speeches.
2. A new chapter (chapter 17) on using visual aids in a speech. This chapter introduces students to various types of visual aids and explains how they should be used while giving a speech.
3. A new chapter (chapter 20) on evocative speaking. This chapter considers the speech to stimulate, as well as the occasional speeches included in the fifth edition.
4. A briefer and simpler development of the Toulmin method for organizing and presenting methods of argumentation (chapter 12)
5. A reorganization of the parts of the communication process that puts the "situation" in the first position, thus clarifying its role as the most important part of the process (chapter 1)

6. A new unit on the use of emotions in persuasive speaking (chapter 19)
7. Four new speeches in Appendix B
8. New examples and research findings

Acknowledgments

I am indebted to the following individuals, who reviewed this project and contributed to the development of this edition: Marvin De Boer, University of Central Arkansas; Madeline Keaveney, California State University, Chico; Robert E. Pruett, Wright State University; James Monroe Stewart, Tennessee Technological University; Warren Ulrich, University of Northern Iowa.

Introduction

The Value of Studying Speech Communication

Rhetorical theory has its roots deep in antiquity. Almost 3,000 years before the birth of Christ, a book written in Egypt, *The Precepts of Kagemni and Ptah-Hotep,* offered rules for speaking in certain situations. Homer's *Iliad* and *Odyssey* both record speeches made by major characters and give testimony of the esteem in which speech making was held. The development of a substantial theory of rhetoric didn't come, however, until a widespread need for the ability of self-expression arose in the fifth century B.C.

On the island of Sicily, ruled for a number of years by tyrants, the people revolted and deposed the tyrants. As a result of the confusion over rival property claims and questionable citizenship rights, many Sicilians were required to go to court to plead their own cases, in the custom of the day. From the necessity of this situation, Corax and his pupil Tisias are commonly credited with preparing what is considered to be the first manual on public speaking. They defined rhetoric as the art of persuasion, designated five parts for a persuasive speech—proem, narration, argument, subsidiary remarks, and peroration—and explained the use of probability for rhetorical arguments.

As the people of Athens, Greece, developed democratic government in the fourth century B.C., the need arose for theorists and teachers of the art of rhetoric. Teachers of public speaking, known as Sophists, became numerous. Some entered the profession for the money they could make, others because they had a sincere interest in helping people develop the ability to speak effectively. Upset by the practices of some Sophists, Plato attempted to belittle their accomplishments and the significance of rhetoric. Ultimately, however, he was forced to acknowledge its importance, and in the *Phaedrus* he set forth a theoretical skeleton of rhetoric that still can be defended. One of his students, Aristotle, then wrote *The Rhetoric,* which is as applicable today as it was then.

With these early rhetorical principles, the Greek people were able to participate more effectively in their newly created democratic society. In the approximately 2,500 years since then, thousands of critics and theorists have expanded, clarified, and improved rhetorical principles.

Those of us who understand rhetorical principles today can meet our responsibilities as citizens. We can analyze public issues, identify valid and invalid arguments, evaluate evidence, and organize the positions on current problems.

Understanding the following principles will increase your appreciation of this course. First, speakers are made, not born. Public speaking is a learned skill. This isn't to deny that some people are able to use the principles more skillfully than others, but whether that is due to inborn traits or to growing up in an environment that fostered and developed those skills is not clear. What we do know is that taking a public speaking course improves one's speaking abilities, so be assured that, at the end of this course, if you've practiced the principles presented, you'll be a better and more effective speaker.

Wendell Phillips, the renowned antislavery agitator, began his speech training at Boston Latin School, where he "distinguished himself" in public speaking. Following graduation Phillips entered Harvard College, "where . . . rhetoric and oratory were a highly important part of the curriculum, being, in fact, the only field in which students were required to take work through the entire four years."[1] After graduation Phillips entered Harvard Law School, where he continued "his training in speechmaking in the Moot Court."[2] Thus, "he had a thorough training in rhetoric, oratory, and declamation in Harvard College." In fact, one of his biographers says that this training "was the foundation of his later success as a public speaker."[3]

Woodrow Wilson's earliest ambition was to be a leader. In his view, oratory was "the first tool of leadership: 'Its object is persuasion and conviction—the control of other minds. . . .' "[4] To prepare himself as a speaker, he became a member of a debating society at Davidson College, delivering orations and participating in debates. Later, at Princeton University, he actively participated in a debating society and, while a law student at the University of Virginia, was an active member of the Jefferson debating society. Thus did he develop and hone the skills that were to make him a highly effective public speaker.

John C. Calhoun obtained his earliest formal education at the age of thirteen from a school run by his brother-in-law. A Friday afternoon debating club offered the opportunity for his first formal training in public speaking. Two years later he entered Yale University as a junior. There he participated in disputations that occurred "twice each week during the junior and senior years."[5] As a member of one of the debating societies, he had ample opportunity to improve his speaking ability.

Following graduation from Yale University, he enrolled in Judge Reeve's law school at Litchfield, Connecticut. His participation in the law school debating society, according to Calhoun, "added to his powers of extemporaneous debating."[6]

These examples are not unusual. If space permitted, many more could be added. If you want to become an effective public speaker, you must work at carefully learning the principles and diligently practicing their use.

The second rhetorical principle is that understanding speech communication principles makes you a more effective citizen in a democratic society. Edwin J. Delattre, then director of the National Humanities Faculty in Concord, Massachusetts, said in 1977 that "practice in reading, writing, speaking, listening . . . enables us to think more rigorously and to imagine more abundantly. These activities free us to possibilities that are new, at least to us, and they unbind us from portions of our ignorance about living well."[7]

With the knowledge of and ability to use the principles of public speaking, you can speak out on the issues you deem important. That gives you influence on the vital decisions made by citizens in a democracy. In addition, your knowledge of those principles enables you to recognize and publicize the fallacious and devious tactics of demagogues. Thus, not only are you able to weaken or nullify the influence of those who use illegitimate methods, you're also able to present your arguments in ethical, responsible, and valid ways. The ultimate result is government policies based on legitimate evidence, sound reasoning, and effective argumentation.

Third, improving your speaking ability will make you a more effective and confident participant in your occupation as well as in society. John M. Harbert III, a civil engineer who has business interests around the world, hires many engineers but says, "Only a select few will reach senior management." He observes that those "few aren't necessarily more knowledgeable than the others. . . . The difference is that they have developed the skill to communicate. All the knowledge in the world is useless unless you can share it."[8] In the late 1970s, an American Council on Education task force made essentially the same point. After studying higher education, they concluded that associate and bachelor degrees "should attest to at least . . . three types of accomplishment." One of those types of accomplishment, the Council said, is "competence in analytical, *communication* [italics added], quantitative, and synthesizing skills."[9]

In a recent study, two business administration professors noted that 90 percent of their respondents testified "that the ability to communicate orally was very important . . . and only one percent indicated that the ability to communicate orally was not important." One hundred percent of their respondents reported that the ability to communicate orally was "very important to success" in the following "job categories: clerical/secretarial, marketing, personnel, production/plant management, public relations, and teaching." The respondents also indicated that they spent approximately 37 percent "of their work time speaking, 19 percent listening, 16 percent writing, and 13 percent reading." These respondents strongly confirm the value of oral communication in their daily lives.[10]

One professional personnel consultant advises clients to "be sure you do not ignore communications and 'people' skills—written and oral. These are important at almost everything you do." She points out that young workers frequently find that their technical skills help them most at the beginning of their careers. Later, however, "people" skills are the most important. "Ultimately," she says, "someone with moderately good technical skills and very good people skills will outshine the techno-whizzes who have let their ability to communicate droop." She advises those who have ignored communication skills, therefore, to "develop public speaking skills."[11]

As you improve your skills, you'll gain the confidence needed to participate more actively in discussions of public policy. As you participate more, you will begin to notice that others are paying attention to your contributions and supporting positions that you advocate. You will begin to notice that your personal influence on decisions is increasing. People will not only want to hear what you have to say, they will actively seek your counsel if you have not voluntarily offered it.

The fourth principle is that developing individual citizens' speech skills is essential to democratic society. There will always be people who prefer a form of government that grants them maximum power and authority. Some of them will have sufficient speaking skills to confuse and mislead many others into helping set up a form of government that provides minimum influence for the many and maximum authority for the few. The presence of a large number of citizens who have the speaking ability to oppose these self-interested authoritarians will help persuade other less informed citizens to reject these potential self-interested leaders.

Fifth, speech is basic to social intercourse. The ability to communicate ideas orally becomes more crucial daily because most of our contacts with others involve speech communication. Our associates make judgments about our intellect, our abilities, our motivations, our knowledge, and our sociability on the basis of our spoken communication. Many surveys have shown that speaking and listening constitute more than one-half of our communication experiences each day.

Think for a minute of how you carry on relationships with other people. It's predominantly with speech. In your discussions you discover that you have mutual interests and concerns with others. A bond immediately begins to develop between you and them. Without speech, neither you nor they might have been able to discover those mutual concerns. Speech, therefore, enables you to develop relationships with other people.

But, you say, conversation is not public speaking. True, but the principles used in developing an effective speech are the same principles used in conversational speech. In good conversation you must be concerned about the topics you introduce; you have to think about how you're going to organize the information you present, what supporting materials you'll use for the ideas you introduce into the conversation, what language will be appropriate for the person you're talking to, and how you're going to use your voice to emphasize ideas and communicate meaning to your conversational partner.

Someone has said that a public speech should be an extended conversation. That position is not totally valid, but a good public speech has many of the qualities of a good conversation—and a good conversation has many of the qualities of a good speech.

Sixth, developing effective oral communication is a necessary ingredient of a liberal education. Only people who have acquired the ability to communicate orally can be considered to have completed a liberal education. In his inaugural address as president of Susquehanna University, Jonathan C. Messerli noted that any definition of a liberal education "will include the need to help students learn how to think, how to communicate, and how to have something to communicate."[12]

Notes

1. Willard Hayes Yaeger, "Wendell Phillips," in *History and Criticism of American Public Address,* ed. W. Norwood Brigance (New York: McGraw-Hill Book Co., Inc., 1943), I, 330. Used by permission.
2. *Ibid.,* I, 332.
3. *Ibid.,* I, 333.
4. Dayton David McKean, "Woodrow Wilson," in *History and Criticism of American Public Address,* ed. W. Norwood Brigance (New York: McGraw-Hill Book Co., Inc., 1943), II, 968–71. Used by permission.
5. Herbert L. Curry, "John C. Calhoun," in *History and Criticism of American Public Address,* ed. W. Norwood Brigance (New York: McGraw-Hill Book Co., Inc., 1943), II, 640–41. Used by permission.
6. *Ibid.,* II, 641–42.
7. Edwin J. Delattre, "The Humanities Can Irrigate Deserts," *The Chronicle of Higher Education,* October 11, 1977, p. 32. Excerpted from *The Chronicle of Higher Education.* Reprinted with permission.
8. *The Birmingham News,* May 7, 1979, p. 22. Used by permission.
9. *The Chronicle of Higher Education,* February 6, 1978, p. 9. Excerpted from *The Chronicle of Higher Education.* Reprinted with permission.
10. Martha H. Rader and Alan P. Wunsch, *Journal of Business Communication,* 17 (1980):35. Used by permission.
11. Ruth Walker, "Earnings: Raw Material for Your Financial Plans," *The Birmingham News,* February 24, 1985, p. 5-B.
12. Jonathan C. Messerli, "Church and State: the Limited Partners of Church-Related Colleges," *The Chronicle of Higher Education,* May 1, 1978, p. 40. Used by permission.

PART 1

BASIC CONSIDERATIONS

CHAPTER 1

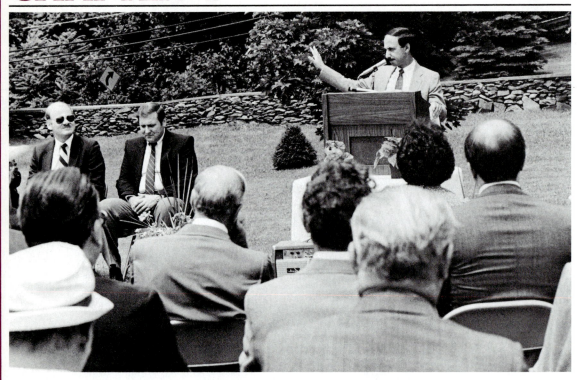

The Communication Process

Why is human communication a subject of study in so many disciplines? A moment's reflection tells us: it touches human beings daily. Through intrapersonal communication we consider a personal problem and devise a solution to it. Through interpersonal communication we tell friends about memorable experiences, a stranger obtains directions to the home of a friend, a parent lets a child know he is loved, an air traffic controller talks an airliner safely onto the runway through rain and fog. Through public communication we present to a local service club the details of a new company policy to establish better relations with the community.

What happens if communication is faulty? Sometimes very little. If you order an egg over-easy and the one you get is scrambled, little harm is done. But if an air traffic controller's report that the altitude of an airplane is one hundred feet is received as two hundred feet, a tragic crash may occur. If a parent's message of love is not received clearly by a child, a serious personality problem may develop.

Not only is communication important in conveying information, it is also an important problem-solving device. By means of arbitration, labor and management explore each other's positions and usually resolve their differences. Using small group communication, a city council analyzes the city's need for a new airport, examines various proposals, and adopts what it considers the best solution. By means of public speeches, supporters and opponents can take their cases to the voters.

Some, recognizing its importance, have suggested communication as a cure-all for solving problems in our society. Thus we hear almost daily that if only two groups could "communicate," they could resolve their problems. Without denying the importance of communication, we know it won't automatically solve every problem in our world. In some instances, it may even increase the difficulty by revealing that differences are greater than assumed.

Human communication takes many forms, such as interviews, conversations, small group communication, public communication, and mass communication. In this book, we'll concentrate on one of these forms: public communication.

Credibility and the Communicator

The main theme of this book is that successful acts of communication—whether from one to one, to a few, or to many—depend on the credibility of ideas.

When democratic government came to ancient Athens, and all citizens were given the right to address the Assembly, many found themselves unable to take advantage of the privilege because they had not been taught to speak effectively.

Soon, teachers of rhetoric, or speech communication, were numerous in Athens. Known as Sophists, some of those teachers considered the principles they taught as a means of giving effectiveness to the speaker. Aristotle—one of the most important of all writers on rhetoric—believed, on the other hand, that *speech communication principles are a means of giving effectiveness to the speaker's ideas*. That concept will be pervasive in this book.

The student of speech communication who learns the principles of creating the credibility of ideas is apt to communicate with others more effectively and to analyze the communication attempts of others more intelligently. The credibility of ideas may stem from several sources: the message content, the organization of the message, the language of the communication effort, the communication situation, the communicator's delivery, or the communicator's attributes. Credibility is seldom created by a single factor alone. Usually several factors must work together.

The remainder of this book discusses the principles by which you can establish the effectiveness and credibility of your ideas.

Definition of Communication

Communication is the process by which we develop and share meaning. This definition precludes no form of human communication—from two people developing and sharing meaning for the sheer joy of communicating, to the public communicator developing and sharing meaning in order to influence the attitudes and behaviors of others.

Figure 1.1 shows the elements that are involved in the communication process. Before discussing those elements, however, we need to clarify their roles and relationships by considering six characteristics of the process itself.

1. Communication is *dynamic* rather than static. The elements act individually, but also interact with each other. Communication is not a single act, but a number of actions that produce certain effects that in turn produce results, and so on. In any communicative effort, therefore, you must constantly be aware of the other elements involved and continually adapt to their changes.
2. It is *continuous*. There is a continuity of each of the parts. Your understanding of the world begins the day you are born and continues until the day you die. Throughout this time you communicate with others, and they communicate with you. Even as you express ideas to a listener, your mutual understanding of those ideas is developing, as a result of both the listener's response to them and your own reaction to that listener's response. Furthermore, communication goes on after you and the listener go your separate ways, as each of you continues to think about and respond to what the other said and did. There is no beginning and no end to communication. Though your death may end your role as receiver, it does not stop your role as source.
3. It is *complex*. Many naively perceive the act of speech communication as a simple one: somebody speaks and somebody listens. Therefore, they reason, communication has taken place. Initiating efforts to communicate may be easy, but achieving communication is difficult.

Figure 1.1
A model of the speech communication process.

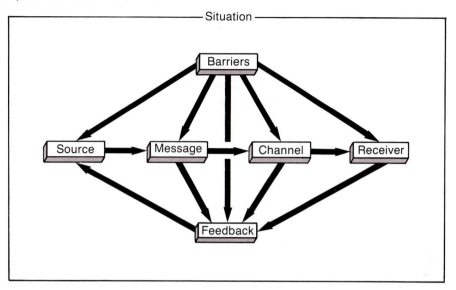

Some even speak of the transfer of ideas from one person to another. Nothing could be further from the truth. Don't expect to transfer your ideas to another; the best that can be done is to stimulate a hearer to think about your expressed meaning. Even if you cause the listener to think, you can't always make him or her think about the meaning you have in mind, because communication occurs at many levels and reflects many influences. The listener may not be stimulated to think about the meaning in the way you wanted.

4. It is *irreversible*. Just as the process of turning iron into steel can't be reversed, the process of communication can't be turned back. If you call a friend an offensive name and later apologize, the effect can't be totally erased. Once a message has been sent and received, the effect it produces becomes a factor in all later messages.

5. It is *nonsequential*. The elements in the communication process aren't necessarily in any particular order. They may occur in any sequence—linear, circular, or any other—or they may occur in a random order. The positions of the parts in the communication model in figure 1.1 are constantly interchanging. For example, the model shows the source before the message, yet the message may have been developing in the source's mind long before it is presented to another person. The placement of barriers in the figure doesn't clearly demonstrate that the barriers can start to block the message even before the source begins. Also, the figure doesn't indicate that the message and channel are

interrelated and generally are inseparable. Moreover, feedback can begin before the source starts a message, although the figure doesn't show this.

6. It is *unrepeatable*. We can't re-create an act of communication. Since participants are changed because of it, they can't repeat the process because they bring altered meanings to any later acts of communication. If you miss a class lecture, for example, there is no way you can get the same information; no classmates' notes will have all the information, nor will the professor be able to repeat the lecture for you because the verbal and nonverbal interactions that came from your classmates will be missing. As Heraclitus said long ago, a person can't step into the same river twice because both are different the second time. Because other factors in an act of communication don't remain static, their changes also prevent the repetition of communication.[1]

In short, communication is a process consisting of a number of independent and interdependent steps leading to the attainment of an end. In speech communication that end is the developing and sharing of some specific meaning. Never let the simplicity of the end obscure the complexity of the process.

Elements of the Speech Communication Process

The complex process of speech communication must be understood if effective, meaningful communication is to occur. We can grasp the process better if we break it into its constituent parts and diagram them in a model as in figure 1.1. Are we to interpret this model literally? No, it is *analogous* with the communication process, not a replica of it. We must also keep in mind that the speech communication process is different from certain biological processes in which the parts cannot be interchanged and must occur in a fixed sequence. Understand that, in some important ways, we distort the communication process when we discuss the elements in isolation. Basically there are seven elements in the process: (1) the situation, (2) the source, (3) the message, (4) the channel, (5) the receiver, (6) barriers, and (7) feedback.

The Situation   We'll begin with the situation, since it is the single most influential element in the speech communication process. It not only binds the other elements together, but also largely fixes their characteristics. The situation often determines who the speaker will be. On the floor of the Senate, no one except a senator or the chaplain can be a speaker. In a local church on Sunday morning, certain areas in the church may be limited to the clergy. Other situations are less structured in determining the speaker, but the situation, to a large extent, limits who will be permitted or motivated to speak. The kind of people who will be present also is influenced by the situation. Few nonchurch members, and still fewer atheists, will be present at the Sunday morning church service. Democratic political rallies attract few Republicans; Republican political rallies attract few Democrats.

Even the message is affected by the situation. It may affect what is or isn't said, how the message is organized, what language is appropriate. A message inappropriate to the situation may have a negative effect instead of the positive effect it would have in an appropriate situation.

Our mood is affected by the situation. Your mood at an orientation lecture is different from that of students in a classroom listening to a lecture, and both will be quite different from the one at a football rally. If you fail to adapt your message to the situation, you stand little chance of being a credible speaker.

The situation affects the polarization of an audience. Polarization occurs when listeners focus their attention intensely on the speaker. An auditorium affects polarization by causing listeners to sit facing the speaker, whereas listeners standing at an outdoor speech may face in several directions easily. Music, especially martial music, preceding the speech facilitates focusing attention on the speaker. Decoration of the meeting place with colored bunting, organizational symbols, or nationalistic symbols helps in polarizing an audience. A podium that puts the speaker above the level of the listeners, or lighting that directs the focal point to the speaker, makes it easier for the listeners to attend to the speaker. On the other hand, a barren-looking room or one that has a wide, open space between the listeners and the speaker makes it more difficult for polarization to occur.

The channel chosen for the transmission of the message depends on the situation. Without an amplifying system, a face-to-face speech cannot be given to an audience of fifty thousand in a football stadium. Yet the use of an amplifying system to aid in talking to an audience of twenty-five in a small room appears ludicrous.

Feedback is influenced by the situation. If there are fifty thousand people present, it is impossible for the speaker to perceive most of the responses of the hearers. If the speech is given from a practically empty studio to a television audience, there is no feedback for the speaker to perceive. If the speech is given to a class of graduate students who have some expertise on the topic, the speaker will probably receive much highly sophisticated feedback from listeners.

The Source

The source in speech communication is the person who makes the decision to communicate. As a communicator you may decide to communicate with yourself (intrapersonal speech communication), with another person (interpersonal speech communication), or with a number of other persons (public communication). You may have one or more of three intents: (1) *to inform,* as when you explain to a neighbor how to clean his car's carburetor; (2) *to entertain,* as when you tell an acquaintance about an interesting and humorous experience; (3) *to persuade,* as when you explain to a friend reasons for majoring in engineering. In some instances you may have more than one purpose because you are talking to more than one audience. A labor leader explaining to the union members how an impending strike will be carried out if negotiations break down is attempting to inform them. If television cameras are present to carry these remarks to the nation, however, the labor leader may be trying to persuade management and the public that the union is serious and unyielding in its contract demands.

You determine the purpose of a speech. Even if you give a speech to inform or entertain and the listeners end up being persuaded, the purpose of the speech is still to inform or to entertain. Or you may give a speech to persuade, but the listeners may only be informed. In some instances your purpose may be to persuade, but the speech is given as an informative one. Although many informative and persuasive speeches use communicative principles similarly, there are some speeches in which the principles are applied in different ways, as explained in chapters 12 and 15.

You are limited to the information you have accumulated on the topic through experience and investigation. Your ability to generate a message is further restricted by your perceptions, thoughts, and feelings.

Significantly influencing the impact of the message will be characteristics that make you appealing or unappealing to the particular audience being addressed. If you have a poor image with a specific group of listeners, change or explain it. If you have a good image, take advantage of it.

Determine the meaning you want to convey to the particular receivers. Your **The Message**
message should consist of your ideas, attitudes, and values. It can be communicated in a number of different forms: *written*—an essay, letter, poem, drama, political pamphlet; *oral*—a conversation, interview, group discussion, debate, informal speech, formal speech; *nonverbal*—music, painting, sculpture, and action. From one point of view, these forms are channels for a message. In fact, however, the form and the ideas are united, and together become the message.

Speech is the most proficient form of communication. Horowitz and Newman had forty subjects speak and write for two minutes after thinking about a given topic for thirty seconds. The results showed that spoken communication produced significantly more ideas and subordinate ideas than written communication, even when the time limit for writing was extended to twelve minutes.[2] When speaking was compared with handwriting, typing, and stenotyping, it again proved more proficient.[3]

You can also use nonverbal communication, which is meaning created by bodily action, facial expression, vocal inflection, and other nonlanguage sounds. Whether you want to or not, you usually communicate nonverbally, and it may be more important than the verbal communication.

We frequently force a receiver to resolve conflicting verbal and nonverbal cues. The response to these different cues will vary according to such factors as the age group of the receiver and the sex of the source. One group of experimenters found that children believe verbal cues more than nonverbal ones. Children interpreted comments more negatively than adults when adult women made critical comments while smiling. The children tended to ignore the nonverbal cue, the smile, whereas it caused adults to interpret the message as neutral. All subjects, children and adult, responded more to the conflicting nonverbal cues of a woman than to similar cues from a man. Bugental and her colleagues pointed out "that if a woman frowned and said something complimentary in a pleasant tone of voice, her sincerity was doubted—her communication was rated as neutral at best and was described as sarcastic." When the same cues were given by a man, the message "was rated positively" and he was described "as sincere or complimentary."[4]

This book will help you learn to communicate by conveying ideas mainly in the form of an informal or a formal oral message, although many of the principles are applicable in other forms of communication. Put your message together so the listeners attend to your ideas, believe them, and respond in the desired way. Be concerned about your specific ideas, organize them clearly, choose precise language, and present the message so the listener focuses on your meaning.

You may consider the channel for speech communication from two points of **The Channel**
view. First, the channel is the means by which you transmit an oral message to a listener. Two senses are involved—hearing and sight. Air waves carry

vibrations created by your voice to the outer ear of the listener. These vibrations create nerve impulses that travel to the listener's brain for interpretation into your original sounds and words. Meanwhile, light waves carry your image and actions to the receiver's eye. Nerve impulses then travel to the visual center of the brain, where the sensation becomes perception. Thus these aural and visual cues transmit the communicative stimuli from you to the receiver.

Second, the channel is the type of speech communication you use. You may speak in a face-to-face situation with no artificial aids, in a face-to-face situation with the aid of an amplifying system, from a radio studio to an unseen audience who cannot see you, from a TV studio to an unseen audience who can see you, or to a live audience with the message being transmitted by radio or TV to an unseen audience.

Whatever channel you use to transmit the message, adapt your speaking to make the most effective use of the particular channel. If you're using the telephone, you may have no concern for eye contact and bodily action. In a face-to-face situation, however, direct eye contact and effective use of bodily action are necessary.

The Receiver

A receiver is any person who perceives the message. It may not be the person for whom the message was intended. Determine who the receivers will be and what are their characteristics: age, sex, education, economic status, characteristics in common, memberships in organizations, occupational backgrounds, concerns about contemporary problems, amount of information on the topic of the message—as much as, more than, or less than you. Will the majority be opposed, neutral, or favorable toward your topic and purpose? If opposed, will they be strongly or mildly opposed? If favorable, will they be strongly or mildly favorable? If neutral, what kind of neutrality is it? Neutrality for some means they're undecided; they haven't made up their minds. These listeners may be moved to a new position. Neutrality may be a committed position based on careful deliberation. McGinnies found, for example, that many Japanese students were committed to a position of neutrality on the issue of the cold war between the United States and the USSR. This wasn't an attitude held because they didn't know or didn't care, but a firmly committed attitude arrived at and held deliberately.[5]

With the above information in hand, decide how much and what kind of information to include and how to convey it to the listeners in order to achieve your purpose.

Unless the people for whom the message is intended are listening, communication will be either nonexistent or distorted. Those who can and do listen will attempt to decode the message. Words will be interpreted to have a particular meaning, which may or may not be the same as you intended. Or the listener may see certain actions and attach a specific meaning to them. The meaning attached can vary from person to person and group to group.

After the receiver has decoded the message and decided what the intended meaning is, he or she makes some kind of response to it: he or she may ignore it, reject it, applaud it, boo it, behave in opposition to it, or behave in accord with it.

Barriers sometimes interfere with the communicative process. What are barriers? They are any factors that cause an incorrect meaning, or no meaning, to be communicated to a receiver.

Barriers to Communication

In most cases you want to communicate a meaning that accurately reflects both the reality of the topic under discussion and your attitude toward that reality. Sometimes, however, you're prevented from perceiving the reality of a situation because of your personal biases or attitudes, ignorance or lack of some information, or inability to perceive the events. For example, you may believe that all Southerners are racists, so when you meet someone with a Southern dialect, you may avoid that person even though she or he is not a bigot. On other occasions, you may have arrived at a meaning that is consistent with reality, but be unable to communicate that meaning to a listener because of an inadequate vocabulary. Or you may possess certain characteristics that cause the listener to focus on you rather than on the message. All these things can cause barriers in the source because they prevent effective communication.

How do you create barriers? You may organize the message so poorly the listener simply can't comprehend its meaning. You may develop the ideas so poorly the listener finds them unbelievable. You may choose a word, such as "ain't," that stirs in the listener reactions detrimental to your purpose, or you may select an ambiguous word that leaves the listener confused or with an understanding different from the one intended. You may deliver the message in such a way that the listener can't focus on its substance but is distracted by irrelevant and meaningless actions.

Interference may occur in the channel of the communication—a baby crying in the audience, a loud sound outside the room, a room that is too hot. Anything that interferes with the receiver's perception of the source, such as a lectern that is too high for the speaker or an improperly used microphone, can become an interference in the channel. For example, some speakers turn alternately away from and toward the microphone, causing the loudness level to change drastically. Some become so enamored of the mike that they talk to it rather than to the listeners. Some set up distracting noises by handling the mike, smacking their lips, pounding on the lectern, or rattling notes close by—all sounds that are magnified by the public address system.

Barriers may exist within the listeners. A person who had little sleep the night before may be unable to concentrate on your statements. One who had an unpleasant argument at home before coming to the speech may relive that controversy instead of attending to you. An individual may be in pain and unable to focus on your thoughts. Obviously, these problems are beyond your control, but they are barriers that the listener can often eliminate or overcome. Other barriers may exist in the listener, however, which you can affect. Some listeners may have had unpleasant experiences that certain words cause them to recall; you can avoid those words if you have previously analyzed the audience and are aware of this situation. Some may react unfavorably to incorrect grammar, nonfluencies, or a monotonous voice.

Feedback

Feedback refers to the listeners' reactions and responses that you perceive. By adapting to this feedback, you're able to communicate more precisely. Feedback begins when you go in front of an audience, even before you say anything, and continues until you and the audience part. In many instances feedback continues even after you and the listeners have gone to other activities. Such feedback comes in the form of printed comment, letters, and public opinion polls, which provide information about your efforts.

Some have described the communicative process as circular—the speaker verbalizes certain thoughts and ideas, the listener responds, the speaker perceives the response, the speaker verbalizes new thoughts adapted to the listener's response, and the cycle continues. Dance, however, has suggested that the communicative process is not circular, but helical. He means that the response of the listener never finds you, the speaker, where you were when you stated the idea that caused the listener's response. You have moved on, and since the feedback never returns to exactly the same point as that from which the original statement began, the process cannot be circular. Dance conceives of the process as ever moving to a higher plateau; consequently, he describes it as a helical or spiral process, as shown in figure 1.2.[6]

Basic Considerations

Figure 1.2

A helical spiral as a representation of human communication. Dance's helical spiral graphically demonstrates that communication is an on-going process, as feedback from the listener returns to a speaker who has moved on from the point at which the feedback was instigated. From Human Communication Theory: Original Essays, *edited by Frank E. X. Dance. Copyright © 1967 by Holt, Rinehart & Winston, Inc. Reprinted by permission of Holt, Rinehart & Winston, Inc.*

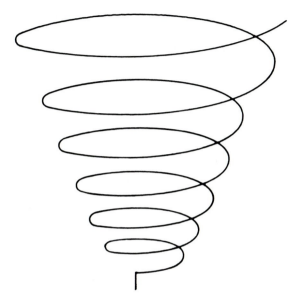

If we keep in mind that it is merely an analogy to clarify the communicative process, then viewing the process as helical can be helpful, because this model does stress that feedback always finds the speaker at a different point from that to which the feedback pertains. However, it is misleading to let the helical model make us believe that communication is always moving to a higher plateau, for feedback can force you, the speaker, backward, instead of letting you spiral upward.

What can cause you to regress? You may misinterpret the feedback. The listener's action may not be a response to you or your message. For example, you may see a key member of the audience lean over and put his head in his hands. Although the action may simply reflect fatigue on the part of the receiver, you may interpret the action to mean you have just said something the listener dislikes. A frown may indicate disapproval of what you are saying, or it may mean that the listener just experienced the pangs of indigestion. Even if the response is to your message, you may not recognize it as such or may misinterpret its meaning. A listener's whispered comment, which causes the neighbor to smile and nod, may be interpreted as a favorable reaction. The listener, however, may have said, "I think he's crazy," to which the second listener nodded agreement.

Whether feedback causes communication to advance or regress, it is an important part of the process. It helps you perceive whether your ideas are being understood, accepted, or attended to. You can't afford to be ignorant of, or to ignore, feedback from listeners.

Summary

Although communication is not a panacea for the world's ills, it's extremely important because it permits people to transmit instructions, convey feelings and attitudes, and cope in a rational way with problems that confront us.

The most effective communicator develops credibility to aid in communication, the process by which we develop meaning and share it with others.

To better control our communication, we must understand the communication process itself, which is dynamic, continuous, complex, irreversible, nonsequential, and unrepeatable. There are seven elements in the communicative process: (1) The situation, (2) the source, (3) the message, (4) the channel, (5) the receiver, (6) barriers, and (7) feedback. But we must remember that no part can be entirely isolated from the others. With an appreciation and understanding of these elements, you can proceed rationally to improve your communicative efforts.

Exercises

1. Analyze the classroom in which you are to speak. Describe how you would arrange it for maximal and minimal support to aid in establishing your credibility.
2. Describe barriers to effective communication that exist in your classroom situation. Explain how you as a speaker plan to cope with them to prevent their affecting your credibility.
3. Analyze the receivers in your classroom: What attributes of theirs must you consider for your next speaking assignment? In what ways will you adapt to these characteristics to improve your credibility?
4. Attend a public lecture on campus. Describe the feedback available to the speaker. Explain in what ways this speaker used it to enhance his or her credibility and in what ways he or she failed to use it.
5. Using the same speech, describe the content of the speech. What kinds of supporting materials did the speaker use? statistics? examples? personal experiences? testimony? opinion polls? Were sources of the content provided? Did you feel that the content was credible? Why or why not?
6. Analyze a communicative effort of one of your classmates. Which elements of the communicative process did this classmate consider in establishing credibility? Which did he or she not consider?

Notes

1. Although there are differences, this discussion of the communicative process relies heavily upon that of Dean C. Barnlund. He believes communication is circular; I believe it is nonsequential. See D. C. Barnlund, "A Transactional Model of Communication," in K. K. Sereno and C. D. Mortensen, eds., *Foundations of Communication Theory* (New York: Harper & Row, 1970), pp. 83–102.
2. M. W. Horowitz and J. B. Newman, "Spoken and Written Expression: An Experimental Analysis," *Journal of Abnormal and Social Psychology* 68 (1964):640–47.
3. M. W. Horowitz and A. Berkowitz, "Structural Advantage of the Mechanism of Spoken Expression as a Factor in Differences in Spoken and Written Expression," *Perceptual and Motor Skills* 19 (1964):619–25.
4. D. E. Bugental, J. W. Kaswan, and L. R. Love, "Perception of Contradictory Meanings Conveyed by Verbal and Nonverbal Channels," *Journal of Personality and Social Psychology* 16 (1970):647–55.
5. E. McGinnies, "Studies in Persuasion: III. Reactions of Japanese Students to One-Sided and Two-Sided Communications," *Journal of Social Psychology* 70 (1966):87–93.
6. F. E. X. Dance, *Human Communication Theory* (New York: Holt, Rinehart & Winston, 1967), pp. 295–96.

CHAPTER 2

The First Speech

In a short time, before you've had a chance to read much of this book, you'll be asked to prepare and deliver your first speech. You may be unduly concerned about this first speech. For many, it will be your first effort and you may not feel ready to prepare and give a speech because you've never given one before. Undoubtedly you've given parts of a speech before. For example, you have told someone of an exciting, boring, or unusual experience you have had. In relating that experience you used some of the same principles used in making a speech. Once you realize that you have often used many of the principles before, you'll understand that giving a speech isn't such a difficult task. The important thing is to learn the principles that make a speech different from relating a single experience. This chapter will explain how to prepare and present that first speech.

Approach the First Speech with a Positive Attitude

First, recognize the benefits that this speech will have for you. It will permit the other students in class to get to know you better. They can see how you think, how you react to unexpected happenings in the situation, whether you have a sense of humor, or what experiences you have had. It will give you an opportunity to affect their thought processes. You can introduce them to new information that will affect how they think about the topic on which you speak. Never overlook the influence that an effective speaker has on listeners' beliefs and attitudes.

Second, this first speech will begin to develop and hone the public speaking skills that will be so valuable to you for the rest of your life. The principles you learn will help you to argue cogently a political position; how to explain clearly a procedure; how to present enthusiastically a new idea to a colleague or supervisor.

Select a Subject for Your Speech

First, select the subject area from which you'll draw your specific topic for the speech. Make a list of subjects you're interested in, then check those on which you've had experience. Your best choice will generally be an area in which you've had experience—scouting, cheerleading, student government, or political campaigns. Next, consider your potential audience. Since your classmates will be your audience, it won't be difficult to ascertain the information you need about their interests, experiences, and knowledge. This will be one of the most homogeneous audiences you'll ever address. Learn everything you can about your classmates and identify appropriate subjects. The final factor in selecting a subject is the occasion, which for you is a classroom assignment. Be sure you've met the requirements stated by your professor, such as type of speech, time limits, and so on.

Now that you've considered your interests, knowledge, and experience; your listeners' interests, knowledge, and experience; and the occasion of the speech, you're ready to select your subject.

Perhaps you had experience as a cheerleader in high school, and you decide that would be a good topic to speak on. Think about the experiences (funny, exciting, happy, sad) you had as a cheerleader. Think about your attitudes and convictions toward cheerleading. As a result of these thoughts, you may decide that you don't want to tell your listeners how to be a cheerleader, however, because probably none of them will ever be one. Give your classmates some information that will be meaningful. Focus on an aspect of cheerleading that will help them understand what cheerleaders do or what they accomplish. Or focus on facets of cheerleading that are relevant to people in other occupations, such as teachers, salespersons, ministers, or nurses.

One of the values of this first speech is to let your classmates begin to understand and know something about you. For example, you might decide to tell them something about what you learned from cheerleading.

Develop Your Purpose and Supporting Materials

First, phrase a sentence that tells specifically what you're going to say about your subject. This is called a purpose (or thesis) sentence, topic sentence, or central idea sentence. It tells the audience specifically what you're going to talk about. Phrase it in the following way: "This morning I want to talk to you about three things I learned from cheerleading."

Second, consider the main ideas to develop the purpose sentence. In this case, you might decide there were six things you learned from cheerleading: leadership, sportsmanship, cooperation, imagination, friendliness, enthusiasm. Realize you can't develop six main ideas in the time allotted for your first speech, so develop only three. Select the ideas you're going to use, phrase each into a complete sentence. These will be the main points in the body of your speech.

Third, develop supporting materials for your main points. Three types are: *facts, statistics,* and *testimony.* Methods of developing them are: definition, comparison, description, classification, narration, restatement, and explanation. These give life and vitality to your ideas. Narration tells a story, and stories are what people like to hear, because they give flesh and blood to your points. Stories also hold the attention of listeners because people are usually curious to know how a story will end.

Define your points, then give an example of each. Find testimony supporting any of your points. Go to the library and find your topic in relevant sources. Check your subject in the card catalog for any books that deal with it. Next, check the *Readers' Guide to Periodical Literature* and the *Social Science Index* for periodical articles on your subject. These indexes should provide all the information you need. Focus on personal experiences as the primary method of developing each point. This should increase your credibility because you'll establish personal experience with the topic, as well as research.

Organize the Speech

When you've completed the above three phases, you'll have the purpose sentence and the body of your speech. Add an introduction and conclusion. The outline of these four parts will look like this:

   I. Introduction
  II. Purpose Sentence: This morning I want to explain to you three qualities that cheerleading taught me.
 III. Body of the speech
    A. Cheerleading taught me leadership.
      1. Definition of leadership.
      2. Testimony concerning leadership.
      3. Personal experience with leadership.
    B. Cheerleading taught me sportsmanship.
      1. Definition of sportsmanship.
      2. Example of sportsmanship.
      3. Personal experience with sportsmanship.
    C. Cheerleading taught me imagination.
      1. Definition of imagination.
      2. Example of imagination.
      3. Personal experience with imagination.
 IV. Conclusion

    After completion of the body of your speech, you're ready to prepare an introduction and conclusion. You can't prepare them earlier because you won't know what to introduce and conclude until you have completed the body of the speech.

In the introduction, your primary purpose is to get the attention of the listeners. You can do one of several things: explain the relevance of this topic to your audience; relate a memorable experience; describe the importance of the topic for you or your listeners; or relate a humorous event. Keep it brief, to the point, and well prepared. Your first and most important impression on the listeners occurs here.

In the conclusion, summarize what you've said, focus on a humorous aspect, or challenge the listeners to use the information. Keep the conclusion brief, relevant, and well prepared. The conclusion provides the final impression for the listeners and will greatly affect their reaction to your speech.

Develop Language

Don't be misled by the heading of this unit. You shouldn't develop, in the sense of fixing permanently or even semipermanently, the language you'll use to present the speech. Develop several ways of phrasing the ideas you're going to present. On occasion you may want to create a strikingly original way of expressing your idea, and use that sequence of words each time you present the speech. Just don't let it begin to sound memorized. Generally, avoid a habitual use of language in presenting the same speech.

Be primarily concerned about two aspects of language: familiarity and clarity. Primarily use words you're accustomed to using. Don't, however, use incorrect or inappropriate words, even if you use them in other situations. Don't try to impress your listeners by using "big" or unfamiliar words. Use your own vocabulary that is appropriate. The words you're accustomed to using will flow more easily and give a sense of naturalness to your speech.

Choose words that clearly express your ideas. Think of synonyms that convey the same idea, so you'll have a choice of words when you give the speech. If you stress familiarity and clarity of language, you'll have no problems in communicating in this first speech.

Practicing the Speech

Prepare delivery of your speech by practicing it. Don't write out the speech. Using your prepared outline, practice talking about each of the points that you have decided to include in the speech. A speech that sounds memorized has little chance of being effective. Moreover, it is difficult to make adjustments and adaptations with a memorized speech. Each time you practice the speech, vary the wording so you don't memorize it. By using different wording each time you practice the speech, you'll remain calm even if you forget a particular word when you actually give the speech. Since you'll have used different words each time you practiced, you'll have several words to choose from. When you deliver your speech to the audience, you won't have to worry about forgetting what you want to say, because you'll have a reservoir of words for each of your main ideas. As a result, your language will have spontaneity; it won't sound memorized. You'll sound as though you're conversing with the audience.

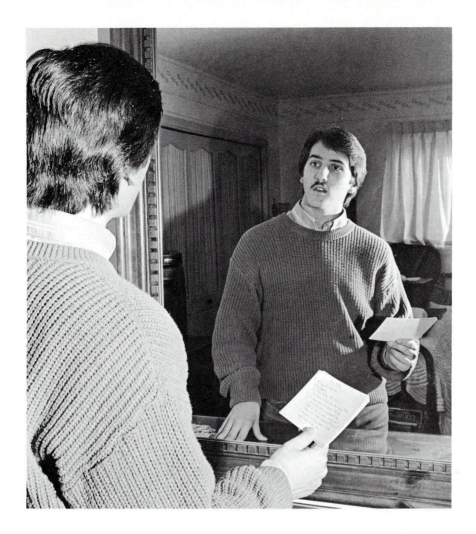

To practice your speech, prepare key word outline on four-by-six cards. Three-by-five note cards are less desirable because they hold so little information you must have a large number. The resultant shuffling of the cards gives listeners the impression you're heavily dependent on your notes. By practicing from a key word outline, you'll naturally vary your language each time you practice. That will help you develop a conversational mode of delivery, reduce your dependence on your notes, and provide a larger number of words to choose from to express your ideas.

Delivering the Speech

Your first appearance in front of the audience is extremely important. Walk purposely and confidently to the lectern, lay your notes on it, look at your listeners, and begin your speech in a confident tone of voice. If you don't have a lectern, go to the center of the podium, look at your listeners, and then begin your speech. Remember, your personality and character are important. They can have as strong an impact on your listeners as any words and ideas you utter, so don't be afraid to reveal them to your listeners.

Speaking Behavior

Maintain eye contact with your listeners. Look them straight in the eyes, not at their foreheads or chins or chests. Avoid nervous mannerisms: shifting weight from side to side, playing with note cards, saying "uh," putting your hands in your pockets and taking them out, rattling coins or keys in pockets. Don't influence the listeners negatively by apologizing for your speech effort. If your apology is for something you should have done and didn't, then the apology is insufficient. If it is for something over which you had no control, then it is irrelevant. In either case, no apology is necessary.

Use plenty of signposts in the speech to tell your listeners where you've been and where you're going. These are important because listeners can't go back over the material the way a reader can. Examples of signposts are: "My first point . . ." "Let me move on to my second point," "however," "nevertheless," "furthermore," "moreover," "therefore," "consequently." Examples of summaries are: "I have presented three reasons . . ." "The point I have tried to make is . . ." "Let me summarize. . . ."

Voice

Speak in a firm, clear voice. If the listeners can't hear you, you're not communicating with them. Vary the pitch, rate, and loudness in keeping with the meaning of your statement. Avoid memorizing the speech during practice.

Use a conversational tone. The resulting spontaneity and intimacy will contribute to improved communication. Using a conversational mode doesn't mean you should speak as you do in conversation but that you should use the qualities characteristic of effective conversation.

First, good conversationalists must adjust to the public speaking situation. Volume must be increased; gestures enlarged so they are easily seen; and speaking rate adapted to the acoustics of the room.

Second, some people are poor conversationalists—they speak too low, speak in a monotone, muffle their articulation, use too many vocalized pauses, speak too slowly or too fast. If these ineffective methods are used in speaking to an audience, the speaker will be just as ineffective as he or she is in conversation.

What, then, are those qualities that are present in effective conversation? James Winans says,

> You will have carried over into your public delivery the most desirable
> qualities of conversational speaking when you maintain upon the platform—
>
> 1. Full realization of the content of your words as you utter them, and
> 2. A lively sense of communication.[1]

Directness, enthusiasm, absence of self-consciousness, a communicative attitude—these are the qualities of the "conversational mode." If you move mechanically through words you have memorized or written on note cards, you often lose the vitality of tone that is present when you turn your thoughts into words as you proceed through the speech. Language becomes more informal when you use a "conversational mode." More personal pronouns—*I, you, me, we, our, your*—are used, contributing to the impression that you are talking directly to each listener.

Conclusion

The conclusion is the final impression you leave with your listeners. Make it a good one! Prepare it carefully. Avoid notes, so you can look directly at the members of your audience during the final moments of your speech. Don't rush. When you have completed your conclusion, pause briefly before leaving the podium. Then walk confidently and positively to your seat. Don't, by facial expressions or bodily actions, indicate displeasure with your effort. The listeners may think you have done an outstanding job, so don't influence them negatively after the speech is over. Unless you requested to speak to the group, don't say "thank you" at the end of your speech. In most cases, any statement of appreciation should come from those whom you addressed. Sometimes, however, a "thank you" maintains audience rapport and appreciation for the speaker.

Criticism of the Speech

Following completion of your speech or a group of speeches, there will probably be a period of oral criticism by your professor and your classmates. Depending on your attitude and that of your classmates, this can be a constructive or traumatic experience. Listen positively to the comments. Realize that most of the people in the class will be sympathetic to your efforts. Recognize that critics are able to perceive things you can't. If they identify problems you don't know how to correct, ask for suggestions. Consider this criticism period as a time to begin preparation for the next speech. Write down the important comments so you can begin working on them immediately.

Finally, consider this first speech an opportunity—to get to present yourself to your classmates, to begin to develop speech skills that will serve you for the rest of your life, and to read and react to the reactions of your listeners.

Summary

In developing your first speech, maintain a positive attitude. Keep in mind that your information is new to your classmates. Select a subject you know something about and on which you've had experience. Develop a specific purpose, identify main ideas, and support them with as much personal experience as possible. Organize the speech into four main parts: introduction, purpose sentence, body, and conclusion. Consider the language: Be sure you've chosen words that communicate your main ideas accurately and clearly. Practice the speech until you're comfortably familiar with it. Deliver the speech confidently in a conversational tone with good eye contact and effective body actions. Accept criticism after the speech positively and consider this criticism period as a beginning of preparation for the next speech.

Exercises

1. Read at least one of the student speeches in Appendix B. Identify the elements that made the speech appropriate to that student. Do you feel the student knew what he or she was talking about? What made you feel that way? Do you consider the speech an effective one? Why or why not?
2. Read one of the nonstudent speeches. Does the speaker use any of the methods that the student speaker did? Does the speaker use any methods not used by the student speaker? Do you consider the speech a good one? Why or why not?

Note

1. J. A. Winans, *Speech-Making* (New York: D. Apppleton-Century Co., 1938), p. 25.

CHAPTER 3

Understanding Performance Apprehension

Seventy-five percent of the respondents in a recent poll identified giving a speech as a cause of social anxiety, the second highest ranking out of ten events.[1] In fact, a look at the ten events reveals that all ten involve and depend on communication. For most beginning speakers, performance apprehension, or stage fright as it is popularly called, is a well-known but little understood phenomenon. The purpose of this chapter is to dispel the mystery of performance apprehension and assist in your mental preparation for a communicative effort. An understanding of the nature and causes of performance apprehension will aid you in coping with, intelligently using, and benefiting from this psychological and physiological reaction.

The Term *Stage Fright* Is a Misnomer

An understanding of stage fright begins with the knowledge that the term *stage fright* is unclear. As a matter of fact, speech teachers have been unable to devise a clear, consistent, meaningful definition of stage fright. Much experimental research has been conducted on this problem, but even here researchers have failed to define the term. "The measuring instrument in a stage fright experiment is not only the measurement of the stage fright, it is the definition as well."[2] Three measuring instruments have been used to assess "the amount of fright a speaker says he has, the amount his audience says he has, and the amount a meter says he has." The important fact is that these three instruments have very little relationship to one another. They "operate with only moderate interdependence during the course of a public speech."[3]

Stage fright is a misnomer because the inclusion of the term *fright* implies fear is present. Some have even defined the reaction as fear. This book contends, however, that a person with so-called stage fright is not experiencing fear, but anxiety or apprehension about the performance. The speaker's personal feelings about the quality of the speaking effort and its outcome causes anxiety or tension. Psychologists Shaffer and Shoben clearly differentiate between fear and anxiety:

> The feeling-tone of anxiety is much like that of fear, but the two emotions can be distinguished in a number of ways. Typically, fear is evoked by a present and external stimulus, such as a ferocious dog or a narrowly escaped accident. Anxiety usually relates to the anticipation of a future situation, an apprehension of a probable pain, loss, or threat. Also anxiety is most often stimulated by qualities of a person himself rather than by external events. A boy *fears* a larger bully but has *anxiety* about his own strength, competence, or acceptance in the group. Anxiety is therefore a relatively late-emerging emotional pattern, since it depends upon some ability to foresee the future and upon some degree of socially acquired evaluation of one's self.[4]

In this book, then, stage fright will be defined as *a normal form of anxiety, or emotional tension, occurring in anyone confronted with a situation in which the performance is important and the outcome uncertain.* It should be noted that this definition doesn't restrict the reaction to speakers or to certain speakers. What we are really talking about is *performance apprehension.*

Performance Apprehension Is Not Peculiar to Certain People

Unfortunately, the terms *stage fright* or *communication apprehension* imply that this reaction is an abnormal one and peculiar to certain people on the stage—public speakers and actors—or persons involved in some act of communication. The truth is the reaction is not abnormal and is not peculiar to any group; it is found in many people—athletes before an athletic event, actors and musicians before a performance, teachers before a class, job applicants before an interview. In 1988, professional golfer Paul Azinger, the Player of the Year in 1987, led after the third round of the PGA National Championship. He said, "I've been here before. . . . I'll be nervous tomorrow."[5] A former professional golfer, Dennis Walters, who became a paraplegic as a result of a freak golf cart accident, now gives exhibitions sitting on a special seat attached to a golf cart. Walters reports: "I still get nervous before a show, but it's a good kind of nervous."[6]

Malcolm Boyd, who has written more than twenty books, including *Are You Running with Me, Jesus?* and *The Underground Church,* reports: "I used to have a fear of public speaking. When I had to say anything in a meeting or had to introduce other people, I sweated and couldn't concentrate. . . . I got myself invited as a speaker to various community meetings. . . . After a half-dozen such speaking engagements—agonizing for me—I began to enjoy public speaking. When I was asked to address 10,000 men and women at a national convention, the experience was both successful and personally satisfying."[7]

"In the spring of 1989, Jimmy Johnson, the highly successful football coach of the University of Miami Hurricanes, was named the head coach of the Dallas Cowboys professional team.

"Jimmy Johnson was nervous. His hands sweated and his mouth was dry.

"He was about to walk into a room of 83 professional football players as their boss, replacing one of the biggest names in the game, Tom Landry.

" 'I just tried to be myself,' Johnson said. . . . Things weren't as uneasy as I thought they were going to be before I stepped in there.' "[8]

The chief pilot of Air Force One, the plane that flew President Reagan wherever he wanted to go, responded to questions about his job: "You bet I was nervous the first time I took it up," he said, "and I still am. Every time. But if I wasn't, it would be time to get out. I have butterflies and if I didn't, that means I'm not concentrating. That person in the back is the most important man in the world."[9]

Rex Harrison, who was an actor on stage and screen for more than sixty-three years, won many honors for his acting ability. Yet, " 'Every night,' he says, admitting that it never gets any better, 'I suppose if you don't have stage fright you go on like a flat pancake.' He's philosophical. 'You deal with it,' he says. 'It's your profession.' "[10]

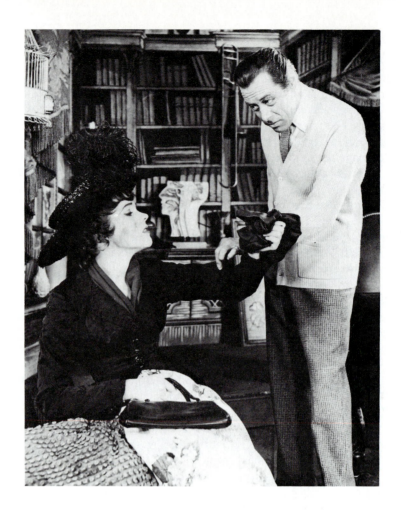

It seems clear that performance apprehension is not peculiar to speakers. This reaction is not unusual, even for experienced speakers. Some beginning speakers think they alone have this response. Rest assured, you are in large and good company. In a study of two groups of college students, 210 in one group and 277 in the second group, "fifty-six percent of the first group and 61 percent of the second group listed some form of nervousness as one of their speech problems." In another study of 512 high school speech students, "seventy-four percent of them judged themselves to be at least somewhat nervous when speaking."[11] Although different students experience performance apprehension in varying degrees, Low and Sheets, on the basis of their research, concluded, "No significant differences were found between students with the most stage fright and students with the least stage fright in: 1. General intelligence. 2. Quantitative reasoning ability. 3. The more important phases of personality. 4. Their interest in the fields of science, mechanics, nature, and business."[12]

You don't have to worry about being abnormal, therefore, because you experience more emotional tension than some of your classmates.

Experienced speakers also have emotional tension prior to a speaking engagement. After studying thirty experienced public speakers, including lawyers, ministers, businessmen, educators, and state supreme court judges, Wrenchley concluded that "seventy-six percent of the interviewees stated that they did have stage fright or, as many termed it, a nervousness or tension before speaking."[13] Coincidentally, Kniseley also reported after studying sixty prominent speakers that 76 percent experienced some form of performance apprehension.[14] An examination of Wrenchley's data reveals that 76 percent is a conservative conclusion on her part, for only one speaker gave a categorically negative answer.

It is interesting to read some of the replies from experienced speakers.

Speaker #3: Yes, a little nervous until I get started. Never had stage fright so badly that I have been blocked. I generally know what I want to say and as soon as I get into it, the tension leaves. I don't particularly like to speak, but am like Fanny Hurst about writing, "Never happy when I'm writing, much unhappier when I'm not."

Speaker #4: Oh, yes, definitely. People who do not talk do not realize. One who is perfectly relaxed isn't so apt to do so well. Most artists are very nervous. Every speaker who is experienced goes through different stages of stage fright. Much of it is dispelled after the speech is under way.

Speaker #10: Always a little nervous, and it was my joy to know that W. J. Bryan was always nervous. One never retires from the mental strain or apprehension with a large or small audience. I have always had it but have learned to do away with it. Am as free as a bird when I'm really in my speech.

Speaker #26: Yes, and everyone has it. That is excellent speakers do.[15]

Before his State of the Union address to Congress and the nation in 1983, President Reagan "admitted to feeling stage jitters akin to those he experienced during his acting days."[16]

Take comfort, then, knowing the phenomenon we call stage fright is not peculiar to certain people, or even to certain groups of people. The reactions occur in athletes, actors, musicians, teachers, speakers—in short, they occur in anyone who is confronted with a situation in which the performance is important and the outcome uncertain.

Performance Apprehension Causes Helpful Physiological Reactions

This emotional tension, or anxiety, results in a physiological reaction that prepares the body for a better physical and mental effort. Located within the human body are organs designed to function only when triggered by what is perceived to be an emergency situation. Just as it would be wasteful and inefficient for an automobile engine to use all its 350 horsepower when the car was going twenty-five miles an hour, so it would be wasteful and inefficient for the human body to operate at peak efficiency under normal circumstances.

Figure 3.1
When the body perceives an emergency situation, certain organs in the body begin to prepare it for a better physical and mental effort.

When an emergency is perceived, these organs go into action. Adrenalin is pumped into the system, increasing the muscles' vitality and reaction time. Larger quantities of sugar are released from the pancreas and converted into energy, giving the body greater strength to cope with physical problems. Numerous red corpuscles are discharged into the bloodstream from the spleen. Breathing is quickened, thus bringing in more oxygen and expelling the carbon dioxide more rapidly. The pulse rate speeds up so that more fresh blood arrives at the muscles, the heart, the brain, and the central nervous system with larger quantities of oxygen. Blood is diverted from its normal process of picking up digested food from the stomach and intestines and is now directed to the muscles, heart, brain, and central nervous system to provide these organs with more oxygen and energy. The brain thus thinks with greater clarity, perceptiveness, and quickness; the muscles exert a more intense physical effort; the central nervous system reacts more quickly. Because of these physiological changes, the human body performs at a much higher level than under normal conditions. (See figure 3.1.)

A few years ago newspapers carried an account of a mother who lifted a small foreign car off her son on whom it had fallen. While his mother held the car, the son scrambled to safety. The mother performed this amazing physical feat even though she stood less than five feet in height and weighed less than 100 pounds. Undoubtedly the emergency organs of the body enabled that mother to aid her son so well.

A number of years ago a woman lifted—not once, but twice—a slab of marble weighing approximately 300 pounds that was lying on a child. Normally she couldn't lift a hundred pounds, but under these extreme circumstances the emergency organs of her body enabled her to lift a weight several times what she normally could.

These examples show how physiological changes can help a person cope with situations better if he or she will just learn to use them. They can also help a speaker. The novelist I. A. R. Wylie tells how she discovered the power of these reactions.

> When I first came to the United States and found out that my publishers expected me to make a speech at a public dinner, I was almost sick with fear. I had never made a speech in my life; in a group of people I was tongue-tied with shyness. To my amazement I found myself speaking fluently, telling stories, sounding—as I was told afterward—like a practiced speaker. I had, in fact, been scared right out of myself to the discovery of someone I hadn't dreamed existed. Now after many years of practice I am, I suppose, really a practiced speaker. But I rarely rise to my feet without a throat constricted with terror and a furiously thumping heart. When, for some reason, I *am* cool and self-assured the speech is always a failure. I need fear to spur me on.[17]

Greg Norman, the Australian golfer, now understands the value of this emotional tension. In the summer of 1986, he led the U.S. Open tournament by one stroke at the beginning of the final round. He played poorly and did not win the tournament. Later in the summer, he led the British Open by one stroke at the beginning of the final round. This time, however, he increased his lead to five strokes and won the tournament. In talking to reporters after the tournament, Norman said, "I wanted to be nervous today . . . I wasn't nervous on the final day of the U.S. Open, and I was flat. . . . (Today) I didn't tell my wife I was nervous. But I was. . . ."[18]

It is important to note, however, that *these reactions don't take place if there is no uncertainty within the individual over the outcome of the performance or if the outcome is considered unimportant.* Poor speech efforts result from this factor. William Jennings Bryan, outstanding speaker of the first part of this century who gave literally thousands of speeches, reported that he failed to experience "butterflies in his stomach" on only one occasion. And, he said, that was the worst speech he ever gave.

Performance Apprehension Can Be Harmful

To say performance apprehension is helpful is not to say it can't be harmful, for it can. Too much anxiety, or emotional tension, may result in extreme physiological reactions. A college football player recalled his experience in his first varsity game in high school. Shortly before the game was to begin, the coach informed him that he was to be responsible for the opening kickoff. On taking the field, the referee, apparently sensing his nervous tension, came over to him and said: "Son, just keep your eyes on that ball, and when you hear my whistle, run up there and kick it as far as you can." With that, the young player fixed his concentration on the ball ready on the tee. Hearing a whistle, he ran forward, kicked the ball, and watched it sail off on the longest kick he had ever made. He was running after it as hard as he could when he suddenly realized he was the only person moving. From the darkness around him he heard the voice of his coach yelling, "Stop! Stop!" The whistle he had heard was the whistle of the band director beginning the national anthem.

Obviously, this youthful football player had received too much help from his emergency organs. Most of us have witnessed the inexperienced speaker who goes blank or whose voice becomes tremulous or whose hands shake so badly he or she can't hold his or her notes or gesture properly. It seems safe to conclude, then, that performance apprehension can be harmful. It can be harmful because the speaker gets too much help. This can occur for two reasons.

First, it can occur because your experience is too limited for the significance of the performance. The football player above, for example, performed beyond his limited experience when he was asked to make the kickoff in his first varsity game. If you were asked to give your first speech over nationwide television, that would be too great a responsibility for your limited experience. A background of success in less important situations must be experienced before coping with important ones.

Avoid significant speaking situations until successful minor ones have been experienced. This is a value you receive from your speech course. You can gain experience before your peers. Only your grade in the course and your standing among peers are influenced by these speeches—a job promotion doesn't depend on your effort.

A second factor making performance apprehension harmful is the failure to understand the origin of the rapid breathing, the moist palms, the butterflies in the stomach, and the other physiological changes. That brings us, then, to the means by which you may control performance apprehension.

Performance Apprehension Can Be Controlled

Many beginning speakers, and even some experienced ones, ask "How can I get rid of speech apprehension?" The answer is you don't want to get rid of it—you want to control it. The emotional tension, or anxiety, is a beneficial reaction for the public speaker. Harry Emerson Fosdick, an early radio minister, was fully aware of the importance of these reactions.

> Impatient to meet his audience face to face, he often had to take sedatives on Saturday night in order to get his rest for Sunday's adventure. "Not anxiety, but tension that was a stimulus" caused him to be "aroused." In his judgment, "Any man who isn't tense before he speaks can't speak. Fear is not something to be feared, but something to be sublimated."[19]

After a penetrating study, Robinson concluded: *The complete absence of feelings of apprehension is neither normal nor a desirable state.*[20] With this fact in mind, let's examine seven ways in which you can learn to control performance apprehension.

**Develop Proper
Attitude toward
Performance
Apprehension**

The first way to control performance apprehension is to develop the proper attitude toward it. Realize the physiological changes are normal and prepare you for a better effort, both physically and mentally. Knowing the anxiety, or emotional tension, before a speech is beneficial and arms you with a healthy attitude, which eliminates the process causing too much performance apprehension.

When you first perceive the situation as an important one, a message goes out from the central nervous system activating the emergency organs. Many speakers misinterpret the physiological changes as indicating the situation is getting worse. Thus, another message goes from the central nervous system to the emergency organs. The increase in the physiological changes causes the speaker to conclude the situation is worse and so the cycle goes until the speaker can no longer control the responses.

With the right attitude, however, the whole process is altered. As soon as the first physiological changes occur, you interpret them as indicating you're going to be ready for this speech, that these changes will increase your power of concentration, improve your thinking ability, and make your perceptive processes more acute. As a result, no other messages go out from the central nervous system and the physiological changes remain at a beneficial and controllable level.

**Get as Much
Experience as Possible**

A second factor helping you control performance apprehension is experience. It doesn't have to be limited to public speaking occasions but can come from speaking in a broad variety of situations. Low and Sheets, in comparing students with the most performance apprehension to those with the least, found that the former—

1. Have not engaged in as much platform speaking activity.
2. Have not participated as much in extracurricular and social activities.
3. Have difficulty in making an adequate social adjustment.
4. Have less linguistic ability.
5. Have less interest in activities that involve self-expression in verbal activities and in work involving judgment and the supervision of others.[21]

The more experience you have, the more confidence you develop in your ability to perform successfully. Every successful speaking effort helps you with future assignments. The wider and more varied the experience, the more confident you'll be that you have confronted a situation in some way comparable to the present assignment. After studying students in a college speech course, Henrikson wrote that his study agreed "with previous investigations in indicating that speech training promotes confidence in the speaking situation." According to students he studied, the most important factor in lowering performance apprehension was *practice* (68.8%).[22] Knowing you have spoken successfully in past situations reduces your uncertainties about the outcome of the anticipated performance, resulting in less complicated anxiety and less

Figure 3.2
Thorough preparation is a strong antidote for performance apprehension.

performance apprehension. Researchers have also discovered through measurements of physiological reactions that experienced sport parachutists have greater emotional control than novices,[23] and experienced divers in underwater exploration develop an increasing ability to cope with the stresses of their environment.[24]

Third, good preparation helps control performance apprehension. If you're worrying about what you're going to say, how you're going to say it, and what the outcome will be, you'll have more emotional tension than if you have to worry only about the outcome. Select your topic with care, do any necessary preliminary thinking, complete your research, organize the materials logically and psychologically to achieve your purpose and to suit this particular audience; then practice your speech. Kniseley reported that, among the prominent speakers in his study who experienced some form of apprehension, 70 percent said their primary method of coping with it was through thorough preparation.[25] (See figure 3.2.)

Prepare Well for the Speech

Evidence indicates you should practice your speech until you overlearn it. University of Illinois psychologists discovered that actors who overlearned their parts found apprehension helpful, whereas actors who underlearned their parts found apprehension harmful.[26] For the speaker, of course, overlearning refers to ideas, not to a particular sequence of words.

Thorough preparation gives you confidence you have something to say and know how to say it. Anxiety about the outcome won't be complicated by concern about adequate preparation.

Use Bodily Action

Once in the speaking situation, bodily action can become a fourth means of controlling performance apprehension. Many speakers interpret shaking of the hands and trembling of the knees as evidence of fear. It isn't fear, but the homeostatic process of the body dissipating excess energy that causes the trembling of certain limbs. Recall when you have narrowly averted a serious accident. You might have been driving down a main thoroughfare when another car darted in from a side street. Avoiding an accident, you found your hands trembling so much you could hardly clutch the steering wheel. This is the same (homeostatic) process in both instances. The body attempts to maintain a constant balance. Just as the body perspires to cause a cooling process when there is danger of body temperature increasing above 98.6 degrees, so the body dissipates excess energy that is not being used. When the emergency organs prepare the body for a superhuman physical effort and no physical exertions are necessary, the body is left with this excess energy, which it must dissipate. This dissipation takes the form of trembling muscles.

Many speakers, interpreting these reactions as fear, grab the sides of the speaker's stand or shove their hands into their pockets, hoping clenched fists will stop the trembling. But they won't. Inhibiting the dissipation of excess energy in one set of muscles means that another set will do the job. This may mean trembling of the knees or a shaking vocal tone.

The best solution is to use this excess energy in a constructive way: for gestures and bodily movement. This not only rids the body of excess energy, but also aids in effective communication. With respect to this point, Lomas has made a keen observation: "If bodily action is to have therapeutic value for stage fright, that value must come through training received *before* speaking, not from anything the student may do *while* speaking."[27] You must have practiced the gestures and bodily action so their use will be automatic during the speech. If you have to think about using gestures and actions because of emotional tension, the situation becomes more complex and may increase your excitement.

Concentrate on Communication

Fifth, a speaker gains control over performance apprehension by concentrating on communicating with the listeners. Talk to almost any athlete and he or she will tell you the "butterflies" disappear as soon as the game begins—with the first tackle or block, when the ball is tipped off, when the pitcher throws the first pitch, when the starter's gun sounds. He or she doesn't have time to think about her- or himself because he or she is too busy playing the game. Evonne Goolagong, the sensational Australian tennis player who won the Women's Wimbledon Cup in 1971 at the age of nineteen, reported to news reporters after the finals that she was nervous before the match began. "But," she said, "as soon as I got out there I forgot my nerves and started playing."[28]

You must play the game. As soon as you begin speaking, observe the reactions of your listeners and make an effort to adapt to their reactions. Look for friendly faces. They can reassure you, but avoid the appealing temptation to talk predominantly to the genial ones. Communicate with all the listeners. Ask yourself, "Are these people hearing and understanding what I'm saying? Are they responding in the ways I desire?" If you're concentrating on communication, you have no time for yourself. Wrenchley's study of apprehension in thirty experienced speakers revealed that "seventy percent of those interviewed" forget performance apprehension reactions as they get involved in speaking. Let the speakers describe the process.

> Speaker #27: Yes, I generally lose the feeling after I get started in my speech. I have learned to concentrate on my subject rather than on myself. Experience has also helped.
> Speaker #28: Yes, I overcome it as I proceed. I'm completely relaxed when I get into my subject. Concentration and thinking about the content relaxes me.[29]

Sixth, performance apprehension can be controlled by remembering the physiological upheavals taking place are internal and cannot be perceived by most listeners—at times not even by expert listeners. Three scholars studied the overt signs of speaking apprehension and concluded that "analysis of individual ratings revealed such gross inaccuracies as to suggest that a speech teacher can place little faith in her unsupported judgment as to the emotions felt by a given student in a given speech."[30] Research substantiated this point. Clevenger concluded that "the consistency with which judges' ratings ran below introspective accounts of speaking apprehension suggests that *a group of observers tends to notice less disruption in the speaker than the speaker reports having experienced.*"[31]

So, as a beginning speaker, remember, the only way listeners become aware of your emotional tension, or anxiety, is for you to tell them in some way, either verbally or nonverbally. Since most listeners place greater reliance in a speaker who appears confident, poised, unruffled, and at ease (the means for developing these attributes are explained in chapter 15), refrain from commenting on your emotional tension unless some overt behavior makes it obvious you are suffering from this problem. Speakers have frequently begun talks with a reference to their nervousness when none of the listeners had any inkling of the problem. Such references distract the listeners from the main subject to be developed in the speech and diminish the listeners' estimate of the speaker's skill, experience, and confidence.

Of course, if you are holding notes and the trembling of your hands obviously reveals emotional tension, you can often relieve the tension by referring to it humorously. But remember: don't mention it unless it is obvious, and then don't apologize for it.

Remember Physiological Reactions Are Unseen

Understanding Performance Apprehension

Remember Listeners Want You to Succeed

A seventh means of controlling performance apprehension is to realize listeners are friendly people who generally want you to succeed. Knowing the audience is friendly should give you greater confidence in presenting your speech. An outward display of confidence may not make you feel better; it will increase your credibility.

Summary

Five main ideas should be remembered from this discussion of performance apprehension. 1. Stage fright is a misnomer. Although some authors imply or say directly that stage fright is a form of fear, this book presents the view that it represents an increase in tension caused by heightened drive or motivation as one approaches the performance situation. When one considers reports by trained professional athletes, musicians, and actors, it seems clear that apprehension in these individuals is more a reflection of high drive than of disorganizing fear. As we approach the critical situation, drives increase and are often experienced as tension. 2. Performance apprehension is not peculiar to certain individuals or groups of people but is a normal form of anxiety, or emotional tension, occurring in anyone confronted with a situation in which the performance is important and the outcome uncertain. 3. Performance apprehension causes helpful physiological reactions that can prepare you for more effective mental and physical efforts. 4. Performance apprehension can be harmful if you fail to understand it properly and control it. 5. Performance apprehension can be controlled by developing a proper attitude toward it, by getting much experience in a broad variety of speaking situations, by preparing well for any speaking effort, by using effective bodily action in presenting the speech, by remembering that the physiological reactions are unseen by listeners, and by remembering that listeners generally want to see you succeed.

Notes

1. *The Opelika-Auburn News,* March 17, 1985, p. A–4.
2. T. Clevenger, Jr., "A Synthesis of Experimental Research in Stage Fright," *Quarterly Journal of Speech* 45 (1959):135.
3. Ibid., pp. 135–38.
4. L. F. Shaffer and E. J. Shoben, Jr., *The Psychology of Adjustment* (Boston: Houghton Mifflin Co., 1956), p. 49.
5. Bob Green, "Ace helps Azinger keep PGA advantage," Associated Press, *The Birmingham News,* August 14, 1988 p. 1B.
6. Jim Martin, "Golf," *The Birmingham News,* October 25, 1987, p. 20B.
7. Malcolm Boyd, "How I Overcame Three Fears," *Parade Magazine,* July, 1988, p. 8.
8. *The Opelika-Auburn News,* March 29, 1989, p. B–4. By permission of Associated Press.
9. Jim Martin, "Golf," *The Birmingham News,* September 29, 1985, p. 17B.

10. Marilyn Berger, "Still a Perfectionist and Delighted to Hear It," *The New York Times,* November 19, 1989, p. 5. Used by permission.

11. F. H. Knower, "A Study of Speech Attitudes and Adjustments," *Speech Monographs* 5 (1938):131.

12. G. M. Low and B. V. Sheets, "The Relation of Psychometric Factors to Stage Fright," *Speech Monographs* 18 (1951):271.

13. E. D. O. Wrenchley, "A Study of Stage Fright Attacks in a Selected Group of Experienced Speakers," M.A. thesis, University of Denver, 1948, p. 36.

14. W. A. Kniseley, "An Investigation of the Phenomenon of Stage Fright in Certain Prominent Speakers," Ph.D. diss., University of Southern California, 1950, p. 90.

15. Wrenchley, "Study of Stage Fright Attacks," pp. 36–39.

16. *Birmingham News,* January 26, 1983.

17. I. A. R. Wylie, "I Enjoy Myself Most When I'm Scared," *The Reader's Digest,* March 1953, p. 18.

18. "1986 British Open," July 21, 1986. © 1986 Associated Press. Used by permission.

19. R. C. McCall, "Harry Emerson Fosdick: Paragon and Paradox," *Quarterly Journal of Speech* 39 (1953):289.

20. E. R. Robinson, "What Can the Speech Teacher Do about Students' Stage Fright?" *Speech Teacher* 8 (1959):10.

21. Low and Sheets, "Relation of Psychometric Factors to Stage Fright," p. 271.

22. E. H. Henrikson, "Some Effects on Stage Fright of a Course in Speech," *Quarterly Journal of Speech* 29 (1943):491.

23. S. Epstein, "Toward a Unified Theory of Anxiety," in *Progress in Experimental Personality Research,* ed. B. A. Maher (New York: Academic Press, 1967), p. 31.

24. R. Radloff and R. Helmreich, *Groups under Stress: Psychological Research in Sealab II* (New York: Appleton-Century-Crofts, 1968), p. 87.

25. Kniseley, "Investigation of the Phenomenon of Stage Fright," p. 106.

26. "Eureka," *Theatre Arts,* July 1956, p. 11.

27. C. W. Lomas, "Stage Fright," *Quarterly Journal of Speech* 30 (1944):482.

28. AP dispatch, *Durham Morning Herald,* July 3, 1971.

29. Wrenchley, "Study of Stage Fright Attacks," pp. 57–60.

30. M. Dickens, F. Gibson, and C. Prall, "An Experimental Study of the Overt Manifestations of Stage Fright," *Speech Monographs* 17 (1950):47.

31. Clevenger, "Synthesis of Experimental Research," p. 137.

CHAPTER 4

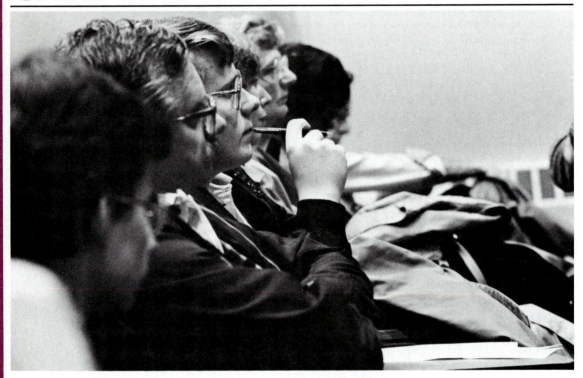

Responsibilities of Receivers:
Effective Listening

An Alabama state legislator recently appointed to Secretary of State indicated his understanding that effective communication rests on the listener as well as the speaker. He "said he hopes he never loses a political belief he has held for a long time.

" 'I have a real good ability to listen. The truth of the matter, that's why I've had such great success in the Senate, because I listen to these folks.

"Most leaders think all leading is talking, and that's not it at all. Most great leaders have a good ability to listen and act.' "[1]

The effective communicator must be both a good listener and a good speaker. A listener's refusal to listen stops communication as effectively as the refusal of a source to speak. This is not to deny that each of us has the right to refuse to listen to any speaker or any message. We don't have to communicate with anyone, speaker or listener.

A recent study of college students revealed they devoted 52.5 percent of their communication day to listening, 16.3 percent to speaking, 17.3 percent to reading, and 13.9 percent to writing.[2] Although most of our communicative activity involves speaking and listening, formal education from kindergarten through high school focuses on reading and writing skills. It isn't surprising, then, that the average person can recall only about 50 percent of the information heard—even when tested immediately after receiving information orally.[3] Thus, even when we're highly motivated to listen, we're frequently "poor" listeners because we have little training in how to meet our obligations as listeners. In this chapter we consider the act of listening, what the speaker can do to aid listening, and what the listener can do to improve listening.

The Act of Listening

The act of listening involves four distinct processes: receiving, perceiving, interpreting, and responding.

The first listening process, receiving, consists of two aspects: seeing and hearing. Seeing, says one scholar of vision, "is, first and foremost, an information-processing task."[4] That precisely defines the role of vision in listening. Seeing is important to listening because it enables us to observe the nonverbal forms of communication: facial expression, gestures, bodily movement. It's also important in recognizing sounds and words. Visual cues such as movement of the lips and tongue assist in identifying some sounds, such as *f, th, t, p,* that are not readily perceived without observation of the facial cues.

Receiving

Effective receiving involves good eyesight. Anatomical processes operate the pupils and eyelids. The optical process changes the shape and focus of the lens so that near and distant objects are brought into focus. A photochemical process converts the light that strikes the retina into nerve impulses that are transmitted by a neurophysiological process through the optic nerve to the brain to be analyzed. Recent research indicates that some of the information is processed in the visual system itself; however, most of the processing occurs in the brain.

Receiving also involves hearing, a neurophysiological process that also requires a working mechanism. If a person is deaf, listening is prevented because hearing cannot occur. Sound is produced when something vibrates in a medium such as air. When a person vibrates the vocal folds, sound waves are created that carry to the outer ear of another person, where they travel down the external auditory canal to the tympanum, a thin membrane stretched tight across the opening into the middle ear. The tympanum vibrates in consonance with the air waves and transmits these vibrations, by means of three tiny bones (the malleus, incus, and stapes), to the oval window. The membrane covering the oval window moves in and out in concert with the tympanum, causing fluid in the inner ear to move. The movement of this fluid generates nerve signals that are transmitted by the eighth cranial nerve to the brain where they are interpreted as sounds. In this manner we "hear" all sounds that make their way to our outer ear, although we are not consciously aware of all of them.

Perceiving

That brings us to perceiving, the second process involved in listening. When we're listening to one set of vibrations striking our eardrum, we're generally not conscious of other vibrations also striking it. When we sit in our homes and watch the evening news, we listen to the commentator by focusing our attention on the vibrations from his or her voice and not the vibrations coming from voices in the next room even though they strike our eardrums. We can listen to those voices, however, simply by shifting our attention to them. It isn't enough to hear sounds in the environment, we must perceive them by focusing attention on the ones we want to listen to. Of course, there are some stimuli that are so dominant we cannot avoid perceiving them.

How can we control attention? By external factors (characteristics of the stimulus) or by internal factors (attitudes, expectations, desires of the individual). What do we mean by attention? "The essence of paying attention is simple," say Carver and Scheier. "It is noticing something, mentally picking it up, processing it." They then admit, however, that defining attention is not easy.[5] Although there is currently much controversy about the nature of attention and exactly how it works and when it begins, we can profitably use the definition given by Wolvin and Coakley: attention is "the focused perception of stimuli."[6]

Interpreting

Once we have received and perceived the visual and aural symbols, we then begin the third listening process: interpreting. We interpret the meaning of sounds as best we can. We recognize them as belonging to some category, such as music, noise, or speech. If we interpret the sounds as speech, we next interpret the meaning of those speech sounds. We may be unable to interpret the meaning, however, if the speech includes words we don't know or if it's in a foreign language we don't understand. If it's language we know, we try to determine the intended meaning. We must interpret not only the language, however, but also the meaning of the nonverbal communication.

Because communication is a transactional process—one in which all communicators are actively involved—the fourth process, responding, is important and necessary. Listening is defined as "that moving of a person made . . . in response to . . . the spoken word of another person." A person responding to the speech communication of others exhibits listening "by an organized set of movements." These responses cause speakers to be affected by listeners.[7] Listening should be an active, involved process. Respond overtly and process actively ideas received. You can't simply be a recorder; you must interpret the meaning of the words and respond internally and externally to them. Unless you do, the transactional nature of communication can't be achieved. Once you have responded, you have completed the act of listening. Receiving messages, therefore, is largely an involuntary process, whereas perceiving, interpreting, and responding are predominantly voluntary processes.

What happens in the cognitive processing of oral messages? We don't clearly understand. Research indicates that listening is primarily a function of general mental ability.[8] It appears that lecture-comprehension listening is "more closely related to measures of general mental ability," whereas short-term listening ability "seems more closely related to measures of oral performance."[9] It appears we don't yet understand how the processes involved in listening operate.[10]

What, then, can the speaker do to improve listening? Consider the possibilities. Receiving ability can't be changed except by artificial means. Interpreting involves cognitive processing, which some say we don't understand. Probably the best way a speaker can aid interpretation is to organize a message clearly, state it in clear language, and deliver it effectively. We are left, then, with the second and fourth listening processes, perceiving and responding. Here is where we can control our own listening habits and efforts and influence those of others. Speakers can assist listeners in perceiving the message, and listeners can improve their perception of and response to messages. In the next two sections, we look first at what the speaker can do to improve listening and then at what the receiver can do to improve listening.

How the Speaker Can Improve Listening

To talk about affecting the listening of others is to talk about attention. You can improve listening, therefore, by increasing listeners' attention. What are the factors that affect attention?

Under most conditions, we have the ability to decide what we listen to, what we focus on, how we interpret it, and how we respond to it. There are certain factors, however, that make it easier for us to listen to certain stimuli.

All things being equal, a moving object attracts attention away from a nonmoving object. On a clear night, for example, which captures your attention, a falling star or all the apparently stationary ones? In a wooded area, on the other hand, you can stand near a rabbit for several minutes and not see it unless it moves.

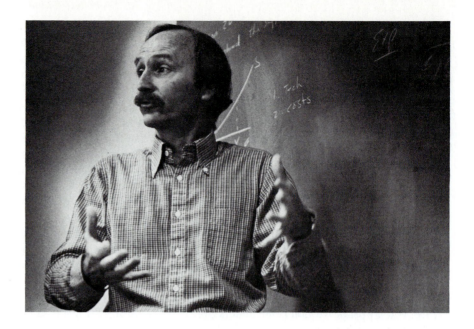

Movement is also important psychologically. It brings change to the situation. "Normal consciousness, perception, and thought can be maintained only in a constantly changing environment." Unless there is change, "the capacity of adults to concentrate deteriorates, attention fluctuates and lapses, and normal perception fades."[11]

Use this principle to assist your listeners in attending to your speech rather than other stimuli in the environment. Achieve movement in the speech by having it well organized and keeping that organization readily apparent to the listeners. Making clear the progression through the main ideas gives a sense of movement to the speech. Use stories that have movement in them to develop your ideas. In addition, use physical movement: reflect your ideas with appropriate facial expressions; gesture; walk about the podium in a meaningful way. Walk over and talk to the listeners on your left, then to those on your right, then return to the lectern and talk from there.

Repetition

We are attracted to a stimulus we have experienced many times because of its repetition and familiarity. Do you find yourself singing the words or humming the tune of an advertising jingle you've heard repeatedly?

Capitalize on this principle by previewing your main points, stating them when you develop each of them, and summarizing them at the end. You can restate your main points or important ideas. Repeat them as you stated them initially or restate them in different words. You can also restate them by using testimony from someone who has said the same thing. If that person happens to be a highly credible source, the impact of the restatement is increased. Use repetition by choosing words that are familiar to your listeners; this has the effect of restatement.

The larger a stimulus, the more likely we are to be attracted to it. Have you **Size** had a loud noise literally jerk your attention from something you were engrossed in?

Take advantage of this factor by at least occasionally using the largest gestures that are appropriate. You can also use a loudness level that makes your speech the dominant sound in the situation, and you can increase the loudness level to indicate more important information or ideas.

Utilize the concept of size by demonstrating or referring to the enormity of the problem you are discussing. Describe how widespread the problem is, how many people are affected by it, the large amounts of money that have to be spent on it, the many harmful effects that result from it.

We are prone to attend to those stimuli that exhibit great energy, strength, or **Intensity** vehemence. Any object, activity, thought, or feeling whose characteristics are extreme in degree possesses intensity.

Achieve intensity in speeches by exhibiting emotions appropriate to your words. Maintain physical alertness and use crisp, energetic gestures to communicate intensity. Your language can convey a feeling of intensity. Use active sentences, rather than passive ones, and use action verbs. Since a slow rate conveys a relaxed feeling, speak faster to develop intensity.

A stimulus is unusual or unique if it stands out in comparison to others, is rare **Novelty** or unusual, has no equal, or is the only one. A small object in the midst of large objects attracts our attention because of its unusual size. An object we have never seen before gets our attention because of its novelty.

How can you achieve novelty in a speech? Present a new or original analysis of the topic. Phrase your ideas in colorful and memorable ways. Tell your listeners things they don't know. Use variety in supporting materials, language, and delivery.

Stimuli that affect our personal needs and specific interests attract our atten- **Personal Needs** tion to a greater degree than those in which we have no interest. To create **and Interests** greater interest, show how your proposal will affect the personal needs and interests of your hearers. Show that what you are advocating will improve economic conditions in the community, enlarge educational facilities, provide additional cultural opportunities, or promote racial harmony and cooperation.

Enhance the benefits of your proposal by showing how the present situation or one advocated by others will not meet the personal needs and interests of your listeners as well as your plan will.

People seem naturally attracted to conflict. Our interest is piqued and we want **Conflict** to know the outcome.

Identify opponents of your proposal and show why they oppose it and how they would profit from failure to adopt it. Then show how most people would gain from your proposal. This will establish direct conflict between you and your opponents. Since personal conflict is most attention-getting, challenge your opponents to answer criticisms.

Uncertainty

We are attracted to those situations involving uncertainty. Have you ever lost interest in going to a football game because you felt that your team was undermatched or overmatched with an opponent? But if you feel that either team can win, you want to be there to resolve the uncertainty.

Color

Bright colors attract us more than dull colors. Notice how the appearance of a redbird gets your attention while that of a sparrow generally does not.

Female speakers can use bright colors in their dress much more easily than males can. Males can generally use bright colored ties but not suits. On one occasion a visiting professor at a university arrived at his lecture wearing a bright, luminous green suit. The next day a student said, "When the speaker first came in yesterday, I thought he was a used car salesman." Keep in mind that you don't want to attract unfavorable attention.

Can color be used in other ways? Yes, if you are using visual aids with your speech, they can be made attractively appealing by using colors to differentiate the parts.

How the Listener Can Improve Listening

Does full responsibility for communication have to be assumed by a speaker? No, but even a cooperative listener can hinder communication with poor listening habits. The following suggestions, therefore, should help you meet your communicative responsibilities as a listener.

Purposeful Listening

Just as a speaker approaches a communicative situation with a purpose in mind, you should approach listening with a purpose. Otherwise, you won't know what type of behavior is appropriate. When you go to a classroom lecture, you go to be informed. That means you'll probably want to take notes on the lecture. When you go to a nightclub to hear a comedian, or when you sit down with friends for a pleasant evening of conversation, you listen for entertainment and enjoyment. Wherever you go, you should go with a listening purpose in mind. Then you know how to react to the information and how to process it. You don't take notes when your purpose is to be entertained or inspired. You do take notes when you want to be instructed or to recall the information.

Active Listening

Communicating a message to a receiver is not like transferring water from one bottle to another. You can't sit passively and let a speaker "pour" a message into your brain. Listening is an active process. You must receive, perceive, interpret, and respond to what the speaker is saying. What do the speaker's statements mean to you? to others? As an active listener, you must listen "with more or less total self—including your special senses, attitudes, beliefs, feelings, and intuitions."[12]

Can you create mental images of what the speaker is saying? As the speaker describes the scarred and barren land resulting from strip mining, can you visualize it? Can you empathize with the speaker's anger at the cruel abuse of children by disturbed parents?

Active listening isn't easy. It requires physical, mental, and emotional involvement. Active listening is work. Our physical and mental involvement in listening is clear when we're sick with a cold or tired from losing a night's sleep. Then we discover it's difficult to listen with a high degree of concentration.

Capitalize on the difference between the speaking rate and the thinking rate in a constructive way. Although the speaking rate may vary from about one hundred to almost three hundred words per minute, the average speaking rate is about 125 to 150 words per minute. Our thinking rate, however, is approximately four times that. This means we have about four hundred words per minute to play around with while listening to the normal speaker. If we're not careful, those extra thinking words will be used to go off on tangents, even to entirely new topics. This extra thinking time can be used constructively, however, by elaborating on what the speaker is saying. This can be accomplished in a number of ways. Look ahead to what the speaker is going to say (although you must be careful not to get so far ahead of the speaker that you lose track of what is being said and get lost). Summarize frequently in your mind what has been said. Keep the central idea in mind and relate the speaker's words to it. Identify the main points and the speaker's organizational pattern. Evaluate the evidence. (1) Is it accurate? (2) Is it current? (3) Are the sources objective ones? (4) Does the evidence presented give a complete analysis of the subject? But keep moving with the speaker. If you focus too long on one topic, you may suddenly discover you haven't been listening to the speaker. Then you may find you can no longer understand what is being said.

Respond to the speaker's words and actions. Smile when the speaker says something pleasant; frown when something is unclear; nod your head to indicate agreement; applaud to show approval. A meaningful response reveals your active involvement.

Objective Listening

We selectively perceive the stimuli around us. Do we want to perceive selectively? Not necessarily, but we are forced to because we can't simultaneously perceive multiple stimuli. Consequently, we perceive certain stimuli and disregard others because of our background, attitudes, interests, previous experiences, values, and other factors. Although our perceptions are necessarily selective, we must, in our role as receivers in the communicative process, consciously strive to avoid misperceiving or misinterpreting information we receive.

The first step in avoiding communication problems caused by selective perception is to identify your attitudes toward the speaker and the subject. Do you admire the speaker a great deal? If so, then resolve that your admiration won't prevent your listening carefully and impartially to the ideas and evidence. Do you approach a communicative situation with a preconceived attitude? Don't assume you will hear nothing worthwhile because the speaker is going to speak in favor of an idea, such as labor unions, that you oppose. Listen to what the speaker has to say. You may learn something that will give you a new perspective on labor unions. Are you aware that your attitude on the subject is opposed to that of the speaker? Then resolve that you won't reject unheard the ideas and evidence presented. Apply the same standards of evaluation that you would to a speech supporting a position you favor: Are the sources valid ones? Is the evidence consistent with familiar information? Is the evidence up-to-date?

Avoid letting your emotions get overly aroused by anything the speaker says. Do certain terms, such as "male chauvinist," "redneck," "abortion," four-letter words, or religious and racial epithets, cause you to explode emotionally? Are you then unable to respond rationally to what the speaker has said previously? Are you also unable to listen effectively to what follows? The objective listener guards against an emotional overreaction to these "signal" words.

Don't let other people around you have an effect on your listening. The process of listening changes in the presence of others. Their inattention may cause you to do a poor job of listening. Their negative responses can cause your listening to be more critical, or their positive responses may make your listening less critical. Maintain as much objectivity as possible in evaluating the speaker's ideas.

Constructive Listening

It is often easy to listen destructively. Have you made fun of an occasion? Have you criticized a speaker's dress, pronunciation, hometown, or organization? Have you sneered at a speaker's failure to use effectively the principles of communication? As undesirable as these things may be, we can't let them cause us to overlook important information. Peer behind the external factors and evaluate what the speaker is saying. Overcome noise and distractions by attempting to discover personal value in what is being said. Ask yourself, "How is this information relevant to me? What can I gain from listening?"

Have you found it difficult to keep an open mind about a speaker's idea because of his or her personal commitments or prejudices? Instead of closing your mind to the speaker or focusing on areas of disagreement, look for points of agreement and emphasize them. Then an open mind will allow you to expand your knowledge of a topic.

Try to pick out the central idea and organizational pattern of the speech. Not all speakers will clearly identify their central idea for you. Some won't because they are unfamiliar with basic principles of communication, some because they want to obscure their true purpose. Decide whether you need to listen for general ideas or specific details. In some cases it is imperative to get the specific details. If someone is giving you complicated directions about how to use a home computer, listen carefully for the specific details. In other instances, it'll be easy to get lost in a maze of facts if you focus too much on specifics; then you'll miss the general ideas as well as the details. In many communicative situations, the general ideas are more important than the details.

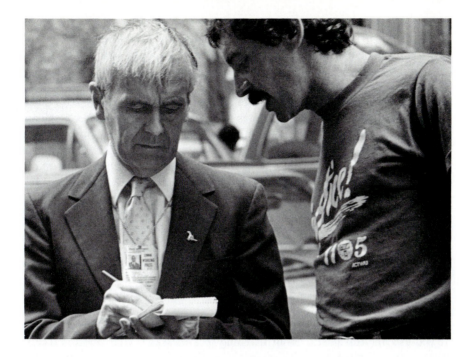

We filter the external world into our system by directing our attention to particular stimuli in our surroundings. When we want to filter out a stimulus, we simply direct our attention elsewhere. In a communicative situation, unless we direct our attention to the speaker we effectively filter out the message. Some people are skillful at faking attention. They assume an alert posture, look in the direction of the speaker with an attentive expression, shift the brain into neutral, and let it roam. Daydreaming may be a pleasant diversion, but it interferes with communication. Do you tend to daydream during speeches or conferences? It may help to take a pencil and pad with you even though you don't actually need the notes. Taking a few notes can keep you concentrating on the communication. When you take notes, do you insist on outlining them? Don't! Some messages are not organized so they can be outlined. If you insist on imposing order on disorganized messages, you'll not only be frustrated, you'll also get hopelessly lost and miss what the speaker has to say.

Avoid behavior distracting to you and others. Do you whisper to friends around you? You may miss an idea that is crucial to understanding the message. Do you work on other projects while involved in a communication activity? Do you avoid eye contact with the speaker? Eye contact improves the communication process for both speaker and listener.

Learn to cope with distractions that occur. Concentrate on the speaker and thus filter out the stimuli coming from noisy neighbors, crying babies, or creaking water pipes. Whether or not these stimuli disturb us is frequently a

Attentive Listening

matter of attitude. If we are annoyed by a crying baby, we have difficulty filtering out the noise. But if we don't get annoyed, it is fairly easy to shut out that disturbance. Most people can read a newspaper with a radio or television on. Similarly, with practice, you can learn to overcome distractions in a communicative situation.

Listening attentively means attending not only to the verbal cues of the speaker, but to the nonverbal ones as well. Observing the speaker's various nonverbal cues will increase the understanding of the message. Sometimes the speaker doesn't communicate the true message verbally. On those occasions, the nonverbal cues—a frown, a smile, a vocal inflection, a pause, a nervous gesture—may reveal the true message. These nonverbal methods of communication are discussed in detail in chapter 15.

Very little motivates a speaker as well as an attentive listener, even if the listener is hostile. The reward of knowing someone is receptive to the message frequently provides the needed incentive to continue the communicative effort.

Meet your obligation by attending to the speaker. Only in this way can you broaden your horizons, and only in this way can the speaker have an opportunity to communicate.

Enthusiastic Listening

If you are unenthusiastic about listening to a message, your mind is free to wander. You'll have difficulty maintaining the necessary interest to achieve good communication. If you are unenthusiastic about the person speaking, forget who is talking and focus on the topic. Examine the credibility of the content; don't allow your low regard for the speaker to interfere with your reception of the ideas. If you are unenthusiastic about the subject, make an effort to discover its relevance to you. Think of ways you can apply the information in your own activities. Can you use the information in one of your college courses? Can you use it in the part-time job you now have? Will you be able to use it in your future work? Is the speaker saying anything that you can use to enjoy life more? In some instances you may want to create enthusiasm by focusing on a negative feature. For example, because you oppose the speaker's position, you'll want to know what he or she is saying in order to counter that position. Sometimes you may just have to remember that even unpleasant tasks need to be finished.

Ethical Responsibilities of Listeners

Listeners also have ethical responsibilities in communication situations. Adherence to the following principles will help you meet your responsibilities as a listener and will ensure that all participants engage in valid and ethical communication.

1. Although total objectivity is impossible, you should process what the speaker says as objectively as you can.

2. Listen with an open mind. Don't come to a communication situation with your mind made up. You may find that the speaker has information that will change your mind.
3. Give the speaker the benefit of the doubt until you have clearly established that the speaker has acted unethically by presenting false information.
4. If you hear something you dislike or disagree with, you have a right to boo briefly, but you don't have the right to boo so loud and long that the speaker can't continue speaking and the other listeners can't hear.
5. Grant the speaker the right to approach a topic or a position from a different point of view from you or your friends. Don't reject the speaker's position until you have heard it explained.

If, as a listener, you follow these few ethical guidelines, you will help safeguard communication's role in a democratic society.

Summary _____

Listening is a necessary component of communication. The act of listening involves four distinct processes: receiving, perceiving, interpreting, and responding.

Both the speaker and the listener can take action to improve listening. The speaker can improve listeners' perception by utilizing factors that affect attention: movement, repetition, size, intensity, novelty, conflict, uncertainty, and color.

The listener can improve the processes by listening purposefully, actively, objectively, constructively, attentively, and enthusiastically.

Exercises _____

1. Attend a lecture on campus with another member of the class. Sit in different parts of the room. Without conferring with one another, report what you heard to the class.
2. Divide the class into dyads (two-person units). Let one member of each dyad tell about a recent trip. The other member of each dyad should avoid listening to the speaker. After several minutes, the instructor should bring the class back together and let the members discuss the experience.
3. Assign three class members to listen to student speeches. Let one concentrate on the effectiveness of the speakers, one on the ineffectiveness of the speakers, and one on whatever seems appropriate. Let each student report to the class.
4. Attend a lecture and observe the behavior of listeners. Describe both positive and negative behavior that you witness.

Notes

1. Tom Lindley, "Perry Hand's Dad Was Cool to Political Talk," *The Birmingham News/Birmingham Post Herald,* p. 6A, April 15, 1989.
2. L. Barker, R. Edwards, C. Gaines, K. Gladney, and F. Holley, "An Investigation of Proportional Time Spent in Various Communication Activities by College Students," *Journal of Applied Communication Research* 8 (1980):104–06.
3. R. G. Nichols, "Do You Know How to Listen? Practical Help in a Modern Age," *Speech Teacher* 10 (1961):120.
4. D. Marr, *Vision* (San Francisco: W. H. Freeman and Co., 1982), p. 3. Used by permission of W. H. Freeman and Co.
5. C. S. Carver and M. F. Scheier, *Attention and Self-Regulation* (New York: Springer-Verlag, 1981), p. 33.
6. A. D. Wolvin and C. G. Coakley, *Listening* (Dubuque, Iowa: Wm. C. Brown Company Publishers, 1982), p. 40. Used by permission.
7. F. H. Ernst, Jr., *Who's Listening?* (Vallejo, Calif.: Addresso'set, 1973), pp. 27, 37. Used by permission.
8. C. M. Kelly, "Listening: Complex of Activities—And a Unitary Skill," *Speech Monographs* 34 (1967):464.
9. R. N. Bostrom and E. S. Waldhart, "Components in Listening Behavior: The Role of Short-Term Memory," *Human Communication Research* 6 (1980):226.
10. R. N. Bostrom and C. L. Bryant, "Factors in the Retention of Information Presented Orally: The Role of Short-Term Listening," *Western Journal of Speech Communication* 44 (1980):145.
11. M. D. Vernon, *The Psychology of Perception,* 2nd ed. (London: Pelican Books, 1971), p. 173. © M. D. Vernon, 1962, 1971. By permission of Penguin Books, Ltd.
12. D. Barbara, "On Listening—the Role of the Ear in Psychic Life," *Today's Speech* 5 (1957):12.

CHAPTER 5

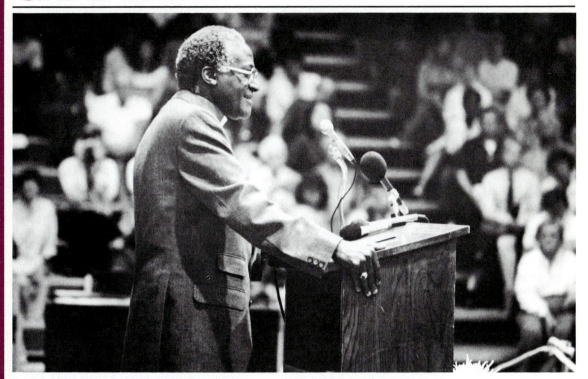

Responsibilities of Speakers: Ethical Dimensions

It is not easy today to discuss ethical responsibilities. "Extenuating circumstances" are used to defend and explain unethical, immoral, and even illegal behavior. Yet the nature and role of oral communication demand that attention be paid to ethical considerations. The skilled and prominent public speaker exerts a greater than normal influence on the conduct of human affairs. An irresponsible speaker can cause harmful decisions to be made.

As we turn our attention to ethical problems in communication, however, we find it almost impossible to get anyone today to think seriously of absolute, legalistic, or "natural law" rules of ethical responsibility. Most people accept the relativistic philosophy that each instance must be decided on its own merits, that the situation must be taken into consideration in evaluating the ethical principles involved. This creates problems for the theorist trying to define the ethical responsibilities of a public speaker.

Amorality of Speech Communication Principles

Further complicating the speaker's task is the fact that speech communication principles are amoral principles—they can be used for either good or evil purposes. Because these principles *are* sometimes used by speakers to achieve immoral ends, some have criticized and condemned the principles themselves. But this is no more valid than the criticism that automobiles are evil because drunken drivers use them to destroy property and kill human beings. It's the user of speech communication principles who determines the ethics: you may use the principles in irresponsible ways to attain some evil purpose or in moral ways to attain a generally accepted good purpose.

Before going any further, we should define ethics. Ethics is concerned "with questions about the meaning of 'good' and 'bad,' 'right' and 'wrong,' and 'moral obligation.' "[1]

Does this book acknowledge the amoral nature of communication principles? Yes. Does it assume an amoral attitude toward their use? Definitely not! Communication professors can't ensure that their students will use principles learned in their course for honest purposes, but the aim of this book and most speech teachers is to instill in students the habit of speaking responsibly. Speakers have ethical responsibilities that must be accepted if human communication is to play its most meaningful role in our society.

Some have argued that the freedom to speak in a democratic society ensures that false statements will be revealed by competing speakers; the unethical speaker will be detected and rejected. This point of view overlooks two important factors. First, it places the responsibility for one's actions on someone else. The speaker can thus justify the use of bad logic or invalid evidence by rationalizing that it is the opponents' responsibility to recognize and publicize it; if no one identifies it, the speaker's conscience is clear. Second, this position assumes that competing points of view will be presented equally well by sources that are equally prestigious. Yet we know only too well that these two criteria are rarely met. A message from the president generally receives far greater attention than one from a senator. And a private citizen has little chance against a public official. We're all too familiar with the false charge of a public official against a citizen blazoned across the front page of a newspaper only to have the retraction, a week later, buried in a brief paragraph well inside the newspaper. In a democratic society speakers must assume responsibility for their communicative efforts.

Lack of trust in public officials has already become a serious problem in our society. The ordinary citizen, who has little access to the actual facts of most controversies, is in a state of confusion over the charges and counter-charges presented. Whom should we believe? If this situation continues, the lack of trust could become so enormous that no speaker will be free of it. When that happens, information and persuasion as means of problem-solving in a democratic society will have lost much of their force.

Furthermore, a democratic society is based on the assumption that, given the information, the majority of people can make better decisions for the general welfare than can a single individual or a small group of individuals. When the public receives inaccurate or inadequate information, however, decisions no longer relate to reality. In such cases, the basic foundation on which democracy rests ceases to function. If people are led to wrong decisions too often because of faulty information or fallacious reasoning, there is clear danger they'll become disillusioned and either stop participating in the voting process or begin making decisions on irrelevant bases such as ethnic background or personality. With too many wrong decisions there is the tragic possibility that people will lose faith in the democratic process itself and reject it for what they believe are more reliable methods: dictatorship, oligarchy, anarchy.

Ethical Bases

What are the bases for determining the ethical nature of oral communications? Some are considered in the remainder of this chapter.

Ends and Means

Some maintain that the end justifies the means. In other words, if a speaker attempts to persuade others to adopt a course of action deemed honorable, just, or desirable, then that speaker may use whatever means are available: distorting evidence, concealing motives, twisting reasoning, and making emotional appeals that prevent the rational thought processes of listeners from operating. The leaders of the Inquisition were convinced that the "truth" of Christianity was so indisputable that heretics should be identified, forced to admit their guilt, and to disavow their heresies. To achieve that "good end," they used the rack and other forms of torture to ensure that heresy was discredited. In this century Hitler used the "big lie" to persuade the German people to accept the programs of the Third Reich. Hitler justified the use of any means to achieve what he considered good social ends.

Unfortunately, this approach is based on one highly questionable assumption: that a given speaker has either the ability or the right to decide for others what is a good end. For example, some are so concerned about the danger of lung cancer and heart disease from cigarette smoking that they justify any means to discourage or prevent others from smoking. Yet some doctors have pointed out that smoking actually relieves nervous tension and anxieties for some people, thus possibly allowing them to live longer, healthier lives than if they did nothing to alleviate their tensions or turned to other means such as alcohol or hard drugs. Other doctors, however, have recently noted the harm that is done to children and other bystanders who inhale secondary tobacco smoke. This knowledge must certainly inhibit the freedom of others to smoke. Except in those instances where the choice is harmful to other members of society, however, who, other than the affected individual or individuals, has the right to determine what is a good end? The purpose of persuasion is to convince others that the speaker's objective is a good one. The only ethical method would be to present the strongest legitimate case possible and let each individual decide whether the end is good.

The speaker who follows the philosophy that the end justifies the means may hold one of three attitudes: (1) "The opposing side is stronger and cannot be defeated unless deceit is used." If that is true, something must be wrong with the end sought. The solution is for the speaker to reconsider his or her position, not to attempt to sell the weaker side by deception. (2) "Advocates of the opposing position are more skillful in persuading." Aristotle observed that truth would prevail if presented as skillfully as falsehood. If it is true that opposing speakers are more skillful, an advocate should improve speech skills instead of compensating with duplicity. (3) "The people to be persuaded are too stupid, too ignorant, or too motivated by baser emotions to be affected by truth." If this is the case, a speaker might make a more significant contribution to their welfare by engaging in an educational, informative effort. Then the listeners will have the ability to draw valid conclusions, and their commitment to the speaker's purpose will probably be longer lived. Moreover, if a speaker persuades through deceit, then the next skillful con artist to pass through the community may undo all the speaker's work.

Advocates should strive for good ends. What, after all, can be said for a speaker who supports evil ends—even through ethical and legitimate means? If we condone the use of unethical and illegitimate means for good ends, we are confronted with a society whose advocates either propose evil ends or use evil methods, hardly a society one would cherish living in.

As an oral communicator, always be concerned about the ends you advocate, not for the purpose of deciding the means to be used, but to be certain in your own conscience that your ends are justifiable, supported by the best evidence and reasoning you can find. Be sure your proposals won't harm others. Make sure your ends are consistent with the highest values of society, for as Thonssen, Baird, and Braden observe, "Speech is justified only if it betters society."[2]

Social Utility

Another means sometimes proposed for determining what is acceptable is the concept of social utility, which is ultimately concerned with "the *survival potential* of the group . . . involved."[3] The speaker determines which proposals to promote on the basis of which will do the most good for the group concerned.

Basic Considerations

Certainly an advocate must consider, as one criterion, whether a proposal will contribute to the benefits of the specific group. One of the difficulties in applying this standard is defining the group. Is it all humanity? Is it one nation? Is it one geographical section of a nation? Is it an ethnic group? But even after the group has been defined, the social utility approach can never be used as the sole criterion for selecting a position. Under the guidance of the greatest good for the survival potential of the group, one could justify Hitler's policy of exterminating Jews or the suppression of freedom in China.

The speaker must be concerned, therefore, about more than what is the greatest good for the group. Some policies and programs must be rejected because of the negative effects they have on a minority or another group, whereas others are desirable because of the good they do for a minority or another group.

Situation ethics, whose most noted proponent today is Joseph Fletcher, is based on the belief there are no natural laws to be followed absolutely—each individual situation must be examined to determine what is the good thing to do. Although some assume the individual making the decision has no principles to guide behavior except the situation in which one finds oneself, Fletcher makes clear that "the situationist enters into every decision-making situation fully armed with the ethical maxims of his community and its heritage."[4] From the framework of these ethical principles, whether they be Judeo-Christian, Moslem, or whatever, the individual decides what is the most loving thing to do, for (says Fletcher) "Loving actions are the *only* conduct permissible."[5] The love he is talking about is an attitude, not sentiment or emotion. It is the agapeic love, which "is neighbor-concerned, outgoing, not self-concerned or selective."[6] Four factors must be taken into consideration by the situationist in making a decision. (1) What *end* is desired? (2) What *means* are to be used to attain the end? (3) What *motive* is behind the act? (4) What *consequences* will result from the action?[7]

On the surface, situation ethics seems a reasonable, rational approach to the problem of determining ethical behavior, and some examples of situation ethics in action evoke little opposition from most people. For example, if an individual is confronted by an escaped convict who wants to know the home address of an intended murder victim, the situationist says the individual would do a good, loving thing by lying. Few would argue with this analysis.

But as the situation becomes more complex, situation ethics seems less clear-cut in its appropriateness and its rightness. One of Fletcher's examples is that of two mothers on different wagon trains going west. Because the wagons are being trailed by Indians, the cries of each mother's infant child pose a danger to the entire wagon train. One mother copes with this problem by choking her baby to death with her own hands, thus allowing the wagon train to arrive safely at the fort. The other mother simply tries to quiet the baby's crying, but is unsuccessful, and the Indians wipe out the entire group. Although asking the rhetorical question, "Which woman made the right decision?" Fletcher clearly implies that the one who saved the train at the expense

Situation Ethics

of the baby's life did the most loving thing because only one life was lost to save many. Many people would argue, however, that the mother who refused to murder her innocent, defenseless infant did the most loving thing. And many adults would not want their own lives saved in such a manner.

As a matter of fact, Fletcher himself provides a contradictory example when he refers to the expedition of Scott to the South Pole. When the men encountered trouble and had to return in haste to the coast, one of them was injured. Because carrying the stretcher slowed them down, Scott was faced with the choice of abandoning the injured man to save the others or continuing to carry him and risk all their lives. Scott chose the latter course, and all died. And Fletcher praises Scott, provided he "was not simply legalistic in his decision. . . ."[8]

Situation ethics seems to have an unsettling ability to justify diverse decisions. Situation ethics seems able to rationalize decisions and actions that stem from selfish and deceitful reasons.

An extremely vulnerable aspect of situation ethics is that it requires a high degree of sophistication in reasoning, objectivity in analysis, and an unusual breadth of perspective to exist in combination within a single individual. These attributes rarely occur singly in human beings.

Credibility-Centered Ethics

This book recommends that speakers adopt credibility-centered ethics. Since listeners hold you responsible for what you say and do in your messages, anything that lowers your credibility can either nullify or minimize the impact of your speech. Approach your communicative effort with the objective of demonstrating your competence and trustworthiness.

In 1986 it was discovered that President Ronald Reagan, who for several years had been critical of other nations for selling military arms to Iran, had been doing that very thing. People then rejected his argument that Iran's size and location made it an important and critical country in the Middle East because Reagan's actions suggested that his arguments had been used for deceitful purposes. As a result of the contradiction of his words and his actions, Reagan's credibility was damaged.

Avoid any possibility that listeners won't believe your messages. Because the following principles are approved by most societies, and because they result in the most valid ideas, observe them in developing and presenting messages to other people.

1. Formulate programs and policies only after a thorough examination of the available evidence. From all the available evidence, construct and present a rational basis for whatever policies and programs you advocate. If you have been unable to scrutinize some important relevant data, admit it and avoid implying you have investigated evidence that you haven't. Examine the empirical evidence, but don't ignore the evidence of experience, recognizing that experience adds a dimension unavailable from any other source.

2. Avoid fabricating or distorting evidence to make it support your position. If the evidence won't support your position, honest thinking demands that you alter that position to be consistent with the available evidence. Reject those who justify the use of falsehoods in persuasive speaking because society condones such practices as a doctor's not telling a patient he or she has a fatal disease. Such situations are not analogous to a communicator trying to persuade others to adopt a policy or a program.

3. Don't knowingly use fallacious or unsound reasoning. If you innocently make an error in reasoning, your ethics shouldn't be criticized. Since it is more difficult to assess ethical responsibilities in the use of reasoning than in the use of evidence, you should be given every benefit of the doubt before you are accused of unethical reasoning. But don't take advantage of this consideration by consciously using unsound reasoning and then, after you are detected, claiming that it was an innocent mistake.

4. Don't conceal an association with a group whose activities you're evaluating or advocating. Evaluating the activities of an organization without acknowledging an attachment to it creates an image of objectivity that distorts your statements and deceives your listeners.

5. Give credit to the sources of evidence. Don't present ideas that originated with others as though they are your own.

6. Don't abandon your own sincerely held convictions to say something pleasing to your audience. Understand that adaptation is an important ingredient of effective communication, but adapt to listeners only in whatever ways you legitimately can. Don't distort evidence or misrepresent your position or that of any group you represent in order to gain favor with particular listeners.

7. Don't imply or claim knowledge or experience you don't have. If your information is incomplete and your experience limited, admit it.

8. Don't simplify a subject to such an extent that listeners fail to comprehend its complexities. Obviously, in any communication on a complicated topic a certain amount of simplification results from selecting some ideas and materials to present while eliminating others. But never leave listeners unaware of any aspects important to the policy or program under discussion.

9. Don't arouse emotions on irrelevant bases to get listeners to accept or reject a proposal. Emotions are legitimately involved in decision making when they pertain to the topic being discussed but not when they are irrelevant. It's appropriate for those who support busing to integrate schools to arouse emotions by referring to the harm done to children who receive an inadequate education. It's also appropriate for those who oppose busing of children away from their neighborhood schools to arouse emotions by referring to the harm done to children who spend unnecessary time riding a bus each day. It's *not* appropriate for opponents to arouse emotions toward busing by calling it a "communist plot," *unless* they have definite evidence that it is.

If you follow these principles of credibility-centered ethics, your reputation should grow as a responsible, ethical communicator, and people will turn to you more and more for advice and leadership. Later chapters explain the principles of speech communication enabling you to develop the full potential of your reputation for credibility.

Summary

Since speech communication principles are amoral, they may be used for good or evil purposes. Because the power of speech in a free society is so awesome, however, speech communication teachers can't tolerate an amoral attitude toward its use. Anyone who uses communication must be concerned about its ethical nature.

We have seen in this chapter it isn't easy to establish a base on which to judge the ethical nature of communication. Judging on the basis of ends and means creates problems that aren't avoided with the bases of social utility and situation ethics. In the final analysis, credibility-centered ethics seems to offer the best means of establishing a dependable basis for promoting ethical communication.

Exercises

1. Read the speech in Appendix B entitled "Omissions Hurt CEO Ethics Rating," by John F. Budd, Jr. What is the author trying to say about ethics and corporations or organizations? Do you agree or disagree? If you were the adviser to the CEO of an organization, would you use any ideas developed by Budd? Are there any that you wouldn't use? Why or why not?

2. Write an essay describing the ethical conduct you deem appropriate for a speaker on your campus. How does that conduct contribute to the creation of credibility?

3. Name a contemporary speaker whom you consider credible. How do his or her ethics contribute to credibility?

4. Name a contemporary speaker whose credibility you question. What role do his or her ethics play in your judgment?

5. Name a political speaker who has, in your judgment, demonstrated a responsible attitude. Describe particular speeches or portions of speeches that caused you to think this person responsible.

6. You are the administrative assistant to a congressional representative from a district in which the state university is located. Your boss recently voted against a bill providing for federal support of higher education. You have been assigned to go to the campus to explain your chief's action. How would you do this in a credible and ethical way?

7. You are the information officer for the Pentagon. The United States is at war with another nation and an important campaign is now under way. An element of the army has been badly beaten. Although unaware of the extent of the damage, the enemy would be aided significantly, both militarily and psychologically, if they knew of it. Since a newspaper reporter has reported rumors of the defeat, the news media are now clamoring for a reply from you. What do you do?

Notes

1. T. R. Nilsen, *Ethics of Speech Communication* (Indianapolis: Bobbs-Merrill, 1966), p. 1.
2. L. Thonssen, A. C. Baird, and W. W. Braden, *Speech Criticism* (New York: Ronald Press, 1970), p. 452.
3. W. L. Brembeck and W. S. Howell, *Persuasion* (New York: Prentice-Hall, 1952), p. 455.
4. J. Fletcher, *Situation Ethics* (Philadelphia: Westminster Press, 1966), p. 26.
5. Ibid., p. 51.
6. Ibid., p. 103.
7. Ibid., pp. 127–28.
8. Ibid., p. 136.

CHAPTER 6

Creating Credibility

Columnist Patrick J. Buchanan was amazed that Pope John Paul II was "clasped to America's bosom" when he visited the United States in the fall of 1979.

Answering his own question, "How is it that a man with a message so unacceptable to the many—on contraception, abortion, divorce—can be so welcomed in the heart of the nation?" Buchanan wrote, "One answer can be found in the character of the man."[1] Columnist Charles Bartlett observed that "One thing is clear: the Pope has a gift for inspiring trust."[2] Character and trustworthiness—these are the qualities that develop credibility. As the credibility theme of this book indicates, ethos is particularly important to effective public speakers.

Definition of Ethos

Ethos, according to Aristotle, is the impression the speaker makes with his or her communication. Today we refer to it as the image of the speaker held by a particular listener. Aristotle considered ethos the most powerful factor in persuasion.[3] Modern research supports Aristotle's observation. Experimental studies have consistently revealed that although persuasive messages attributed to sources with low ethos produce opinion change, these same messages generally produce more attitude change when attributed to a source with high ethos.

Does ethos exist in you? No, it's in the eyes of the beholder. Ethos doesn't exist independently of you, however. Listeners' attitudes interact with your attributes to determine their attitude toward you. A university professor may be a nationally recognized scholar in a particular field, but in a city where university professors are held in low esteem, personal attainments as a scholar contribute nothing to ethos, and may in fact lower it. In another community, however, where university professors are held in high esteem, scholarly achievements enhance ethos. The same speaker, therefore, may have high ethos with some audiences and low ethos with others.

Not only does ethos vary from audience to audience, but, as shown in figure 6.1, it is a dynamic process. Your ethos varies every time you make an intelligent or unintelligent statement, a temperate or intemperate statement, a selfish or unselfish statement. Be aware that everything you say or do in a speaking situation has an effect on your ethos.

Two researchers showed clearly how a speaker's ethos can change during a speech. They measured the ethos of Malcolm X before, several times during, and after a speech to a predominantly white college audience. Of the eight measurements taken during the speech, the first—taken just after an opening prayer—showed a highly significant favorable shift. In remaining measurements, however, Malcolm X's ethos first went down, up twice, then consistently downward until the measurement taken after the speech was significantly lower than the first one made at the beginning of the speech.[4]

Figure 6.1

Ethos is not a static phenomenon, as revealed by this graph of the relationship between different events and Nixon's changing popularity.

From The Gallup Opinion Index, *Report 111 (September 1974), p. 12. Used by permission.*

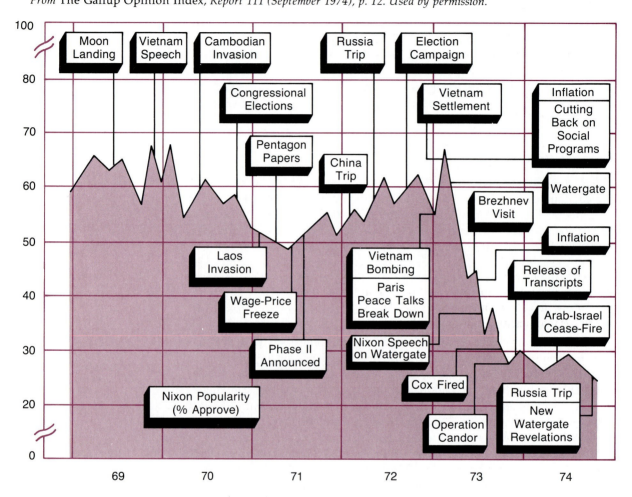

The change in the image of Jack Nicklaus demonstrates the dynamic nature of ethos. Early in his career he was called "Fat Jack" by golf spectators, and his wife lamented that it seemed she was the only one at a tournament pulling for "Fat Jack." With a slimmed-down physique, youthful clothes, a mod haircut, and a winning record, he suddenly became the "Golden Bear," and sports writers reported that he had become a sex symbol for females. His ethos was definitely enhanced!

Aristotle required that ethos "be created by the speech itself, and not left to depend upon an antecedent impression that the speaker is this or that kind of man."[5] Although it's certainly true you should use available techniques in speech to enhance your ethos, it's unrealistic to attempt to divorce the listeners' reactions to your communicative effort from their prior attitudes toward you. Most speakers are known for something—efficiency or inefficiency, maturity or immaturity—and that produces an image in others' minds. Whatever your image, you bring it to the communicative situation, and it either contributes or detracts from your effectiveness. By bringing positive ethos to the speaking occasion, you build credibility for your ideas and make them more easily accepted by the listeners.

Not only can you use your ethos to get your ideas accepted, you can also use speech to improve your ethos. Politicians have been using speeches to increase their ethos for a long time. They approve issues favored by their constituents, thus putting ethos in the bank. Then, when they have to take stands antithetical to their constituents on other issues, they draw on this reserve.[6]

Speakers improve their ethos in the speech itself by saying things that listeners like. McGinnies used the same speaker to present six different tape-recorded persuasive communications to students at four Japanese universities: a pro-American and pro-Soviet communication on the cold war; a pro-American and a pro-Soviet communication on the Cuban missile crisis; a communication favoring American submarine visits to Japanese ports; and a communication presenting arguments both for and against such visitations. Following the message, the students completed a questionnaire revealing their attitudes toward the speaker. The results showed that the message affected what they thought about the speaker. Although it was the same speaker delivering each message, one group of students thought the speaker, defending the role of the United States in the cold war, was significantly "more honest, sincere, interesting, strong, informed, and intelligent" than the speaker presenting the pro-Soviet argument.[7] The statements reflected their pro-American thoughts and caused the students to think more highly of the speaker.

Is ethos affected by the presence or absence of communication skills in the presentation of a speech? It appears so. Nine versions of a speech were tape-recorded with various numbers and types of nonfluencies occurring in each. Each student rated the credibility of the speaker in each of the versions. The results showed that increases in nonfluencies decreased the speaker's credibility.[8]

A speaker's ethos contributes to and is affected by a speech's impact. If your prespeech ethos is high, it should favorably influence the listener to accept your ideas. If, however, your speech contains statements that are obviously absurd, or if your ideas are opposite to those of the listeners, then the negative reaction may be so strong among the listeners that your postspeech ethos will be lowered. Even in this case there is generally a positive effect on listener attitudes toward the ideas. If you have positive ethos and you speak on an issue toward which the listeners are negative, there is a tendency for the listeners' attitudes to become less positive toward you and less negative toward your ideas. On the other hand, if you have negative ethos and you discuss issues toward which the listeners are positive, there is a tendency for the listeners' attitudes to become less negative toward you and less positive toward the issue.[9]

Sources of Ethos

If you are to take advantage of your existing ethos—use it when possible, build it when necessary, ignore it when feasible—you must understand the sources of ethos. "There are three things that gain our belief," wrote Aristotle, "namely, intelligence, character, and goodwill."[10] Present-day researchers have identified from two to twenty-one factors as the sources of ethos.[11]

Admittedly, determining the sources of ethos is complex, and there is also interaction among the speaker, the audience, the occasion, and the speech itself. In fact, after studying listeners' perceptions of the sources of ethos in three different situations—a lecture in a classroom, a speech to a social organization, and a sermon in a church—two researchers concluded that the sources of ethos are not the same over different situations.[12] Nevertheless, experimental evidence, supported by observation, indicates five main sources from which a speaker may derive ethos: *competence, trustworthiness, similarity, attraction,* and *sincerity.* These dimensions may not be mutually exclusive—they may overlap—but it is helpful to approach ethos from different focuses.

Competence refers to factors indicating the speaker is a source of valid information. Included are experience, age, leadership offices or titles, educational background, and other significant factors. It is sufficient that you seem to know what you are talking about. You don't have to be an expert to be considered competent.[13]

In the classic study on ethos, Haiman measured the attitudes of a group of college students toward compulsory health insurance on a nationwide basis. Dividing the students into three sections, he presented a recorded speech in which the speaker was identified first as the surgeon general of the United States, second as the secretary general of the Communist party in the United States, and third as a sophomore speech major (which the speaker in all three cases truly was) at Northwestern University. Attitude scales administered after the speech found a significant positive shift of opinion for those who thought they were hearing the surgeon general. There was a positive, less than significant, shift for those who thought they were hearing the sophomore student. Those who thought they were listening to a communist made a negative, though not significant, shift from the position advocated in the speech.[14] Although other factors were involved, undoubtedly one of the important factors influencing those who believed they were hearing the surgeon general was the belief that he was qualified to speak on this subject.

Competence as a specific source of credibility was accidentally identified. Establishing levels of credibility for various sources by pretests, two scholars presented assorted persuasive messages from different sources. Opinion change in the direction advocated occurred significantly more often with the high-ethos source than with the low-ethos sources. One exception stood out. The message, arguing that TV would cause a decline in the number of movie theaters, was attributed to *Fortune* magazine in the high-credible situation and to a movie gossip columnist in the low-credible situation. Surprisingly, the subjects changed their attitudes more when the message was attributed to the movie columnist than when it was attributed to *Fortune*. Apparently, the subjects generally considered *Fortune* to be a more credible source, but when faced with the specific topic, they felt that the movie columnist would be more competent to gauge the impact of TV on movie theaters.[15] Attempt to establish your knowledge on the subject of the speech if you're going to be an effective speaker.

Since competence is probably the most important dimension of ethos,[16] avoid topics you don't know. For you, this is a particular source of difficulty. You must generally develop your competence through the information on your topic. Not only must you develop competence on your subjects, you must skillfully make the hearers aware of your competence.

Even speakers with high ethos recognize they must make listeners aware of their competence. Former Surgeon General of the United States, C. Everett Koop, made his audience aware of his competence to deal with the specific problem of violence in children.

> . . . I believe the pediatrician has a unique relationship with children and
> with parents. You gain certain insights about individuals and families that
> other physicians may not have the chance to see.

I base that opinion, by the way, on the reflections of my own career of 35 years in pediatric surgery. Dealing with the young children who were my patients I saw firsthand the stresses of childhood and was aware of both the strengths and weaknesses of children trying to cope. I also had to understand the families of those children. I had to gain their confidence and win them as allies in the battle to help their children.

In the process, I think I began to understand a great deal about the contemporary family.

I tried to absorb that information and then focus it upon the problem to be solved by surgery. Sometimes, when it was clear to me that I was gaining insights into a serious family problem not directly related to the surgery, I would be open and available to that family, just in case they wanted to talk it through. But, I knew that I lacked a clear understanding of the need for me to become involved and to what extent I should become involved and what I might hope to accomplish.

Now, after looking at the data from my new vantage point as surgeon general, and appreciating the special access to and relationship with the American family that pediatricians do enjoy, I think my message to you today on violence in our society and its effects on children and families is appropriate and necessary.[17]

James B. Conant, former president of Harvard University and a critic of the system of secondary education in the United States, revealed his competence to discuss education by referring to his experiences and his accomplishments. Early in his speech he called attention to his experiences when he said,

There has been a good deal of talk in recent years about the need for a national educational policy. As I have studied public education in this country at all levels, I have become more and more convinced that the phrase a national educational policy is misleading.

Later he called attention to his accomplishments:

In a book published last year entitled *Shaping Educational Policy,* I answered this question in the affirmative. I suggested that the states enter into a compact or agreement to establish a commission which would be a planning commission with no administrative authority and thus differ from some of the regional boards.

In referring to statistics concerning dropout rates from school Conant said, "I have referred to these in my book *The Education of American Teachers,* and would merely like to repeat here what I have written in that book."[18]

Few college students have written books to which they can refer to increase ethos, but you can refer to books you have read to demonstrate your competence to talk on the subject of your speech.

These are some factors—knowledge, experience, and accomplishments—you can use to establish your competence on an issue. Be careful, however, that you don't seem to be boasting, for this can destroy the impact of your positive attributes. Provide information about your competence to the person introducing you; that will seem to be more objective. However, information establishing your competence has greater impact if provided at the pertinent point in your speech.

A second source of ethos is *trustworthiness,* or the appearance that the speaker gives of being honest, just, and objective. Avoid any appearance of self-interest in the outcome of the speaking effort. Most people are suspicious of a speaker whose self-interest will be served by the proposal advocated. Clear objectivity on your part will enhance your ethos. This fact was clearly demonstrated by researchers who presented a message to subjects from a convicted criminal. When the message advocated greater individual freedom and opposed greater power for police, little attitude change occurred. When the message advocated greater powers for police, there was a large attitude change. Clearly, in the latter instance, the subjects perceived the source of the communication as arguing against his own self-interest and changed opinion in the direction he favored even though he was originally a low-ethos source. The researchers conclude that when a low-prestige source argues against his own self-interest, he is "even more effective than a high-prestige communicator presenting the same argument."[19]

Trustworthiness

A study of the impact of orientation films for servicemen in World War II indicated the serviceman's estimate of the objectivity of the film affected his response to it. Those who thought the films were propaganda were less likely to accept them than those who thought their purpose was informational.[20] Increase your ethos by making listeners aware of your objectivity or lack of self-interest.

By making clear his candidness and implying his lack of hypocrisy, Attorney General Robert F. Kennedy demonstrated his trustworthiness in a speech to faculty and students at the University of Georgia during the time when civil rights was a particularly sensitive issue in the South.

> I have many friends in the United States Senate who are Southerners. Many of these friendships stem from my work as counsel for the Senate Rackets Committee, headed by Senator John McClellan of Arkansas for whom I have the greatest admiration and affection.
>
> If these Southern friends of mine are representative Southerners—and I believe they are—I do not pretend that they believe with me on everything or that I agree with them on everything. But, knowing them as I do, I am convinced of this:
>
> Southerners have a special respect for candor and plain talk. They certainly don't like hypocrisy. So, in discussing this third major problem, I must tell you candidly what our policies are going to be in the field of civil rights and why.[21]

In a 1961 speech to the National Association of Broadcasters, Newton Minow, then the new chairman of the FCC, made obvious his objectivity and his lack of self-interest:

> It would not surprise me if some of you had expected me to come here today and say in effect, "Clean up your own house or the government will do it for you."
>
> Well, in a limited sense, you would be right—I've just said it. But I want to say to you earnestly that it is not in that spirit that I come before you today, nor is it in that spirit that I intend to serve the FCC.
>
> I am in Washington to help broadcasting, not to harm it; to strengthen it, not weaken it; to reward it, not punish it; to encourage it, not threaten it; to stimulate it, not censor it.
>
> Above all, I am here to uphold and protect the public interest.[22]

A recent study of American values in the 1980s asked people to identify the least admired leader. Ranking Nixon first, respondents named dishonesty as the quality "they least admire in him." When asked to identify the quality of a leader they consider most important, the public overwhelmingly cited honesty.[23] A study of trustworthiness and ethos concluded that, despite other qualities, a speaker considered untrustworthy is viewed as a questionable source.[24]

Similarity

A *similarity* of attitudes or other factors between you and the audience in related and even nonrelated factors increases your ethos and makes it easier to gain acceptance for your ideas. During the Vietnam War, some protestors complicated their persuasive efforts by flaunting attitudes and behavior that alienated the very people they wanted to persuade. In the eyes of many Americans, the ethos of some protestors was tarnished by their waving of Viet Cong flags, disrespect for the American flag, use of foul language, disregard for others' rights, nudity, public participation in sexual activity, and other actions. These actions clearly emphasized the *dissimilarity* between certain protestors and those Americans who didn't approve of their beliefs and actions. Fully aware of this loss of ethos, many politicians in the 1970 elections refused to let young people who had become identified with the protest movement go out and campaign among the general public. They simply relegated them to doing clerical tasks in the back rooms.

It's difficult to overcome differences between yourself and your auditors on an issue you want to discuss. If, at the same time, you must overcome differences on a number of other related or unrelated factors, you have little chance to succeed in changing listeners' attitudes. Find and stress all the similarities with your listeners that you can. Thus you'll be able to build credibility for your ideas.

Successful politicians and other speakers have known and used for hundreds of years the "common ground" approach—the stressing of the similarities between speaker and audience. Kenneth Burke emphasized this point when he noted that, "You persuade a man only insofar as you can talk his language by speech, gesture, tonality, order, image, attitude, idea, *identifying* your way with his."[25] In the 1980 presidential campaign, both Carter and Reagan attempted to establish their similarities to southern voters. Carter tried to create a bond of similarity with southern audiences when he opened his campaign in Alabama on Labor Day, telling his audience: "It's good to be home." Then he further stressed his similarity by saying he was happy to be with friends "who don't talk with an accent." On the other hand, Reagan stressed his similarity in political attitudes. His campaign argued that there was greater philosophical similarity between southerners and Reagan than between them and Carter, even though Carter was from the South.

Although unrelated points of similarity are effective in increasing the ethos of the source, related items of similarity are the most effective. Berscheid presented a speaker as having attitudes similar to the audience in the field of education and dissimilar in the field of international affairs. To another audience she presented the speaker as having dissimilar ideas to theirs in the field of education and similar attitudes in the field of international affairs. Half of each audience then received a message on education and half received a message on international affairs. The most effective message for changing attitudes was the one in which the similarity was in the same area as the message.[26] Attempt to establish similarities in areas relevant to the subject of your speech.

As a persuasive speaker you don't have to rely on information given before the speech to develop common ground with your listeners; develop the similarities in the speech itself. Examining the attitudes of college students on a number of topics, Weiss discovered most of them were for fluoridation, but not strongly in favor of it. He also discovered they were almost unanimously in favor of academic freedom. Consequently, he prepared a communication opposing water fluoridation and favoring academic freedom. One group of students was exposed to the message favoring academic freedom before they were given the message opposing water fluoridation. A second group was exposed to a neutral communication before receiving the message opposing water fluoridation. Attitude scales collected immediately after the fluoridation speeches revealed that those students who were first exposed to the message on academic freedom accepted the attitudes against fluoridation more than those who were first exposed to the neutral message.[27]

Any similarity between the speaker and audience may be used to build ethos for the speaker. Notice how the president of the Pharmaceutical Manufacturers Association, speaking to representatives at an annual meeting of the American Land Title Association, undoubtedly enhanced his ethos by focusing on a similarity between his professional group and that of his audience:

> Perhaps I ought to confess that when I first received the invitation to appear here, I was somewhat daunted. I wondered why an organization whose wide interests lie in real estate development and underwriting title insurance would want to hear from a representative of the manufacturers of pharmaceuticals. Then I learned that your industry may be the object of a Congressional investigation in the foreseeable future.
>
> This, of course, is something with which the pharmaceutical industry has had long and painful experience, and the scars to prove it. We have been investigated, on and off, for ten solid years and the end is not in sight.
>
> There may be one or two exceptions which do not come readily to mind but I believe we are probably the most thoroughly investigated industry in the country today.
>
> My subject "The Congressional Hearing" allows me to review this decade of inquiry, and to offer you some comments and thoughts based on our experiences which may prove helpful to you at some later time.[28]

Attraction

Attraction refers to the orientation of one person toward another person. Newcomb observes that although it is normal to consider attraction equivalent to "liking," he prefers to think of it "in somewhat broader terms. Thus respect, admiration, and dependence all refer to positive person-to-person orientation, and yet any of these may be associated with either positive or negative liking." *Attraction,* then, refers to any relationship with another person that causes "approach rather than avoidance, moving toward rather than against or away from."[29]

One source of negative or positive attraction seems to be racial prejudice or the absence of it. Aronson and Golden had four speakers—a white engineer, a black engineer, a white dishwasher, and a black dishwasher—discuss the worth and significance of arithmetic with white fifth-grade students. Questionnaires revealing any change in attitude toward arithmetic were completed following the speech. The results showed the white engineer and the black engineer were equally persuasive, and both were significantly more persuasive than the black dishwasher. Although neither was significantly more effective than the white dishwasher, the latter was more effective than the black dishwasher. When the experimenters divided the subjects into "prejudiced" and "unprejudiced" categories, they discovered there was not only a "tendency for prejudiced individuals to be undersusceptible to the influence of a Negro communicator, but there was also a tendency for unprejudiced subjects to be oversusceptible to the influence of a Negro communicator."[30]

A second source of attraction is appearance. In front of a group of subjects who were being asked to fill out a questionnaire, the experimenters called for a volunteer to reply to the questionnaire aloud. A female confederate, who had already been coached, "volunteered." In one condition of the experiment, she "was made up to look extremely attractive. She wore chic, tight-fitting clothing; her hair was modishly coiffured; she wore becoming makeup." In the other condition, "the same confederate was made up to look repulsive. She wore loose, ugly, ill-fitting clothing; her hair was messy; her makeup was conspicuously absent; the trace of a moustache was etched on her upper lip; her complexion was oily and unwholesome looking." The results showed that the attractive communicator was more effective in changing the attitudes of the subjects.[31]

A third source of attraction is recognition by another person of positive aspects of one's self-concept. If a person considers herself to be intelligent and another person compliments her intelligence, the first person tends to be attracted to the other. In other words, we like those who like us for what we consider to be the right reasons. A clear distinction must be made, however, between flattery and liking. We frequently hear the statement "Flattery will get you everywhere." Not necessarily—only if the compliments are perceived as genuine.

A fourth source of attraction is fulfilling attributes. If a woman plays a violin, a man who likes violin music but doesn't play the instrument may be attracted to her. The man is fulfilled by listening to the music, and the woman is fulfilled by having someone listen while she plays. In other instances, opposites may attract one another. A woman who is forceful and domineering and a man who is meek and mild may be attracted to one another because each finds the relationship fulfilling. Factors causing the listeners to like or be attracted to you may be stressed in order to increase your ethos.

Sincerity

Although listeners aren't always able to differentiate between a speaker's genuine and feigned sincerity, they do respond more favorably to what they *perceive* as sincerity on the part of the speaker. Hildreth had speakers present speeches on topics in which they believed and on topics in which they did not believe. Listeners were asked to determine the sincerity of each speaker and to rate his or her effectiveness. Although unable to distinguish between sincere and insincere speakers, hearers rated as most effective those speakers perceived as sincere.[32]

In practical as well as experimental situations, speakers who mean what they say are rated more credible by listeners. Listeners were asked who won the presidential debates in 1960; then they were asked why they thought Kennedy or Nixon was better. One of the three reasons cited was the speaker's sincerity.[33]

An admirer of Lincoln reported that she had long been interested in the most important element of Lincoln's "success as a speaker." Finally, she asked the question of Paul Angle, a noted authority on Lincoln. He replied: "Lincoln's transparent honesty and sincerity was the impressive characteristic of his oratorical style. I believe he created the impression of sincerity by complete honesty in dealing with his opponent."[34]

Recent evidence demonstrates the importance of sincerity in obtaining a favorable response from others. A list of 555 trait names was presented to subjects with instructions "to think of a person being described by each word and to rate the word according to how much they would like the person." The word receiving the highest likeableness rating was *sincerity*.[35]

Basic Considerations

The late President Harry S Truman, recognizing the immense importance of this quality to a speaker, declared that "Sincerity, honesty, and a straight-forward manner are more important than special talent or polish."[36]

Without undermining in any way the importance of sincerity or the veracity of Mr. Truman's testimony, let it be noted that it doesn't have to be an either/or situation. The polished speaker can be sincere, honest, and straightforward, and the sincere, honest, straightforward speaker can develop polish.

When you are *perceived* as sincere, you lend credibility to your ideas. And you have an ethical responsibility to *be* sincere.

Summary

Ethos is the listener's perceived image of the speaker. It is a function not only of who you are, but also of the listeners' attitudes toward your attributes. Thus you have only partial control over your ethos. In the final analysis, it isn't your abilities, accomplishments, and attributes that determine your ethos, but the estimate of those factors made by listeners.

You should recognize that ethos plays an important role in the degree to which your speaking will influence listeners. Although the accumulated evidence seems to indicate that a well-developed speech can change the attitudes of listeners despite the low ethos of the speaker, it also quite clearly shows that the same speech will have a more significant impact if presented by a speaker with high ethos. The development of ethos will do much to create credibility for your ideas.

The sources of ethos are many and complex, but research indicates that five main sources are *competence* of the speaker, *trustworthiness* of the speaker, *similarity* between the speaker and listeners, *attraction* of the speaker to the audience, and perceived *sincerity* of the speaker.

Exercises

1. Analyze the speaking of a contemporary politician. In what ways does he or she use ethos to retain or improve credibility? What does this person do that makes you believe that he or she (a) knows what he or she is talking about, (b) is trustworthy, (c) is similar to you, or (d) has traits that are attractive to you?
2. Attend a lecture on campus. Describe the ways in which the lecturer attempted to develop similarities between the listeners and himself or herself. Did this affect the speaker's credibility? Why or why not?
3. Select one of the sources of ethos discussed in this chapter and explain in detail how you can use it in your next speech to increase your credibility.
4. Discuss the practice of responding to the speaker's "image." In what ways is this an unfair method of determining a speaker's credibility? In what ways a fair method?
5. List three contemporary speakers who evince sincerity in speaking. Explain what causes you to think they are sincere.

Notes ————————————————————————————

1. Patrick J. Buchanan, "The Dividing Line," *Birmingham News,* October 12, 1979. Used by permission.
2. Charles Bartlett, "News Focus," *Birmingham News,* October 2, 1979. Used by permission.
3. L. Cooper, *The Rhetoric of Aristotle* (New York: D. Appleton-Century Co., 1932), pp. 8–9.
4. R. D. Brooks and T. M. Scheidel, "Speech as Process: A Case Study," *Speech Monographs* 35 (1968):1–7.
5. Cooper, *Rhetoric of Aristotle,* pp. 8–9.
6. J. C. McCroskey, "Ethos, Credibility and Communication in the Real World," *North Carolina Journal of Speech* 4 (Spring 1971):24–31.
7. E. McGinnies, "Studies in Persuasion: V. Perceptions of a Speaker as Related to Communication Content," *Journal of Social Psychology* 75 (1968):21–33.
8. G. R. Miller and M. A. Hewgill, "The Effect of Variations in Nonfluency on Audience Ratings of Source Credibility," *Quarterly Journal of Speech* 50 (1964):36–44.
9. C. E. Osgood and P. H. Tannenbaum, "The Principle of Congruity in the Prediction of Attitude Change," *Psychological Review* 62 (1955):42–55.
10. Cooper, *Rhetoric of Aristotle,* p. 92.
11. C. I. Hovland, I. L. Janis, and H. H. Kelley, *Communication and Persuasion* (New Haven: Yale University Press, 1953), chap. 2; D. K. Berlo, J. B. Lemert, and R. J. Mertz, "Dimensions for Evaluating the Acceptability of Message Sources," *Public Opinion Quarterly* 33 (1969–70):563–76; J. C. McCroskey, "Scales for the Measurement of Ethos," *Speech Monographs* 33 (1966):65–72; J. L. Whitehead, Jr., "Factors of Source Credibility," *Quarterly Journal of Speech* 54 (1968):59–63; D. Schweitzer and G. P. Ginsburg, "Factors of Communicator Credibility," in *Problems of Social Psychology,* ed. C. C. Backman and P. F. Secord (New York: McGraw-Hill, 1966), pp. 94–102; W. J. McGuire, "The Nature of Attitudes and Attitude Change," *The Handbook of Social Psychology,* ed. G. Lindzey and E. Aronson (Reading, Mass.: Addison-Wesley Publishing Co., 1969), 3:179.
12. R. F. Applebaum and K. W. E. Anatol, "The Factor Structure of Source Credibility as a Function of the Speaking Situation," *Speech Monographs* 39 (1972):216–22.
13. Whitehead, "Factors of Source Credibility," p. 60.
14. F. S. Haiman, "An Experimental Study of the Effects of Ethos in Public Speaking," *Speech Monographs* 16 (1949):190–202.
15. C. I. Hovland and W. Weiss, "The Influence of Source Credibility on Communication Effectiveness," *Public Opinion Quarterly* 15 (1951):635–50. See also Kelman and Hovland, " 'Reinstatement' of the Communicator," pp. 327–35; E. Aronson, J. A. Turner, and J. M. Carlsmith, "Communicator Credibility and Communicator Discrepancy as Determinants of Opinion Change," *Journal of Abnormal and Social Psychology* 67 (1963):31–36.
16. D. G. Bock and T. J. Saine, "The Impact of Source Credibility, Attitude Valence, and Task Sensitization on Trait Errors in Speech Evaluation," *Speech Monographs* 42 (1975):235.
17. C. Everett Koop, "Violence and Public Health," Owen Peterson, ed., *Representative American Speeches, 1982–1983* (New York: The H. W. Wilson Co., 1983), pp. 210–11.

18. J. B. Conant, "The Role of the States in Education," *Vital Speeches of the Day* 31 (1965):686–88.

19. E. Walster, E. Aronson, and D. Abrahams, "On Increasing the Persuasiveness of a Low Prestige Communicator," *Journal of Experimental Social Psychology* 2 (1966):325–42.

20. Hovland et al., *Communication and Persuasion,* p. 24.

21. R. F. Kennedy, "Law Day Address—University of Georgia," from *Rights for Americans: The Speeches of Robert F. Kennedy,* ed. Thomas A. Hopkins, copyright © 1964 by Thomas A. Hopkins, reprinted by permission of The Bobbs-Merrill Company, Inc., pp. 17–26.

22. N. N. Minow, "The Vast Wasteland," from Newton N. Minow, *Equal Time: The Private Broadcaster and the Public Interest,* ed. Lawrence Laurent (New York: Atheneum Publishers, 1964), p. 50. Used by permission of Atheneum Publishers.

23. *The Connecticut Mutual Life Report on American Values in the '80s: The Impact of Belief* (Hartford: Connecticut Mutual Life Insurance Co., 1981), pp. 193–95.

24. R. G. Smith, "Source Credibility Context Effects," *Speech Monographs* 40 (1973):309.

25. K. Burke, *A Rhetoric of Motives* (New York: Prentice-Hall, 1950), p. 55. See also E. Burnstein, E. Stotland, and A. Zander, "Similarity to a Model and Self-Evaluation," *Journal of Abnormal and Social Psychology* 62 (1961):257–64.

26. E. Berscheid, "Opinion Change and Communicator—Communicatee Similarity and Dissimilarity," *Journal of Personality and Social Psychology* 4 (1966):670–80.

27. W. Weiss, "Opinion Congruence with a Negative Source on One Issue as a Factor Influencing Agreement on Another Issue," *Journal of Abnormal and Social Psychology* 54 (1957):180–86.

28. C. J. Stetler, "The Congressional Hearing," *Vital Speeches of the Day* 36 (1969–70):53–56.

29. T. M. Newcomb, *The Acquaintance Process* (New York: Holt, Rinehart & Winston, 1961), pp. 6–7.

30. E. Aronson and B. Golden, "The Effect of Relevant and Irrelevant Aspects of Communicator Credibility on Opinion Change," *Journal of Personality* 30 (1962):135–46.

31. J. Mills and E. Aronson, "Opinion Change as a Function of the Communicator's Attractiveness and Desire to Influence," *Journal of Personality and Social Psychology* 1 (1965):173–77.

32. R. A. Hildreth, "An Experimental Study of Audiences' Ability to Distinguish between Sincere and Insincere Speeches," Ph. D. diss., University of Southern California, 1953.

33. S. Kraus, ed., *The Great Debates* (Bloomington: Indiana University Press, 1962), p. 198.

34. M. F. Berry, "Lincoln—The Speaker: Part II," *Quarterly Journal of Speech* 17 (1931):187.

35. N. H. Anderson, "Likeableness Ratings of 555 Personality-Trait Words," *Journal of Personality and Social Psychology* 9 (1968):272–79.

36. E. E. White and C. R. Henderlider, "What Harry S Truman Told Us about His Speaking," *Quarterly Journal of Speech* 40 (1954):39.

CHAPTER 7

Understanding and Adapting to Listeners

Attitudes are the wellsprings from which behavior flows. This is not to contend that the development, arousal, or holding of an attitude will result in a specific behavior related to that attitude. Other factors may intervene. A person may believe strongly in the necessity of saving gasoline, but the fear of flying and a desire to take a vacation 2,000 miles away may motivate that individual to drive that distance, using many gallons of gasoline. Or a person who believes drugs are harmful may not express that attitude when everyone in the group begins smoking marijuana. Consequently, you may arouse an old attitude or develop a new one and still not produce the behavior desired. Nevertheless, the existence of an attitude does create pressure within the individual to behave in a manner consistent with that attitude. With an effect similar to that of credibility, activating an attitude in a listener enhances your chances of causing the desired behavior. To understand how to activate attitudes, you must know what they are and how they operate.

Definition of Attitude

Many definitions of attitudes exist. This book defines one as "an evaluation or feeling reaction."[1] As three authors explain:

> *Attitudes* refer to the stands the individual upholds and cherishes about objects, issues, persons, groups, or institutions. The referents of a person's attitudes may be a "way of life"; economic, political, or religious institutions; family, school, or government. We are speaking of the individual's attitudes when we refer to his holding in high esteem his own family, his own school, his own party, his own religion, with all the emotional and affective overtones these terms imply. We refer to his attitudes when we say he holds other groups, other schools, other parties or religions in a less favorable light or at a safe distance (as "safe" is defined by his attitudes).[2]

An attitude differs from a motive in that an attitude persists, whereas a motive comes and goes, and its strength depends on a drive state. Thus a person may have a favorable attitude toward the eating of rabbit. Though the attitude remains constant, the person won't ordinarily eat rabbit until the hunger motive occurs. Another individual may have an unfavorable attitude toward eating rabbit. If this person has been in the forest several days without food, the hunger motive may be cause to overlook this attitude in order to satisfy the hunger. Nevertheless, unless eating rabbit causes some change, the original unfavorable attitude toward the eating of rabbit will persist.

An attitude is also different from a belief in that a belief is more cognitively oriented. A belief is based, or seemingly based, on factual information. That the United States has a universal system of free education is a belief. That the universal system of free education in the United States is worthwhile is an attitude. That the United States has a democratic form of government is a belief. That the democratic form of government in the United States is beneficial is an attitude. Thus an attitude involves judgment, evaluation, feeling.

An opinion is defined as the verbalization of an attitude. It may or may not accurately reflect the attitude underlying it, but in many instances it is the only index we have to a person's attitudes. At least the opinion constitutes what the individual wants the world to think his or her attitude is.

Components of Attitude

An attitude has three components: the cognitive, the affective, and the behavioral. Its *cognitive* aspect consists of the perceptions, thoughts, and beliefs a person has about a particular class of objects. It doesn't matter whether these perceptions, thoughts, and beliefs are accurate or inaccurate. For the person who has them, they constitute "knowledge." If the athletes you have known have been dumb, then for you athletes are dumb. If someone has lived in a community where businesspeople have been corrupt, then for that person businesspeople are corrupt. What can you do to change attitudes? You can provide information. It can be very important in changing and forming attitudes, especially if it is credible information previously unknown to the listener.

The *affective* component consists of the feelings an individual has about an object. These feelings may be favorable or unfavorable and may be measured physiologically. College students listened to complimentary or derogatory statements about ethnic groups while their galvanic skin response (GSR) was measured. Most students' GSRs were greater while they were hearing a derogatory statement about a group they liked than while hearing a derogatory statement about a group toward which they were neutral. The GSRs were also greater when the students were listening to complimentary statements about groups they disliked than when listening to complimentary statements about groups toward which they were neutral.[3] After determining the attitudes of a group of university students toward the church, Dickson and McGinnies measured the students' GSRs while letting them hear recorded statements praising or criticizing the church. Regardless of the individual student's attitude toward the church, the GSR was greater when the statement heard contradicted the student's attitude than when the statement agreed with it.[4] From this evidence and everyday observation, McGinnies, concluded "that attitudes do have emotional support, and that the emotional component is more apparent when someone's attitudes are attacked than when they are supported."[5] Speakers who attack objects or concepts cause a greater emotional response among their hearers than speakers who make positive statements about their proposals.

The *behavioral* component refers to the actions that a person adopts in relation to an object or concept because of an attitude or group of attitudes. Although no person's behavior correlates directly with attitudes, there is good evidence now that behavior and attitudes are more positively related than had been previously thought. For example, when people are reminded of their experience with an object, there is a greater tendency for behavior to be related to their attitude toward that object. In one study, for example, subjects were asked about their attitudes toward religion. Prior to being asked, however, some of the subjects were asked to complete a ninety-item checklist describing their religious behavior in the past year. Approximately thirty days later, all the subjects were requested to describe their recent religious behavior. Those who had completed the checklist revealed generally higher correlations between attitude and behavior. Those who had not filled out the checklist had significantly lower attitude-behavior correlations. Thus, it appears that attitudes and behavior are more closely related if subjects are reminded of their past behavior.[6]

Well-conducted public opinion polls, by virtue of their accuracy in predicting what actions people will take on such issues as voting, have demonstrated an impressive correlation between attitudes and behavior.

Several factors affect the consistency between attitudes and behavior. First, the strength of the attitude is important. The greater the strength, the more likely is a person's behavior to reflect that attitude. Second, the way in which the attitude is formed affects the correlation between it and behavior. Attitudes created by direct experience tend to correlate more highly with behavior than those developed by indirect experience ("reading or being told about the attitude object").[7] Third, the social acceptance of an attitude influences whether behavior will reflect it. A person who is prejudiced against a particular group of people will be less likely to reflect that prejudice in behavior if the people with whom he or she is currently associating are opposed to that particular prejudice.[8]

Two factors sometimes give the impression that behavior is unrelated to attitudes. First, time may have elapsed between the expression of an attitude and its expected behavioral component, and the attitude may no longer be held at the time of the expected behavior. Second, an expected behavior doesn't necessarily follow from one specific attitude. For example, you may like college football, but that doesn't mean you'll support the relaxing of academic standards to make an all-American player eligible. If it's concluded that your behavior doesn't reflect your attitude, it's because a behavior was expected that doesn't necessarily follow from your attitude.[9]

Characteristics of Attitudes

Attitudes have distinctive characteristics. First, the *intensity,* or strength, of an attitude may vary, since it involves a judgment, an emotional reaction, which may be strong or mild, or varying degrees in between. The person who considers nuclear weapons dangerous may hold that attitude strongly, moderately, or mildly. The intensity of the attitude may well be reflected in that person's behavior. Citizens who join in marches against the use of animals for experimental research probably have stronger attitudes against cruelty to animals than those who stay home.

A second important characteristic of attitude is its *centrality* to the whole attitude system. It may be peripheral, or it may be a vital part of the person's attitude system. If a person who has a favorable attitude toward athletics is a football coach, then that attitude will lie close to the center of the person's attitude system. To disturb that attitude would be to disturb many other attitudes. If the person is a businesswoman advising high school athletes, that attitude will be important to her but not as vital as to the coach. A disturbance of this attitude would probably not affect many of her attitudes. Other attitudes will play a more important role in determining her behavior.

Third, attitudes may be *salient* or nonsalient. An attitude is salient if the immediate situation causes you to be aware of it. For example, you may dislike intensely a professor on your campus. But, on most occasions that attitude is not salient and you are not consciously aware of it. If someone begins to talk about that professor, however, or you are forced to take her class, then the attitude becomes salient and you become aware of it.

Fourth, attitudes have *direction*—they may be positive or negative. An individual may have a favorable or unfavorable attitude toward the Strategic Defense Initiative (SDI or Star Wars). The positive attitude will cause that person to "approach" SDI—for example, to support higher taxes for military spending. The negative attitude will cause someone to "avoid" SDI—to oppose higher taxes for military spending.

Fifth, attitudes have differing levels of *stability*. They tend to grow more fixed the longer they are held. Since young people have held most attitudes only a short time, they are more flexible, as demonstrated in their greater willingness to accept new proposals or new concepts. Older persons, having held attitudes a longer time, are generally less willing to change. Accumulated evidence clearly shows this to be true for political affiliation, in which the increasing rigidity of attitudes affects behavior. There is a decline in the probability that people will change their political parties as they get older.[10]

Sixth, attitudes have varying degrees of *clarity*. We define the clarity of an attitude as the width of a person's latitude of acceptance. An attitude with a high degree of clarity reduces the number of positions a person finds acceptable. An attitude with a low degree of clarity increases the number of positions a person finds acceptable.

The six characteristics of attitudes—intensity, centrality, salience, direction, stability, and clarity—are important to the oral communicator. You need to know how these characteristics apply to the attitudes held by your listeners if you are to deal meaningfully with them and to establish credibility for your ideas. Only a careful, intensive analysis of your listeners prior to the communicative effort can provide this important information.

Formation of Attitudes

Within the past two decades theories have developed to account for and predict the formation and change of attitudes. None has proved wholly satisfactory. "Subsequent research will undoubtedly make these theoretical orientations appear more and more inadequate."[11]

On the assumption that attitude formation and change are complex processes dependent on individual differences as well as on contextual factors, this book argues that attitudes may be formed or changed at any age from a variety of causes. Without getting involved in the dispute over which theory is best, it is maintained that most attitudes stem from one or more of the following three causes: (1) one's environment, (2) one's self-interest, and (3) one's desire for cognitive consistency.

Our environment plays an important role in determining our attitudes. Communication, both verbal and nonverbal, is a prime vehicle in the process. As children we begin early to adopt attitudes from those around us. There is a strong correlation between the attitudes of children and their parents.[12] A 1968 national survey of high school seniors disclosed that when both parents held the same political beliefs, 76 percent of the seniors held those same beliefs.[13] Attitudes are acquired by imitation, either conscious or unconscious. We like the people around us and want to be like them, and one important way to be like them is to adopt their attitudes.

Some attitudes are the result of deliberate cultivation, primarily through oral communication. Religious attitudes are consciously taught in synagogues, temples, and churches. New recruits into military service undergo training to

Environment

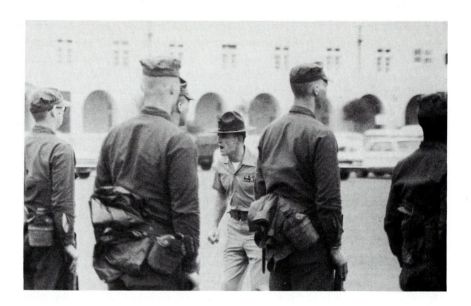

develop specific attitudes toward discipline, fighting, and being shot at. The Boy Scouts and the 4-H Clubs in the United States, the Komsomol in the Soviet Union, the pioneer youth movements in Israel, though different in a number of respects, have a common concern: they aim, in part, to challenge adolescents to give a high priority to the performance of public service roles. This includes the performance of acts of good citizenship, the discussion of social issues and consideration of the idea that, in an emergency, they should volunteer for difficult and dangerous assignments. They offer an organizational framework for young people to play approved adultlike roles, to acquire self-confidence, and to undergo a rite of passage into a more mature status. The program includes work and adventure, indoctrination and self-expression, study and instruction, which the sponsoring adult-making agency views as relevant preparation for becoming a reliable person.[14]

Self-Interest

Our self-interest causes many attitudes to develop. A child learns attitudes through being rewarded for some behaviors and punished for others. Adults also develop and hold attitudes as a result of rewards and punishments. An employee changes political affiliation to conform to that of the boss because it removes an area of discord between them and will likely mean quicker promotions and larger salary increases.

One of the reasons young people in the early 1990s support the present system is they perceive the system operating in their self-interest. The more material possessions people have, the more they stand to lose by a destruction of the established order. It is no accident that most of the radical revolutionaries are among those who have "dropped out" of society; since they have few material possessions—little self-interest at stake—they have little to lose by destruction of "the system." Reference groups—those whose standards or norms influence a person's attitude—exert enormous pressure on a person's attitudes because self-interest demands conformity to group values in order to remain a member in good standing with peers.

Our desire for cognitive consistency causes many attitudes to be formed or altered. This process is known by a number of names: dissonance theory, congruency theory, balance theory.[15] It is nothing more than homeostasis (automatic efforts of the body to maintain a constant, normal state) on the cognitive level, similar in type to the homeostasis that takes place on the physiological level. Just as the body attempts to restore balance to the bodily temperature by sweating in a hot environment, so we attempt to restore balance to our attitudinal system when two or more attitudes become imbalanced. Significantly, when an imbalance occurs in a person's attitude system, it generally means that "some *new state of balance* will come about—not just any old change, at random, but a change that is orderly because it follows the principle of balance."[16]

Cognitive Consistency

For example, if a person whom we admire makes a statement praising an object we detest, we are faced with a cognitively inconsistent situation. To restore the consistency, we have a number of alternatives. We may decide we were in error in our judgment of the individual and develop a negative attitude toward that person. We may decide we were in error about the object and develop a positive attitude toward it. We may decide we were in error about our judgment of both the individual and the object and develop a less positive attitude toward the person and a less negative attitude toward the object. Another alternative is to deny the reality of the situation, which in this instance would be to deny that the person made the statement. This allows us to maintain our cognitive consistency. This alternative is not available, however, unless there is ambiguity about the reality of the situation. This allows us to maintain our cognitive consistency. You may cause attitude change, however, simply by removing the ambiguities of a situation so that a listener's cognitive inconsistency becomes obvious.

Another alternative is to acknowledge the inconsistency exists, but deny its importance. For example, you have a favorable attitude toward a person who has made a positive statement about an object for which you have a negative attitude. You simply maintain that your attitude toward that object is insignificant and unrelated to your relationship with that person. So you quit thinking about the imbalanced attitudes. You may be able to effect attitude change, therefore, by bringing cognitive inconsistency to a conscious level and setting forth its significance.

A final alternative is that the imbalance persists and no attitude change occurs. This is possible, but unlikely because it makes most people uncomfortable. In fact, the imbalance motivates most people to eliminate the factors causing discomfort.[17]

Audience Analysis

An important advantage of human communication is that you can adapt your message to the specific situation and the particular receiver. The message thus acquires greater credibility because it is more appropriate.

In order to adapt your speaking to particular listeners, you must understand not only the theoretical bases of attitudes but also what specific attitudes are held by your listeners. For this reason, a careful audience analysis must be made for each speaking occasion. Audience analysis is the identification of those characteristics of the listeners—including their needs, wants, beliefs, attitudes, experiences, knowledge, and values—that influence the way they will probably respond to the speaker's message.

Analyzing the Attitudes of Potential Listeners

In the ideal situation, you would analyze the attitudes of each member of an audience, developing a thorough knowledge of each person. Except in a classroom situation, you will only rarely know beforehand precisely who will be in the audience. At best, you will generally know only that the listeners will come from certain areas of the city, county, state, or nation. Even if the exact composition of an audience can be determined, it is normally impractical to meet all listeners in advance to discover their attitudes regarding the speech topic.

When the exact membership of an audience is unknown, you can still find information to draw inferences about the population from which the audience will be drawn. The validity of those inferences will determine the value of the audience analysis. To analyze an expected audience, use one of two methods: a demographic analysis or a purpose-oriented analysis.[18]

Demographic Analysis

A demographic analysis considers salient characteristics of the potential hearers to derive inferences about their attitudes. These inferences then permit you to make strategic choices about subjects, materials, and methods to be used in the specific communicative situation. Some of the more common questions to be asked are discussed below.

Age What is the *age* of the listeners? Age affects an individual's interests, motivations, values, attitudes, and other factors. In the last few years, some commentators have talked about a "generation gap" as though it were a new phenomenon. In fact, it has existed as long as human beings have, although some periods draw more attention to it than others. Some 2,500 years ago, Aristotle described the characteristics of people in their youth, middle age, and old age. His descriptions are amazingly apt even today. Note, for example, his description of youth:

> Young men have strong desires, and whatever they desire they are prone to do. Of the bodily desires the one they let govern them the most is the sexual; here they lack self-control. They are shifting and unsteady in their desires, which are vehement for a time, but soon relinquished; for the longings of youth are keen rather than deep—are like sick people's fits of hunger and thirst. The young are passionate, quick to anger, and apt to give way to

it. . . . They love both honor and victory more than they love money. Indeed, they care next to nothing about money, for they have not yet learned what the want of it means. . . . The young think no evil [are not cynical], but believe in human goodness, for as yet they have seen many examples of vice. They are trustful, for as yet they have not been often deceived. . . . They live their lives for the most part in hope [anticipation], as hope is of the future and memory of the past; and for young men the future is long, the past but short. . . . They are high-minded [have lofty aspirations]; first, because they have not yet been humbled by life, nor come to know the force of circumstances; and secondly, because high-mindedness means thinking oneself fitted for great things, and this again is characteristic of the hopeful. In their actions they prefer honor to expediency; for their lives are rather lives of good impulse. . . . All their mistakes are on the side of intensity and excess. . . . They carry everything too far; they love to excess, they hate to excess—and so in all else. They think they know everything, and are positive about everything; indeed, this is why they always carry their doings too far.[19]

On the other hand, notes Aristotle, the characteristics of elderly men "for the most part are the opposite of these."[20] As he did for all subjects, Aristotle applied the principle of the golden mean to this topic of age when he said: "As for men in the prime of life, their character evidently will be intermediate between these two, exempt from the excess of either young or old."[21]

An important fact to note is that age has a significant effect on the stability of a person's attitudes. Young people's attitudes are more likely to be unstable simply because, in general, they have been held for a shorter period of time. Since older people generally will have held their attitudes for a longer time, theirs will generally be more stable.

Sex What is the *sex* of the listeners? You need this information to determine whether your audience includes both men and women or just one sex. Just a few years ago, researchers reported that women succumbed to group pressures more than men, were less willing to express their views on public affairs than men, and were more persuasible than men; that married women tended to accept the political affiliation of their husbands when it conflicted with that of their parents; and that women were less interested than men in the economy, business, sports, and politics. These statements may have been generally valid at one time, but their validity is highly questionable today.

Women currently do most things men do. They're enrolled in all the service academies; they participate in intercollegiate athletics; they're active in mass communication; they seek and win political office; they hold leadership posts in education and business. These role models have altered the attitudes of many women, especially young girls. In the future, we'll have to look at factors other than sex of the listeners.

Education What is the *educational level* of the listeners? The amount of education people possess influences their interest and participation in politics and community affairs. It affects the amount of knowledge they have about current events and world affairs, their expectations for the future, the amount of confidence they have in their ability to control events, and the consistency of their stated beliefs in democratic principles with actions involving those principles. It affects tolerance for others in the general population and influences the stability, intensity, and consistency of attitudes. People's educational level influences whether changes in attitudes come primarily because of new information, or whether group pressures and authoritative opinions are the major factors. Critical thinking ability and vocabulary level are affected by educational level. Finally, educational level influences people's awareness of the political system, their detachment from it, the degree of alienation resulting from policies of the system, and their place in it.

Political philosophy What is the *political philosophy* or ideology of the listeners? Does this refer to the political party the listeners belong to? Not at all! There are in both major political parties individuals with differing political philosophies. Two political observers concluded: "Conservatives are only somewhat more likely to be Republican than Democrat, and Democrats are not much more likely to be liberal than conservative."[22] Almost equal numbers of independents are liberal, conservative, and moderate. The political philosophy or ideology of an individual affects attitudes toward government spending, restrictions on business, national defense, individual freedom, busing to achieve integration, public work programs, abortion on demand, and a more relaxed relationship with Communist nations.

Audience homogeneity How *homogeneous* are the listeners? If the people are greatly similar, it will be easier to find speech content that is acceptable to the majority. If all the listeners are farmers, they'll be a rather homogeneous group. If half are farmers and half are urbanites, there will be considerable heterogeneity. If a third are farmers, a third urbanites, and a third suburbanites, there will be a great deal of heterogeneity. In a college speech course, the classroom audience is relatively homogeneous. The students are all about the same age, have essentially the same level of education, come from the same general geographical area, and are generally motivated to achieve. Although a classroom audience certainly has heterogeneous features, the number of similar factors offers many ways for you to adapt the message.

Cultural interests What are the *cultural interests* of the listeners? Is this related to the educational level? In many ways it is; in others, it is not. People in two areas with the same general educational level can have entirely different cultural interests. Are the people of the area interested in the arts—Is there a symphony orchestra in the area? A museum of fine arts? An art gallery? Or are the people of the area strongly interested in sports—Are there professional teams in various sports? A stock car racetrack?

Are there a number of bookstores in the area, indicating that the people read frequently? What kind of books sell best in the area? What kind of magazines do the people read: *Reader's Digest, Harper's, Atlantic, People, The Wilson Quarterly, Sport?*

Are people of the area widely traveled, or do few travel outside the area? Are they familiar with cultural activities in other areas, or are they predominantly provincial in their knowledge and interests?

All these aspects of cultural interests will affect the attitudes of the people who might be in an audience.

Ethnic background What is the *ethnicity* of the listeners? Until recently it was considered un-American by some to have a sense of cultural identity. The United States was supposed to be the great "melting pot," which took in immigrants and produced Americans. In the last few years, however, it has become acceptable and popular to recognize that various ethnic groups do in fact exist and retain particular cultural traits.

There are many different ethnic groups in the United States, including Arab, Chinese, French, German, Greek, Scandinavian, Japanese, Turkish, Vietnamese, and Indian (or, as some would say, "Native Americans"). The six major ethnic groups now identified in the United States are (1) black Americans, who are about 11 percent of the population; (2) Hispanic Americans (including Cubans, Mexicans, and Puerto Ricans), who make up about

5 percent; (3) Jewish-Americans, who constitute approximately 2.9 percent; (4) Irish Americans, who amount to about 6.5 percent; (5) Slavic-Americans who make up about 2.5 percent; and (6) Italian Americans, who constitute about 3.5 percent.[23] The ethnicity of individuals influences their political philosophy, political party affiliation, voting habits, occupation, economic status, assimilation into the general population, and attitude toward other American groups.

Economic status   What is the *economic status* of the listeners? Economic level has a definite impact on the programs and policies in which a person is interested. Attitudes toward the government, political philosophy, and the like are affected. Someone who is just eking out a subsistence level of existence is not interested in the fluctuations of the stock market. A low-income person's attitudes toward welfare programs are different from those of a high-income individual. Economic level affects attitudes toward labor unions, business, and religion. People with lower incomes tend to be less motivated and feel more alienated and powerless than those with higher incomes. Whether these psychological feelings are a cause or an effect of poverty is not entirely clear, but they are a factor with which you must deal.

Religion   What is the *religious affiliation* of the hearers? Protestants, Catholics, and Jews have strikingly different attitudes toward government, divorce, the Middle East, abortion, and other public issues. Do all or most of the members of the audience hold the same religious beliefs? How strong or intense are their religious commitments? You must determine whether there are members of the audience who hold no religious beliefs. Unless you have this information, you may make comments or include data that will offend some or most of your audience.

Group interest   Is there a common *group interest?* Some groups are held together by a common bond even though in many other respects the members are dissimilar. A group such as the Sierra Club, for example, may be made up of homemakers, students, doctors, lawyers, businesspersons, and laborers who have a multiplicity of attitudes about many subjects. As members of the Sierra Club, however, they all have a strong interest in, and positive attitudes toward, the conservation of natural resources. This will influence their reaction to any topic, idea, or proposal that affects the use of natural resources.

Audience occupations   What is the *occupation* of the listeners? White-collar workers have different attitudes and interests from blue-collar workers. Educators don't hold the same attitudes as lawyers. Doctors differ from farmers. Truck drivers' attitudes and interests differ from those of police officers. Employed people have different concerns from full-time students. An argument highly persuasive with one of these groups may be self-defeating with another group. An idea in a speech may be better understood and accepted if it is related to the listeners' jobs.

Residence What is the *place of residence* of the listeners? Do they reside in the city, in the suburbs, or on farms? Do they live in the South, the North, the Midwest, or the Far West? Each of these areas affects a person's attitudes and interests. A farmer in the South and one in the Midwest will have attitudes in common because of their occupation. But a farmer in the Midwest will probably have little knowledge of growing cotton and tobacco, whereas a farmer in the South will have little interest in growing wheat. A farmer and a city dweller in the South will have a number of common attitudes and interests because they live in the South. But they'll also have a number of differences because of where they live within the region.

Listener knowledge What *knowledge* do listeners have about the topic to be discussed? Information possessed by the listener on the topic will determine the intellectual level at which you can function. A speech on geology to high school students must be developed at a lower level than one given to a group of Ph.D.s in geology.

Obviously, there can be interrelationships or overlapping of these various demographic factors. Sometimes one demographic trait will cancel out another. To seek the answers to all these questions about any one audience will provide much duplicative data. Nevertheless, it's better to have several pieces of information that duplicate one another than to be missing a vital bit of data that might make the difference between success and failure as a speaker. The more thorough the demographic analysis, the more complete your information will be and, consequently, the more accurate the inferences you make about the audience.

Purpose-Oriented Analysis

This method of audience analysis begins from a totally different perspective. Instead of seeking answers to a number of questions about various traits of listeners, the purpose-oriented analysis asks the question: What about my audience is important to the purpose of my speech? Purpose-oriented analysis can be viewed as an extension or specific application of demographic analysis that focuses on the effects of a particular topic and relevant attitudes of a particular group of receivers. Rather than attempting to understand listeners in general, purpose-oriented analysis attempts to assess the receiver's potential reactions to a particular speech topic and speaking purpose or goal. If you are going to speak on tax reform, for example, you want to ask a number of questions related to your listeners and taxes. What is the income level of the listeners? What is their attitude toward taxes? What is their attitude toward government? How much do they know about present income tax laws? What is their interpretation of the term *tax reform*? What is their concept of the purpose of income taxes—to pay for government or to redistribute wealth? The answers to these and similar questions will tell you where to begin development of the topic and how best to present it.

Listeners' motivations An important question you must ask is—How does my purpose in this speech relate to the motivations of my listeners? A quick review of Maslow's hierarchy of needs as motivating factors may help reveal the relevance of this question. Maslow sets forth five different levels of needs: (1) physiological needs—hunger, thirst, sex; (2) safety needs—security, stability, protection, freedom from fear; (3) belongingness and love needs—friends, sweetheart, wife, children; (4) esteem needs—strength, achievement, adequacy, competence, reputation, status, fame, recognition; and (5) self-actualization need—necessity to be what one can be. Maslow observes that people are not necessarily motivated by only one of these needs; there can be a multiple-need motivation of behavior.[24] In Maslow's scheme, human needs and motivations are thought to be arranged in a hierarchical order. That is, listeners will not generally be influenced by appeals to esteem or self-actualization unless other more basic drives such as physiological or safety needs are already satisfied. Whether listeners are motivated by single or by multiple needs, you must consider the speech purpose in relation to their motivations.

Listeners' emotions Another important question to ask is—How does my purpose in this speech relate to the emotions of the listeners? One psychologist has classified emotions into four categories: (1) goal-related emotions—joy, anger, grief, and fear; (2) emotions related to sensory stimulation—pain, pleasure, disgust, revulsion, and delight; (3) emotions related to the self-concept—shame, guilt, pride, satisfaction, and self-abasement; and (4) emotions directed toward other people—love, hate, resentment, affection, and jealousy.[25] Obviously, these categories are not mutually exclusive; anger and fear, for example, may be directed at other people. Nevertheless, the categories are reasonable and make it easier to understand the origin of emotions. To be well-prepared, you must know whether your purpose will allay or aggravate any of these emotions.

The occasion Finally, you will want to answer the question How does the purpose of my speech relate to the occasion? The listeners' states of mind are affected by the occasion and the time. If the occasion is a festive one, it will certainly affect the attitudes and behavior of the listeners. If the occasion is to commemorate Lincoln's birthday, the hearers will expect you to relate the speech to that event. If a speech is scheduled for midmorning, hearers generally will be alert and attentive. It will thus be easier to get them to respond behaviorally, if that is the purpose. In addition, listeners will be able to follow carefully constructed and complex chains of reasoning more easily than at other times. After a banquet, on the other hand, listeners will be less alert because of the physiological processes taking place; they'll have more difficulty attending to closely reasoned arguments than would the morning audience. You need to understand, then, all the ways in which the speech purpose and the occasion may or may not be related.

The purpose-oriented analysis continues throughout the development of the speech. For every idea and piece of supporting material that is considered, you must ask the question: *What* about my audience is important to my purpose in using this?

The ability to obtain data about a specific group of listeners is affected by two main factors: (1) The greater the geographical area from which the listeners are drawn, the more difficult it is to obtain data, and (2) The more unfamiliar you are with the area in which the speech is to be given, the more difficult it is to accumulate data.

Obtaining Data about Listeners' Attitudes

With these difficulties in obtaining data in mind, it should be understood that the following sources aren't always available to you. Nevertheless, make use of whatever sources you can to learn as much as possible about potential listeners.

One of the most important mass media sources of general information is the newspaper(s) of the area in which the speech will be given. The front page provides data about major events. The editorial page gives interpretations of major events and issues, and generally, by the way the editorials are written, reveals whether the writer is in accord with or in opposition to majority opinion. The business section and the classified section give important clues about the economic activity of the community, and the entertainment section tells a great deal about its cultural level. Most newspapers also include a "Letters to the Editor" section, which often can offer important clues to public opinion. This

Mass Media

section must be used cautiously, however, as the letters can also be misleading. Sometimes special interest groups organize letter-writing campaigns, so what looks like a spontaneous outpouring of community sentiment is in fact a small, well-organized effort. Another problem is that every community produces habitual letter writers whose attitudes are not typical of the community. Newspapers themselves create a potential booby trap for anyone trying to infer community attitudes from letters to the editor. Although many newspapers print letters for each position on an issue according to the ratio of letters received, other newspapers follow what they consider an evenhanded policy and print an equal number of letters for each position, regardless of the number they receive. Used with care, however, newspapers are an important and valuable source of information about a community and its people. Newspapers provide greater detail and in-depth coverage than any other mass media source.

If you are going into a new community to speak, it is wise to order a subscription to a local newspaper approximately a month before the speech. This will inform you of what is happening in the area and allow you to add "local color" to your speech by referring to pertinent events.

Radio and television are also important mass media sources of information. Local news programs offer insight into the interests and problems of an area. Local talk shows give a hint of the attitudes of the region.

The Organization

Find out about the nature of the organization to which you are to speak. If it has a publication, read some copies of it to learn what goals and values the members cherish. Determine the issues the organization is concerned about. Try to discover the nature of the people who belong to the group. If possible, attend a meeting to get a feel of the group's interests and attitudes.

Conversations

Much can be learned through conversations with local people who are familiar with people and events in the area. If you live in the area in which the speech is to be given, you'll have many opportunities to talk with local people. Business leaders, educators, and ministers, for example, can give vital insight into prevalent attitudes. If you are speaking in an area other than your home community, don't overlook the most important source of information: the person or committee that invites you to speak. Interview them in great depth. Using both demographic and purpose-oriented analyses, devise as many questions as you possibly can to learn as much as they can tell you. If you can talk to others who have spoken to the group, they may be able to provide important insights into the audience's attitudes and beliefs. Finally, do not forget taxi drivers; most have a wealth of information.

Public Opinion Polls

Scientific methods for ascertaining public opinion were first utilized by George Gallup. Using those procedures, he has been amazingly accurate in predicting the results of political campaigns since 1936.[26] One of the major reasons for the success of both the Gallup and Roper organizations in polling public opinion is that neither has ever accepted a job as pollster for an organization or political candidate. They take polls on public issues and sell the results to whatever person or agency is interested. Some pollsters, on the other hand, assist or work for particular groups or specific political candidates. The danger in this practice is that the pollster's conscious or unconscious desire to please the employer may bias obtained results or conclusions.

Caution must be observed in using polls. They provide valid results only when questions are carefully designed, respondents randomly chosen, and nonverbal cues slanting carefully designed questions are avoided.

Important information can be gleaned from well-conducted polls. Politicians and advertisers frequently use polls to plan their campaigns. Analysis of their target group by polls enables them to make vital decisions.

Two important problems confront many speakers who want to use polls to aid in obtaining information about an audience: (1) there may not be a poll available on the specific issue for the particular group; and (2) the cost of conducting a valid poll may be prohibitive.

Some important sources of polls are the following: (1) *Public Opinion Quarterly,* a periodical that publishes polls from various sources; (2) *The Gallup Report,* which contains results of Gallup polls; (3) *Public Affairs Information Service,* which indexes various polls under the heading "Public Opinion Polls"; (4) *Gallup International Public Opinion Polls, France, 1937–1975;* (5) *Gallup International Public Opinion Polls, United Kingdom, 1937–1975.*

Audience Adaptation

Audience adaptation may be defined as the actions taken as a result of audience analysis, in order to develop maximum credibility. The practice of adapting messages to specific hearers has long been an important part of human communication. Does this mean that you should say what you think the receivers want to hear, regardless of your own beliefs and convictions? Critics point out that many leaders in all fields wait for the most recent public opinion poll to tell them what a majority of people think, then rush out to advocate those policies. Don't compromise your principles by making statements you don't believe. To do so would damage your credibility. Effective audience adaptation doesn't involve a compromise of principles. It does require a concern for listeners and a sensitivity to their needs, wants, and values.

After investigating an issue and collecting and analyzing all available evidence (including public opinion), form whatever conclusions are valid, *regardless of public opinion.* In deciding what ideas to use and the order in which to present them, be sensitive to the beliefs, attitudes, interests, mores, wants, values, and desires of an audience. Thus, you use all the information obtained from audience analysis to help in preparing and presenting the most effective message for the particular receiver.

Figure 7.1
Continuum of audience attitude.

Cast your ideas in the form most acceptable to the particular persons you are addressing. Audience adaptation should occur at three times: *before* the speech, when audience analysis helps you select the subject and prepare the message in certain ways; *during* the speech, as you interpret audience feedback and adjust your presentation accordingly; and *after* the speech, when—with a view toward future speech making—you revise and change the speech on the basis of all available final impressions of successes and mistakes.

Adaptation before the Speech

Adaptation to the audience begins immediately after the commitment to speak has been made.

Selection of Subject

The subject chosen for a speech should be one that will be appropriate to the speaker, the occasion, and the audience. In the 1976 presidential campaign, Jimmy Carter displayed consummate skill in speaking to various audiences. His subjects were matched with great "care to the particular audience—Navy talk in Norfolk, parochial school aid in Pittsburgh, Arab boycotts to B'nai B'rith."[27]

Once you have chosen the subject you can determine the specific purpose and adapt it to the particular listeners. One of the first things you need to know is the attitude of your listeners toward the particular topic you are considering. Members of an audience may be generally classified as hostile, neutral or apathetic, or friendly toward your subject. Obviously, there are degrees within each of these categories, so we may range the members along a continuum similar to that in figure 7.1.

You may be considering a speech against subsidized intercollegiate athletics. On your campus, however, you know there is overwhelming support for subsidized athletics. Moreover, research indicates that the members of your speech class reflect the campus opinion. If you give a speech advocating abandonment of a subsidized athletic program, it will obviously be received with considerable hostility. Instead of advocating abolishment of subsidized athletics, change your topic to the cost of a subsidized athletic program. In developing this topic, avoid criticizing a subsidized program and focus on factual data that would prevent personalties or attitudes—yours or your listeners'— from becoming involved. Use as much evidence as you can from sources respected by your listeners. In this way, you identify a problem for your listeners but don't offer a solution. This approach would be consistent with research findings revealing that as the opposition of an audience increases, the effective speaker uses "fewer solution arguments" and "more problem arguments."[28]

Once the specific topic has been chosen, you can select particular supporting ideas or arguments on the basis of their compatibility with the specific listeners. For example, a controversy may be raging in your area about where to locate a new highway. In speaking in favor of a particular route to a group such as the Sierra Club, focus the speech on the fact that the route you favor would disturb the natural environment less than others. On the other hand, if the hearers are members of an economics club, focus on the fact that the proposed route would be less costly.

Supporting Materials

Listeners' attitudes and knowledge can help you shape the supporting evidence used in the speech. Select testimony from experts whom the listeners respect and admire. If you're talking to union members about the need for the United States to maintain a strong defense, cite someone like George Meany, the late president of the AFL-CIO. Choose examples relevant to the audience's interests, knowledge, and experience. If you're talking to a group of business leaders about the need for honesty in everyday affairs, use illustrations (detailed examples) or specific instances (undetailed examples) of people in business who have practiced the kind of honesty you're talking about.

Frequently, you can make a message more acceptable to listeners by adapting the order of the ideas to their predispositions. When addressing a hostile audience, it is advisable to employ an *indirect* organizational pattern, that is, begin with ideas and arguments based on values and premises that the speaker and listeners share before introducing potentially objectionable issues.

Organization

Your purpose may be to argue for a decrease in defense spending. The audience, however, may be in favor of defense spending. In this instance, you may prepare them by beginning with a discussion of the relaxation of world tensions as a result of the activities of Gorbachev and President Bush. You may refer to the actions of both men to eliminate some weapons systems. You may point out that both countries, for various reasons, have reduced military spending. Finally, you can argue that world peace will be jeopardized if we increase our military spending while Russia is reducing hers. The hostility of the listeners toward reduced defense spending may then be sufficiently softened for them to consider your arguments in a more unbiased way.

To a friendly audience, you should adopt a more *direct* organizational plan and begin with the argument that world peace will be jeopardized unless the United States decreases its defense spending sufficiently to maintain a balance of power. There will probably be no need to discuss the need for a balance of power between the Communist and non-Communist nations. The fact that the listeners are favorable toward reduced defense spending indicates they have probably already accepted that argument.

Adaptation during the Speech

Adaptation during the speech is just as important as that prior to the speech. Sometimes it is more so.

Verbal and Nonverbal Cues from Listeners

Feedback begins as soon as you appear in front of the audience. Perceive it and adapt to it.

Nonverbal cues may indicate the listeners are having difficulty understanding your ideas. A puzzled expression on the face of some listeners may show a need for clarification of your meaning. You may use another example, explain more fully an example that has been used, define a technical term, or shift to a different pattern of organization.

Facial expression, eye contact, and bodily action provide nonverbal cues about the audience's acceptance or rejection of the ideas. If you perceive rejection, adapt by offering additional supporting material to make it easier for the listeners to agree with your position. In some instances opposition to your ideas may be so strong that the audience provides verbal cues. Sometimes you can cope with this by lowering the volume of your voice until it becomes difficult for the listeners to hear you. Wendell Phillips, the great antislavery agitator, used this technique effectively on one occasion.

> Often called before howling mobs, who had come to the lecture-room to prevent him from being heard, and who would shout and sing to drown his voice, he never failed to subdue them in a short time. . . . One illustration of his power and tact occurred in Boston. The majority of the audience was hostile. They yelled and sang and completely drowned his voice. The reporters were seated in a row just under the platform, in the place where the orchestra play in an ordinary theatre. Phillips made no attempt to address the howling audience, but bent over and seemed to be speaking in a low tone to the reporters. By and by the curiosity of the howling audience was excited; they ceased to clamor and tried to hear what he was saying to the reporters. Phillips looked at them and said quietly:
>
> "Go on, gentlemen, go on. I do not need your ears. Through these pencils I speak to thirty millions of people."
>
> Not a voice was raised again. The mob had found its master and stayed whipped until he sat down.[29]

Note any feedback that indicates the attention of the listeners is lagging. Adaptation can regain their attention. Be sure you're talking with them, not at them. Use more nonverbal behavior—more physical action, more varied vocal behavior. Move closer to the listeners, even to the point of moving among them. Sometimes an unmalicious interruption may direct attention away from the speaker. A witty, caustic, ironic, or similar comment may sometimes be just the thing to return attention to the speaker. A noted Civil War historian visiting a southern university was addressing a class of students on the defeat of the southern forces. One student, who was a wit, suddenly called out: "I am so proud of the southern effort that I keep the Confederate flag with me." He then held up his foot to reveal his socks into which had been woven a Confederate flag. Without a moment's hesitation, the lecturer replied: "That just goes to prove my point, that ultimately the Confederate flag went down to 'de' feet." The lecturer's quick retort mastered the brief interruption and held the attention of his hearers so that he had no difficulty in continuing his lecture. Not everyone has such a quick wit, but if you have it, use it.

Sometimes changes in the occasion demand that you adapt in some way. Several years ago, as the commencement exercises began in an outdoor amphitheater on a college campus, lightning began to play on the horizon, the distant rumble of thunder could be heard, and the wind began to blow. The president of the college, analyzing the situation and adapting to the changed conditions, decided to reverse the order of events and award the diplomas before the commencement address was given. By the time the main speaker was introduced, lightning could be seen clearly overhead, thunder claps had become distinct, and the wind smelled of fresh rain. The speaker announced that he was as afraid of lightning as anyone and that if it got closer he would cut his speech short and run for cover with everyone else. With that he plunged into his prepared manuscript, and one listener whispered to another: "That means we're here for the duration." As the impending storm drew nearer, the members of the audience became increasingly apprehensive and began to grow restless and noisy. An almost steady line of people moved from their seats to the exits and hastily departed. Despite these changed conditions and the obvious inattention of the listeners, the speaker read page after page of his manuscript until he reached the last word on the last page. The situation cried out for the speaker to present his main points, summarize, and sit down. If he had adapted to the changed conditions, the listeners would have been grateful for his willingness to be sensitive for their concerns. Unfortunately, they retained only negative memories because those who remained until the end were caught in a downpour.

Sometimes the room becomes overheated during a speech. You may ask someone to open some windows or turn down the thermostat. A sudden noise in the vicinity may require a comment or explanation from you.

Adaptation doesn't end with the speech; it's a continuing process. Why would you want to adapt *after* giving a speech? Because, even though you may not give the same speech twice, you frequently speak on the same topic a number of times. Consequently, you want to know what you can do differently the next time to make a speech on that subject more effective. In addition, you'll want to improve your speech-making ability in general. Several sources of feedback provide aid in adapting a speech to the next audience.

The most obvious source of feedback is your own perceptions of what did and didn't work as expected. Knowing that something didn't work isn't sufficient, however. After the speech, try to find out why it didn't work. Consider all possibilities and try to deduce as accurately as possible the cause or causes for the success or failure of any part of the speech.

Changes in the Occasion

Adaptation after the Speech

Analyze Your Own Perceptions

Consult Other People

Listen to the comments of family and friends. They can provide constructive criticism on the basis of their observations and what they heard others saying. If you can, find out the reactions of opponents of your position. Their comments may not be unbiased, but they can't be ignored. Consideration of the valid ones can yield useful insights and possibly valuable results for future speaking situations.

Other students and the instructor are important sources of feedback after a classroom speech. Listen to the comments of fellow students, even those that hurt. What do they say about the subject of your speech, the organization, the supporting materials used to develop the subject, the language, the nonverbal presentation? Don't take the criticism personally and resolve not to be upset by negative comments, even those that seem to be maliciously motivated. In a friendly way, ask the critic what you could have done to eliminate the perceived faults.

If your instructor fills out a rating sheet for each speech, analyze it. In which areas did you get your highest ratings, in which the lowest? For your next speech, remember to continue doing what you did in the area where you got your highest rating. If the rating can be improved, use the instructor's comments as a basis for changes. Analyze the instructor's comments to find ways of improving the area of lowest rating. Concentrate on making improvements in that area. After each speech, compare your rating with that of previous speeches. In that way, you can see where your strengths are, where your weaknesses are, and where your possibilities for improvement are.

Consider Media Reactions

A third source of feedback after the speech may be the comments and criticisms of reporters in some of the mass media. Since the efforts of most students and many other speakers do not merit attention from the media, this isn't generally a source of feedback. If such feedback is available, however, you certainly must evaluate whatever appraisal is made.

Summary

You must have an understanding of attitudes to take full advantage of the available means of persuasion in building credibility. An attitude is defined as a tendency to respond favorably or unfavorably to a class of objects or a concept.

An attitude is composed of three ingredients: the *cognitive,* consisting of the perceptions, thoughts, and beliefs a person has about a particular class of objects or concepts; the *affective,* consisting of the feelings an individual has about a particular object or concept; and the *behavioral,* consisting of the behavior of an individual with respect to a class of objects or concept because of the attitude.

Six characteristics of attitudes seem apparent. An attitude may be weak or strong; it may be central or peripheral to the individual's attitude system; it may be salient or nonsalient; it may be positive or negative; it may be stable or unstable; and it may have a high or low degree of clarity.

Although a number of theories attempt to account for the formation and change of attitudes, you would be wise to take the position that such development can be attributed to one or more of three causes: an individual's (1) environment, (2) self-interest, (3) desire for cognitive consistency.

Using either a demographic analysis or a purpose-oriented analysis, analyze an audience in order to identify those characteristics of the listeners that influence their probable response to your message.

The media, conversations with other people, the organization to be addressed, and public opinion polls are four important sources of information about the attitudes of potential listeners.

The information obtained from the audience analysis is used to prepare and present the most effective message for the particular receiver. An ongoing process, audience adaptation occurs before, during, and after the speech.

Exercises

1. You are planning a speech to a group of listeners who are opposed to your point of view. What can you do to make your position credible to them?
2. Describe one of your classmate's attitudes in terms of the characteristics of an attitude discussed in this chapter.
3. Name one of your classmate's attitudes that you must consider in the next speech you give. In what ways will that attitude determine what you say? What you do not say? How can you use that attitude to improve your credibility?
4. Select one of your attitudes and describe in detail how you think it was formed.
5. Prepare a written description of the demographic characteristics of your classroom audience.
6. Attend a lecture on campus. Write a description of the ways in which the speaker adapted and failed to adapt to the audience.

Notes

1. L. Berkowitz, *A Survey of Social Psychology,* 2d ed. (New York: Holt, Rinehart & Winston, 1980), p. 275. Reprinted by permission of Holt, Rinehart & Winston, CBS College Publishing.
2. C. W. Sherif, M. Sherif, and R. E. Nebergall, *Attitude and Attitude Change* (Philadelphia: W. B. Saunders Co., 1965), p. 4.
3. J. B. Cooper, "Emotion in Prejudice," *Science* 130 (1959):314–18.
4. H. W. Dickson and E. McGinnies, "Affectivity in the Arousal of Attitudes as Measured by Galvanic Skin Response," *American Journal of Psychology* 79 (1966):584–89.
5. E. McGinnies, *Social Behavior: A Functional Analysis* (Boston: Houghton Mifflin Co., 1970), p. 302.

6. M. P. Zanna, J. M. Olson, and R. H. Fazio, "Self-Perception and Attitude-Behavior Consistency," *Personality and Social Psychology Bulletin* 7 (1981):252–56.

7. R. H. Fazio and M. P. Zanna, "Direct Experience and Attitude-Behavior Consistency," in *Advances in Experimental Social Psychology,* ed. L. Berkowitz, vol. 14 (New York: Academic Press, 1981), pp. 163–65.

8. D. W. Rajecki, *Attitudes: Themes and Advances* (Sunderland, Mass.: Sinauer Associates, Inc., 1982), p. 77.

9. Ibid.

10. A. Campbell, P. E. Converse, W. E. Miller, and D. E. Stokes, *The American Voter* (New York: John Wiley & Sons, 1960), pp. 160–67.

11. C. A. Insko, *Theories of Attitude Change* (New York: Appleton-Century-Crofts, 1967), p. 348.

12. T. M. Newcomb and G. Svehla, "Intra-family Relationships in Attitude," *Sociometry* 1 (1937):180–205. The correlation coefficients were war, .44; communism, .56; religion, .63.

13. M. K. Jennings and R. G. Niemi, "The Transmission of Political Values from Parent to Child," *American Political Science Review* 62 (1968):169–84.

14. J. W. Eaton, *Influencing the Youth Culture* (Beverly Hills, Calif.: Sage Publications, 1970), pp. 21–22.

15. For a discussion, analysis, and evaluation of the various cognitive consistency theories, see Insko, *Theories of Attitude Change.*

16. T. M. Newcomb, R. H. Turner, and P. E. Converse, *Social Psychology* (New York: Holt, Rinehart & Winston, 1965), p. 130.

17. Ibid., p. 131.

18. T. Clevenger, Jr., *Audience Analysis* (Indianapolis: Bobbs-Merrill Co., 1966), pp. 43–48.

19. Lane Cooper, trans., *The Rhetoric of Aristotle* (New York: D. Appleton-Century Co., 1932), pp. 132–34.

20. Ibid., p. 134.

21. Ibid., p. 136.

22. W. H. Flanigan and N. H. Zingle, *Political Behavior of the American Electorate* (Boston: Allyn and Bacon, 1975), pp. 114–15.

23. M. R. Levy and M. S. Kramer, *The Ethnic Factor* (New York: Simon & Schuster, 1972).

24. A. H. Maslow, *Motivation and Personality* (New York: Harper & Row, Publishers, 1970), pp. 35–58, 149–80.

25. R. B. Levy, *You and Your Behavior* (Boston: Holbrook Press, 1975), p. 189.

26. G. Gallup, *The Sophisticated Poll Watcher's Guide* (Ephrata, Pa.: Science Press, 1972), p. 215.

27. D. S. Broder, "Computer Telling Carter What to Say," *Opelika-Auburn News,* September 15, 1976. Used by permission.

28. M. D. Hazen and S. B. Kiesler, "Communication Strategies Affected by Audience Opposition, Feedback and Persuasibility," *Speech Monographs* 42 (1975):59.

29. Major J. B. Pond, *Eccentricities of Genius* (New York: G. W. Dillingham Company, 1900), pp. 7–8.

PART 2

PREPARATION

CHAPTER 8

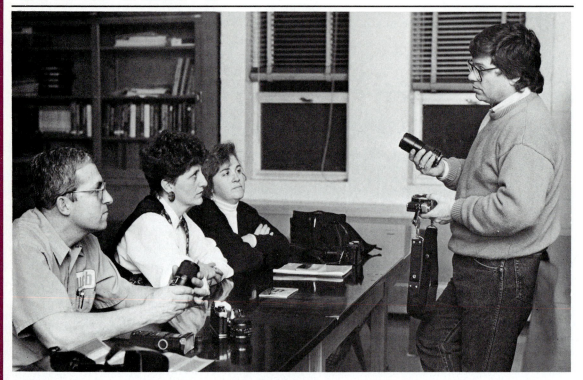

Selecting the Subject
and the Purpose

You will be tempted to say, as other students have, "Professor, if you'll just assign me a topic for my speech assignment, it'll give me more time to work on this speech, and I'll be happy to speak on whatever you tell me to." Your professor will have to decline your request because no person—no matter how informed about speech communication principles—can tell another person what topic to speak on. Your professor can assist in selecting a subject, though, if you simply ask some pertinent questions. As these questions are answered, you'll become aware of potential subjects and can then select one.

In this chapter you'll learn what questions to ask so you don't burden your professor with helping you make your decision. After you finish this course, you'll no longer have easy access to help from your professor.

Sometimes the topic for a speech is supplied by the group inviting the speaker. They wish to hear that person because he or she has some information or a particular point of view. In other instances, a speaker is invited because of his or her position or renown as a speaker, but no natural subject suggests itself. Faced with this situation, some speakers simply reach into their mind and pull out a subject, with little or no thought about its appropriateness for the particular speaking engagement. Such methods sometimes result in successful speeches, but the odds of selecting an effective subject are enhanced if the selection process is more methodical.

In preparing any speech, carefully select the subject, determine the general purpose, and choose the specific purpose.

The Speech Subject

The first opportunity to take positive action to establish your credibility occurs when you select a subject for your speech. That choice determines whether you develop credibility at the outset or labor through the speech with the handicap of an inappropriate subject. Making an effective choice of subject requires considering three factors: (1) the speaker, (2) the occasion, and (3) the audience.

The Speaker

Begin by considering yourself. The answers to a series of questions will be helpful in selecting an appropriate subject.

What are you interested in? The things you're interested in are those things you like to do, such as playing tennis, backpacking, making handmade jewelry, visiting Revolutionary War battlefields, or working with Girl Scouts. Make a list of these interests. By drawing on these topics, speaking will be more fun. Not only is it more enjoyable to talk about topics in which you are interested, but you're then presenting genuine feelings and convictions. That is what listeners are interested in—your attitudes, your perceptions, your point of view. In addition, the enthusiasm you feel when discussing a topic you're concerned about is conveyed to the listeners who, in turn, become more interested in the speech.

What experiences have you had? There are two kinds of experience: actual and vicarious. Actual experience refers to things you have done. Vicarious experience is that which you obtain indirectly, as through reading a book, seeing a movie, hearing a speech. Vicarious experience can be enjoyable, but actual experience provides knowledge and insights not found in a book or any other source. Take the list you prepared of the things you're interested in and underscore those on which you have had actual experience. These will be the best subjects on which to speak.

Speaking from personal experience has several advantages. You can express the material in your own words, and you don't have to worry about trying to interpret the meaning of another person's statement. The material has a freshness because the listeners won't have heard it before, at least not from your point of view. Almost any subject can be made interesting if you draw materials from your own experiences.

What knowledge do you have? Unfortunately, some speakers ask only the first two questions and don't ask this one. But interest and experience aren't enough without knowledge. William Norwood Brigance, an outstanding speech professor for many years, asserted that a speaker "must earn the right to give every speech."[1] He meant that you have a responsibility to learn everything you can about any subject on which you plan to give a speech. It is a waste of the listeners' time to talk on a subject about which you know so little you are unable to offer anything useful or new. For that reason, interest and experience are not enough. For example, you may have become a skydiver only recently. You have much interest in your new hobby and some brief experience, but you simply haven't had time to acquire much information. This is not yet a topic for a speech. It will be in time, so be patient. Don't think these last remarks mean that you must know everything or nearly everything about a topic in order to use it in a speech.

Research is essential to provide knowledge for your speech. When you don't yet know enough to speak, or the specific topic chosen covers an aspect of the subject about which you know relatively little, or the subject is one on which new information is currently being developed, research is necessary. Before speaking on a subject, you should put your current information or any new information in perspective.

In considering your knowledge, don't forget the other college courses you have had or are taking. A topic you have studied and discussed in sociology or psychology, for example, may be developed into a subject for a speech assignment. A term paper in political science may be transformed into a speech. Notice the emphasis is on changing whatever information you possess into appropriate form for a speech. A term paper is not a speech; neither is an essay. You must make the necessary changes and additions to produce a speech. You will also probably have to do additional research.

Consider groups or organizations to which you belong. You may be a member of the Pershing Rifles, the marching band, the foreign relations club, or some other group. Few nonmembers know much about any of these groups. A speech about some phase of such a group may not only be interesting and informative, it may also create potential new members.

What does your audience know about you? What expectations will they have? They may expect you to speak on a certain subject. If you don't, they may be disappointed. On some occasions, your range of choices may be limited because the listeners are aware of your interests and knowledge and expect you to speak on a subject within your known expertise. In most instances, you won't want to disappoint them. If they know that you're an expert on China, they'll probably expect you to speak on some aspect of China. Give them what they want.

Occasionally, however, you can delightfully surprise your listeners by speaking on an unexpected subject. In one college speech class, for example, a tall, burly basketball player created instant attention for his first speech when he began: "I know that athletes are supposed to be interested only in athletics. Since I am a member of the basketball team, you probably expect me to talk about some phase of the game. I won't deny that basketball is one of the two major interests that I have. I have great love for two activities: basketball and art. And art is what I want to talk to you about this morning."

A second factor you must consider in selecting a subject is the occasion. People aren't the same in all places; they aren't even the same at different times in the same place. Unless you consider the occasion in selecting a subject, you minimize your chances of communicating effectively. The answers to the following five questions will help in choosing a subject appropriate to the specific occasion.

The Occasion

What is the nature of the occasion? Put another way, *why* are these people coming together on this day, at this time, in this place, to hear me speak? You may discover, for example, that there is nothing special about the occasion. The listeners may be convening simply because this is a regular meeting of their service club—Kiwanis, Lions, Rotary—and they always meet at the same time and place. And except for a few meetings when special activities occur, they always have a different speaker, one of whom is you. In other instances, the audience may be gathering for a special occasion. It may be Veterans Day or Martin Luther King's birthday. You may have been invited to speak to the local Democrats because it's Thomas Jefferson's birthday or the local Republicans because it's Abraham Lincoln's birthday.

What kind of mood will the occasion encourage? If the occasion is one to celebrate the final payment on the debt of a church, the mood will be happy and the subject should be one that matches the joy of the occasion. If the occasion is to commemorate the death of some person who was a member of the group or was associated with it, the mood will be somber. Again, the subject should be one that matches the sadness of the occasion.

If the subject of the speech is inconsistent with the mood of the occasion, listeners will have difficulty shifting their mood to coincide with that of the speech. Think, for example, of a time when you were looking forward to an important social event. Anticipation increased daily. Then the afternoon of the event, you were informed that your host had become ill—nothing so serious you needed to worry about his welfare, but serious enough to prevent his giving the party. But your mood was set to have fun; even though you had some studying to do, you couldn't really concentrate on it because your mood was set to be carefree and happy. This is the difficult kind of shift required of listeners when a speaker's subject is inconsistent with their mood.

What are the time limits of the speech? Some program planners will voluntarily tell you of important time limitations, but many won't unless you ask. Never make any assumptions. Insist that the person in charge of the program give you precise time limits. Beware of the program planners who are very cavalier about time limits. When asked how long the speech should be, they will reply: "Oh, about twenty minutes," or "Oh, whatever you need." But time limits are extremely important. You can't rationally select a subject unless you know how much time you'll have. A subject excellent for a five-minute speech may be unsatisfactory for a twenty-minute speech. Unobserved time limits can ruin a speech, even one that is otherwise very good. Some organizations are conscientious about the length of their meetings and adjourn promptly at the appointed time. Service clubs that hold luncheon meetings, for example, have members who must be back to work on time. Any speaker going past the adjournment time will be looking at the backs of members as they depart. Select a subject you can develop clearly and thoroughly in the time allotted. Some students get angry at professors who strictly enforce time limits on classroom speeches. But this is a discipline you must develop; be appreciative of the professor's help.

What will the program consist of? There are a number of reasons for asking this question. A most important one is that it provides a check on the time limits suggested by the program planner. Some program planners, like some speakers, are poor organizers and assign too little time for each program activity. Since the speaker is generally the last activity, any deficit of time will come from the speech. If you have seen a copy of the entire program beforehand, however, you may realize that the time limits for the speech appear to be unrealistic, and you can select a subject that can be developed in a shorter time or expanded through additional supporting material if the promised time materializes. Being aware of the entire program also allows you to prepare appropriate adaptations and references. Sometimes, in fact, the rest of the program or some part of it may suggest a subject that will enhance the effectiveness of your speech. And it may be a subject that would not otherwise have occurred to you.

What is the nature of the place where the speech will be given? Will the speech be inside or outside? Will the audience be sitting or standing? Will the members of the audience be free to come and go? If so, you may have to avoid a subject that would be more challenging and select one that will be more interesting in order to hold the listeners in the audience. Will there be a place to display visual aids? If not, that may eliminate some topics from consideration. Are the seats comfortable or uncomfortable? Will you have to use a microphone? If so, will there be one available? What kind of lectern is available? Will you be able to use notes? If not, some subjects may not be practicable for that situation.

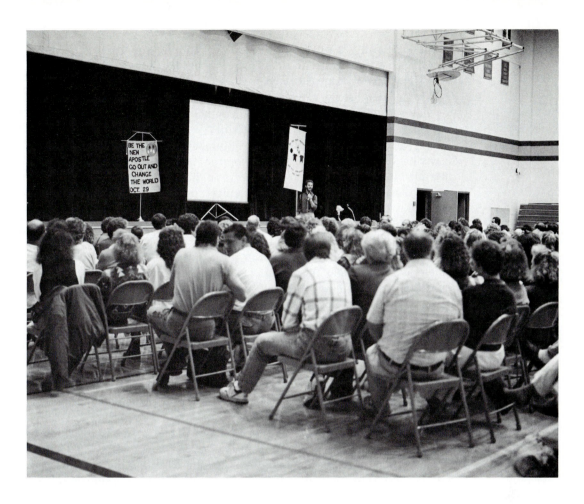

The third factor in selecting a subject is the audience. Four questions can provide information about the audience that will significantly improve the selection of a subject.

The Audience

What are the important demographic features of the listeners? We have already discussed in chapter 7 the methods of analyzing an audience. That information will be vitally important in selecting a subject. You'll need to know the age, sex, educational level, political philosophy, homogeneity, ethnicity, economic status, religious affiliation, group interest, occupation, and place of residence of your expected auditors. A knowledge of important demographic factors allows you to determine, through inference, what topics or subjects the audience will consider interesting and worthwhile.

Why are the listeners present for the speech? You'll need to know why your listeners are present to hear your speech. Have they come voluntarily or were they compelled to come? If the listeners have attended voluntarily, that indicates interest on their part in some aspect of the situation. Careful analysis may reveal that motivation, which in turn may suggest an appropriate subject.

Listeners who attend involuntarily, on the other hand, may have a certain amount of hostility that will make it more difficult for you to develop rapport with them. Any subject that might increase that hostility should be avoided.

What are the listeners interested in? You'll need to know the concerns of your potential listeners. What issues are important to them at the moment? In what ways will those issues affect them, politically, socially, economically, religiously, educationally?

If your hearers are bankers, they'll probably be interested in hearing a discussion of the effects of manipulating the money supply. Farmers will be interested in hearing about new fertilizers on the market or improved ways of getting their products to market. Law enforcement officers will be interested in innovative methods of tracking fugitives. Members of a photography club will be interested in learning about a new film-processing method.

In most instances you want to choose a topic of interest to your listeners. On other occasions, you may choose a topic because the audience isn't interested in it. For example, the potential audience may have little interest in participating in political activities, but your analysis indicates their self-interest would be better served if they became involved in political activities. Thus, you select a subject encouraging your listeners to become active politically.

What do the listeners know? You can't expect to know more about the subject you choose than *every* member of the audience. But you must know more than most. If you don't, you'll probably lose the attention of the listeners in a short time. When selecting a topic and deciding on your development or treatment of that subject, consider the general level of the audience as well as their knowledge of your speech topic.

Never talk down to or treat an audience condescendingly by choosing an elementary subject. Choose one that respects the listeners' intellectual ability. It is better to aim too high than too low. Select a subject challenging your listeners as well as your ability as a speaker to present the subject so they can understand and appreciate it.

The General Purpose

Once you have chosen a subject, you must determine the general purpose of the speech, in other words, the general response you want the listeners to make. You may choose from among three general purposes: to entertain, to inform, and to persuade.

To Entertain

If your purpose is to entertain, you simply want the listeners to relax and enjoy the occasion. The speech may also make your listeners aware of some idea, but that is a supplementary effect. The main function of the speech is to amuse, enthrall, or divert. Many different methods can be used to entertain. The vivid description of an interesting place can be entertaining. The suspenseful narration of an exciting adventure can be entertaining. One of the most frequently used methods of entertaining is humor.

Most people enjoy humor if it is appropriate to the occasion and the subject. It must be used with care, however. It should never be offensive to any of the listeners. If directed at people, ideas, or anything the audience respects, it should poke fun gently and in a conciliatory way, rather than with biting satire or a derogatory attitude. It should be perceived as humorous; few things are more deadly to a speaker's cause than humor unappreciated.

Almost any subject can be made entertaining if the speaker uses ingenuity and creative thinking. The speech to entertain is especially appropriate in after-dinner situations where members of the audience are less than alert and are not interested in following closely reasoned arguments. They just want to be amused.

If your purpose is to inform, then your main goal is to make clear to your listeners the material you are presenting and enable them to comprehend the ideas. A central or primary requirement of an informative speech is that it must present new information to the listeners. An informative speech can, and probably should, be entertaining, but it should never pursue amusement as its main objective. You will have failed as an informative speaker if the listeners can't recall at least the main ideas of the speech.

To Inform

You generally have one of four objectives in mind with a persuasive message: to create a new belief or attitude, to change the direction of an existing attitude, to increase the intensity of an existing attitude, or to obtain a behavioral response.

To Persuade

First, you may want to create a new attitude on the part of your listeners. For example, you may want to develop an awareness of the neglect of elderly people in many nursing homes.

Creating a New Attitude

Second, you may want to change the direction of an existing attitude. This means changing an attitude from positive to negative, or vice versa. You might change the direction of an existing attitude by persuading your classmates that "big time" football is an anachronism, or that taxes should be increased to provide greater support for education.

Changing an Existing Attitude's Direction

Third, you may want to increase the intensity of an existing attitude, such as making a positive attitude more strongly positive, a negative attitude more strongly negative, or a neutral attitude more strongly neutral. In the 1988 presidential election, both political parties used this technique. Democrats attempted to increase the general public's perception that Bush was a wimp. Republicans attempted to increase negative attitudes toward Dukakis as unrealistic in the treatment of convicts.

Changing an Existing Attitude's Intensity

Finally, you may try to persuade an audience to behave in some way. In an election, politicians attempt to persuade the electorate that it will be advantageous for them to go to the polls on election day. Thus, their speeches attempt to go beyond mere intellectual agreement and influence the audience's

Obtaining a Behavioral Response

overt behavior in some way. Two questions must be answered before you prepare a speech seeking a behavioral response: (1) Does the audience have the capability to act on this subject? It would be unrealistic, for example, for you to attempt to persuade your classmates to dismiss the president of your school. Your classmates don't have that capability. You could persuade them, however, to sign a petition to be presented to the Board of Trustees asking that they replace the president. The members of the audience have the capability to sign the petition; the Board of Trustees has the capability to dismiss the president. (2) Is the proposed action practicable? A petition to the Board of Trustees asking that each faculty member be given a 30 percent increase in salary would not be practicable for most schools; even though the board has the authority to make such a decision, the money is not available.

It should be noted that the distinction between an informative and persuasive speech is not always clear-cut. First, informative speeches can be persuasive. Learning new information is frequently sufficient to cause a change in attitudes and behavior. When people were told there was a relationship between smoking and lung cancer, some stopped smoking. Others began to use less salt in their food when they learned salt may cause high blood pressure. Second, persuasive speeches use information to persuade. In fact, the methods of presenting information are the same, whether the purpose of the speech is to persuade or to inform. The methods of informing aren't exclusive to informative speaking. This explains why an intended persuasive speech may succeed in informing an audience but fail to persuade them, whereas a speech designed primarily to inform may have persuasive effects. Third, some informative speeches are given to accomplish covert persuasion. Some companies, such as public utilities, conduct advertising campaigns and maintain a speakers' bureau to inform interested groups about company programs and activities. Their ultimate purpose, however, is to develop goodwill for the company. In other words, their underlying purpose is subtly or indirectly to increase public approval of the company.

The persuasive speech generally must also be informative to be effective, and it may also be entertaining. Nevertheless, the persuasive speaker uses these other methods simply as means to an end.

The Specific Purpose

Once the general purpose has been determined, turn your attention to the specific purpose of the speech.

Whereas the general purpose identifies the type of general response you want the listeners to make, the specific purpose identifies the particular objective of a given speech. The specific purpose should then be cast into an appropriately worded and precise purpose sentence. The following examples may help to clarify the difference between the two kinds of purpose:

Subject: Voting
General Purpose: To entertain

Specific Purpose: To describe the reactions of voters who supported losing
    candidates

Subject: Voting
General Purpose: To inform
Specific Purpose: To explain how to cast an absentee ballot in California

Subject: Voting
General Purpose: To persuade (actuate)
Specific Purpose: To persuade the local Democrats to vote a straight ticket

A specific purpose ensures that you've narrowed the subject for the spec-
ified time limits. Some think a speech can be expanded or contracted simply
by adding or omitting supporting materials. It's true you can make slight
changes in the length of a speech. But a significant change can't be achieved
in this way. To reduce a twenty-minute speech to a five-minute speech by eliminating supporting materials will leave only a skeleton of a speech. To make
a length change of any magnitude, you must change the specific purpose to
one covering a complete segment of the twenty-minute speech. For example,
your specific purpose for a twenty-minute speech might be to explain the factors that produce a successful golf shot. Your main points might be these:

A. The grip
B. The stance
C. The swing

If you reduce this speech to five minutes and retain all these main points, you
will be able to present very little worthwhile information. But if you narrow
the speech by making your specific purpose to explain just one of those three
main points, you can still say approximately as much about that one point as
you could in a twenty-minute speech devoted to all three main points. (This
example also clearly illustrates the importance of determining the time limits
for your speech well in advance.)

Deciding on the specific purpose is also important because it helps you
prepare the speech. After selecting the subject, decide what you intend to discuss specifically in this particular speech. This eliminates much unnecessary
work from the preparation of the speech. For example, shortly after beginning
work on a speech, you'll probably go to the library to do research. In reading
an article, you may discover some interesting information. But every piece of
interesting information won't be relevant to your purpose. If you've determined your specific purpose, you'll know immediately whether you should
transfer the information to a note card for use in the speech. If you haven't
decided on your purpose, all you can do is record the material in hopes it will
be relevant to whatever specific purpose you ultimately choose. Once you determine your purpose, you may find a significant number of your notes are
irrelevant and must be discarded. If your specific purpose had been clearly
stated first, valuable time, which could have been spent in gathering pertinent
data, wouldn't have been wasted.

Suggested Speech Topics

Listed below are some suggested topics for informative and persuasive speeches. Some of the topics listed under one heading could just as easily be listed under the other heading. Some of the topics will need to be narrowed to fit the time limits available. At the least, these few topics will provide a starting point for finding a subject for your speeches.

Informative Speeches

Découpage	How the instant camera works
Rappelling	Card tricks
Clog dancing	Selling real estate
Racketball	Laser beams
Using a microscope	Soccer
Karate	Handmade jewelry
The Bermuda Triangle	Arts and crafts fairs
Transcendental meditation	Rummage sales
Repotting a plant	Selecting a tennis racket
Warming up for jogging	Caring for a hi-fi stereo record
Bypass heart surgery	Home smoke detectors
Cooking crepes	Astrology
Gripping a golf club	Home computers
Swinging a tennis racket	Stock market
Skydiving	The Marsh Arabs
Pruning a peach tree	The diadem butterfly
Skinning a frog	The flat tax
Magnet schools	A co-op program
Values clarification	Marathon running

Persuasive Speeches

Strip mining	Railroad passenger service
Teenage alcoholism	Pollution
Child abuse	Fishing rights
Wife abuse	Overcrowded national parks
Abortion	Energy crisis
Gun control	Divorce
Reinstatement of the military draft	Airbags for automobiles
Vegetarianism	Mandatory seatbelt laws
Fuel shortage	Athletic scholarships for women
Poverty	Academy Awards
Crime	Violence on television
Zoning restrictions	Sex on television
Crime victims' rights	Animal rights

Preparation

Summary

Selecting a speech subject is one of the most important decisions you can make. The subject is frequently the determining factor in the success or failure of a speech. Making an effective choice of subject requires the consideration of three factors: (1) the speaker, (2) the occasion, and (3) the audience.

Begin with yourself, considering your interests, experiences, and knowledge, and the audience's expectations of you.

A more effective subject will be selected if you also determine the nature and mood of the occasion, the time limits of the speech, the other events on the program, and the nature of the place where the speech will be given.

The chances of selecting a subject appropriate to the audience will be enhanced if you ascertain the important demographic features of the listeners, why they are present for the speech, what they are interested in, and what they know.

After choosing the subject, decide upon the general purpose (to entertain, to inform, to persuade) and the specific purpose (the particular objective for the speech).

Exercises

1. Prepare a list of topics in which you are interested. Prepare a list of topics in which your classmates are interested. On the basis of knowledge possessed by you and your classmates, identify from the two lists three common topics on which you could speak to the class.
2. For each of the three topics identified in exercise 1, determine a specific purpose for a speech for each of the three general purposes.
3. Phrase a specific purpose and list the main ideas to develop it for a twenty-minute speech. Then, using the same topic, phrase a specific purpose and list the main ideas to develop it for a seven-minute speech.
4. Identify two or three areas of the topic in exercise 3 that you need to research for a speech. Collect evidence on 5 four-by-six index cards to be turned in.
5. Explain how a speech subject you choose for a classroom speech could create credibility for you.

Notes

1. W. N. Brigance, *Speech: Its Techniques and Disciplines in a Free Society*, 2d ed. (New York: Appleton-Century-Crofts, 1961), pp. 35–37.

CHAPTER 9

Understanding Methods of Presentation

You can use one of four methods in presenting a speech to an audience. Each has certain strengths and certain weaknesses; each is more appropriate in specific situations; and one method may be better suited to an individual than the others. You have the responsibility of assessing the circumstances, evaluating the methods of presentation, and determining which is more effective for your specific occasion, your audience, and yourself.

Extemporaneous Speaking

Extemporaneous doesn't mean speaking without preparation. Extemporaneous speeches result from a carefully prepared effort. Select your topic carefully, limit it to an idea that can be developed in the time available, phrase a statement of purpose, decide on the main points needed to develop the purpose, gather and select supporting materials for the main points, think about the language to use, and prepare an introduction and conclusion. Then practice the speech a number of times. Does this mean you'll couch your thoughts in the specific sequence of words to be used in presenting the speech? No, you'll make the exact choice of words and construction of sentences largely during the act of communicating directly with your listeners.

The extemporaneous method of presentation has distinct advantages. It is generally the most effective method of delivering a speech and is usually preferred by experienced speakers. In an interview with two speech communication scholars, the late President Harry Truman said

Advantages of the Extemporaneous Method

> If I had my choice, I would always speak extemporaneously. However, as President I was compelled to read most of my speeches. While I feel less strained than I used to, I'm still not completely at home when I have to read from a text. Like almost everyone else, I talk more effectively than I read. As I have said, sometimes I try to get away from the formality of a text by inserting ad-libbed comments. Even in formal Presidential addresses I often strayed from the official copy.[1]

The extemporaneous speech leaves you free to develop and maintain direct contact with listeners. Since only occasional glances at notes are necessary, you can look directly at listeners the rest of the time. You can utilize the same behavior apparent in good conversational speech. Speaking extemporaneously also leaves you relatively free to use bodily action and gestures. You can move away from the lectern because you're not tied to a written manuscript.

You generally have a greater tendency to use an oral style when you speak extemporaneously. Norman Thomas, perennial Socialist candidate for president during the first half of the twentieth century, evidenced an awareness of this:

> It cannot be too strongly insisted that the written and spoken word, while they have much in common, are by no means the same. The speaker is concerned with the particular group before him; he is not speaking to a scattered group

of readers or to posterity. Sometimes he can communicate more effectively by repetition, intonation, gesture, unfinished sentence. I have often winced at stenographic reports of speeches which had gone over well enough to receive much applause. But I am convinced that I would have made a mistake to have read a smoother speech.[2]

Having to think about the ideas as you phrase them usually results in a more direct, conversational style. And you may get some of the advantages of preparation by memorizing precisely stated portions of the speech. Some speakers prepare their introduction and conclusion and learn them thoroughly in order to begin and end the speech smoothly and effectively. William E. Borah, senator from Idaho from 1907 to 1940 and an effective speaker, is reported to have "memorized choice sentences" he wanted to use while speaking extemporaneously.[3]

An advantage of the extemporaneous method is you are better able to adjust and adapt to the audience and the situation. You don't have to worry about being unable to break into a specific sequence of words you are giving from memory or reading from a manuscript. It is easier to restate your ideas in different words if it appears the listeners don't understand, to offer additional supporting material if what you have given appears inadequate, to comment on some unexpected occurrence in the speech situation. Norman Vincent Peale reported: "I prepare only a pattern or sequence of ideas and leave the exact expression of those ideas to the inspiration of the moment. I find that reading or memorizing a speech injures spontaneity. Without spontaneity there can be little rapport between the speaker and his audience."[4]

Disadvantages of the Extemporaneous Method

Does the extemporaneous method have any weaknesses? Yes, language can be less precise. Frequently the most apt word doesn't occur to you, so a synonym is taken that has a slightly different meaning. Phrases and sentences may be less polished because you can't study the construction and rewrite for clarity and aptness of expression.

Speaking extemporaneously makes it more difficult to observe the time limits in a speaking situation. Since no practice session is the same as the actual speaking situation, you can never be sure you're going to use the same number of words and the same amount of time. With practice, however, your timing can be close.

You can get so emotionally involved in the speaking situation that you get carried away and say things you don't mean. The give-and-take between you and the audience may cause you to make remarks that calm deliberation would tell you were ill-advised. Against the counsel of his advisers, President Andrew Jackson spoke extemporaneously and let his audiences guide and influence his speeches in his ill-fated "Swing Around the Circle" in 1866. He found himself responding to listener's reactions with replies that created the impression of a reckless, egotistical person.

Preparing to speak extemporaneously can give a false sense of security. Since you don't have to prepare a written form of the speech, you may decide there is little to worry about. You may rely too much on the inspiration of the moment and not make the necessary preparation.

Speaking extemporaneously can result in a jerky, halting, nonfluent speech instead of a fluent rate. You may hesitate in order to think of the best word to communicate your meaning. Too much of this, especially if filled with "uhs" and "and-uhs," can disrupt the communicative process and cause the listener to lose interest in what you have to say.

May you use notes when you speak? Your professor will set the policy for your class. If permitted, be sure they don't interfere with communication. One of the best ways to use notes is to prepare them on note cards, preferably four by six inches, which can be held easily in the hand and slipped into a coat pocket or purse. They are easier to carry to the speaking situation and can be held unobtrusively in your hand if there is no lectern. If there is a lectern you can move away from it if you desire. If holding the cards in your hands interferes with gesturing, slip them into a pocket, or gesture with the cards in one hand.

Note cards should be held to a minimum. Put only an outline of key words and phrases on the cards. If you use more, you'll spend most of your time shuffling and looking at note cards instead of at the listeners.

Material on the cards should be printed, written clearly, or typed. Deciphering notes in front of an audience is distracting. Use only one side, and number the cards to prevent them from getting out of order.

Reading from a Manuscript

A speech to be read from manuscript is written out in its entirety. A common error to avoid is the tendency to write an essay. Even though the speech is written, it must conform to all the principles of good speech making. One of the best ways to prevent a speech from sounding like an essay is to use an oral, conversational style, not a written style. Former television news commentator David Brinkley advised aspiring news broadcasters, "In writing news for broadcasting, it's important to remember that what you're writing is conversation—not words to be printed but words to be spoken, and there is a great difference. The most important requirements are clarity, simplicity and brevity. It's harder to do it that way, but the results are worth the effort."[5]

Your instructor will tell you which type of presentation you're to use in your classroom speeches. It is best not to prepare a speech to read from a manuscript until you have mastered the extemporaneous method of presentation. Most students have been trained in writing much more than in speaking. After you have mastered the extemporaneous method and have developed an oral style that has become habitual, it will be easier to write a speech retaining the spontaneity of conversational speech. The absence of this quality is a frequent fault of written speeches.

Using a manuscript in the speaking situation is more effective if certain guidelines are followed. The manuscript must be clearly legible. It should be typed with either double or triple spacing. Most people find that triple spacing makes for easier reading at the lectern. The typescript is also more easily read if nothing but capitals are used. This prevents you from having to squint at the manuscript or bend over the lectern in order to read the speech.

A speech to be read from a manuscript must be practiced diligently. Develop a strong familiarity with it so you can read it with the proper meaning and establish direct eye contact with your listeners.

When reading the speech, avoid bending your head to look at the manuscript. Learn to glance at the page so the audience won't be distracted.

Avoid sounding as if you are reading the manuscript; sound as if you are talking to the listeners. One important way to achieve a conversational style is to avoid the type of reading in which every sound is accented. Children read in this manner: The—boy—was—playing—with—the—marbles. In normal conversation, however, only rarely would more than three words in that sentence be accented; generally the sentence would be divided into two thought units: Thə boy—wəz playing wi-thə marbles. Learn to accent the sounds and words that merit emphasis and let those that don't remain unaccented. Get the same kind of elision in your speech as in your conversational speaking.

Turning the pages of the manuscript can be distracting if you aren't careful. It is best not to turn the pages as they are completed. Slide the top page across the lectern to the other side. With practice this can be done unobtrusively. If you slide each page over when you're about half through that page, you'll be able to accomplish the movement from page to page with a minimum of disturbance.

Are gestures needed in reading a speech from a manuscript? Yes, make a conscious effort to use gestures and avoid letting the manuscript set up a barrier between you and the audience.

Advantages of Reading a Speech

Reading a speech has several advantages. The language can be more precise than in an extemporaneous presentation. Sentences can be recast to develop clarity. A dictionary and thesaurus can be consulted to select the precise word to communicate intended meaning. The fireside chats of Franklin D. Roosevelt, noted for their clarity of expression, went through numerous drafts before they achieved the qualities characterizing them in their actual presentation.

Not only can language be made delicately precise, it can also be polished to express ideas more vividly and felicitously. Consciously manipulate language to take advantage of stylistic devices such as alliteration and periodic sentences. Avoid sequences of sounds and words that are difficult to pronounce. It is not always possible to accomplish these in an extemporaneous delivery.

Reading a manuscript permits you to conform to the time limits with much greater precision and ease than when you are speaking extemporaneously. You can time the speech during practice sessions and edit it to within a few seconds of the prescribed time limit.

Despite its advantages, there are problems in manuscript reading that make it an ineffective speaking method. A speaker reading a manuscript finds it extremely difficult to adapt to changing conditions in the situation. Senator Borah "felt that a manuscript gave him a sense of restriction and rigidity."[6]

This is not to say that adjustments can't be made. A comparison of Franklin D. Roosevelt's reading text with the actual recorded speech reveals many interpolations made during the presentation of his speeches. Crowell counted "172 instances of spontaneous alteration" in one speech and she reported that this was not atypical.[7] An example of Roosevelt's ability to deviate

Disadvantages of Reading a Speech

from the prepared text is demonstrated in the following example. Those words in italics were added in delivery; those in parentheses were in the prepared text but omitted in delivery:

> *Secretary Ickes, Governor Hoey, Governor Cooper and our neighbor, Governor Maybank of South Carolina, and my friends from all the states: I have listened with attention and great interest to the thousands of varieties of plants and trees and fishes and animals that Governor Cooper told us about, but he failed to mention the hundreds of thousands of species of human animals that come to the park.*
>
> Here in the Great Smokies, we (meet today) *have come together* to dedicate these mountains, and streams and forests, *the thousands of them,* to the service of the *millions of* American people. We are living under governments (which) *that* are proving their devotion to national parks. The Governors of North Carolina and of Tennessee have greatly helped us, and the Secretary of the Interior is so active that he has today ready for dedication *a number of other great National* (two more) parks—*like* Kings Canyon in California and the Olympic National Park in the State of Washington, *the Isle Park up in Michigan and, over here, the Great Cavern of Tennessee,* and soon, I hope, *he will have another one for us to dedicate* (a third,) the Big Bend Park *away down* in Texas, *close to the Mexican Line.*[8]

Roosevelt was a man of unusual speaking ability, however, and many speakers find it difficult to make even the relatively minor changes in a manuscript speech that Roosevelt made. To make major changes and adaptations becomes, for many speakers, a monumental task.

A harmful aspect of reading a speech from manuscript is its disruption of communication between speaker and listener. Despite familiarity with a manuscript, your eye contact is more limited than when speaking extemporaneously. It is difficult to keep your place in a manuscript and maintain eye contact.

Moreover, you are more definitely bound to the lectern and your manuscript; consequently, your freedom to gesture and move about the podium or around the lectern is hampered. If you perceive the necessity of moving to one end of the platform to talk more directly to a particular segment of your audience, you must either ignore that need or resort to the rather awkward solution of picking up your manuscript and carrying it with you.

Finally, unless you are skilled at reading aloud, you'll find it difficult to read a speech from manuscript in a conversational manner.

Comparison with Extemporaneous Method

Despite obstacles in effectively reading a speech from manuscript, evidence indicates the two methods are equally effective in informing an audience. Note, however, that this is different from holding the interest of an audience and developing credibility for a speaker. Investigators did discover, however, that one speaker was more effective with one method than with the other. Consequently, they caution against indiscriminately recommending one method over the other. "As common sense perhaps should have suggested all along, the statement in textbooks that the extemporaneous method is superior to reading should be revised to read: *Some speakers are more effective extemporaneously than they are when using a manuscript, and some use both methods with equal effectiveness.*"[9] Since only skilled speakers were used in this experiment, the conclusions cannot be extended to beginning speakers.

Speaking from Memory

The memorized speech differs from both the extemporaneous and the manuscript speech because it is completely written before coming to the speech occasion. It is committed to memory and no written copy is used.

The memorized speech offers several advantages. You can roam about the platform and use as much bodily action and as many gestures as you wish. Since you use no notes or manuscript, you are freer to use bodily action in delivering the memorized speech than with any other method.

Advantages of the Memorized Presentation

The absence of notes or a manuscript allows you to maintain the most direct communication of any method of presentation. You can look at listeners because you have no notes to read from. You can move to any part of the platform for better contact with some or all of the listeners without worrying about notes that would normally be on the lectern.

Like the manuscript speech, the prior preparation of the memorized speech enables you to achieve a more precise use of language, to be more accurate and more colorful. This is especially helpful when you want to be sure you don't accidentally use a word giving the wrong impression to the listeners.

Also, as in the manuscript speech, the memorized speech permits you to conform more precisely to the time limits. The length of a memorized speech will vary by only a few seconds from one occasion to another.

Despite the advantages of the memorized speech, there are several weaknesses. Those who have heard schoolboy orators with memorized pieces know how artificial and unmoving those efforts can be. The spontaneity that results from thinking about your ideas and phrasing them as you talk is sometimes lacking in a memorized speech. Your mind is focused on a particular sequence of words rather than on the ideas themselves; this is frequently reflected in your voice and manner.

Disadvantages of the Memorized Presentation

Probably the greatest objection to memorization arises from the obstacles it raises against adaptation to the specific situation. Once a sequence of words has been learned, it is extremely difficult for many people to insert additional words. Consequently, if anything happens in the situation that demands a spontaneous response, it is difficult to alter the memorized material. Yet some speakers can. Although Rufus Choate and Chauncy M. Depew, outstanding lawyers of the nineteenth century, "wrote their speeches, neither of them . . . used notes in their delivery. Both reproduced what they had written with fidelity and were" skillful at making their speeches seem spontaneous "by witty and appropriate interjections, obviously inspired by the occasion."[10]

Another weakness, which also occurs in the manuscript speech, is the danger that the ideas will be presented in a written rather than oral style. This is not a direct result of the speech being memorized, however; it is the result of the speech being written beforehand. Consequently, when using the memorized method, pay special attention to style and make a conscious effort to write in an oral style.

A final and sometimes prohibitive weakness of memorization is that some individuals have great difficulty in memorizing material. Although techniques are available to aid a person's memory, these methods don't always produce the results claimed by their proponents. Susan B. Anthony, foremost advocate of women's rights, temperance, and other causes in the nineteenth century, found memorization difficult. The first time she was to make a major speech for woman's suffrage, "She paced up and down for hours trying to commit the speech to memory, but all in vain. It was impossible for her, then or later, ever to memorize exact words. For this reason most of her speeches were given from notes, never being presented in quite the same way."[11] If you have difficulty in memorizing exactly, avoid this method of speech presentation.

Impromptu Speaking

A truly impromptu speech is one for which the speaker has had no prior warning. No specific preparation has been made and no previous planning of the speech was possible, although this doesn't mean the impromptu speech is unorganized. If the topic for the speech is also one on which the speaker has had little or no experience and has little or no knowledge, it won't be much of a speech. The speaker would better serve himself, and speech making in general, if he or she gracefully declined the opportunity to speak.

On occasion, impromptu speeches may be unavoidable. In a meeting, for example, an unexpected discussion of a topic may call for an informed member of the group to speak on some phase of the topic. Or, occasionally, a person may be intrigued by some unanticipated event about which he or she has information and decides to talk about it. This happened to poet Robert Frost on one of his lecture tours:

> Once, at a midwestern college, just before he was to begin a lecture, someone piqued him by a reference to Plato's "Republic," and he launched off on a remarkable impromptu excursus on Plato. Yet what appears to be impromptu usually has a long foreground. A longtime reader of Plato who puts down no notes, keeps no journal, he was ready, and the occasion was right.[12]

With quick thinking and application of certain principles in such instances as these, an acceptable speech can be made.

Organizing an Impromptu Speech

The organization of an impromptu speech should begin the same as any other speech: phrase the central idea in a clearly worded, simple, declarative sentence. In many instances, choosing a statement of specific purpose for an impromptu speech will be easier than for any other type because the request or need for an impromptu effort will be an outgrowth of a specific discussion and a specific request. On rare occasions you may receive a general request for an impromptu speech and must choose and word the statement of purpose yourself.

Once you have decided on the thesis sentence, divide the topic into some logical sections to be used as the main points of the speech. If called upon to discuss, for example, politics in the state of Indiana, you might use as your thesis "The changing political structure in Indiana is beneficial." You might show that the changes are beneficial by using a syllogistic development with the following three points:

1. The political changes occurring across the United States are beneficial.
2. Similar political changes are occurring in Indiana.
3. Therefore, the political changes in Indiana are beneficial.

The divisions used can be developed with appropriate supporting material you can recall. Technical or strange terms should be defined. Attempt to cite at least one example for each main point, and if you can recall any testimony, statistics, or humorous anecdotes, use them to develop your ideas more fully.

Like any other speech, most impromptu speeches need an introduction to get the attention of the hearers, gain their goodwill, and start them thinking about the subject. In many instances, however, an impromptu speech doesn't need

Starting an Impromptu Speech

an introduction. Any discussion that leads to a request for an impromptu speech is, in effect, an introduction to the speech. Since the people present have indicated their interest in the topic, demonstrated their goodwill toward the speaker by asking him or her to speak, and have their attention focused on him or her, all the speaker needs to do is launch immediately into the statement of purpose and begin development of it. On other occasions the request to make an impromptu speech will be completely unexpected. In such an instance an introduction of the speech is much more necessary, even if it serves no other purpose than to give you a moment longer to organize your thoughts.

A number of means are available in introducing an impromptu speech. You may relate to what a previous speaker has said, to something the presiding officer has said, or to what an authority has said. You may begin by repeating a question that was asked or with a brief anecdote or some pertinent statistics. The one thing you must not do as an impromptu speaker is to begin with an apology for your lack of preparation. An apology sounds as though you are begging for sympathy.

Ending an Impromptu Speech

The conclusion of an impromptu speech will rarely be as polished as the conclusion of a prepared speech. Nevertheless, attempt to focus your listeners' thoughts for a final time on the central idea of the speech. You may simply summarize the main points, restate the original question, explain the significance of your ideas to the listeners, or repeat and amplify the main idea with authoritative testimony.

Anticipating an Impromptu Speech

Not all impromptu requests have to result in impromptu speeches; many times you can successfully anticipate the request and be prepared for it. A person who is known to give speeches frequently must realize that if someone is going to be singled out for an impromptu speech, there is a strong likelihood she or he will be that person. Knowing this, she or he will go prepared. As a matter of fact, some known speakers never go anyplace without an "emergency" speech in mind.

Even if you do little public speaking, you can analyze the situation beforehand to determine if there is any likelihood you will be asked to speak. If you are attending a going-away dinner for a close personal friend of many years, anticipate being asked to make a few remarks about your friend. Before leaving home, therefore, select two or three main ideas you would like to emphasize about your friend and recall one or two interesting anecdotes to illustrate each point. Then, if you are asked to speak, you won't be unprepared.

Advantages of an Impromptu Speech

It is difficult to talk about advantages of the impromptu method. Ordinarily this method is used because the speaker is unexpectedly asked to speak and has no other choice. Most speakers caught in this predicament will verify there are few advantages. The impromptu speech may seem to have all the advantages of the extemporaneous method—direct contact with listeners, free use of bodily action and gestures, easy adaptation to situations, and tendency to

Preparation

use an oral style. A closer look reveals that the impromptu speaker is so involved in determining what to say and how to organize it that he or she has little time to devote to these factors.

If used in the educational situation carefully and discriminatingly, however, the impromptu speech can have value. It can teach you to think quickly on your feet, which, let's hope, will be transferred to other speaking occasions when you are called on to think quickly.

Although the impromptu method has a number of disadvantages (absence of careful selection of main ideas, lack of research to develop ideas, lack of thoughtful choice of language), there is one basic cause for a poor speech: the lack of careful preparation for the speech.

Disadvantages of an Impromptu Speech

Summary

This chapter has presented the strengths and weaknesses of four methods of presenting a speech. The different methods have been developed as though they are largely discrete and mutually exclusive. In fact, however, any speech may use more than one method. The extemporaneous speaker frequently has committed to memory or written on a note card a choice way of stating a particular part of the speech. Speakers using a manuscript or giving a speech from memory frequently make extemporaneous adaptations to the particular audience or situation. The truly effective speaker, therefore, must be capable of using all of these methods.

Finally, each of the methods of presentation has both advantages and disadvantages. The advantages of extemporaneous speaking are that it permits direct contact with listeners, encourages free use of bodily actions and gestures, allows easy adaptation to the situation, and invites use of an oral style. The disadvantages are that the language may be less precise, time limits are more difficult to observe, the speaker may say something unintended, the speaker may rely too heavily on the inspiration of the moment and not prepare properly, and the speaker's fluency may be adversely affected.

The advantages of reading from a manuscript are that language can be more precise, language can be more polished, time limits can be conformed to more easily, and there is no worry about what is going to be said. The disadvantages of reading from a manuscript are that it makes adaptation difficult, can interfere with direct communication, requires a skilled reader, and encourages use of a written style.

The advantages of speaking from memory are that it permits complete freedom in body action, direct communication, precise use of language, and easy conformance to time limits. The disadvantages of speaking from memory are that it tends to sound memorized, makes adaptation difficult, encourages use of a written style, and it is difficult for some people to memorize.

The only advantage of impromptu speaking is that it teaches the ability to think quickly on one's feet. Impromptu speaking has many disadvantages, but the basic one is a lack of careful preparation.

Notes

1. E. E. White and C. R. Henderlider, "What Harry S Truman Told Us About His Speaking," *Quarterly Journal of Speech* 40 (1954):39.
2. N. Thomas, "Random Reflections on Public Speaking," *Quarterly Journal of Speech* 40 (1954):149.
3. W. W. Braden, "The Bases of William E. Borah's Speech Preparation," *Quarterly Journal of Speech* 33 (1947):29.
4. E. E. White and C. R. Henderlider, "What Norman Vincent Peale Told Us About His Speaking," *Quarterly Journal of Speech* 40 (1954):414–15.
5. David Brinkley, *Richmond News Leader* May 22, 1956. Used by permission.
6. A. E. Whitehead, "The Oratory of William Edgar Borah," *Quarterly Journal of Speech* 32 (1949):296.
7. L. Crowell, "Word Changes Introduced Ad Libitum in Five Speeches by Franklin Delano Roosevelt," *Speech Monographs* 25 (1958):230.
8. E. Brandenburg, "The Preparation of Frankln D. Roosevelt's Speeches," *Quarterly Journal of Speech* 35 (1949):219–20.
9. H. W. Hildebrandt and W. W. Stevens, "Manuscript and Extemporaneous Delivery in Communicating Information," *Speech Monographs* 30 (1963):372.
10. H. W. Taft, *Kindred Arts: Conversation and Public Speaking* (New York: Macmillan Publishing Co., 1929), p. 91. Used by permission.
11. E. E. McDavitt, "Susan B. Anthony, Reformer and Speaker," *Quarterly Journal of Speech* 30 (1944):176.
12. Reginald L. Cook, "Notes on Frost the Lecturer," *Quarterly Journal of Speech* 42 (1956):129.

CHAPTER 10

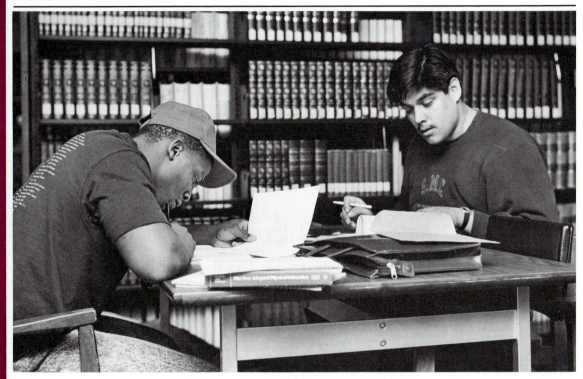

Researching a Speech Topic

Generally when you are called on to make a speech, you'll speak on a familiar topic. In some instances, however, you may be asked by a group to prepare and present a talk on a topic on which you have little information. In that case you may have to do considerable research to prepare for the speech. Usually, however, you'll be asked to speak on a topic on which you are knowledgeable and experienced. Still, you'll probably have to do some research to fill in weak areas and to bring your information up-to-date. This chapter is designed to help you find the sources of information you need for whatever speech you are going to make. Four general sources may be consulted in the search for ideas and evidence: (1) personal experience, (2) interviews, (3) documents, and (4) library resources.

Personal Experience

Begin with your own knowledge and experiences. The use of personal experience has a number of virtues. First, it's easier to talk about. You don't have to remember what someone else has said or written; you're talking about things you have done. Rely on your own vocabulary to describe the experiences. If you're relating what someone else has said or written, you're restricted to repeating the exact words of that person or to finding synonyms for those words. You can't go beyond the words of that other person, which makes it more difficult to use your own vocabulary.

A second advantage of personal experience is that the information is new to listeners unless you have talked to the group previously or have published the material someplace where the listeners could have read it. Thus, you can use personal experience without any concern about whether the listeners are familiar with the content. Even if you're talking about experiences that others have talked about to this same group, it is still fresh information because no two people perceive the same things in a given situation, and no two people react in the same way to the stimuli they perceive.

But the most important advantage of using personal experience is that it contributes to your credibility, thus causing greater attitude change on the part of the listeners. Ostermeier presented to subjects persuasive messages in which he varied the number of self-reference materials (defined as firsthand personal experiences) and the number of prestige reference materials (defined as the firsthand experience of others). The results of the study showed that increasing the number of self-references caused the subjects to perceive the source as being more competent and trustworthy, and it caused the subjects to change their attitudes more. Ostermeier concludes that an audience considers personal experience "direct information" about the speaker, whereas firsthand experiences of others are considered "indirect information."[1]

Canadian statesman Lester Pearson used an effective personal experience to present a point in his speech accepting the Nobel Peace Prize in 1957:

> I have, therefore, had compelling reasons, and some opportunity, to think about peace; to ponder over our failures since 1914 to establish it, and to shudder at the possible consequences if we continue to fail.

I remember particularly one poignant illustration of the futility and tragedy of war. It was concerned, not with the blood and sacrifice of battles from 1914 to 1918, but with civilian destruction in London in 1941 during its ordeal by bombing.

It was a quiet Sunday morning after a shattering night of fire and death. I was walking past the smoking ruins of houses that had been bombed and burned during the night. The day before they had been a neat row of humble, red brick, workmen's dwellings. They were now rubble except for the front wall of one building, which may have been some kind of community club, and on which there was a plaque that read "Sacred to the memory of the men of Alice Street who died for peace during the Great War, 1914–1918." The children and grandchildren of those men of Alice Street had now in their turn been sacrificed in the Greater War, 1939–1945. For peace? There are times when it does not seem so.[2]

Interviews

Interviews with knowledgeable and experienced persons in the surrounding community shouldn't be overlooked as valuable sources of information. As a college student, you have an unparalleled opportunity to consult experts and near experts. And most professors will be happy to talk to you if the interview is conducted in the proper way. Using the following four guidelines should make for a happier and more productive interview.

First, make a prior appointment for the interview. This will save you time and effort. Anyone knowledgeable or important enough to be interviewed will generally have many obligations. Without a definite appointment, you may find yourself making several trips before the person is free to see you. Making an appointment also indicates respect for the person you want to interview. The appointment indicates you put some thought into the decision to conduct the interview; you didn't just drop by because you had a spur-of-the-moment inspiration.

Second, conduct interviews only after most of the other research has been completed. There is no need to take up someone's valuable time with questions that can be answered by reading a book or a periodical article. Moreover, in your reading you may find information you don't understand. In the interview you can then get help with that material. You may also find that you have difficulty in locating information about certain facets of your topic. You can start your interview by asking the person being interviewed for information in those areas. If the interviewee can't or doesn't want to provide the information, then you can ask her or him to suggest some sources. If the interview is held too early in the research effort, however, you lack the knowledge to ask some important questions.

Third, take specific questions to the interview. Avoid asking a general question, such as "Tell me what you know about growing watermelons." If you're consulting an expert, that person doesn't have time to answer that one question. An interview should involve specific questions to which you have been unable to find answers. This doesn't mean you can't ask questions suggested by the interviewee's replies to your prepared questions, or other remarks. It simply means you go to the interview knowing the important questions you need to ask.

Fourth, conduct the interview with sensitivity. Show respect for the respondent's feelings and privacy. After the Alaskan earthquake of 1964, some survivors were immediately flown back to Seattle. The memory of one insensitive television reporter still lingers. Thrusting a microphone into the face of one woman as she disembarked from the plane, he asked: "How did you feel when you saw your husband and sons disappear into the hole in the ground?" Remember that most people don't like to give personal information. Many citizens resented the 1970 census because the questionnaire included so many questions seeking personal and family data. If you need or desire such information, present the first personal question gingerly and be prepared to move to another line of questioning at the first hint of displeasure by the respondent.

Documents

Actual documents are another important source of information. Pictures (especially the negatives, because prints may have been falsified), deeds, or contracts are documents that can furnish significant evidence. A college basketball player denied reports during the 1970–71 season that he had already signed a contract with the Pittsburgh Condors. At the end of the season when he signed with another basketball team, the Pittsburgh management produced in court a signed contract, on the basis of which the NCAA voided the record of his college team and reclaimed from the school the financial share of the NCAA tournament it had received.

Documents are generally too small to be perceived by listeners in a speaking situation. Nevertheless, the fact that you have them in your possession can be persuasive. If desirable, you can hold them up during the speech and offer to let any listener examine them after the speech. If some documents happen to be large enough to be readable by the entire audience, they can be used as visual aids.

Library Resources

Even the most knowledgeable person will frequently want to do some research to check some point on which his or her memory is fuzzy or to check the latest data on a specific topic. The less knowledgeable speaker will have to do considerable research. A number of library materials provide valuable information. Some of these sources provide factual data themselves; others recommend sources of information.

Begin your research on the topic you have chosen in your school library. It is one of the best sources because as a general rule the academic library is the largest in a community or region. Academic libraries are also generally open for longer hours than other libraries—on weekends and late at night; in some instances, all night. After you have used your library, investigate others in the area for information not available in your college library.

If your library is not computerized, go to the card catalog and find the topic of your speech in the appropriate alphabetic area. Browse through that section and record the call numbers of the newest books. Then go to the stacks and browse through the books you have listed, plus any others that appear worthwhile. If you want to use the latest book available on your topic, go to the *Cumulative Book Index*. Once you have identified the newest book, you can go to the card catalog to see whether the book is in your library.

If your library is on a computerized system, use the search options on the computer terminal to identify, on your selected subject, available books that are in your library. A widely used system is LUIS, Library User Information Service. Other systems are very similar. The terminal screen should have on it the following information:

Search Options	*Commands*	
To search by	TITLE:	= T
	AUTHOR:	= A
	SUBJECT:	= S

Thus, if you're looking for a book whose title you recall, you would type on the screen at the proper location the following: T = Ends of Power. If the book is in your library, the following information will immediately appear on the terminal screen: the author's name, the title of the book, the date of publication, the publisher, and the call number to find the book. If you know the name of the author, but not the name of the book, you would type on the terminal screen: A = Bruce Catton. All books written by Bruce Catton would then be listed on the terminal screen so you could identify the one in which you were interested. If you are interested in what is available in your library on a specific topic, you should type S = Boer War. All works in your library on the Boer War would appear on the terminal screen.

After you have located the books you want, by title, author, or subject, you may in many computerized libraries go to a terminal that is connected to a printer and print out the books listed under the heading you have chosen. With your list you can go to the stacks and select the books you think will be most helpful in developing your speech.

You can also consult the *Subject Guide to Books in Print* to identify books on the topic you're considering for your speech. This will identify any published books on your subject. You can then check to see if these books are in your library.

You will also want to include any periodical articles that are pertinent to your topic. These can be found in the *Reader's Guide to Periodical Literature*, which is generally housed in the Humanities division of the library. It indexes approximately 130 current, popular periodicals, such as *Time, Harper's Magazine,* and *Fortune.* Articles are listed under subject headings, title of article, and author's name.

References to specialized topics may be found in a number of books: *Where To Find What,* by James M. Hillard, refers to books on topics from A through Z, such as Allergies, Civil Rights, Grasses, Linguistics, Reptiles, Treaties, and Zoos. *Where To Find More,* also by James M. Hillard, identifies additional books on a wide range of topics from A through Z, such as Butterflies, Earthquakes, Lotteries, Religions, and Wines. *How To Do Library Research,* by Robert B. Downs, also identifies a large number of reference books about such subjects as periodicals, words, places, people, literary works, history, reptiles, and ships and shipping.

Sources of Data

Many libraries have accumulated special collections that can cast light on a topic you are interested in. Check other libraries for any special collections. Other possible sources for information are hospitals and clinics; federal and state agencies; consulates and embassies; chambers of commerce; trade, professional and hobby associations.[3]

Some published sources provide specific data about various topics of interest.

Statistical Abstract of the United States is an annual publication of the Bureau of Census of the Department of Commerce. It is the most reliable source of statistics available, containing statistical information on practically every phase of life in the United States. More than thirty chapters provide information on such topics as education, labor force, employment and earnings, prices, communication, and population. Included is statistical information gathered from a wide variety of sources, identified in footnotes that frequently suggest additional sources for consultation.

Statesman's Year Book is an annual publication providing specific and significant data on every nation in the world (as well as on major international organizations). Discussed are such things as type of government, governmental expenditures, educational programs, type and quantity of industrial goods produced, type and quantity of agricultural goods. Where a nation consists of governmental subunits, such as states in the United States and provinces in Canada, the information is given, not only for the country as a whole, but also for each individual subunit.

The Congressional Record provides a text of each speech given in Congress. You should know, however, that the members of Congress have the freedom to alter the text from that delivered on the floor of the Senate or the House of Representatives. They may delete some things they said and they may add statements they did not make.

Facts on File is a weekly summary of world news. In addition to its *News Digest* published weekly, a cumulative index published twice each month provides a complete reference to all *News Digests* of the current year.

Vertical File is a collection of various pamphlets and clippings filed under specific and general topics. The folders holding the materials are generally kept in filing cabinets. The clippings are from newspapers, magazines, and other published sources you would generally not see because it would require examination of such a wide range of materials. The H. W. Wilson Company publishes a *Vertical File Index* each month except August.

What They Said is an annual volume of quotations spoken by persons of "fame and influence" on a wide variety of topics. The statements are organized by specific topics under three major headings: national affairs, international affairs, and general. An index of speakers is included.

Current Biography, Directory of American Scholars, Dictionary of American Biography, Dictionary of National Biography (British), *Webster's Biographical Dictionary* (includes pronunciations), *International Who's Who, Who's Who, Who's Who in America, Who's Who in the East, Who's Who in the South and Southwest, Who's Who in the West, Who's Who in the Midwest, Who's Who Among Black Americans, Who's Who of American Women*—all these works offer a speaker valuable sources of biographical information.

Biographical Information

Various indexes are available that identify sources of data that may be pertinent to your topic.

Humanities Index indexes approximately 260 periodicals of a scholarly bent in various fields classified as the humanities. Articles may be found under the author's name and subject heading.

Indexes to Sources of Data

Social Sciences Index is an index to articles in approximately 150 periodicals in various social sciences. Articles are listed under author's name and subject heading. Prior to 1974, *Humanities Index* and *Social Science Index* formed the *Social Sciences and Humanities Index,* which was known as the *International Index to Periodicals* until 1965.

The Education Index indexes (by author and subject) approximately 200 selected books, government documents, yearbooks, and periodical articles on the subject of education that were published in the English language during the period covered by the specific volume.

The Art Index indexes (by author and title) all books, government documents, and periodical articles on the broad subject field of art that were published in the English language during the period covered by the specific volume.

The International Index to Periodicals provides a listing of articles from noted journals around the world.

Public Affairs Information Service Bulletin is an index to pamphlets, books, government documents, "and other useful library material (in the English Language) in the field of economics and public affairs."

The New York Times Index is an index to all the stories, listed by alphabetical headings, which have appeared in the *New York Times.* Not only is it an important guide to information in the *New York Times,* it's extremely valuable in helping to locate information in other newspapers that aren't indexed! By finding the date a story appeared in the *New York Times,* you can then work around that date in any local newspaper in which you are interested.

The Monthly Catalog of the United States Government Publications indexes all government documents. Although it's a little confusing to use, it is often worth the effort, since some of the government documents frequently contain information found in no other source.

The *Index to Journals in Communication Studies* catalogs the fourteen major periodicals in the various fields of communication.

Encyclopedias

Knowing Where To Look by Lois Horowitz is an excellent source to find a wide range of information on a large number of subjects. In twenty-three chapters the author describes/identifies, in addition to the old standbys of information, such sources as magazines, newspapers, government documents, microfilm, addresses, statistics, quotations, and legal information. She also explains how to use the computer to find information, how to find original material, and how to locate experts.

These sources provide information on all branches of knowledge. Not infrequently, they offer a comprehensive discussion of a specific branch of knowledge.

Three general encyclopedias commonly found in college libraries are *Encyclopaedia Britannica, Encyclopedia Americana,* and *Collier's Encyclopedia.* The references are kept up-to-date by supplements issued on an irregular basis. Some of the articles are followed by brief reference lists.

Afro-American Encyclopedia is a ten-volume set that "covers black life, history, politics, culture, education, etc., in Africa, the United States, West Indies, Canada, and Latin America."[4]

Jewish Encyclopedia is a twelve-volume work that covers "Jewish history, culture, literature, etc., up to the time of its publication."[5]

Recording Research Information

As you do research on your speech topic, you should collect the information on four-by-six or five-by-eight index cards. Record on each card information from only one source and pertaining to only a single topic. Figures 10.1 and 10.2 show sample note cards with information recorded from a book and a periodical article. Don't put the headings on the cards when you record the information on them. Wait until you have collected most of your evidence. In that way you'll have a better idea of what the headings ought to be. Even then you should put the headings on each card in pencil, so you can easily change the heading if necessary or desirable. Be sure to record the source, date, and page number of information on the note card. Some put the bibliographical information on the back of the card. Be sure you put quotation marks around any material that is directly quoted. That way you'll never make a mistake of using a statement that is not yours without giving credit to the source. Develop a uniform method for recording data on the note cards and for filing them. It is much easier to use your cards when they are uniform.

Now that you have collected your information from the various sources, it's time to prepare a bibliography for the development of your speech. The following is a model bibliography for a proposed speech on China.

Bibliography on China

1. R. Bernstein. "A Journey of Conscience," *The New York Times Magazine,* April 16, 1989, pp. 22–25.
2. S. Bialer, "Reform: Moscow vs. Beijing," *US News and World Report,* February 6, 1989, 106:32–33.
3. A Deming, "We All Want Change" (Chinese students take to the streets), *Newsweek,* May 1, 1989, 133:40–41.
4. D. Duder, "China's 'Me Generation,' " *US News and World Report,* December 12, 1988, 105:25–28.
5. E. N. Luttwak, " 'A' is for Autonomy," *The New Republic,* April 17, 1989, 200:15–16.
6. R. Seidelman, "More Than Just Chinese Racism" (Anti-African demonstrations by Chinese students), *The Nation,* February 13, 1989, 248:195–196.
7. "Forcing Change on a Reluctant China," (Student Protests), *US News and World Report,* May 8, 1989, 106:42.

Figure 10.1
Sample note card: information taken from a book.

```
EDUCATION:  Focus on False Values

"As evidenced by their conspicuous and wholesale absence
from virtually every one of these reports and proposals,
we have obviously relegated all the moral and civic (read
"civilizing") values of education to the very back seat
of the big yellow bus--if indeed they are still being
allowed to ride at all--while prominently seated up front
are the real necessities, those which give primacy to our
economic needs, our escalating technological needs; in
short those that are unabashedly utilitarian." p. 81
Author:  Jeffrey R. Holland
Title: "A 'Notion' at Risk:  The Greater Crisis in
American Education," in Representative American Speeches,
1984-1985
Publisher:  The H. W. Wilson Company, 1985
```

Figure 10.2
Sample note card: information taken from a periodical article.

```
SPORTS:  Drug Use by Athletes

The pileup of revelations about drugs in sports raises
issues beyond the propriety of testing.  Big time univer-
sity athletic programs have come under fire for allegedly
placing sports competition--and the revenue it garners--
ahead of educational ideals.  In professional sports, the
big leagues may be in danger of alienating fans permanent-
ly if the perception grows that players are unable or
unwilling to tackle the drug problem.  "We have to restore
public confidence in the game," says Don Shula, head
coach of the Miami Dolphins.  "We must do everything
possible to show fans that the game is drug free.  This
is a battle we have to win, and the players, coaches,
and owners must join together to win it."  pp. 52-53
Author:  Jacob V. Lamar Jr.
Title:  "Scoring off the Field"
Periodical:  Time, August 25, 1986
```

Summary

Research is an important part of preparing a speech. It is the means of providing support for your ideas and giving the listeners specific information about the topic you discuss in your speech. Important sources of information are your own personal experiences, interviews with knowledgeable and experienced people, documents, and library resources.

Notes

1. T. H. Ostermeier, "Effects of Type and Frequency of Reference upon Perceived Source Credibility and Attitude Change," *Speech Monographs* 34 (1967):137–44.
2. L. B. Pearson, *The Four Faces of Peace* (New York: Sidney Hillman Foundation, n.d.), p. 4. Used by permission.
3. Lois Horowitz, *Knowing Where To Look,* Writers Digest Book, Cincinnati, Ohio, 1984, pp. 22–25.
4. Horowitz, *Knowing Where To Look,* p. 108.
5. Horowitz, *Knowing Where To Look,* p. 108.

CHAPTER 11

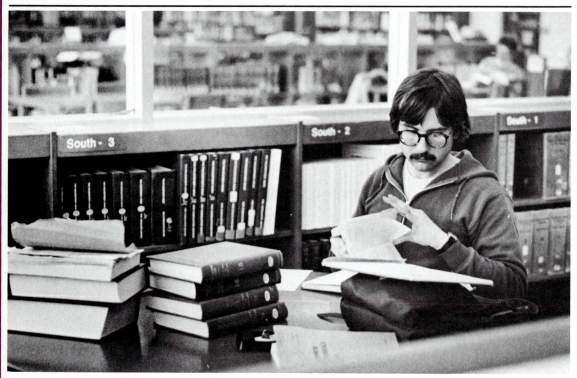

Developing Content

Content is all the information used in developing the speaker's statement of purpose. Acceptance or rejection of the content ultimately determines whether or not listeners respond in the manner desired by the speaker. Listeners are more likely to find the content credible, and therefore acceptable, if it possesses one or more of the following four attributes: (1) it is consistent with or coincides with their own knowledge or attitudes, (2) it is consistent with their experiences, (3) it originates from a speaker who is a highly credible source, or (4) it includes specific and credible content.

What is credible content? Credibility of content occurs on two levels. The first level is concerned with whether the content is *worthy* of belief on the basis of evidence and reasoning, regardless of whether it *is* believed. For example, the idea that was beginning to develop in the fifteenth century that the world was round was *worthy* of belief, even though many at that time did not believe it.

The second level of credibility is whether the content is *persuasive* to, or *believable* by, the listener. In early 1987, for example, despite President Reagan's denials, public opinion polls revealed that a majority of Americans believed that he had authorized secret shipments of military equipment to Iran to gain release of American hostages in Lebanon and had known of the diversion of funds from those arms sales to the Nicaraguan rebels.

The responsible and effective speaker tries to select content that is credible on two levels: it is not only *worthy* of belief, it is also *believable* or *persuasive* to the particular audience.

Ideas Consistent with Listeners' Knowledge and Attitudes

Statements or ideas consistent with knowledge and attitudes are accepted as credible. For example, the idea that work is an ennobling and necessary activity of humankind has long been held by most people in this country as a sacred principle. Any speaker making statements consistent with the "work ethic" would find many believing the statements merely because they consider the "ethic" itself valid. Without getting involved in the rightness or wrongness of the beliefs, we can think of a number that have long been held in this country: patriotism is good; democracy is the best form of government; freedom of speech is vital; freedom of religion is a right of all people; private enterprise is preferable to government ownership.

Anyone praising these or other such attitudes, or making statements consistent with them, is likely to strengthen his or her credibility. The speaker who stands in front of a labor union convention and says, "The product of American labor is what has made this country great," doesn't have to prove that claim. The listeners believe it in the marrow of their bones. The speaker who says to a business convention, "The ingenuity of American business leaders is responsible for the development and strength of the free enterprise system in this country," won't have this claim questioned. The speaker who comments to a group of college students that "Young people of today are better informed and more mature than any previous generation of young people," doesn't have to support that claim. In each instance, the listeners believe these statements deep down inside. Audiences require no proof when a speaker makes statements wholly consistent with their beliefs or attitudes. The ethical speaker, however, must share these beliefs and have evidence to support their validity.

Don't make a statement unless you believe it and can provide supporting evidence if needed. In these instances, the speaker's claim is acceptable because of the audience's implicit belief, which serves as both evidence and warrant. In other cases, the evidence or warrant may be stated explicitly. Thus a belief or attitude of the listener is used as the basis for other statements. If you're talking to a group that believes federal public works programs should be used to reduce unemployment, you may cite as evidence the unemployment rate and then present the claim that a federal public works program should be enacted immediately. You don't have to state explicitly your warrant that a federal works program is an effective method to reduce unemployment, nor do you have to prove it, because the listeners already believe it.

On the other hand, you can also use the knowledge of the listeners as evidence. If the audience knows that Richard Smith was drunk when he had an automobile accident last week, you can omit the evidence and go directly to the claim that "Richard Smith's drunkenness caused him to have the accident." You probably won't even have to state or develop the warrant that "Drunken drivers are prone to have accidents."

Constantly be alert for audience knowledge and attitudes you can use as evidence and warrants for the claims you are going to make in your speeches.

Use the methods explained in chapter 7 for analyzing the audience to which you are going to speak. With the materials that these audience analyses provide, you should become highly knowledgeable about the listeners' beliefs and attitudes, enabling you to know which statements you must prove, which need no proof, and which can serve as the basis for other statements.

Ideas Consistent with Listeners' Experience

We accept as real those things we actually experience. We believe our senses cannot betray us—a concept that one psychologist has called "primitive credulity." Each witness on the stand in a courtroom is convinced his or her account of events is the accurate one; after all, he or she perceived them through his or her own senses. If we hear an idea consistent with our experiences, we find it credible. On the other hand, we find unbelievable an idea that is inconsistent with our experiences. The fact that most academic theorists have never had actual experience in their field causes many practitioners to disbelieve their advice when it runs counter to experience. That is why businesspersons have said of certain economic theorists: "She can say that because she has never met a payroll." Or a journalist may say of a journalism professor: "If he had ever put a newspaper to bed, he wouldn't say that." Farmers frequently express contempt for agricultural officials when they come out from

Washington to give advice. One of the reasons for this attitude is that some of the advice runs counter to their own experiences. Credible ideas or statements are those that are consistent with our own experiences.

Show how your ideas are consistent with your listeners' experiences.

Ideas from a Respected or Authoritative Source

Because we consider our close friends trustworthy, we tend to believe what they tell us. We believe those things told us by authorities we respect because we believe their qualifications lend validity to their statements. We give special credence to authoritative statements or ideas when there is general agreement among the experts. The difficulty comes when there is a division among respectable and qualified authorities. One of the problems the public has had in deciding on a number of issues in recent years is that eminent and qualified authorities have been on both sides of these issues. Thus we have had outstanding experts testify for and against the building of nuclear reactor plants, the establishment of space colonies, the development of the Strategic Defense Initiative (the so-called Star Wars defense), the necessity to interrogate accused criminals without the presence of counsel. Despite these problems, authoritative testimony remains our most important and frequent source of information. We can't know by experience, reasoning, or intuition what is going on today in Moscow, Berlin, or Tokyo, so we accept the account in the afternoon newspaper as accurate, unless or until we have reason to question it. Since we can't know by any other method that Queen Elizabeth I of England lived, we accept the word of historians that she did. To make your ideas and statements credible, seek confirmation from sources held in high esteem by members of your audience.

Specific and Credible Evidence

The significant issues confronting our communities, our nation, and our world should be decided, not on the basis of people's beliefs and attitudes or on the basis of an individual's ethos, but on the basis of a careful scrutiny of the available evidence coupled with rational thought processes. Evidence thus serves an important function: it is the means by which reasonable persons establish and verify their ideas. Consequently, as a speaker committed to an intellectual or logical development of your ideas, seek to include sufficient valid evidence to demonstrate their veracity. Be certain that any evidence cited is credible on both levels—it is *worthy* of belief by careful thinkers, and it is believable by the particular audience to which you are speaking.

A number of experimental studies on the use of evidence in speaking have been conducted. Some indicated that evidence made a significant difference in changing attitudes;[1] some found that evidence made a difference in changing attitudes, although not a significant one;[2] others found that evidence made no difference.[3]

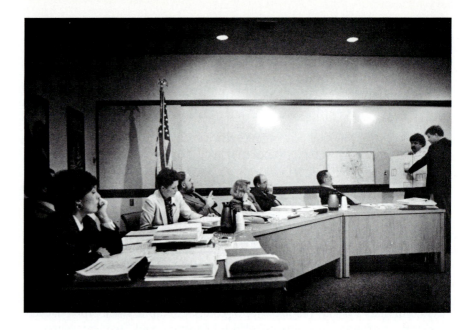

The conflicting results were a puzzle until recently when it was suggested that ethos might be a confounding element in some of these studies.[4] Specifically, it was speculated that when the classroom instructor is the sponsor of research with students, the instructor's ethos is transferred to the message. Thus, a message that lacks evidence is still effective in changing attitudes because of the effect of the instructor's ethos. Holtzman subjected the theory to experimental scrutiny, preparing two forms of a speech, one with and one without evidence. Each speech was then presented to a different class by a sponsor who was unfamiliar to the students. Each speech was also presented to two classes with their own instructor as the sponsor. The results supported the theory. When the sponsor was unfamiliar, the speech with evidence shifted the attitudes of the students significantly more than the speech without evidence. But when the instructor was the sponsor, there was no significant difference in the effect of the two speeches. In other words, the high ethos of the instructor caused the speech with no evidence to be just as effective as the speech with evidence.[5]

Two descriptive studies of the use of evidence by high-ethos speakers have confirmed that these speakers use little evidence. In four major foreign policy speeches given in 1950–51 by Dean Acheson and Senator Robert A. Taft, the investigator found only five pieces of authoritative or statistical evidence.[6] Brandes investigated the use of evidence by "high-ranking" and "low-ranking" senators and found no differences between them, mainly because neither group used much evidence.[7] If this seems a contradiction, remember that even a "low-ranking" senator has high ethos compared with most speakers.

High ethos is so important in creating credibility for content that you must make whatever attempts are appropriate to develop high ethos for yourself. Chapter 6 presented five sources of ethos; use the appropriate ones whenever possible.

Although some early experimental studies indicated that the inclusion of evidence did not increase the persuasiveness of a speech, recent investigations suggest that the issue is complex, and that there are situations in which evidence is necessary if the speaker is to be effective in changing attitudes.

The remainder of this chapter is concerned with (1) instances in which evidence is helpful, (2) ways in which evidence should be used, and (3) types of evidence that can be used.

First, evidence helps to change attitudes when the speaker has low ethos with the audience, *if* the speech is well delivered. When speeches with and without evidence were prepared and presented to subjects by low- and high-ethos speakers using good and poor delivery, it was discovered that the addition of evidence made a significant difference in changing attitudes "only in the low-ethos—good delivery treatment."[8]

Instances in Which Evidence Is Helpful

Second, evidence is helpful if the ethos of the speaker needs to be improved. Using written messages on both questions of fact and policy with different levels of support—specific factual evidence, nonspecific factual evidence, and no evidence—Kline compared the effects on both low and high levels of intelligence. The results showed that all subjects exposed to the messages with specific factual evidence rated the authors of the messages as significantly higher on competence and trustworthiness than did the subjects exposed to the messages with nonspecific factual evidence or no evidence.[9]

Third, attitude change by a speech is sustained over a period of time more effectively if the speech includes evidence to support the claims.[10] Apparently, attitude change resulting from the impact of the speaker's ethos or the use of audience knowledge and beliefs lacks the foundation to withstand the influence of opposing evidence and speakers. The lack of substance leaves the listener vulnerable to opposing messages. It may be that evidence serves as a bulwark for the speaker's ideas when the listeners begin to have second thoughts about the speech or are confronted by opposing messages from other sources or other speakers with equally high ethos.

Fourth, evidence appears to operate as an effective immunizing agent against subsequent counterpersuasion. Two versions of both a pro and con speech on the same topic were prepared. One version of each included evidence and the other included no evidence. With the ethos of the speaker manipulated as high or low, the various versions of the speech were presented to subjects in alternating sequences. Invariably, the listeners who first heard the speech with evidence changed their attitudes more in the direction advocated by the speech than did those listeners who first heard the speech with no evidence. The high-credibility speaker lost credibility in the eyes of listeners when presenting a speech with no evidence following one in which evidence was used.[11]

How Evidence Should Be Used

To be effective in changing the attitudes of listeners, evidence should be used in the following ways: (1) qualifications of the source of the evidence should be cited, (2) evidence should be specific, and (3) evidence should be substantially unfamiliar to the listeners.

Cite Qualifications of Evidence Source

If the source of the evidence is to be cited, it will be more effective if you also present the qualifications of that source. Simply adding the source gives evidence no more effectiveness in changing attitudes than merely giving the evidence. One study even discovered that adding the source without its qualifications made the speech less effective than when the evidence alone was used to support the arguments.[12] Some studies have found that supporting assertions with evidence alone was just as effective as giving the evidence with the source and its qualifications.[13]

Although it may appear from these studies that it's unnecessary to cite sources of evidence, there are other reasons for doing so. Give proper credit to sources to avoid accusations of plagiarism, and give the qualifications of sources to avoid lessening the impact of the message.

Use Specific Evidence

Evidence should be presented specifically; it shouldn't be converted into general terms. If you have figures showing that 80 percent of the families in the United States have an adequate diet, don't say, "Most families in the United States have an adequate diet." Instead say, "Eighty percent of the families in the United States have an adequate diet." Specific evidence is important because it gives an impression of more precise support for your claims than general evidence does. Moreover, the more specific the data, the more concrete your ideas will be. Something is concrete when it can be perceived by one or more of the senses. Although you can't cause an actual perception as a result of your statements, you can evoke a mental image of a sensory perception. Thus, if you say something is soft as velvet, the listener has a mental perception of the feel of velvet, *if* he has ever touched velvet. Of course if he has never touched velvet, your words mean nothing to him. It is for this reason you must present material that will evoke *familiar* sensory perceptions. Concrete data are important because we understand better those objects that we have sensorily perceived. Abstract statements and ideas are hard to comprehend because an abstraction is incapable of being perceived by the senses. Thus, we can talk about such things as loyalty, liberalism, or love, but nobody can see, feel, hear, taste, or smell any of these things.

After studying the comparative impact of messages using specific, nonspecific, or no evidence, Kline concluded that for most topics, the effectiveness of nonspecific evidence "appears to be about midway between that of specific and that of no evidence. For other topics, nonspecific evidence appears little if any more effective than no evidence and for other topics it seems just as effective as specific evidence."[14]

Experimental research has not yet identified the precise nature of those infrequent topics on which nonspecific evidence is as effective as specific evidence. Use specific evidence, therefore, to achieve maximum effectiveness of a message.

Evidence used to support statements in a speech should be fresh and unfamiliar to the particular listeners. Audience analysis enables you to determine which specific materials are familiar and which are unfamiliar. Experimental studies haven't clearly confirmed the advantage of unfamiliar evidence, but McCroskey concluded that currently it is more justifiable to assume unfamiliar evidence has an advantage over familiar evidence than to assume that unfamiliar evidence is not more effective.[15] A moment's reflection should convince us of the importance of unfamiliar evidence. Most of us have been exasperated at a speaker who has told us nothing we didn't already know. The usual feeling after such a speech is that we have wasted our time. But the most important reason for presenting unfamiliar information is that most people have already adjusted their attitudes to accommodate the information they possess; therefore, if you are to effect attitude change, you should provide either new information or a new analysis of old information.

Use Unfamiliar Evidence

"Evidence," according to one authority, "consists of those data that are intended to induce a sense of belief in the proposition which the data purportedly support."[16] Three general types of evidence are available: (1) opinion of others, (2) statistics, and (3) factual data.

Types of Evidence

Three types of opinion of others can be identified: (1) public opinion, (2) expert testimony, and (3) lay testimony.

Opinion of Others

Public opinion Public opinion is what the majority of people in a given geographical location believe on a given issue at a given time. Thus, there can be public opinion on permitting abortion on demand in the United States, on selling wheat to Russia in the Midwest, on toxic waste dump sites in North Carolina, on teacher education programs in California, on the building of a horse racing track in Birmingham, Alabama. You must identify the geographical source of the public opinion you are citing.

How can you determine what public, or majority, opinion is? Many times you'll know what it is just by listening to people in your community; opinion can be so strong there can be no mistaking it. Editorials in the newspapers, letters to the editor, and general conversations reveal the prevailing attitudes on a specific issue. In other instances, public opinion is less obvious and you must rely on some objective measuring technique, such as polls, to determine its precise nature.

If the results of polls are used, be sure that such polls were properly conducted. Polls can be ingeniously biased to produce whatever result is desired. The wording of a question can influence the way a respondent will answer it. Burns W. Roper reported that when the SALT II treaty was being debated, a poll by his firm found 33 percent of the respondents favored the treaty. Roper, watching the "NBC News" that night, heard them report that "a just-completed poll showed 68 percent in favor of the SALT treaty—a 35 point difference." The reason for the difference, Roper discovered, was that the NBC poll never mentioned SALT II. It simply asked "whether people would like to see an agreement between the United States and Russia that would reduce the likelihood of a nuclear conflict." Roper called for the press to increase its credibility by telling exactly what questions are asked.[17] There are a few pollsters, like Gallup and Roper, who have established a reputation for objectivity and accuracy by following carefully designed methods and by refusing to associate themselves with either a political candidate or party. These are the type of pollsters you should turn to for evidence to support your claims.

Even after you have uncovered public opinion polls that apparently provide an accurate representation of majority opinion, you're still faced with three problems in using public opinion to support your ideas. First, public opinion may be in error. Frequently, public opinion is based on myths or erroneous information. In 1964, for example, "the Survey Research Center discovered that 64 percent of adults polled remembered voting for John F. Kennedy in 1960."[18] In fact, Kennedy received only 49.7 percent of the votes cast in 1960.

Second, popularity is no indication of the merits of anything. Before you can responsibly use public opinion, you must ascertain that the opinion is consistent with other available evidence and whatever reasoning can be brought to bear on the topic. Public opinion is used because of its psychological or rhetorical value, but it must also meet logical requirements. Third, you are confronted with the fact that majority opinion isn't always effective in persuading others. Hadley Cantril noted that the persuasiveness of majority opinion has frequently been demonstrated in experiments, and is frequently exhibited in everyday life. But, he observed,

> This suggestibility to majority opinion is always highly relative, dependent upon the particular circumstances of the situation, cut across by numerous other influences that may be operative at the moment, and circumscribed by what the individual regards in *his* world. If people are suggestible to majority opinion, why, for example, did they not vote for Landon in 1936, when the widely publicized *Literary Digest* poll showed Landon the choice of the majority? Why do we still have two major political parties in the United States? Why do members of minority groups continue fervently to preach their causes when they know public opinion is ranged against them? Why do new values ever arise at all? Majority opinion is probably effective as a suggestion only when an individual has no clearly structured mental context adequate to interpret a situation and when the majority opinion does not conflict with other frames of reference or ego values.[19]

You can't rely on citation of public opinion alone to get listeners to accept your point of view. Majority opinion can be used only as part of a mixture of evidence.

Expert opinion A second type of testimony is expert opinion. To qualify as expert opinion, two criteria must be met. First, the individual must be expert in the field on which he or she is speaking. It is not enough for a person to be an expert in some field. Thus a businessperson speaking on religious matters is not giving expert opinion; a politician speaking on business matters is not giving expert opinion; a minister speaking on economic matters is not giving expert opinion. Of course, in some instances an individual may be expert in more than one field. Second, the expert testimony must come from one who is unbiased. When economists employed by the AFL-CIO testify, you may expect them to represent labor's point of view. If they present opinions detrimental to labor, they probably won't draw next month's pay from the AFL-CIO. On the other hand, economists employed by the National Association of Manufacturers can be expected to testify favorably to management. If not, they too will probably not receive next month's pay. You must look for experts who at least have the *opportunity* to be objective. University professors are often consulted because their position isn't dependent on their point of view and their scholarly bent generally inclines them toward objectivity. Even here, however, you must be cautious, for professors' conclusions can be prejudiced by their own philosophical view, their political affiliation, or their consulting fees!

There is a tendency for some to believe that expert testimony constitutes proof. Nothing could be further from the truth. In the final analysis, expert testimony constitutes an opinion, nothing more. An educated opinion, to be sure, but an opinion nonetheless. Testimony, therefore, is weak logical proof, even though it may be strong psychological proof because the listeners respect and accept the opinion of the expert cited. As Copi has pointed out,

> If laymen are disputing over some question of physical evidence and one appeals to the testimony of Einstein on the matter, that testimony is very relevant. Although it does not prove the point, it certainly tends to confirm it. This is a relative matter, however, for if experts rather than laymen are disputing over a question in the field in which they are experts, their appeal would be only to the facts and to reason, and any appeal to the authority of another expert would be completely without value as evidence.[20]

Even more important, expert testimony can be partially or totally wrong. One writer on mental hygiene has pointed out that the "mere citation of expert opinion" can't "be taken as an invariably dependable way of disposing" of controversial questions in that field.

> The history of medicine is replete with instances of experts who backed what we now know to have been the wrong opinion. In the seventeenth century there were experts who opposed what Harvey had to teach regarding the circulation of the blood. And Pasteur's troubles with the medical experts of his day are common knowledge. That Charcot, France's leading authority on diseases of the nervous system in the late nineteenth century, refused to endorse the then novel teaching of syphilis as the cause of paresis is also common knowledge among those familiar with the history of paresis.
>   . . . In other words, we are not saying that experts should be ignored but their opinion on *controversial* issues should not be confused with tested knowledge. What they have to say should be taken as presumptive evidence rather than as coercive proof. As applied to our immediate concern—unsettled questions in the field of mental hygiene—this means that such questions cannot be disposed of by appeals to what "Freud taught" or "Adler

advocated" or "MacDougall maintained." Appeal to authority is different from a direct and critical scrutiny of the available evidence. What a "doctor" says is probably more often right than what the "layman" says; but when another "doctor" contradicts the first one, then the poor "layman" may begin to appreciate the difference between fact and opinion, between data and their interpretation, or between symptomatology and diagnosis.[21]

Recently, two journalistic commentators called attention to a number of modern scientific experts who have given incorrect testimony. The following are some of the examples they listed. (1) In 1933, Dr. Ernest Rutherford, English Nobel Prize winning scientist, declared that atomic energy could never be controlled in a useful manner. (2) In 1949, the General Advisory Committee of the U.S. Atomic Energy Commission claimed that it was unfeasible to produce an H-bomb. (3) In 1950, Dr. Vannevar Bush said it was impossible to make accurate intercontinental rockets or ballistic missiles. (4) In 1953, the Lincoln Summer Study, whose membership included Dr. James Killian, Dr. Carl Kaysen, and Dr. Jerome Wiesner, stated without equivocation that Russia could not possibly develop ICBMs "for at least another 10–15 years." (5) In 1962, Dr. Jerome Wiesner declared that Lunar Orbital Rendezvous was unworkable and "too risky for astronauts to attempt."[22] Every one of these predictions, we now know, was inaccurate. Yet at the time the statements were made, there were those who wanted to adopt policies based on the predictions.

The point is clear: Use expert testimony as evidence for psychological reasons, but seek out more substantial evidence to use as logical proof.

Lay testimony Lay testimony, the opinion of one who isn't an expert in the field on which he or she is testifying, doesn't even have the virtue of being a more educated opinion. Nevertheless, there is no denying that some lay testimony is highly persuasive to some groups and, on occasion, may be more correct than expert opinion. Historian Daniel J. Boorstin points out that it was Cotton Mather and his fellow members of the clergy who led the fight to adopt inoculation to eliminate smallpox. Ironically, the doctors of the period were the outstanding opponents of inoculation.[23] A highly respected member of a community may give lay opinions on a number of topics and be listened to with great care.

One feature of testimony, whether it be lay or expert, that has long been recommended by rhetoricians is that the testimony be *reluctant,* which is testimony running counter to the best interests of the one giving the opinion. If the president of the AFL-CIO said that labor unions have too much power in controlling wages, that would be reluctant testimony. If the president of U.S. Steel were to say that steel companies were making too much profit, that would be reluctant testimony. Recent studies indicate that *unbiased* testimony is preferable to reluctant testimony, even though both are more effective than biased opinions.[24]

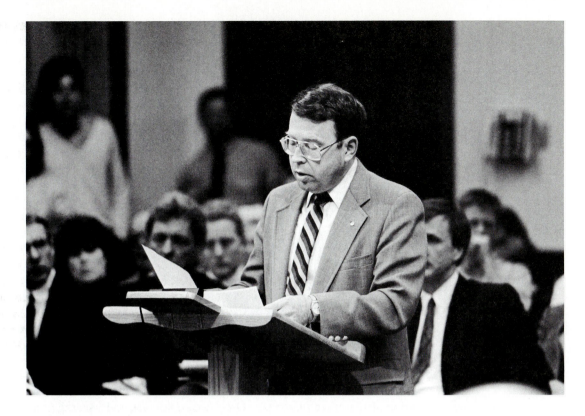

Whether testimony emanates from an expert or a layperson, the crucial question is: Will the listeners accept this person as a credible source? If they won't, it doesn't matter how competent the source is.

"Statistics are lenses through which we form images of our society. . . . Even when they misrepresent reality, they standardize our perceptions of it."[25]

Statistics

Some refer to any quantitative data as statistics, but quantitative data consist of two types: numbers and statistics. Numbers are unorganized, unanalyzed data. They will be discussed under the next unit, factual data.

Statistics are those quantitative data produced "when the data have been organized and analyzed and relationships among them have been stated in summary or relative terms."[26]

Be aware of the varying attitudes that exist toward statistics. At one extreme are those who regard statistics as holy writ. Their attitude is that if data can be reduced to quantitative form, they must be true. After all, the data couldn't be counted if they weren't true. At the other extreme are those who refuse to accept the validity of any statistics. In their view, figures don't lie, but liars figure; as some phrase it, "There are liars, damned liars, and statisticians."

Even though there are invalid statistics, it is also true that some statistics are valid. To know which are valid and which are not, be familiar with their source and know where, when, and under what conditions the statistics were compiled.

One feature of statistics that many don't adequately understand is there is no real referent for a statistic. For example, consider a basketball team whose five starters have the following heights: 6′ 10″, 6′ 8″, 6′ 7″, 6′ 0″, and 6′ 0″. The mean height of the team would be 6′ 5″. Yet there would be no member of the team who would be exactly 6′ 5″. If uniforms were purchased on the basis of the mean height of the team, no uniform would fit. It's like the man who said, "On the average I am comfortable," while standing with one foot on a cake of ice and the other on a hot stove. Unless you recognize that a given statistic may not have a real referent, you may draw unwarranted inferences from it. This is why statistics cannot be classified under factual data: since there is frequently no real referent, statistics can't be considered invariably as fact.

Quantitative data are probably the most effective type of evidence in causing a change in attitudes. Costley used a speech with three different types of content (quantitative data with comparisons, quantitative data without comparisons, no quantitative data). The speech using quantitative data with comparisons to audience experience caused the greatest shift of attitude, but the difference was not significant.[27] Gardiner prepared five different versions of the same persuasive speech, each using a different type of evidence: (1) statistics, (2) testimony, (3) examples, (4) generalizations, and (5) a combination of the other four types. Only two—statistics and generalizations— produced significant shifts, and the most significant shift was caused by the speech using statistics.[28]

If statistics are to be used properly and effectively, there are certain principles you must observe.

Use statistical measures correctly Use the proper label for any measure of central tendency. Although most of us were taught that an average is arrived at by summing all the items and dividing that total by the number of items, this isn't the meaning of the term "average" in statistics. Average, in statistics, is a general term meaning measure of central tendency. There are a number of averages, or measures of central tendency, of which the most commonly used are the mean, the median, and the mode. The mean is an arithmetic computation, the formula for which is $\Sigma X/N$; in other words, what is commonly referred to as the average. The median is the item or class of items occurring at the midpoint between the highest and lowest data, after the data have been placed in rank order. The mode is that datum or class of data that occurs most frequently. In a normal distribution the mean, median, and mode are the same. Correctly identify any measure of central tendency you use. To use the term *average* leaves some confusion about which precise measure you are referring to.

Make no comparison of percentages unless you know the base used in the computation of each percentage was the same; otherwise any comparison is totally invalid. If a student makes 90 on one exam and 99 on the next, she has made a 10 percent improvement. But if another student makes a 60 on the first exam and a 78 on the second, she has made a 30 percent improvement. It is quite clear that any comparison of these two percentages in no way reflects the differences between the two students.

Cite specific sources of statistics In order for the listener to evaluate accurately the statistics presented, provide the specific source. Vague references such as "statistics show," "studies prove," or "statisticians say" will not give needed information. If a speaker goes into an agricultural section of North Carolina and convinces the farmers to use a particular type of seed corn because a study by the U.S. Department of Agriculture showed it improved production, without telling his listeners that the study was conducted in Iowa in 1939, he could cause the farmers to make a serious mistake. Tell your listeners where the statistics were obtained, when they were compiled, and by whom.

Round off statistics where possible It is rarely necessary or practicable to present precise statistics. Remember that listening is a difficult task, much more so than reading. Since it's difficult to comprehend a series of figures in written material, think how much more difficult it is to comprehend them in listening. You generally communicate more with rounded-off statistics than with precise figures. If you use the figure 72.39 percent, you may find that many listeners actually hear the figure as 39 percent, or in hearing the .39 they may miss the first two digits and have no idea what the important number is. To round that number off to "slightly over 72 percent" would make it far easier to comprehend, and it would be even easier to understand if presented as "just under three-fourths."

Convert statistics to concrete data where possible The value of concrete data has already been discussed. Since quantitative data are abstract, they should be made concrete if at all possible. If you are addressing an audience in a wheat-growing area, you may refer to the number of bushels of wheat produced last year. A bushel of wheat isn't abstract to those listeners; it is a very concrete object. But if you're talking to an audience in an area where wheat is not grown, you may want to convert the bushels of wheat to loaves of bread, a concrete object for your listeners. Or you might want to connect the bushels of wheat with some concrete object familiar to the listeners by saying something such as, "The wheat produced last year in this country would fill Shea Stadium level with the top row of seats ten times." In this way some of the abstractness of the statistics is removed.

David Stockman, former director of the Office of Management and Budget, attempted to make budget cuts more concrete to a group of Republicans when he said, "There's plenty of room for more and deeper cuts. . . .

It isn't necessary . . . for the government to spend as much to teach someone a job as it costs a parent to send a son to Harvard—with his own limousine. It isn't necessary to employ one federal bureaucrat for every 26 Indians."[29]

Use statistics sparingly It's easy to use too many statistics. The result is information overload, and listeners won't be able to cope with all the data. At a minimum, one of two results will occur. Either the listener gets the statistical information confused and assigns the statistics to a wrong referent, or the confusion causes the listener to quit listening to the speaker.

Choose only statistics that are important to the comprehension of your ideas. Omit all others even though they may be vivid and interesting.

Factual Data

Factual information, a third form of evidence, must be verifiable by objective measurements (The temperature is 75° today. The left offensive guard for Auburn University weighs 275 pounds.) or by sensory perception (There are three cars in the driveway. Her eyes are blue. The finish on the table is smooth.) or by historical investigation (The stock market crashed on October 29, 1929. The Japanese attacked Pearl Harbor on December 7, 1941. The New York Jets defeated the Baltimore Colts in the Super Bowl in 1970.).

Factual data must be investigated carefully; it may not be as factual as it seems. The objective measuring instruments may be out of order. If a thermometer is broken, it won't give an accurate reading. Weights won't be correct if the scales are out of balance. Or sensory perception may be erroneous. Personal characteristics frequently affect sensory perceptions. Some persons may claim that a pitcher of iced tea is bitter, while others say it isn't. Teenagers listen to music at a level they deem enjoyable, while their parents complain that the music is so loud it hurts their ears. Historical data may be erroneous. Abraham Lincoln is alleged to have written a letter to a Mrs. Bixby whose five sons were killed in the Civil War. Yet one investigator reported that not all of Mrs. Bixby's sons served in the army, nor did all those who served get killed.[30] It would appear, then, that either Lincoln wrote no such letter or, if he did, made a horrendous mistake.

Factual data may be presented in the speech as quantitative data, as simply statements of fact, or as examples.

Quantitative data Quantitative data in the form of numbers are factual data because they have real referents. Thus you use numbers to represent factual data when you say "The population of the United States is 240,468,000." "The president's salary is $200,000." A word of warning, however; numbers can be just as invalid as statistics. One writer reported: "Recently it was authoritatively reported that more than half the money spent on birth control worldwide goes for abortions. That's the kind of number likely to stick in people's minds and influence important decisions, which would be a shame. Given the widespread taboos about birth control and abortion, and the very different economies of socialist and third-world societies, the figure can have been no more than the wildest guess. It should have been presented as a guess."[31] *Time* recently reported that the federal government's Center for Disease Control had "announced that a certain drug company may have infected 5,000 hospital patients with contaminated intravenous solutions, contributing to the deaths of 500 people. When asked how this figure had been determined, a government spokesman said that one estimate of 2,000 was 'unrealistic' and another estimate of 8,000 was 'unfair.' So the authorities split the difference."[32] On its morning news program of April 23, 1982, ABC radio news reported that the severe winter had created 200 million potholes in the United States. Who do you suppose counted those potholes?

Statements of facts Statements of fact are used by the speaker who says "Even numbered interstate highways run east and west, while odd numbered ones run north and south." "The president made a speech on national TV last night." "OPEC has raised the price of oil two dollars a barrel."

An example is the use of a particular case to support another statement by amplifying or extending it. The speaker who made the statement about the numbering of interstate highways might also say "An example is I-95, which runs from Miami, Florida, to Maine." The example, then, supports a more general statement. Examples may be used as specific instances or as illustrations.

A specific instance is an undetailed example. Notice how one speaker used four specific instances to support a generalization: "We know from past experience that it is when the public and private sectors are united in some grand national undertaking that we have been at our best—the Manhattan project, development of synthetic rubber, the railroads in an earlier day, and more recently, NASA. The mix has varied in each of these projects and there is no formula for the future. But certainly, we can achieve energy self-sufficiency only with a program that calls for the best that all of us in the private sector have to offer."[33]

The virtue of specific instances is that several can be presented in a short period of time. Thus if you make a claim about which listeners will have strong reservations, you can supply a number of specific instances rather quickly to weaken those reservations. After hearing several instances it will be more difficult for the hearers to convince themselves that you have based your claim on too few or unrepresentative examples.

An illustration is a detailed example. The late Hubert H. Humphrey, when vice-president, used an effective illustration in a speech in Tampa, Florida, in 1965 concerning the war on poverty.

> I came to Washington seventeen years ago as a freshman senator. During that first year a scene took place in a Senate hearing room that symbolized just what we mean by the Great Society.
>
> A woman from Tennessee, a garment worker, was testifying before seven U.S. senators on behalf of raising the minimum wage to seventy-five cents an hour. At one point, this is what she said:
>
> "My youngest girl she's nine now, goes straight to the piano when we go to a house where they have one. She does want to play the piano so bad. I've

thought that maybe I could save fifty cents or a dollar a week to buy a second-hand piano for her, but I haven't found a way to do it yet. Maybe I've been foolish to talk to you people about music for one of my children when the main question is getting enough to eat and wear, or blankets for the bed, or a chair to sit on. But down in Tennessee we love music, and factory workers don't live by bread alone any more than anyone else does."

Piano lessons for a little Tennessee girl; full, productive lives for our citizens and the places where they live—these are what the war on poverty is all about, what the Great Society is all about. This is what we work for.[34]

Obviously, an illustration is more time-consuming than a specific instance, so if you're developing a controversial claim in a limited amount of time, you'll probably have to forgo the use of illustrations in order to include a number of specific instances. But it's obvious the illustration is more interesting to listen to and gets the listener more involved in the example. If possible, therefore, work some illustrations into your speech.

Summary

The content of a speech aids in developing credibility for your ideas. Content will be acceptable to listeners if it's consistent with or coincides with their knowledge or attitudes, if it's consistent with their experiences, if it emanates from a highly credible source, or if it's supported by specific and credible evidence.

Evidence is helpful in changing attitudes, both immediately and over a period of time; it's helpful in increasing your ethos; and it's helpful in operating as an immunizing agent against subsequent counterpersuasion.

If evidence is to be maximally effective in changing attitudes, it should have the qualifications of the source cited; it should be specific; and it should be unfamiliar to the listeners.

You can use the following general types of evidence to support your claims: (1) opinions of others, (2) statistics, and (3) factual data.

Exercises

1. Prepare a two-minute speech supporting one main point with three specific instances and one interesting illustration.
2. Attend a public lecture on campus. What did the speaker say that was consistent with the listeners' knowledge or attitudes? Did these statements increase or decrease the speaker's credibility? In what ways?
3. Find three pieces of testimony for one of the ideas in your next speech. Evaluate the expertise and objectivity of each source. Will they add to the credibility of your ideas? Why?
4. Find three pieces of factual data for one of the ideas in your next speech. Explain why you can place confidence in the validity of this information. How will this information contribute to the credibility of your claims?

5. Find three pieces of statistical information for one of the ideas in your next speech. Explain how you will conform to the principles for using statistics. Convert one of the statistics into the most concrete form you can. Explain how that concreteness will enhance the credibility of the statistic itself and the claim which it supports.

6. Prepare the questions for some person whom you plan to interview on your next speech topic.

Notes

1. R. S. Cathcart, "An Experimental Study of the Relative Effectiveness of Four Methods of Presenting Evidence," *Speech Monographs* 22 (1955):227–33; E. P. Bettinghaus, Jr., "The Relative Effect of the Use of Testimony in a Persuasive Speech upon the Attitudes of the Listeners," M.A. thesis, Bradley University, 1953. The following study found certain types of evidence to be significantly more effective in changing attitudes: J. C. Gardiner, "An Experimental Study of the Use of Selected Forms of Evidence in Effecting Attitude Change," M.A. thesis, University of Nebraska, 1966.

2. H. Gilkinson, S. F. Paulson, and D. E. Sikkink, "Effects of Order and Authority in an Argumentative Speech," *Quarterly Journal of Speech* 40 (1954):183–92; T. H. Ostermeier, "An Experimental Study on the Type and Frequency of Reference as Used by an Unfamiliar Source in a Message and Its Effect upon Perceived Credibility and Attitude Change," Ph.D. diss., Michigan State University, 1966; D. L. Costley, "An Experimental Study of the Effectiveness of Quantitative Evidence in Speeches of Advocacy," M.A. thesis, University of Oklahoma, 1958.

3. D. C. Anderson, "The Effect of Various Uses of Authoritative Testimony in Persuasive Speaking," M.A. thesis, Ohio State University, 1958; G. A. Wagner, "An Experimental Study of the Relative Effectiveness of Varying Amounts of Evidence in a Persuasive Communication," M.A. thesis, University of Southern Mississippi, 1958; W. R. Dresser, "Studies of the Effects of Satisfactory and Unsatisfactory Evidence in a Speech of Advocacy," Ph.D diss., Northwestern University, 1962.

4. J. C. McCroskey and R. E. Dunham, "Ethos: A Confounding Element in Communication Research," *Speech Monographs* 33 (1966):456–63.

5. P. D. Holtzman, "Confirmation of Ethos as a Confounding Element in Communication Research," *Speech Monographs* 33 (1966):464–66.

6. C. S. Goetsinger, Jr., "An Analysis of the 'Validity' of Reasoning and Evidence in Four Major Foreign Policy Speeches, 1950–51," M.S. thesis, Purdue University, 1952.

7. P. D. Brandes, "Evidence and Its Use by Selected United States Senators," Ph.D. diss., University of Wisconsin, 1953.

8. J. C. McCroskey, *Studies of the Effects of Evidence in Persuasive Communication,* Speech Communications Research Laboratory, Department of Speech, Report SCRL 4–67 (E. Lansing, Mich.: Michigan State University, 1967), p. 42.

9. J. A. Kline, "Interaction of Evidence and Readers' Intelligence on the Effects of Short Messages," *Quarterly Journal of Speech* 55 (1969):407–13.

10. McCroskey, *Studies of the Effects of Evidence,* pp. 39–45. See also T. B. Harte, "The Effects of Evidence in Persuasive Communication," *Central States Speech Journal* 27 (1976):45–46.

11. J. C. McCroskey, "The Effects of Evidence as an Inhibitor of Counterpersuasion," *Speech Monographs* 37 (1970):188–94.

12. R. N. Bostrom and R. K. Tucker, "Evidence, Personality, and Attitude Change," *Speech Monographs* 36 (1969):22–27.

13. H. Gilkinson, S. L. Paulson, and D. E. Sikking. "The Facts on Order and Authority in an Argumentative Speech," *Quarterly Journal of Speech* 40 (1954):183–92; Cathcart, "An Experimental Study"; Bostrom and Tucker, "Evidence, Personality, and Attitude Change."

14. Kline, "Interaction of Evidence," pp. 407–13.

15. McCroskey, *Studies of the Effects of Evidence,* p. 54.

16. G. R. Miller, "Evidence and Argument," in *Perspectives on Argumentation,* eds. G. R. Miller and T. R. Nilsen (Chicago: Scott, Foresman & Co., 1966), p. 25.

17. J. Greenfield, "An Acerbic View," *Birmingham News,* April 25, 1982. Used by permission.

18. D. Gergen and W. Schambra, "Pollsters and Polling," *The Wilson Quarterly* 3 (Spring 1979):70.

19. H. Cantril, *The Psychology of Social Movements* (New York: John Wiley & Sons, 1941), pp. 74–75.

20. I. M. Copi, *Introduction to Logic* (New York: Macmillan Publishing Co., 1953), pp. 60–61.

21. D. B. Klein, *Mental Hygiene* (New York: Henry Holt & Co., 1956), p. 201.

22. Robert S. Allen and John A. Goldsmith, "ABM Debate—Scientists Can Be Wrong," September 1, 1969. Syndicated column. By permission.

23. D. J. Boorstin, *The Americans: The Colonial Experience* (New York: Random House, 1958), pp. 224–25.

24. W. E. Arnold and J. C. McCroskey, "The Credibility of Reluctant Testimony," *Central States Speech Journal* 18 (1967):97–103.

25. William Alonso and Paul Starr, "A Nation of Numbers Watchers," *The Wilson Quarterly* IX (Summer, 1985), 93–96.

26. M. M. Blair, *Elementary Statistics* (New York: Henry Holt & Co., 1944), p. 1.

27. Costley, "An Experimental Study of the Effectiveness of Quantitative Evidence."

28. Gardiner, "An Experimental Study of the Use of Selected Forms."

29. J. M. Perry, "Stockman Dials the Right Number, Soothes GOP Loyalists at Fund-Raiser," *Wall Street Journal,* November 25, 1981. Reprinted by permission of *The Wall Street Journal,* © Dow Jones & Company, Inc. 1981. All rights reserved.

30. C. D. MacDougall, *Hoaxes* (New York: Macmillan Publishing Co., 1940), pp. 161–62.

31. P. Weddle, *Argument: A Guide to Critical Thinking* (New York: McGraw-Hill, 1978), p. 90.

32. "Of Imaginary Numbers," *Time,* August 2, 1971, p. 37. Reprinted by permission from *TIME,* The Weekly Newsmagazine; Copyright Time, Inc.
33. J. F. McGillicuddy, "The Economy, Energy and the President's Proposals," *Vital Speeches of the Day* 45 (1979):708.
34. H. H. Humphrey, "Anniversary of War on Poverty," from *Congressional Digest* 45, no. 3 (March 1966), "The Controversy over the Federal Anti-Poverty Program, Pro & Con": pp. 76, 78, 80. Used by permission.

CHAPTER 12

Using Reasoning

One author defines reasoning, or critical thinking, as *"a process that emphasizes a rational basis for beliefs and provides procedures for analyzing, testing, and evaluating them."*[1] That statement precisely identifies the objective of this chapter. Understanding reasoning will aid you in comprehending others' positions and in explaining clearly your own.

Proving statements involves two processes: citing evidence and reasoning from it. To be meaningful to listeners, evidence must be explained or interpreted. Reasoning establishes a relationship between evidence and the conclusions you draw as a result of that evidence. Thus, looking at the latest FBI crime report, you find that the crime rate was up last year. From that one piece of evidence, you may draw a number of conclusions: (1) penalties for crime should be increased; (2) salaries for law enforcement officials should be increased; (3) penal institutions should be improved; (4) more law enforcement officials should be employed; (5) more judges need to be appointed; (6) the permissive attitudes of judges need to be changed; (7) a better distribution of wealth in the United States must be devised; plus sundry other statements. The movement from evidence to a conclusion is called reasoning. For many listeners the reasoning that produced these conclusions would be clear and acceptable. For others, it would not. In instances when the reasoning is unclear and unacceptable, explain your reasoning until it is clear.

Listeners must perceive as credible the reasoning supporting your statements. This isn't to imply that listeners can determine an argument's validity. They do arrive at a judgment of the speaker's statements, however, and one basis of that judgment is the reasoning involved. We have all heard listeners say of a speaker, "His ideas are too radical" or "His ideas are impractical" or "I couldn't accept his conclusion." These judgments may result from the listeners' inability to identify the specific error in reasoning committed by the speaker, or they may reflect the listeners' attitudes rather than the speaker's reasoning.

Audience analysis and an understanding of the listeners' attitudes will help you identify statements perceived as unbelievable. Despite the listeners' attitudes, be concerned about the validity of the reasoning underlying your statements. Although sound and valid reasoning won't necessarily make a statement credible to a particular listener, it can help develop credibility for your ideas. And for some listeners valid reasoning may be the most important factor in making a statement credible.

Invalid reasoning may have a more far-reaching effect than the immediate speech. Those who recognize fallacious reasoning may conclude, rightly or wrongly, that you're generally guilty of faulty reasoning and refuse to accept the credibility of your statements in future speeches.

Since the validity of your conclusions is dependent on the quality of your reasoning, an effort to establish soundness of your reasoning will generate credibility for your ideas. Structural models are available to help you examine your reasoning processes. This text uses a modification of the Toulmin scheme to help you analyze your reasoning efforts.

Figure 12.1
Sample Toulmin model.

The Toulmin model is a method for analyzing arguments.[2] It is *not* a plan for organizing a speech or even for organizing an argument in a speech.

The Toulmin Model

The Toulmin model may consist of as many as six parts: *claim, evidence, warrant, qualifier, reservation,* and *backing for the warrant.* In this book, however, we're going to be concerned only with three of these parts: *claim, evidence,* and *warrant.* (See Figure 12.1.)

Claim

The claim is the assertion, or conclusion, based on the evidence and the warrant. Claims may be classified under four headings: *designative, definitive, evaluative,* and *actuative.*

A *designative* claim deals with questions of fact—is a thing true? Did John Doe commit burglary? Is General Motors losing market share? A *definitive* claim deals with questions of definition—what is it? Is burning the American flag an act of free speech? Is the economy in a recession? An *evaluative* claim deals with questions of value—what is the merit of a thing? Are American cars built as well as Japanese cars? Do prisons rehabilitate criminals? An *actuative* claim deals with questions of policy—should a certain thing be done? Should all high school graduates be admitted to universities? Should the federal government provide homes for all citizens?

Tracing one example through the different claims may help to clarify the difference among them: The United States has 8 million people unemployed (designative). This unemployment rate constitutes a recession (definitive). This unemployment rate is too high (evaluative). The federal government should adopt a program of public work to lower the unemployment rate (actuative).

No matter what kind of claim is being made, be sure your argument is sound. "A sound argument, a well-grounded or firmly backed claim," says Toulmin, "is one which will stand up to the standard required if it is to deserve a favorable verdict."[3] Whenever you make a claim, be prepared to demonstrate you have made a justifiable one.

Evidence

Types of *evidence* are described in the next chapter. Evidence is extremely important because it determines the soundness of a claim. All available evidence must be examined, not just that which you can conveniently locate or find favorable to a claim. Where the listener accepts the evidence, simply establish the link between the evidence and the claim. In some instances, listeners won't accept the evidence. On those occasions, use a preliminary argument to eliminate listeners' objections to the evidence.

Warrant

The *warrant* is the link between the evidence and the claim, the basic premise upon which the claim rests. The warrant is the reason we consider the claim credible. In order to establish credibility, rely on warrants that are acceptable. If you use evidence that crime rates are increasing to develop a claim that permissive attitudes of judges need to be changed, the listener might well ask how you got from the evidence to that claim. The link is the warrant, in this instance the generalization that crime rates increase because penal institutions aren't rehabilitating convicted criminals. The listener must accept your warrant if it is to be effective in justifying your claim. If the listener finds the warrant unacceptable, you must support and develop it before the claim will be accepted as a sound one.

Some warrants, given the appropriate evidence, justify the claim unequivocally. *Evidence:* Icicles are hanging from the roof. *Claim:* The temperature is 32 or below. *Warrant:* Ice forms when the temperature is 32 or below. Other warrants justify only a tentative claim. *Evidence:* Ducks are flying south. *Claim:* Winter is coming. *Warrant:* Ducks flying south sometimes indicate that winter is coming.

Now that we understand the Toulmin model for analyzing arguments, let's take an actual example of argumentation from a speech and see how it looks in the Toulmin model. The speaker presented his argument in the following manner:

> The achievements of the Cistercian monks serve to illustrate another aspect of modern ecologic philosophy. As I mentioned before, the swamps in which they established their monasteries were unfit for human life because of insects and malaria. But monastic labor, skill, and intelligence converted these dismal swamps into productive agricultural areas, many of which have become centers for civilization. They demonstrate that transforming of the land, when intelligently carried out, is not destructive but, instead, can be a creative art.
>
> My speaking of medieval times in Europe was not meant to convey the impression that only then have there been great achievements in the management of the land. One need only look at the Pennsylvania Dutch country to see a striking demonstration of land that has been created out of

Figure 12.2
Toulmin model: analyzing an argument.

Evidence:
(1) The Cistercian monks changed swamps into productive agricultural areas.
(2) The Pennsylvania Dutch changed forests into a productive area for human life.

Claim:
These instances demonstrate that transforming of the land is not destructive but, instead, can be a creative art.

Warrant:
These instances are typical of what can be done when land is transformed intelligently; in other words, made suitable for both human life and the health of nature.

the forest, that became highly productive, and that has been well preserved. One could cite many similar feats all over the world. But the tendency at present is to determine the use of lands and waters, mountains and valleys, only on the basis of short-range economic benefits. And yet one can safely assert that sacrificing ecological principles on the altar of financial advantage is the road to social disaster, let alone esthetic degradation of the countryside. I shall now present a few remarks about how we can create land. By this I mean taking nature as it is presented to us and trying to do with it something which is both suitable for human life and for the health of nature.[4]

This argument is diagrammed in the Toulmin analysis in figure 12.2.

Notice that in the finished rhetorical effort one piece of evidence is presented, then the claim is stated, and that is followed by another piece of evidence. A strictly logical development of an argument offers all the evidence before the claim, but a rhetorical communication allows you to vary development of the various parts of your arguments.

Types of Reasoning

Argumentation may be from a particular instance to a general principle, from a general principle to a particular instance, or from a particular instance to a particular instance. The claim may be a particular conclusion (a statement that applies to only one instance) or a general conclusion (a statement that applies to a number of instances or a class of objects). Two such arguments are diagrammed in figures 12.3 and 12.4.

Figure 12.3
Toulmin model: argument with a particular claim.

Evidence:
John Williams is a member of the Sierra Club.

Claim:
John Williams is a conservationist.

Warrant:
Members of the Sierra Club are conservationists.

Figure 12.4
Toulmin model: argument with a general claim.

Evidence:
Jane Smith is a member of the Sierra Club.

Claim:
Members of the Sierra Club are conservationists.

Warrant:
Jane Smith, who is a conservationist, is typical of the other members.

Four types of reasoning will now be discussed: reasoning by generalization, reasoning by analogy, reasoning by causal relationships, and reasoning by sign relationships.

By Generalization

When you look at different members of a class of objects and make a statement about the whole class on the basis of those observed, you are engaged in reasoning by generalization. If you examine the records of 20 percent of the students at State University and find that all have total college board scores above 1,000, you may conclude that "Students at State University have total college board scores above 1,000." The soundness of that claim will depend on how well you have met the tests that must be applied to any reasoning by generalization. In order to determine whether reasoning by generalization has produced a proper and credible claim, three basic questions must be answered affirmatively: (1) Are the instances representative of all the members of the class? (2) Has a sufficient number of instances been examined? (3) Can negative instances be accounted for? These are potential reservations to the claim. Let's consider each of these tests.

Are the instances representative of all members of the class? Efforts must be made to avoid bias in selecting the examples. Unfortunately, it is often difficult—especially in the field of public affairs—to select in a scientific way examples of the subjects with which a speaker is normally concerned. You have to take the evidence where you find it. Where feasible, however, the samples must be selected as randomly as possible. In the ideal situation, a *random sample* should be used—that is, *a sample so selected that each member of the class has a theoretical chance of being chosen.* If we stood in front of Memorial Hall on the campus of State University and selected every fifth student who came out of the hall between the hours of 8 A.M. and 12 noon on Thursday, we would have a random sample of students who took classes in the building between the hours of 8 A.M. and 12 noon on Thursday, but we wouldn't have a random sample of students at the university. Nor would we have a random sample of students who took classes there on other days of the week, and we probably wouldn't even have a random sample of students who took classes there on Thursday afternoon. But if we went to the student directory of the university and selected every fifth name, we would then have a random sample of the student body. If the method of selection prevents some members of the class from being chosen, it isn't a random sample. If the sample isn't random, then a significant reservation has been raised, and the propriety of the claim is in serious doubt. Logically, the claim can no longer be maintained. It may in fact be true; nevertheless, it is invalid logically.

Has a sufficient number of samples been used? Unless all members of a class of objects have been examined, you can never know for sure that you have included enough examples. If statistical procedures are applied to the data, the number of samples will determine the margin of error. But if statistical procedures aren't applicable, you must make a subjective judgment about whether the number of examples is sufficient. One thing you know: if you have observed 100 percent of the examples, you have enough. On the other hand, you can be fairly sure you have an insufficient number if you have investigated only 5 to 10 percent of the cases. The difficulty is in determining what number between 10 and 100 percent constitutes a sufficiency when statistical procedures aren't employed. This is why you need to engage in extensive research. As you find more and more consistent evidence, you can develop confidence in the validity of your examples as well as reduce the chance of using any exceptional instances. Because if the listener decides your statements are based on atypical examples, your credibility will be diminished.

Can negative instances be accounted for? In other words, can the examples supporting the generalization be explained? Let's go back to the generalization that "Students at State University have total college board scores above 1,000." Suppose someone says, "Wait a minute, I know two people in one of my classes who have total college board scores under 1,000." If investigation discloses that those two persons are special students who are being allowed to take some courses but are not eligible for graduation, then the negative instances have been accounted for, and the original generalization still stands. If, however, investigation reveals that those two people are bona fide

Figure 12.5
Toulmin model: reasoning by generalization.

Evidence:
James Wilson, Betty Johnson, Tammy Brown are college students who are registered to vote.

Claim:
A large percentage of college students are registered to vote.

Warrant:
These students are typical of most college students.

students, then there are deficiencies in the claim and it must be modified in order to be consistent with the evidence. The validity of this reservation may necessitate the inclusion of a qualifier such as "most."

Now that reasoning by generalization has been explained, you can see what it looks like in the Toulmin model in figure 12.5.

By Analogy

Rather than reasoning from a number of particulars to a general conclusion as in reasoning by generalization, reasoning by analogy reasons from one particular to another particular. For example, a salesman is about to buy a new car, and one of his concerns is how many miles the car will travel per gallon of gasoline. Until he drives several hundred miles he can't know for certain, and since it is a new car, the dealer won't let him drive it the necessary miles. Moreover, there is no previous owner to consult. So he'll be forced to use reasoning by analogy to arrive at a reasonable judgment about the number of miles the car will travel per gallon of gas. He may compare it with the car he now owns, and find the following characteristics shared by the two cars: (1) They are the same make. (2) Each is a four-door sedan. (3) Each has a 165 horsepower, V-6 engine. (4) Each has automatic transmission. (5) Each has air conditioning. (6) Each has power steering. (7) Each has power brakes. (8) Each is blue. (9) Each has a plush interior. (10) Each has steel-belted tires. (11) Each has hidden front headlights. (12) Each has a stereo radio and tape deck. There is, however, one additional piece of known information about his present car: it gives approximately 24 miles per gallon of gas. Our driver now reasons that since the two cars are alike in a number of known respects, he can reasonably expect them to be alike in another unknown respect. So he concludes the new car will give approximately 24 miles per gallon of gas. Thus his reasoning started with only one particular example and extended to only one particular example.

The preceding is a *literal* analogy, which compares two members of the same class. A literal analogy is the only kind that can produce a legitimate claim. A second type is the *figurative* analogy, which compares members of two different classes. A figurative analogy was used by prosecutor Vincent Bugliosi in the murder trial described in his book *Till Death Us Do Part:*

> I think that counsels' problem is that they misconceive what circumstantial evidence is all about. Circumstantial evidence is not, as they claim, like a chain. You could have a chain extending the span of the Atlantic Ocean from Nova Scotia to Bordeaux, France, consisting of millions of links, and with one weak link that chain is broken.
>
> Circumstantial evidence, to the contrary, is like a rope. And each fact is a strand of that rope, and as the prosecution piles one fact upon another we add strands and we add strength to that rope. If one strand breaks—and I am not conceding for a moment that any strand has broken in this case—but if one strand does break, the rope is not broken. The strength of the rope is barely diminished. Why? Because there are so many other strands of almost steel-like strength that the rope is still more than strong enough to bind these two defendants to justice. That's what circumstantial evidence is all about.[5]

Although the figurative analogy doesn't result in a sound claim on its merits, it can be highly effective in getting listeners to understand or accept a point if the analogy is carefully chosen.

In order to determine whether reasoning by analogy permits you to defend the propriety of a claim, two specific questions must be answered affirmatively: (1) Are the compared examples alike in all essential respects? (2) Are differences between the compared examples accounted for? These are potential reservations for the claim. Let's consider these questions.

Are the compared examples alike in all essential respects? Essential respects are those related to the unknown attribute. In other words, some characteristics of a car affect how many miles it goes per gallon of gas; these are the essential respects. Other characteristics don't affect how many miles a car travels per gallon of gasoline; these are the unessential respects. Of the similar characteristics of the two cars cited previously, you'll notice that only the first seven have any influence on gasoline economy. Now the question is: Are there any other essential respects in which the two cars differ? If we discover that the new car has dual four-barrel carburetors whereas the old one has a single two-barrel carburetor, we know this is an essential respect in which the two cars are dissimilar. Therefore, our conclusion that the two cars will give essentially the same number of miles per gallon is an improper claim. The two examples used in reasoning by analogy must be similar in all *essential* respects.

Are differences between the compared instances accounted for? Differences can be accounted for by showing that the differences are in unessential factors. If the two cars are different in color, that is an unessential difference with respect to fuel consumption. If one has hidden front headlights and the other one doesn't, that is an unessential difference. Be prepared, therefore, to

Figure 12.6
Toulmin model: reasoning by analogy.

Evidence:
The construction of interstate highways in State A reduced the number of fatalities from auto accidents.

Claim:
The construction of interstate highways will reduce the number of fatalities from auto accidents in State B

Warrant:
State A is similar to State B in essential respects.

show that any cited differences between two examples are unessential differences. If you can't, the reservation to the claim will stand, and the reasoning by analogy has significant deficiencies in the claim.

Notice how reasoning by analogy looks in the Toulmin model in figure 12.6.

By Causal Relationships

Causal reasoning attempts to show why something happened or is going to happen. If something has happened and we're trying to determine why, this is called effect-to-cause reasoning. If we're trying to maintain that something is going to happen as a result of some specific factors, that is called cause-to-effect reasoning. If, going out to my car one hot July day to leave on a trip that will necessitate my driving 65 miles per hour for six hours on an interstate highway, I notice that my front tires are worn thin, I may reason—from cause-to-effect—that thin tires, a hot day, and fast, steady driving are likely to produce a blowout. Consequently, I may have two new tires installed to avoid my predicted effect. On the other hand, if I fail to see the tires before I leave and four hours later have a blowout, I may reason—from effect-to-cause—that the blowout was caused by the thin tire, hot day, and fast, steady driving.

In order to determine whether causal reasoning has resulted in a correct claim, four specific questions must be answered negatively: (1) Has the fact that two events are related in time been misinterpreted as a causal relationship? (2) Has an immediate cause been misinterpreted as a sufficient cause? (3) Have other factors intervened, or will they intervene, to prevent a normal effect from occurring? (4) Are there other causes that contributed to the effect? These are potential reservations to the claim. Let's consider each of them.

Has the fact that two events are related in time been misinterpreted as a causal relationship? This is what the Romans called the fallacy of *post hoc, ergo propter hoc;* in other words, when one event precedes another, we conclude that the first event actually produced the second one. Superstitions thrive on this kind of reasoning. A person whose path is crossed by a black cat has an accident later in the day and reasons that the cat caused the accident. One of the most entertaining of Ann Landers' columns appeared several years ago. In it a reader lamented that "her life was ruined because of an offensive odor she couldn't get rid of. She made the rounds of nose specialists, endocrinologists, dermatologists, gynecologists—and no one could explain it. She said no friend or relative had ever mentioned the odor, but it was driving her crazy." The following letters were among the 500 received in response by Ann Landers.

> FROM WHEELING: The woman with the "odor " is not sick—she is gifted. I, too, have the ability to smell things that no one else can smell. I can smell animals in the woods and birds flying overhead. I can also smell friends and acquaintances before they enter a room. I first realized I had this gift when I was four years old. I said to my mother, "Grandpa will be here soon." She asked, "How do you know?" I answered, "I can smell him." Sure enough, in five minutes Grandpa arrived. Please tell the woman who wrote not to worry. She's exceptional.
> FROM MARSHALLTOWN, IOWA: Tell the lady with the strange odor to cheer up and she will smell better. Scientists have proved that happy people give off a fragrant scent. Negative brain waves (worry, anger, fear, anxiety) give off unpleasant odors. Animals can smell emotions but most people can't.
> FROM LA PORTE, IND.: The woman who "Nose It All" should stop drinking coffee. The odor that is bothering her is the result of caffeine poisoning.
> FROM JACKSON, MICH.: Tell "Stinky" to put a cup of salt in her bath water.
> FROM JUNEAU, ALASKA: Tell the lady with the odor to sleep with a raw oyster over each eye at night. It's a sure cure.
> FROM LONDON, ONTARIO: Her trouble is not in her mind, Ann, it's in her nose. She should line her nostrils with vaseline every night when she goes to sleep.
> FROM FLINT, MICH.: The lady with the odor problem should change toothpaste and soap. She has an allergy that is throwing her chemistry out of balance.
> FROM DES MOINES: If the woman will stop wearing synthetic fabrics (nylon, acetate, etc.) her odor will disappear. Synthetics stimulate glandular secretions which create odors.[6]

Obviously, the suggested remedies can't be causative factors. These people have confused a prior event with a causal factor. You must avoid this kind of reasoning, for it creates deficiencies in the claim.

Has an immediate cause been misinterpreted as a sufficient cause? An event may serve as a trigger to produce a result, but not be sufficient to cause the effect by itself. A notable example of this kind of mistake is the claim that the assassination of Archduke Francis Ferdinand of Austria at Sarajevo caused World War I. Undoubtedly this event triggered the beginning of the war, but it wouldn't have been sufficient to produce a world war if conditions had not been what they were at that time in Europe. Had conditions been different,

Figure 12.7
Toulmin model: reasoning by causal relationships.

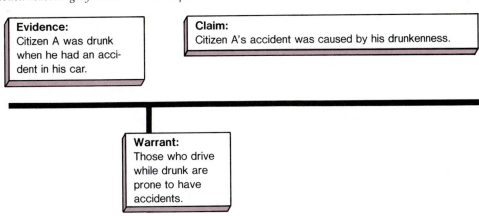

the assassination of Archduke Ferdinand would probably have been little more than a minor ripple among all the world events of the day. You must ask whether the factor you are labeling a cause is one that is sufficient to produce the effect by itself. If not, the propriety of the claim must be questioned.

Have other factors intervened, or will they intervene, to prevent a normal effect from occurring? Whenever you argue a given effect has occurred, or will occur, because of a given cause, be sure that no other factor has been introduced that will alter the relationship of the alleged cause and effect. If a building erected on former marshland collapses, for example, some may offer the claim that the collapse resulted from building it on an unsafe foundation. However, if someone points out that the contractor sank foundation supports fifty feet to solid rock, then the chances are that the fact the land was previously marshland had nothing to do with the collapse of the building.

Are there other causes that have contributed to the effect? Single factors are rarely the cause of an effect. In most instances there are multiple factors. Even when you have cited a number of factors as causes, be sure there are no additional factors that could have contributed to the result. Let's look again at the example of the blowout. It could have resulted from the thin tire, hot day, and fast, steady driving; but it also could have resulted from striking a sharp stone on the highway. All similar factors would have to be ruled out before the blowout could reasonably be blamed on the other three factors.

Figure 12.7 shows how causal reasoning looks in the Toulmin model.

By Sign Relationships

Sign reasoning occurs when we take one event as an indication that a thing is true even though the reason for its being true is not explained. Thus, if we look out the window and see the leaves moving on a tree, we take that as a sign that the wind is blowing. If we hear the sound of water running in the downspout from the gutters on the roof, we infer that it is raining. If we hear the sound of squealing tires on the street, we assume that someone has either had an accident or narrowly averted one. If we see a long line of people standing outside a theater, we deduce that the movie being shown is a popular one. Note that in none of these cases is there an explanation of why the occurrence is true. There is no explanation why it is raining, only the claim that it is.

In order to determine whether sign reasoning permits a claim that is sound on its merits, four specific questions must be answered: (1) Is the sign relationship accidental or coincidental? (2) Is the sign relationship reciprocal? (3) Have special factors intervened that alter normal relationships? (4) Is the sign reliable without the collaboration or concurrence of other signs? These are potential reservations to the claim. Let's consider each of these questions.

Is the sign relationship accidental or coincidental? In other words, is the sign only infrequently associated with the event. Enrollment in a university is taken as a sign that the individual can read and write with reasonable proficiency. Is it only coincidental that the college students we know have these competencies? If it is, the reasoning by sign won't have a high degree of probability, and the claim won't be a correct one.

Is the sign relationship reciprocal? In other words, can either be taken as a sign of the other? If we take enrollment at a university as a sign that the person can read and write with reasonable proficiency, can we also take reading and writing proficiencies as signs that the person is a university student?

Have special factors intervened that alter normal relationships? When we learn that a university student is an athlete, we must ask if some special factor has intervened—athletic ability—that has caused relationships to be altered. If some special factor can be shown to have intervened, the sign relationship to the event is highly improbable, and the propriety of the claim is questionable.

Is the sign reliable without the collaboration or concurrence of other signs? When you look out the window and see the leaves on a tree moving, do you also see a flag waving? If the leaves are moving, but a flag is hanging limp, it may, though not necessarily, mean that the wind is not moving the leaves. Instead someone may be shaking the tree or squirrels may be running on the limbs causing the leaves to move. Of course, it could be that the wind is blowing where the tree is, but not where the flag is. But the presence of a flag hanging limp increases the probability that the moving leaves are not a sign the wind is blowing. The more collaborative or concurrent signs that can be discovered, the more reliable is the claim based on the sign reasoning.

Figure 12.8 is an example of sign reasoning as it appears in the Toulmin model.

Special Fallacies

The term *fallacy* refers to "any trick of logic or language which allows a statement or a claim to be passed off as something it is not."[7] In the previous section, certain tests were suggested for each form of reasoning. If the reasoning is sound, the conclusion reached is sound. But if the reasoning fails to measure up to the tests, a fallacy has crept into the reasoning. A claim based on a fallacy cannot be accepted.

Figure 12.8
Toulmin model: reasoning by sign relationships.

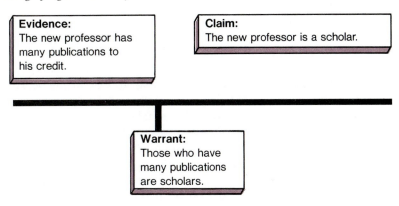

In this section we'll be concerned with *special fallacies*. These special fallacies don't result from invalid use of the methods of reasoning. Instead they are tricky or specious devices that are too frequently used in human communication. Special fallacies involve such things as fallacies in the use of language, source materials, and audience attitudes and values. The special fallacy is a diversionary tactic to draw the audience's attention away from the non-logical basis of the conclusion, like a magician's showy movements used to mask the way he performs illusions. Some of the more common special fallacies are discussed in the following material.

Appeal to Tradition

In this special fallacy, the speaker argues that a position should be maintained because that is the way our people have always done it, or that a position shouldn't be adopted because we've never done it that way before. For a long time, for example, some people in the South contended that Southerners should vote for the Democratic party because their parents and grandparents had voted for it. In other sections of the country, the same appeal was made for the Republican party. Ideally, the voter should examine the case for each party and for each candidate in every election.

Supporting a traditional course of action isn't fallacious when supporting arguments are developed that show it's the best way. When we're asked to accept traditional ways simply because they are traditional, however, that is a fallacy.

Appeal to Ignorance (Argumentum ad ignorantiam)

In this instance, a person argues that because you can't prove what he or she is saying is false, then it must be true. For example, some will say of a person accused of a crime: "Well, I think he is guilty, and he can't prove he is innocent, so he must be guilty." Or a speaker will say: "This is a good proposal I am presenting. Unless someone can prove it is not good, it should be adopted." In both of these cases, however, the burden of proving the case has been assigned to the wrong side. Those who are arguing for a change in policy have the burden to prove there is justification for that change. Thus, a person is innocent until proved guilty, and a proposal isn't adopted until its advocate proves it should be.

Use of Question-Begging

A first type of question-begging is the use of a word that assumes the validity of a charge or point that should be proved. Consider the following examples: "We must get rid of the *bloated* federal bureaucracy." "The *unfair* income tax should be revised." "That *immoral* book should be banned." "Let's defeat this *corrupt* politician." *Bloated, unfair, immoral,* and *corrupt* are all question-begging words. The speaker must prove these implicit and unsupported charges before we can accept the statements.

A second form of question-begging is arguing in a circle. For example, a person might argue: "Education is good because it helps people." When asked why education helps people, the advocate replies, "Because it is good." Then, when asked why it is good, he answers, "Because it helps people." Arguing in a circle is fallacious because it uses two unproven assertions to support each other.

Appeal to Authority (Argumentum ad verecundiam)

Appeal to authority occurs when we're asked to support a position or adopt a policy simply because an authority says we should. For example: "We should cut the appropriations to higher education because our governor says the universities are wasting state funds." The error is compounded when the authority used is not even knowledgeable in the area in which we're asked to accept his or her opinion.

The fallacy of appeal to authority is not to be confused with the legitimate use of authority in developing evidence and reasoning to support a position. When a speaker cites the director of the Highway Patrol as saying a speed limit above 55 miles per hour increases the number of accidents and then gives the statistics the director has collected, that isn't a fallacious appeal to authority.

Attack on a Person (Argumentum ad hominem)

The *ad hominem* fallacy is an attack on the person or the source. A few years ago, for example, when the intercollegiate debate topic called for the cessation of nuclear testing, affirmative teams cited one particular scientist who had discussed the level of radiation resulting from nuclear fallout. In a number of instances, the negative team would ask the question: "Did he give that testimony before or after his stay in a mental hospital?" Notice that the attack is not germane to the testimony given. If one could show that this scientist had erred in using the wrong equipment, that would be a legitimate attack upon him. If one could show that he lacked the proper training or knowledge to use the equipment, that would be a legitimate attack upon him. If one could show that he was actually mentally ill during the collection of that data and that illness had adversely affected his ability to interpret the data, that would be a legitimate attack upon him. But to ask the general question, "Did he give that testimony before or after his stay in a mental hospital?" suggests a connection that must be proved.

Frequently, we hear arguments of speakers answered by such statements as, "Oh, she's a born-again Christian," or "Oh, he's a member of the NAACP," or "She's one of those rabid conservationists," or "He's a Legionnaire." In each case, no effort is made to deal with the specific statement or argument of the individual. It is just assumed that no member of the particular group involved can present a valid argument.

An appeal to emotions asks the listener to accept a position solely for emotional reasons, because of feelings he experiences. A defense attorney uses this fallacy when defending a client accused of embezzling funds: "Members of the jury, this man is your neighbor. He has lived in this community all his life and has never done physical harm to anyone. All of you know his mother. Think of the anguish she will endure if her only son is sent to prison." When we are asked to oppose a space program because there are people in this country who are starving, we are asked to behave in a certain way for an emotional reason.

Appeal to Emotions

Appeal to emotions can also involve an appeal to the listener's prejudice. When listeners are asked to oppose an action because it was "conceived by the Jewish bankers," an appeal to prejudice has been made. When listeners are told that "we must get control of our government away from the WASPs," an appeal to prejudice has occurred. In each of these instances, the listeners responding to the appeal do so because of their distrust or dislike of a particular group of people.

In this fallacy, the argument is made that a policy should be adopted or an argument accepted because the majority of people approve it. In some cases, the speaker doesn't even claim the majority of people approve, but merely says, "The people support this position." "The people" aren't identified. "The people" may be Democrats, Republicans, Communists, or anybody else; we are never told. In other instances, the indeterminate "they" is used, as in, "They support our policy in the Middle East." The appeal is to get on the bandwagon and join the crowd, whoever the crowd is.

Appeal to Popular Approval (Argumentum ad populum)

But the important fallacy in this kind of argument is that even if all the people in the United States favor a position, that doesn't make it valid. When native Japanese-Americans were placed in detention camps at the beginning of World War II, that action was approved by the great majority of Americans. That overwhelming public approval, however, didn't make the policy right.

Summary

One of the ways to develop the credibility to have your ideas accepted is to prove what you say. Proof involves two processes—the use of evidence and the use of reasoning. This chapter has discussed the process of reasoning. The Toulmin model for analyzing reasoning has been used because (1) it doesn't require the certainty that the Aristotelian model does; (2) it places the components of the reasoning process in the open and shows clearly their relationship to one another; and (3) it places the basic premise of the argument, the warrant, in a position where support for it can be developed as a part of the reasoning model.

Only three parts of the Toulmin model are used: (1) evidence, (2) claim, and (3) warrant.

Four types of reasoning were discussed: (1) reasoning by generalization, (2) reasoning by analogy, (3) reasoning by causal relationships, and (4) reasoning by sign relationships.

To draw a proper claim from reasoning by generalization, three questions must be answered affirmatively: (1) Are the instances representative of all members of the class? (2) Have a sufficient number of instances been examined? (3) Can negative instances be accounted for?

Reasoning by analogy produces a sound claim if two questions can be answered affirmatively: (1) Are the compared examples alike in all essential respects? (2) Are differences between the compared examples accounted for?

A correct claim can be arrived at by reasoning from causal relationships if four questions are answered negatively: (1) Has the relationship of two events in time been misinterpreted as a causal relationship? (2) Has an immediate cause been misinterpreted as a sufficient cause? (3) Have other factors intervened to prevent a normal effect from occurring? (4) Are there other causes that contributed to the effect?

If the claim is to be free of deficiences when reasoning by sign relationships, four questions must be answered: (1) Is the sign relationship accidental or coincidental? (2) Is the sign relationship reciprocal? (3) Have special factors intervened that altered normal relationships? (4) Is the sign reliable without the collaboration or concurrence of other signs?

Special fallacies, tricky or specious devices, are used frequently to divert the audience's attention from the logical basis of a conclusion. Some common special fallacies are appeal to tradition, appeal to ignorance, use of question-begging words, appeal to authority, attack on a person, appeal to emotions, and appeal to popular approval.

Exercises

1. In a speech by one of your classmates, find an example of reasoning by generalization. Did you find the generalization credible? Why or why not?
2. Attend a lecture on campus. Analyze the speaker's reasoning. What aspects of this speaker's reasoning caused you to accept his or her ideas as credible? What about this reasoning caused you to doubt the credibility of his or her ideas?

3. Prepare a short speech analyzing a claim, which you didn't consider credible, presented earlier by another member of the class. Explain why the claim didn't seem credible to you.
4. Diagram in the Toulmin model one of your major arguments in your next speech. What parts will you omit in your speech? Why?
5. From letters to the editor of your school or community newspaper, select examples of reasoning that exemplify special fallacies.

Notes

1. Vincent E. Barry, *Invitation to Critical Thinking* (New York: Holt, Rinehart, and Winston, 1984), p. 9. Used by permission.
2. S. Toulmin, *The Uses of Argument* (Cambridge: Cambridge University Press, 1958).
3. Ibid.
4. Rene Dubos, "A Theology of the Earth," in *Representative American Speeches: 1969–1970,* ed. Lester Thonssen (New York: H. W. Wilson Co., 1970), pp. 90–91.
5. V. Bugliosi, *Till Death Us Do Part* (New York: Bantam Books, 1978), pp. 340–41.
6. Ann Landers, "Sleeping with Raw Oyster Over Each Eye Will Cure 'Odor'!" Los Angeles Time Syndicate, *Durham* (N.C.) *Morning Herald,* November 4, 1971, p. 3B. Used by permission.
7. Madsen Pirie, *The Book of the Fallacy* (London: Routledge & Kegan Paul, 1985), p. vii. See also Alex C. Michalos, *Improving your Reasoning* (Englewood Cliffs, New Jersey: Prentice-Hall, 1986), p. 26. Used by permission of the author, title and Routledge & Kegan Paul Publishers.

PART 3

THE SPEECH

CHAPTER 13

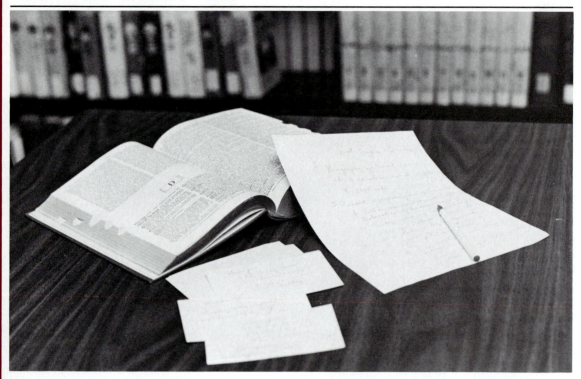

Structuring the Speech

Some evidence indicates that the element of organization is a more important factor than content in a listener's evaluation of a speech.[1] Obviously no one is going to advocate giving speeches without supporting materials, but content alone is insufficient. Improve your chances of developing credibility for your ideas by putting them into some meaningful form.

The Value of Organization

The ability of organization to affect the credibility of a speaker's ideas has been revealed by experimental evidence. Four main values of organization have been identified, any one of which is sufficient to justify the time and labor necessary to produce a well-organized speech.

Organization makes a significant impact on the listener's comprehension of information included in a speech. Studies show that you must be careful about the placement of all organizational elements in a speech. Randomly changing the order of sentences in a well-organized speech revealed that listeners comprehended the unaltered version significantly better than the altered one.[2] Rearranging the "thesis sentence, two major contentions, two subcontentions for each, and two assertions for each subpoint" of an organized speech, adversely affected the listeners' comprehension.[3] Randomly rearranging the paragraphs of a well-organized speech revealed that those who heard the unaltered version comprehended it significantly better than those who heard the altered form.[4] Altering the chronological pattern of rules explaining the game of *Risk* showed that subjects hearing the organized message scored significantly higher on a recall test than those listening to the disorganized version.[5] Varying the order of three basic parts of a speech—attention, need, satisfaction—revealed that comprehension was significantly higher for those who heard the correct version.[6]

Affects Listeners' Comprehension of Message

Be concerned, not only about the order of major parts of a speech but also about placement of paragraphs and sequence of sentences.

Does organization aid only listeners with low levels of ability in comprehending orally communicated messages? On the contrary, a number of studies have revealed that organization is most beneficial to listeners with high levels of ability. Determining the organizational ability of subjects showed that organization increased the comprehension of subjects with high organizational ability more than those with low.[7] A second study measured the linguistic ability of subjects before presenting material in organized and disorganized form and found that "clear organization increased comprehension more among (subjects) with high linguistic ability than among those with middle linguistic ability."[8] A third study showed that clearly organized communications produced better comprehension, which was clearly related to the intellectual ability of the listener.[9]

Thus you can't evade responsibility for organizing a message with the excuse that intelligent listeners can organize the material themselves.

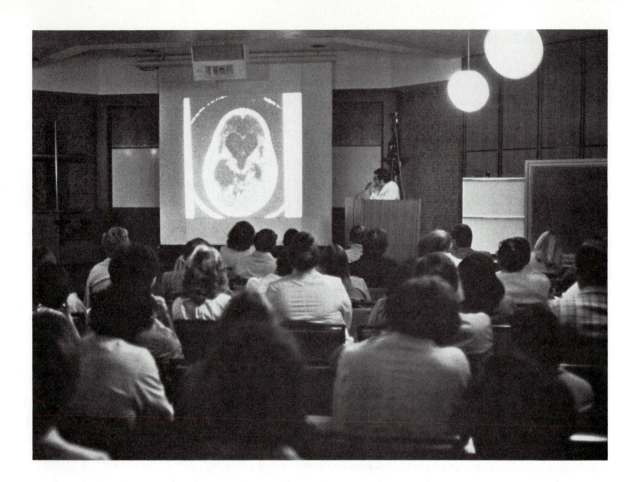

Affects Ethos of the Speaker

Organization increases your ethos or credibility. Using organized and disorganized speeches, two scholars found that subjects who heard the disorganized speech thought significantly less of the speaker afterward.[10] A speaker delivered two forms of the same speech; the only difference between them was that one included eighteen disorganization cues. Although the inclusion of the cues did not significantly lower the speaker's credibility, "there was a significant increase in speaker credibility in the *absence* of speaker disorganization cues."[11] Good organization will not necessarily increase your credibility, but its absence will reduce it.

Affects Attitude Change

Although it appears that organization by itself won't cause a change in attitude, evidence indicates it's a necessary ingredient if a speech is to significantly shift attitudes. Subjects heard four versions of a speech: organized and fluent, organized and nonfluent, disorganized and fluent, disorganized and nonfluent. Only one version, the organized and fluent, caused a significant shift in the attitudes of the listeners.[12] Smith developed a speech that was divided into six main parts: attention, need, satisfaction, visualization, refutation, and action. He varied the organization by transposing one or two parts and also by randomizing the order of the parts. His results showed a negative audience reaction when all parts of the speech were randomized.[13] To maximize your chances of changing listeners' attitudes, organize your speech.

Clear organization prevents listeners from becoming frustrated, especially those with high cognitive need, defined "as a need to structure relevant situations in meaningful, integrated ways." After measuring the cognitive need of subjects, Cohen presented to half of them an ambiguous story; to the other half he presented the same story in structured form. The results revealed that the subjects with high cognitive need experienced significantly more frustration in the ambiguous situation than they did in the structured situation. Those with medium and low cognitive need did not differ in the two conditions. "Thus," concluded Cohen, "the degree of structure becomes more crucial for the individual as the strength of his need for cognition increases."[14]

Affects Listeners' Frustration

Avoid frustrating listeners with high cognitive need; organize your speech. With these points in mind, let's consider the organization of a speech. It includes three distinct processes: (1) selecting the ideas to be used in a particular speech, (2) developing the entity we call a speech, and (3) ordering the main ideas in the body of the speech.

Selection of Ideas

When you analyze a subject, you frequently find many different ideas you can present sincerely and develop with valid evidence and reasoning. Some of these ideas will be more acceptable to one group than to another. For example, different ideas can be used to support increasing efforts to curtail the crime rate in the United States: The high crime rate (1) makes streets unsafe for defenseless citizens, (2) increases prices for consumers, (3) increases the economic burdens of small businesses, (4) increases personal danger to owners of small businesses, (5) causes loss of revenue to cities by deterring tourists and shoppers from coming into the downtown area, and (6) increases the complexities and hazards of police work.

Assuming you could support all these arguments with equal sincerity, use the ones that would be most persuasive to a particular group of listeners. If you were talking to a group of elderly citizens, you would contend that the high crime rate makes our streets unsafe for citizens and increases prices for consumers; to a group of business owners, argue that the high crime rate increases the economic burden of small businesses and increases the personal danger to their owners; to a group of city officials and politicians, assert that the high crime rate causes a loss of revenue to cities by deterring tourists and shoppers from coming into dangerous areas; to a group of law enforcement officers, maintain that the high crime rate increases the complexities and hazards of police work.

An important phase of organization is selecting the arguments you're going to use with a particular audience. This selection of appropriate arguments can be made only after you have carefully analyzed the attitudes and characteristics of the potential hearers.

Development of the Speech

Can the entity we call a speech be created in a number of different ways? Definitely! Aristotle suggested there were only two necessary parts to a speech: (1) state your case (what we call the thesis), and (2) prove it. However, he also observed it was frequently necessary to add two other parts, an exordium (introduction) and a peroration (conclusion). These four basic parts—introduction, thesis, body, and conclusion—make up the entity we call a speech. There are other ways to divide a speech, but we will limit our discussion to these four parts, plus a fifth optional part—the preview.

Although experienced and skillful speakers find it appropriate and desirable on a given occasion to omit one or more of these basic parts, proceed on the assumption that each is absolutely necessary. Once these fundamental procedures have been deeply ingrained in your speaking behavior, they can be altered to deviate from the pattern suggested here. However, in the vast majority of speaking situations you will find these four fundamental parts to be appropriate elements of a speech.

Purposes and types of introductions and conclusions are discussed in the next chapter. At this point let's consider the thesis and body of the speech. The thesis is discussed first because until it is precisely stated there can be no meaningful development of the other parts of a speech.

Purpose Sentence

The purpose sentence—also called the thesis, the statement of central idea, statement sentence, or the subject sentence—normally comes at the end of the introduction, after you have the attention of the listeners. In unusual instances where the listeners' attention is already riveted on the subject or the speaker, the speech may open with the purpose sentence. Otherwise, to begin with a statement of purpose, as some speakers do, is to invite those hearers who have not begun to attend to the speech to miss this most vital part. In some unusual circumstances, the purpose may not be stated until later in the speech, sometimes not until the end. And in some rare cases, the purpose may not be stated at all, even though you have it framed for your own purposes. As we'll see, however, this latter practice creates both practical and ethical problems.

The purpose sentence identifies the topic you want your listeners to focus on in this particular speech. The focus may be on any or all of several things: (1) It may simply focus on what the topic of the speech will be: "This morning I want to explain three objections to the proposal to increase Congressional salaries." (2) It may focus on the meaning you want your listeners to obtain: "This morning I want to show that the proposal to increase Congressional salaries should be defeated." (3) It may focus on the behavioral response you want your listeners to make: "This morning I want to show why you should write your representative to oppose an increase in Congressional salaries." In all these instances, you would discuss the three disadvantages of the proposal to increase Congressional salaries.

The purpose sentence must be explicitly identified so that listeners recognize it. For example, one's purpose sentence might be: "There are three actions the United States can take to improve educational opportunities." In this form, however, many listeners fail to recognize it as the purpose sentence. Therefore, you can present your purpose more explicitly by stating it in a manner similar to this: "This morning I would like to call your attention to three actions the United States can take to improve educational opportunities." Be sure your purpose is stated as a complete sentence.

Why should a speaker be obvious in presenting the purpose? Doesn't this insult the listeners' intelligence? Isn't the speaker talking down to the listeners? The answer to these questions is you must be obvious, not because you belittle the intelligence of hearers or because you're talking down to them, but because this is a method of adapting to oral communication. **Value of the Purpose Sentence**

A writer can provide many cues that will aid in the communication of ideas. Many of these cues aren't available to a speaker. On these pages, for example, the punctuation marks help in determining what words go together in thought units. The period shows that one group of words is related in a sentence. An indentation at the beginning of a sentence indicates that the next group of sentences is going to develop a specific theme. Headings over a group of paragraphs reveal that those paragraphs are related to the idea expressed by the heading.

Since you can use none of these visual guides, use others to provide similar information to listeners. Since you can't put a purpose sentence in visual italics, one of the ways you can emphasize it is to put it in *aural italics*. The statement, "This morning I would like to call to your attention," constitutes the speaker's aural italics. It informs the listeners that this sentence is more important than others around it, that it contains an important idea not to be missed. As writers put main ideas in large, bold print to make them stand out for readers, so speakers should put main ideas in words that make them stand out for listeners. We have accepted without question the need for visual cues to help readers with written material. Surely we must grant speakers the freedom to use aural cues, since listening is a much more difficult task than reading.

The purpose sentence is important not only because it provides significant aural cues for communication, but also helps establish the listeners' *set,* which is a predisposition to focus on specific stimuli and to respond in a particular way.[15] You ask listeners to perceive the data in such a way that they will draw the same conclusions from the data that you do. We know, from both personal observation and experimentation, that individuals don't always perceive data in like ways. Consequently, without a clear purpose sentence, listeners may draw conclusions different from those desired by the speaker.

People's perception may be influenced by a number of factors: attitudes, mental and physical condition at the moment, ability to perceive, knowledge, and recent experiences. The impact of recent experience was clearly demonstrated in a classroom experiment. One group of subjects was told that they were going to be shown words related to boats; a second group was told they were going to be shown words related to animals. The letters SAEL and WHARL were then flashed briefly before them. The first group perceived them as SAIL and WHARF; the second as SEAL and WHALE.[16]

Another experiment demonstrated that value judgments can also be influenced by the *set* of the listeners. The following narrative was presented to three groups of subjects:

> A middle-aged man, his wife, and teenage son live in a public housing development. Their house is adequate for their needs and is superior to anything that they could obtain on the open market at the same price. This development was built by the government to provide housing for underprivileged families and, in order to assure that this low-cost housing is properly used, the regulations require that the resident families have an income under the figure of $2,900.
>
> The man mentioned above has an income just under this amount and his entire income is used in running his household. He has, however, a strong desire to send his son to college and finds that he can obtain a job on weekends with a relative, which would provide enough money for his son's education.
>
> This additional income, however, would require his moving from the housing development and the increased rent would absorb most of his increased income. To provide for his son's education, he takes the job but makes arrangements for this additional income not to be reported. Thus he is able to stay in the low-cost housing and also secure the desired education for his son.

Prior to hearing this narrative, the first group of subjects was told they were going to hear about an ethical issue, the second was told they were going to hear about a social issue, and the third was told they were going to hear about an economic issue. The experimenters discovered that the ethical set "produced a significantly greater negative attitude toward the situation than either the economic or social sets."[17] In other words, the experimenters, by labeling the material to be presented, established a *set* in the listeners that caused them to perceive the stimuli in a manner consistent with the labels.

Use the purpose sentence to create a *set* in listeners toward your ideas and supporting materials. Once this set is established, it is easier for hearers to listen to the material because they have a frame of reference in which to place it. Instead of wondering why certain statements are being made, the listener has a perspective from which to view them. Omitting a purpose sentence or failing to state it clearly leaves the door open for a speech to be perceived differently than desired.

The Speech

The purpose sentence is also important because, in stating explicitly what you're trying to do, it aids in changing attitudes of listeners. A comparison of the use of explicit and implicit conclusions with the degree of commitment of listeners found "that the speech with the explicit conclusion caused significantly more attitude change than the speech with the implicit conclusion."[18] The explicit conclusion was significantly effective in changing the attitude of both noncommitted and highly committed subjects, whereas the implicit conclusion was more persuasive only to those who were strongly committed to the topic. There was a tendency for the neutral and less committed members of the audience to boomerang (change opinion in the opposite direction from that advocated by the speaker) when the implicit conclusion was used. The study concluded an explicit conclusion is more effective in causing attitude change when members of the audience are heterogeneous in their degree of commitment.[19]

Even more important is the finding that direct statement of purpose doesn't alienate those opposed to the purpose. A series of experiments testing the effectiveness of various methods revealed that explicit refutation doesn't necessarily diminish a speech's persuasiveness for listeners who are opposed.[20]

The explicitly stated conclusion is also more effective with the less intelligent members of an audience. Two researchers presented an antiprejudice film to adults and high school students. They hoped that an important message implicitly stated would be detected by the audience. The more intelligent members of the audience were influenced by the message, but the less intelligent ones were not. It was concluded that the implicit form of the message may well have caused it to be inaccessible to the less intelligent members of the audience. The only parts of the message that made any lasting impression were the explicit and specific details.[21]

Finally, the purpose sentence aids in delivering a speech because it gives coherence and unity to the ideas and supporting materials selected for presentation. Numerous experiments by psychologists have demonstrated that organized material is learned more easily and remembered longer than unorganized or disorganized data. Thus, you'll have less need for reliance on notes when the material is coherent and unified.

Statement of Purpose

Once you have determined the purpose sentence and gathered the materials you're going to use in the speech, you may begin to think about how you're going to express that sentence in the speech itself. It may be presented in many different forms; you shouldn't assume that only one, rigid, inflexible way of focusing on the central idea of the speech is appropriate or desirable. One way in which the statement of purpose may be developed is to first tell the listener what the speech is not going to do, then what it is. President Woodrow Wilson used this technique in the speech he gave at the ceremony on July 4, 1913, commemorating the fiftieth anniversary of the Battle of Gettysburg. Since the nature of the occasion demanded little in the way of an introduction, Wilson moved swiftly to a statement of his purpose.

Friends and Fellow Citizens:—I need not tell you what the Battle of Gettysburg meant. These gallant men in blue and gray sit all about us here. Many of them met upon this ground in grim and deadly struggle. Upon these famous fields and hillsides their comrades died about them. In their presence it were an impertinence to discourse upon how the battle went, how it ended, what it signified! But fifty years have gone by since then, and I crave the privilege of speaking to you for a few minutes of what those fifty years have meant.

Another way of presenting the purpose sentence is to introduce it as a question. John C. Calhoun, in the last speech that he gave in the U.S. Senate, used just this method to make clear what his speech was about:

I have, senators, believed from the first that the agitation of the subject of slavery would, if not prevented by some timely and effective measure, end in disunion. Entertaining this opinion, I have, on all proper occasions, endeavored to call the attention of both the two great parties which divide the country, to adopt some such measure to prevent so great a disaster, but without success. The agitation has been permitted to proceed, with almost no attempt to resist it, until it has reached a period when it can no longer be disguised or denied that the Union is in danger. You have thus forced upon you the greatest and the gravest question that ever can come under your consideration: How can the Union be preserved?

Like all phases of a speech, the purpose sentence should be adapted to the specific situation. On occasion this will mean phrasing a purpose sentence that is clear to those who are present when the speech is given, but that does not explicitly delineate the scope of the speech for someone not present. Such an example is found in a speech made by John Marshall in the Virginia convention called to ratify the Constitution. In the debate that ensued, Marshall and Patrick Henry found themselves on opposite sides. Following one of Henry's speeches, Marshall took the floor:

Mr. Chairman:—I conceive that the object of the discussion now before us is, whether democracy or despotism be most eligible. I am sure that those who framed the system submitted to our investigation, and those who now support it intend the establishment and security of the former. The supporters of the Constitution claim the title of being firm friends of the liberty and rights of mankind. They say that they consider it as the best means of protecting liberty. We, sir, idolize democracy. Those who oppose it have bestowed eulogiums on monarchy. We prefer this system to any monarchy, because we are convinced that it has a greater tendency to secure our liberty and promote our happiness. We admire it, because we think it a well regulated democracy: it is recommended to the good people of this country; they are, through us, to declare whether it be such a plan of government as will establish and secure their freedom.

Permit me to attend to what the honorable gentleman, Mr. Henry, has said.

Those unfamiliar with Patrick Henry's speech have little idea of the arguments to be covered by Marshall, but those delegates in the convention who had just heard Henry speak needed no help. The purpose sentence need be no more specific than is required by the particular conditions.

Skillful speakers may use a purpose sentence that doesn't explicitly tell what they are going to do in the speech but instead merely implies the scope and purpose of the speech. As a general rule, avoid using this particular method until you have learned to use purpose sentences well and have gained the ability to make implicative statements that are unambiguous. Nevertheless, the implicative method is a valid one and should be understood. William Jennings Bryan used this technique in his famous lecture "Prince of Peace." After several introductory paragraphs, he came to the one in which he stated, in implied form, his purpose sentence:

> There are honest doubters whose sincerity we recognize and respect, but occasionally I find young men who think it smart to be skeptical; they talk as if it were an evidence of larger intelligence to scoff at creeds and to refuse to connect themselves with churches. They call themselves "Liberal," as if a Christian were narrow-minded. Some go so far as to assert that the "advanced thought of the world" has discarded the idea that there is a God. To these young men I desire to address myself.

Although Bryan does not state his purpose explicitly, it is practically impossible to misinterpret his intentions. If you choose to imply your statement of purpose, it must be done in a manner as unambiguous as that used by Bryan.

The Preview

An optional part of a speech is the preview, an extension of the purpose sentence telling the listeners precisely what main points will be included in the development of your main purpose. The preview may be included as a part of the purpose sentence: "I wish to speak to you this morning about the changes in the educational, recreational, protective, and economic functions of the family during the past century." Or it may be presented in a sentence or two immediately following the purpose sentence: "This morning I'd like to give you a brief outline of a model reading program. Such a reading program includes four elements: one good book each week, a newspaper daily, a magazine of interpretation weekly, and a book review monthly."

What are the advantages of a preview? It enables listeners to see in advance where the speech is going and to interpret supporting materials as they are presented. It also permits listeners to perceive movement in the speech as you progress from one main point to another. Knowing there are only four main points can often give hearers the fortitude to continue listening when, in a long speech, they hear the third or fourth point introduced.

Research on speeches of different organizational quality may have revealed the most important value of a preview: it significantly improved comprehension.[22]

The Body

Once you have settled on a purpose sentence and selected the main ideas to develop it, decide in what sequence to present those ideas. The ideas and development constitute the body of the speech.

Organizing Main Points According to a Stock Pattern

One alternative is to use a stock pattern for ordering the ideas. A number of these are available; six will be discussed on the following pages.

Chronological pattern In this instance the ideas are put together according to their relationship in time. For example, if you decide to speak on the topic "Population Growth," you might assemble the materials in a chronological pattern.

A. Prior to the seventeenth century, population growth was relatively slight.
   1. The food supply was inadequate to support large increases in population growth.
   2. The death rate was high.
   3. The birth rate was not high enough to overcome the death rate.
B. From the seventeenth century to the twentieth century, there was a substantial increase in the world's population.
   1. Medical advances drastically lowered the death rate.
   2. The food supply increased sufficiently to support large increases in population growth.
   3. The birth rate increased.

4. Normal pressures of population growth were relieved by the immigration of the people of many countries to newly discovered and unsettled lands.
C. During the twentieth century, population growth has begun to create problems.
   1. The food supply has failed to keep pace with the increases in population growth.
   2. The continually declining death rate has created social problems.
   3. Normal pressures from population growth are now being experienced because immigration is no longer a viable means of siphoning off people from overpopulated areas.
D. The prognosis for population growth beyond the twentieth century is discouraging.
   1. At present growth rates, the food supply will be insufficient to provide most people with an adequate diet.
   2. Present population growth rates will create a population density so great that living will be uncomfortable.
   3. Present methods for controlling population growth have not proved to be widely effective.

As you can see, the chronological development of the subject provides an understanding of the problem that can't be attained with any other pattern of organization. Instead of moving from past to future as the above example does, it sometimes is more effective to reverse the order of the main points and move from future to past.

Spatial pattern The spatial pattern assembles materials in terms of their relationship in space. An analysis of population growth around the world could be organized in a spatial pattern.

A. There has been population growth in the European nations.
   1. Most European countries have low rates of population increase.
   2. All European countries have low death rates.
   3. Most European countries have a moderately high population density.
B. There has been population growth in the African nations.
   1. Most African countries have high rates of population increase.
   2. All African countries have high death rates.
   3. Most African countries have a low population density.
C. There has been population growth in the Asian nations.
   1. Most Asian countries have high rates of population increase.
   2. The death rate in Asia varies from country to country.
      a. About half of the Asian countries have a low death rate.
      b. About half of the Asian countries have a high death rate.
   3. The population density in Asia is extremely varied.
      a. Some Asian countries have a very low population density.
      b. About half of the Asian countries have a high population density.
      c. Some Asian countries have a moderate population density.

D. There has been population growth in the American nations.
   1. Most American countries have high rates of population increase.
   2. The death rate in America varies from country to country.
      a. Most American countries have a low death rate.
      b. A few American countries have a high death rate.
   3. Most American countries have a relatively low population density.

As you can see from this example, the spatial pattern may order the parts in various ways; any one of the main points may be put first, second, or third. You are free to present them in the order that will best meet your purpose with a particular audience.

Topical pattern   The topical pattern groups ideas according to some classification of natural or conventional parts. If you wanted to discuss the disadvantages of the various methods of deterring population growth, you could use a topical pattern.

A. Deterring population growth by contraception has disadvantages.
   1. It is too expensive for many groups.
   2. It requires voluntary cooperation.
B. Deterring population growth by sterilization has disadvantages.
   1. Most methods are irrevocable.
   2. It requires voluntary cooperation.
   3. It can be used selectively if a compulsory program is adopted.
C. Deterring population growth by abortion has disadvantages.
   1. It violates the religious principles of many.
   2. It can be dangerous to the mother unless performed early in pregnancy.
   3. It uses medical personnel needed for other purposes.
   4. It uses medical facilities needed for other purposes.
   5. It uses medical services needed for other purposes.
D. Deterring population growth by infanticide has disadvantages.
   1. It is repugnant to humanitarian ideals.
   2. It would brutalize the people.
E. Deterring population growth by euthanasia has disadvantages.
   1. It is repugnant to humanitarian ideals.
   2. It would brutalize the people.

In most cases the topical pattern is more effective if the number of topics in the body of the speech exhausts the divisions of the subject. One of the advantages of the topical pattern, however, is that you may develop in a speech only a few selected topics from a longer list. It permits you to avoid discussion of areas of the subject that you deem irrelevant and insignificant for you, the audience, or the occasion. In the preceding example, you might omit D and E, since infanticide and euthanasia are not commonly suggested methods of deterring population growth. An important consideration is that the principle for determining the topics must be consistent. In other words, points A, B, and C can't discuss methods of deterring population growth while points D and E discuss methods of getting people to accept controls on population growth.

Causal pattern The causal pattern organizes materials according to their cause-and-effect relationship. A causal relationship may be concerned with discussing why a particular thing occurred, that is, the factors that caused a particular effect. This is an effect-to-cause relationship. Looking at the factors that have contributed to population growth gives an effect-to-cause pattern.

A. A lowered death rate has contributed to population growth.
   1. Advances in medical science helped to produce a lowered death rate.
   2. The advent of industrialization helped to produce a lowered death rate.
   3. Improvements in the physical environments helped to produce a lowered death rate.
B. Increasing birth rates have contributed to population growth.
   1. Early marriages have increased the birth rates.
   2. More women living through a greater proportion of their child-bearing years has increased the birth rates.
C. An increased food supply has contributed to population growth.
   1. The development of agriculture made possible a greater food supply.
   2. Technological developments increased the food supply.
   3. Machine production made possible an increased food supply.

A causal relationship may be concerned with a discussion of the results or predicted results of a particular factor. This is known as a cause-to-effect relationship. Consideration of the problems arising from population growth gives a cause-to-effect pattern.

A. Population growth retards economic advances.
   1. Population growth depletes savings.
   2. Population growth decreases capital formation.
   3. Population growth hampers investment.
B. Population growth hinders social development.
   1. Population growth increases the percentage of dependent children.
   2. Population growth strains medical services.
   3. Population growth results in inadequate funds for development of transportation.
   4. Population growth results in inadequate funds for the development of communication facilities.
   5. Population growth results in inadequate funds for education.
   6. Population growth results in inadequate funds for recreational facilities.

Before proceeding to the next pattern of organization, it should be pointed out that all symbols of the same type in an outline must use the same pattern. If A and B are parts of a topical analysis, then C and D must also be of the same topical analysis. If 1 and 2 under A are of a time sequence analysis, then 3 and 4 must be of a time sequence analysis.

There is a simple method to help you be sure you're following the same principle in assembling the materials. Assume you have a helper who has the outline of your points, while you have the supporting materials to be fitted into their appropriate places in the outline. To determine where each piece of information goes, the helper will ask a question that will be different for each pattern of organization. If a chronological pattern of organization is being used, the question will be—*when* did it happen? For a spatial pattern, the question will be—*where* is it located? For a topical pattern, the question may take several forms—*what* is it? *which* is it? *how* did it happen? For a causal pattern, the question will be—*why* did it happen? If more than one of these questions can be asked to locate materials under several points headed by similar symbols, you know you have mixed two different patterns of organization.

Problem-solution pattern In the problem-solution pattern you discuss a problem facing a particular group of people, then advocate what you think is the most workable solution to that problem. This can be an effective method of organizing a persuasive speech. Beginning with an analysis of the problem gives listeners the framework from which you arrived at your conclusions. It also indicates that you have made a careful study of the situation and have based your position on an objective, rational analysis. The outline of a speech using the problem-solution pattern might resemble the following:

A. Problem
   1. Historical background of problem.
   2. Nature of problem.
   3. Causes of problem.
   4. Effects of problem.
B. Solution
   1. Explanation of solution.
   2. Explanation of how solution eliminates problem.
   3. Explanation of practicability of solution.
   4. Explanation of advantages of solution.

In a given speech, you might cover only a few of the subtopics in this outline. If your audience has had long experience with the problem, there will be no need to discuss the historical background. In some instances, it might be impossible to isolate specific causes of a problem; obviously, then, you can't discuss them. You must weigh all factors and decide which of these subtopics can and should be included in any particular speech. Although common sense tells us that the order of problem-solution would be preferable to solution-problem, experimental data confirmed it.[23]

Motivated sequence Developed by Alan H. Monroe,[24] and best suited for persuasive speaking, the motivated sequence has five main divisions: *attention, need, satisfaction, visualization,* and *action.* Monroe's motivated sequence is a variant of the problem-solution pattern with the *need* step presenting the problem and the *satisfaction* step developing the solution.

The *attention* step is self-explanatory; it simply involves doing something appropriate to get the favorable attention of the listeners directed to your topic. It is in reality the introduction of the speech, and suggestions for purposes and types of introductions can be found in chapter 14. The *need* step describes the problem either by discussing evils in the present system that need to be eliminated or by showing that the present system should be retained. The *satisfaction* step in a persuasive speech offers a plan that will eliminate the evils presented in the need. The *visualization* step describes the conditions that will prevail once the plan is instituted and the evils of the present system have been abolished. This allows listeners to perceive themselves enjoying the satisfaction of doing, believing, or feeling what you are advocating. The *action* step shows what specific acts should be taken to implement the plan offered in the satisfaction step and requests listeners' approval. It is the conclusion of the speech. I don't recommend the motivated sequence for an informative speech.

The motivated sequence is an excellent pattern of organization for a persuasive speech. Its progression involves the listeners psychologically and moves them naturally to the final phase calling for action. Following is an outline of a speech using the motivated sequence.

A. [*attention*] People are the world's most important product. Planet Earth now has over 5 billion people living on it.
B. [*need*] Overpopulation leads to problems in the world.

1. Population growth has caused food deficits in the world.
   a. Many countries cannot produce sufficient food for their citizens.
   b. Other countries are not always able to make up the deficits.
2. Population growth has created social problems.
   a. Many overpopulated countries have crime problems.
   b. Many overpopulated countries have housing problems.
   c. Many overpopulated countries have health problems.

C. [*satisfaction*] A decrease in birth rate can help solve the problems of overpopulation.
   1. Population growth can be reduced by a decrease in the birth rate.
      a. The United States has brought population growth to almost a zero growth level.
      b. Canada has brought population growth to almost a zero growth level.
      c. Most European countries have brought population growth to almost a zero growth level.
   2. The highly overpopulated nations need to adopt birth control measures.
      a. India needs to curtail the birth rate.
      b. Many African nations need to curtail the birth rate.
      c. Many Asian nations need to curtail the birth rate.

D. [*visualization*] Imagine a world where population growth is curtailed.
   1. With a decrease in population growth, the world can produce sufficient food to eliminate hunger.
   2. With a decrease in population growth, many of the social problems of overpopulated nations can be reduced.

E. [*action*] The time to act is now.
   1. The UN should adopt a worldwide plan for decreasing population growth.
   2. The plan should be financed by a proportional tax levied on all nations.

Transitions

Organization may exist in your mind and may even have been transferred to paper in the form of a preparation outline of your speech, but to be effective that organization must be clear to those who hear the speech. Transitional devices can be used to give unity and coherence to the ideas, to give a sense of movement to the speech, and to emphasize important ideas.

An effective transitional technique is to provide signposts to guide listeners through the ideas. Number main points: "My first point is. . . ." "A second option is. . . ." "Third, let's consider. . . ." The main points can be labeled: "The economic consequences of this program. . . ." "Let's look at the social effects of this proposal. . . ." "This analysis would be deficient if it didn't also discuss the political ramifications."

Give main points a more striking impact by phrasing them in parallel form: "When government officials are corrupt, the efficiency of the government is diminished. . . . When government officials are corrupt, the confidence of the citizens in their government is destroyed. . . . When government officials are corrupt, the moral fiber of society is subverted." Speakers are frequently heard introducing main points with "another reason," "another factor." Avoid the use of "another" to introduce main points: it lacks both the movement and specificity provided by numbers or labels. Subpoints can be numbered or labeled, but different terms should be used to designate main points and subpoints. Otherwise, listeners may become confused trying to find their way among the various ideas.

Almost as bad as unclear organization is organization so stark as to seem skeletal, mechanical, or artificial. To overcome this problem, use transitional words and phrases to make ideas and supporting materials flow easily from one to another. Single words can readily serve as transitional elements: *therefore, nevertheless, furthermore, since, although, however, moreover, consequently, finally, also.* Avoid overuse of these terms. Be especially sensitive to the tendency to overuse "also." Phrases and sentences can be used as transitional bridges from one segment to another: "More than that," "In addition to," "On the other hand," "As a result of this analysis," "Now that we have seen the causes of this problem, we can next look at the consequences," "The economic features, which we have just examined, have a direct bearing upon the social impact of this problem." A thought-provoking transitional method is the rhetorical question: "What do the political ramifications of this proposal have to do with us?" "How will this problem affect us in the next ten years?" "What can we do to prevent the recurrence of these social ills?" These questions cause listeners to begin to think along the lines you desire. Internal summaries give an opportunity to signal the end of one unit, as well as to focus listeners' attention on the main thoughts just developed: "Economically we have seen that this proposal will affect our balance of payments in international trade adversely and will necessitate an increase in deficit spending in domestic affairs. Now let's examine the social impact of this proposal on the nation."

Use variety in transitions. Avoid repetitious transitions. They are self-defeating because they call attention to themselves, and so lose the ability to unify, emphasize, or give a sense of movement to the ideas.

The Preparation Outline

The preparation outline is an important aid. It enables you to plan the major parts of a speech and to check the logical relationship of ideas and supporting materials. Until you have assigned outline symbols to the various parts and ideas, it's frequently difficult to detect logical deficiencies.

The preparation outline is not necessarily—and generally is not—the complete speech, or the speech as it will be delivered. It may or may not include the transitions you use. It may or may not include internal summaries. It generally won't include restatements of ideas or evidence. It should be viewed as little more than the skeleton of the speech, which will be fleshed out when you actually communicate with listeners.

Not only is the preparation outline not the finished speech, it is also not a straitjacket binding your efforts to what is in the outline. Adapt the material in the outline to the response of the particular listeners. As you develop point one of the speech, you may decide it would be more effective to present the planned third point next rather than the one you had put in the outline as the second one. Then you may introduce that second point as the third one, or decide that this audience is not ready for that second point and so omit it altogether. Supporting materials may be handled differently. Testimony quoted verbatim in the preparation outline may be paraphrased in the speech.

Even though the preparation outline isn't the complete speech, it should contain all the ideas and supporting materials to be included in the speech. Unless they're all included, errors in analysis may not be detected. But keep in mind, all materials in the outline don't have to be used in the speech.

The preparation outline shouldn't be confused with notes to be taken to the communicative situation. These two aids exist for different purposes. The preparation outline is to logically analyze all ideas and supporting materials involved in the speech. Notes taken to the lectern are intended to remind you of key ideas and supporting materials. Such notes may be unintelligible to anyone but you. The preparation outline, however, should be clear to others.

Following are some suggestions that may make the production of the preparation outline easier and more beneficial.

1. The outline should have four parts: *introduction, purpose sentence, body,* and *conclusion.* If a *preview* is to be used, it may or may not be included in the outline.
2. These parts should be numbered in sequence: I, II, III, IV. This will continually remind you that these are not independent parts, but are interrelated units of a totality—the entity we call a speech.
3. A consistent set of symbols should be used to represent each part.
   a. Roman numerals usually represent the major parts.
   b. Capital letters indicate the main ideas of each part.
   c. Arabic numerals signify the subpoints of main ideas.
   d. Lowercase letters identify divisions of the subpoints.
   Most outlines won't go beyond this level of division, but if it is necessary to do so, Arabic numerals in parentheses can be used next, followed by lowercase letters in parentheses. Beyond that you can make up your own system!
4. Each succeeding level of symbols should be indented from the previous level:

   I.
     A.
        1.
        2.
     B.
   II.

   This permits you, or anyone else, to perceive at a glance the relationships between the various parts of the outline.

5. Complete sentences should be used for all *main points*. Since the main points are such vital parts of the speech, this ensures that you have spent some time in phrasing them clearly and concisely.
6. The introduction and conclusion may be either written out completely or outlined.
7. Put only one idea after each symbol, or great confusion can result. When two ideas are placed after one symbol, the outline can't demonstrate which of the succeeding subpoints supports each idea. The outline, therefore, will have failed in one of its most important purposes—demonstrating logical relationships.
8. If transitions and summaries are included in the outline, they should be labeled as such. To assign them a symbol destroys the logical framework of the outline.

Many scholars caution that no head in an outline should be supported by only one subhead. This principle doesn't apply, however, when symbols are used to indicate evidence. Some avoid the problem by not using outline symbols before evidence. I prefer the use of symbols, however, because they indicate the relationship of the evidence to the point it supports. Since there are times when only one piece of evidence is necessary or desirable, the speech preparation outline will have only one subhead under some heads.

I. Introduction   **A Sample Outline**
"Since the late 1960s, and especially since the 'oil crisis' of 1973, coal . . . has once more moved onto center stage of the energy scene. Projections of long-term availability and costs of alternative fossil fuels, and better appreciation of technical options for interchanging gas, oil, and coal, have not only led to a consensus that coal will again become an increasingly important component of future energy supplies, but also persuaded many that it will become a preeminent primary energy resource before the end of the century." N. Berkowitz, *An Introduction to Coal Technology* (New York: Academic Press, 1979), p. xi.

II. Purpose Sentence
Today, I want to explain why coal is an important source of future energy in the U.S.

III. Preview
Coal is important for three reasons: (1) It is abundant in the U.S. (2) It can be converted to other usable forms. (3) It would provide economic advantages to the U.S.

IV. Body
   A. Coal is abundant in the U.S.
      1. "Coal is the most abundant energy resource in the U.S. . . . At current demand levels, we have enough coal reserves to last at least 300 years and, at . . . projected 1985 production levels . . . coal reserves could last 150 or more years." *U.S. Energy Demand and Supply 1976–1985: Limited Options, Unlimited Constraints,* March 1978, p. 49.

2. " . . . estimates of coal resources published by the U.S. Geological Survey established a resource base of 3.2 trillion tons, about half of which . . . is usually considered recoverable." James E. McNulty and Clayton G. Bell, "Coal Reserves—Estimates," *Energy Technology Handbook.* 1977, 1–35.

3. "The U.S. Bureau of Mines estimates that 437 billion tons are in deposits that are mineable with current technology at today's prices." W. R. Hibbard, Jr., "Policies and Constraints for Major Expansion of U.S. Coal Production and Utilization," *Annual Review of Energy* 4 (1979):149.

4. An international group, The Workshop on Alternative Energy Strategies, concluded: "Coal has the potential to contribute substantially to future energy supplies. Coal reserves are abundant, but taking advantage of them requires an active program of development by both producers and consumers." James Lust and Lester Lave, "Review of Scenarios of Future U.S. Energy Use," *Annual Review of Energy* 4 (1979):529.

B. Coal can be converted to other usable forms.

1. ". . . there is no technical barrier to immediate gasification of coal or production of methanol from coal." J. R. Bowden, "Prospects for Coal as a Direct Fuel and Its Potential through Application of Liquefaction and Gasification Technology," *Energy Sources—An Interdisciplinary International Journal of Science and Technology* (1976):6.

2. "The Navy has actually run some ships on synthetic fuel created from coal; they found that some adjustments were required but that it could be done." *The National Energy Plan Options under Assumptions of National Security Threat,* Congressional Research Service, Library of Congress for the Subcommittee on Energy and Power, April 1978, p. 44.

3. Airplanes can use fuel from coal. "In 1976 a T-63 engine was operated on JP–5 fuel derived from coal. Engine performance for this test . . . was equivalent to that using JP–5 refined from crude oil." *National Energy Plan Options,* p. 45.

4. Coal "can be gasified to produce a low Btu gas or subsequently modified to synthetic natural gas. Alternatively, the low Btu gas can be improved through removal of the nitrogen to a medium Btu gas, believed by many to be the most suitable and economic form as a feedstock to the chemical industry." Charles Simeons, *Coal: Its Role in Tomorrow's Technology* (New York: Pergamon Press, 1978), p. 142.

C. The greater use of coal would provide economic advantages for the U.S.

1. Coal can reduce the balance of payments.

a. Oil imports send billions of dollars out of the U.S.

        (1) Currently we are importing 45 percent of the oil we use. *Birmingham Post-Herald,* February 8, 1980.

        (2) It is estimated that imported oil cost the U.S. $74 billion in 1979. *Wall Street Journal,* December 21, 1979.

        (3) The outflow of this huge sum of money has an adverse effect on the U.S.

            (a) It contributes significantly to a deficit in our balance of payments, which fuels inflation.

            (b) Our balance of payments deficit for 1979 was approximately $23.5 billion. *Wall Street Journal,* December 31, 1979.

    b. The substitution of coal for oil in the generation of electricity would help to decrease the amount of oil to be imported.

        (1) Coal can be substituted for oil in producing electricity. Harvey Brooks and Jack M. Hollander, "United States Energy Alternatives to 2010 and Beyond: The Conaes Study," *Annual Review of Energy* 4 (1979):32–33.

        (2) "If all public utility boilers were to convert to coal . . . we could save 1.8 million barrels a day; if every industrial boiler converted to coal, we could save more than 3.5 million barrels a day. These two steps alone could save more than half of the oil we now import." Armand Hammer, "Our Dependence on Foreign Imports," *Vital Speeches of the Day* 46 (1979):47.

  2. Increased use of coal would create new jobs.

    a. "U.S. mines are producing more than 750 million tons of coal a year. But they could probably be bringing out 100 millions ton more—if the coal could be used." Charles J. Dibona, "U.S. Energy," *Vital Speeches of the Day* 46 (1979):106.

    b. " . . . it would help to revitalize our domestic coal industry and help to put some thirteen thousand unemployed coal miners back to work and create many thousands of new jobs." Armand Hammer, "Our Dependence on Foreign Imports," *Vital Speeches of the Day* 46 (1979):48.

V. Conclusion

The Workshop on Alternative Energy Statistics, an international study, concluded: "The supply of oil will fail to meet increasing demand before the year 2000, most probably between 1985 and 1995, even if energy prices rise 50 percent above current levels in real terms. Additional constraints on oil production will hasten this shortage, thereby reducing the time available for action on alternatives." Simeons, *Coal,* p. 528. Coal is a realistic alternative energy source for the U.S. because coal is abundant in the U.S., it can be converted to other usable forms, and its use would provide economic advantages.

"Since the late 1960s, and especially since the 'oil crisis' of 1973, coal . . . has once more moved onto center stage of the energy scene. Projections of long-term availability and costs of alternative fossil fuels, and better appreciation of technical options for interchanging gas, oil, and coal, have not only led to a consensus that coal will again become an increasingly important component of future energy supplies, but also persuaded many that it will become a preeminent primary energy resource before the end of the century." That is the conclusion of Professor Berkowitz of the University of Alberta.

I believe Professor Berkowitz is correct in his analysis, and today I want to explain three reasons coal will be an important future source of energy in the U.S.

Coal will be important because: (1) Coal is abundant in the U.S. (2) Coal can be converted to other usable forms. (3) The use of coal would provide economic advantages to the U.S. Because of these factors, the U.S. will be able to decrease its dependence on foreign oil and improve its economic status at home and abroad. Now, let's consider each of these reasons.

First, the U.S. has large supplies of coal. Concluding that, "Coal is the most abundant energy resource in the U.S.," a congressional study projected that coal will last "at least 300 years" at the current level of use. At expected demands in 1985, we have enough coal to last "150 or more years." The U.S. Geological Survey estimates we have "3.2 trillion tons" of coal resources. About half "is usually considered recoverable."

Even more optimistically, Dr. W. R. Hibbard, University Distinguished Professor of Engineering at Virginia Tech, reports that "437 billion tons can be mined by today's methods at today's prices." Even an international group, the Workshop on Alternative Energy Strategies, believes that coal can become an important future energy source if both producers and consumers undertake an active program of development and use in order to take advantage of the abundant coal reserves.

It seems clear, therefore, that the U.S. has ample supplies of coal, that the coal is recoverable, and that it can play an important role in meeting the energy needs of this country. Nevertheless, both consumers and producers will have to adopt more aggressive policies with respect to coal if its potential as an energy source is to be realized.

A second reason that coal is an important source of future energy in the U.S. is that it can be converted to other usable forms. J. R. Bowden, Vice President of Conoco Coal Development Co., argues that "there is no technical barrier to immediate gasification of coal or production of methanol from coal." Supporting that contention are some specific examples of the use of coal-converted fuels. A congressional study revealed that, though some adjustments were necessary, some Navy ships have operated on synthetic fuel made from coal. The same study also disclosed that one type of fuel made from coal ran an airplane jet engine as efficiently as the same type of fuel made from crude oil.

Not only can coal be converted to a liquid fuel, but Charles Simeons, a British industrial consultant and author of the book, *Coal: Its Role in Tomorrow's Technology,* claims that coal can be converted to different forms of gas, one of which can be used by the chemical industry to create other products.

Thus, by testimony and example we have evidence that coal can be converted to other usable forms of energy.

A third reason that coal is an important source of future energy in the U.S. is that it would provide economic advantages. Increased use of coal would keep billions of dollars in the U.S. Currently, we are importing 45 percent of the oil we use. The *Wall Street Journal* of December 21, 1979, estimated that imported oil cost us $74 billion in 1979. The outflow of this huge sum of money fuels inflation because it contributes significantly to a deficit in our balance of payments. The *Wall Street Journal* reported on December 31, 1979, that our balance of payments deficit for 1979 was $23.5 billion. In other words, if we could have cut our oil imports by one-third in 1979, we would have had no deficit in our balance of payments. Think of the effect that would have had on inflation in this country.

The substitution of coal for oil in the generation of electricity would help to decrease the amount of oil to be imported. Professors Harvey Brooks of Harvard University and Jack Hollander of the University of California contend that coal is a practicable substitute for oil in producing electricity. Armand Hammer, chairman of Occidental Petroleum Corporation, has pointed out that "If all public utility boilers were to convert to coal . . . we could save 1.8 million barrels a day." He goes on to say that "if every industrial boiler converted to coal, we could save more than 3.5 million barrels a day." As a result of these two steps alone, says Mr. Hammer, we "could save more than half of the oil we now import." Thus, we could not only eliminate our balance of payments deficit, we could create a balance of payments surplus.

Not only would an increased use of coal have a positive impact on our balance of payments, it would also provide economic advantages by creating new jobs. Charles J. Dibona, president of the American Petroleum Institute, says that though we "are producing more than 750 million tons of coal a year," we "could probably be bringing out 100 million tons more—if the coal could be used." Mr. Hammer believes that increased use of coal "would help . . . our domestic coal industry" by putting "some thirteen thousand unemployed coal miners back to work and" creating "many thousands of new jobs."

In this speech I have explained three reasons that coal is an important source of future energy in the U.S. The Workshop on Alternative Energy Strategies has concluded that "The supply of oil will fail to meet increasing demand before the year 2000, most probably between 1985 and 1995, even if energy prices rise 50 percent above current levels in real terms. Additional constraints on oil production will hasten this shortage, thereby reducing the time available for action on alternatives."

We need not despair about our energy future, however; we only need to take positive action. Coal is a realistic alternative energy source for the U.S. because it is abundant, it can be converted to other usable forms, and its use would provide significant economic advantages.

Differences between Sample Outline and the Speech as Presented

It is obvious there are a number of significant differences between the sample outline and the speech as presented. You shouldn't conclude, however, that all these differences must always exist, or that these are all the differences that may occur. This example is just to give you an idea of the relationship between a preparation outline and the speech as presented. Another factor you must keep in mind is that there is no adaptation in this speech to a particular audience. It is written for a general audience. In presenting it to a specific audience, however, adaptation would be made wherever appropriate. In this example, the following differences may be noted:

1. The outline has no transitional words or phrases; the speech does.
2. The outline has no internal summaries; the speech does. Notice that the summary at the end of point 1 is longer and more detailed because point 1 is more complex than points 2 and 3. Point 2 has only a brief one-sentence summary because the point itself is easily understood and remembered. There is no summary after point 3 because the conclusion includes a summary of the three main points.
3. The outline has detailed bibliographical information for the evidence used; the speech omits much of the bibliographical data and focuses instead on the sources and their qualifications. If someone asked you about some of your information after the speech, you would have the complete bibliographical information in the preparation outline.
4. The symbols in the outline identify the main points; the speech converts those symbols to verbal forms, such as "the first reason."
5. The outline cites evidence in the precise form in which it appears in the original source; the speech paraphrases much of the evidence and presents some in abbreviated quotations. This has two advantages: (a) It presents the evidence in the words of the speaker. (b) It eliminates the need for excessive reliance on note cards in the presentation of the speech.

Summary

Organization, which some evidence reveals as more important than content, is valuable for four reasons: (1) it significantly increases the listener's comprehension of the information; (2) it affects your ethos; (3) it aids in shifting the attitudes of listeners; and (4) it prevents some listeners from becoming frustrated.

Organizing a speech involves three processes: selecting the materials to be used in a particular speech, developing the entity we call a speech, and ordering the main ideas in the body of a speech.

The entity we call a speech usually has four divisions: an introduction, a purpose sentence, a body, and a conclusion. Not infrequently, a fifth optional part, a preview, is also included.

The purpose sentence, telling the audience specifically and explicitly what you want them to focus on in this particular speech, has three values: it provides necessary aural cues for the listener, it establishes the set of the listeners, and it aids you in preparing and delivering your speech. An effective purpose sentence can be stated in various ways.

The main ideas in the body of a speech may be ordered according to stock patterns (chronological, spatial, topical, causal, problem-solution, or motivated sequence). Transitional devices help to make the organization of a speech clear to the listeners by giving unity and coherence to the ideas, conveying a sense of movement to the speech, and emphasizing important ideas.

Exercises

1. Attend an intercollegiate debate. Write a critique of the organization of the speeches. How did it affect the credibility of the debaters?
2. Attend a public lecture on campus. Discuss the speaker's organization. What did this speaker do that made it easier for the listener? What could he or she have done? How did the organization affect the credibility of the ideas?

Notes

1. K. B. Olson, "Content and Form in Public Address: An Analysis of the Relative Influence of the Major Components upon the Listener," M. A. thesis, University of the Pacific, Calif., 1965.
2. E. Thompson, "An Experimental Investigation of the Relative Effectiveness of Organization Structure in Oral Communication," *Southern Speech Journal* 26 (1960):59–69.
3. D. K. Darnell, "The Relation between Sentence Order and Comprehension," *Speech Monographs* 30 (1963):97–100.
4. J. A. Kulgren, "The Effects of Organization upon the Comprehension of a Persuasive-Type Speech," M. A. thesis, Fresno State College, Calif., 1960.
5. C. Spicer and R. E. Bassett, "The Effect of Organization on Learning from an Informative Message," *Southern Speech Communication Journal* 41 (1976):298.
6. F. R. Miller, "An Experiment to Determine the Effect Organization Has on the Immediate and Delayed Recall of Information," M. A. thesis, Miami University, Ohio, 1966.
7. Thompson, "An Experimental Investigation."
8. J. P. Parker, "Some Organizational Variables and Their Effect upon Comprehension," *Journal of Communication* 12 (1962):27–32.

9. D. L. Thistlethwaite, H. de Haan, and J. Kemenetzky, "The Effects of 'Directive' and 'Nondirective' Communication Procedures on Attitudes," *Journal of Abnormal and Social Psychology* 51 (1955):107–13.

10. H. Sharp, Jr., and T. McClung, "Effect of Organization on the Speaker's Ethos," *Speech Monographs* 33 (1966):182–84.

11. E. E. Baker, "The Immediate Effects of Perceived Speaker Disorganization on Speaker Credibility and Audience Attitude Change in Persuasive Speaking," *Western Speech Journal* 29 (1965):148–61.

12. J. C. McCroskey and R. S. Mehrley, "The Effects of Disorganization and Nonfluency on Attitude Change and Source Credibility," *Speech Monographs* 36 (1969):13–21.

13. R. G. Smith, "An Experimental Study of the Effects of Speech Organization upon Attitudes of College Students," *Speech Monographs* 18 (1951):292.

14. A. R. Cohen, E. Stotland, and D. M. Wolfe, "An Experimental Investigation of Need for Cognition," *Journal of Abnormal and Social Psychology* 51 (1955):291–94.

15. P. L. Harriman, *Handbook of Psychological Terms* (Paterson, N.J.: Littlefield, Adams & Co., 1959), p. 168.

16. E. Siipola, "A Group Study of Some Effects of Preparatory Sets," *Psychological Monographs* 46: no. 210 (1935).

17. F. J. Di Vesta and P. Bossart, "The Effects of Sets Induced by Labeling on the Modification of Attitudes," *Journal of Personality* 26 (1958):379–87. See also D. Sears and J. L. Freedman, "Effects of Expected Familiarity with Arguments upon Opinion Change and Selective Exposure," *Journal of Personality and Social Psychology* 2 (1965):420–26.

18. S. L. Tubbs, "Explicit versus Implicit Conclusions and Audience Commitment," *Speech Monographs* 35 (1968):14–19.

19. S. L. Tubbs, "An Experimental Study of an Explicit versus an Implicit Conclusion in a Persuasive Speech, and Degree of Commitment in the Audience," M. A. thesis, Bowling Green State University, Ohio, 1966.

20. D. L. Thistlethwaite, J. Kemenetzky, and H. Schmidt, "Factors Influencing Attitude Change through Refutative Communications," *Speech Monographs* 23 (1956):14–25.

21. E. Cooper and H. Dinerman, "Analysis of the Film 'Don't Be a Sucker': A Study in Communication," *Public Opinion Quarterly* 15 (1951):243–64.

22. J. E. Baird, Jr., "The Effects of Speech Summaries upon Audience Comprehension of Expository Speeches of Varying Quality and Complexity," *Central States Speech Journal* 25 (1974):124–25.

23. C. I. Hovland, *Order of Presentation in Persuasion* (New Haven: Yale University Press, 1961), p. 135.

24. A. H. Monroe and D. Ehninger, *Principles and Types of Speeches* (Glenview, Ill.: Scott, Foresman & Co., 1967), pp. 264–89.

CHAPTER 14

Developing Introductions and Conclusions

Opening and closing remarks are the crucial points of a speech. In the beginning listeners form their initial judgment of the speaker; in the ending they obtain their final impression. If the introduction creates a poor image, the listeners may become prejudiced toward the ideas presented in the body of the speech. If the conclusion leaves a bad final impression, it may nullify the impact of the ideas presented earlier. Most speakers can't afford to communicate a bad impression either at the beginning or end of their speech. For this reason, introductions and conclusions should be prepared with great care and presented well.

When Aristotle said an introduction and conclusion were needed in a speech because of the sorry nature of audiences, he was not so much denigrating humankind as acknowledging that the communicative situation makes certain demands on listeners that require adjustments and adaptations on the part of the speaker. This chapter considers the nature of introductions and conclusions and the ways in which they can be used.

Introductions

Three concerns should dominate the preparation of an introduction for a speech: Will the introduction (1) attract the attention of the listeners; (2) either improve your ethos with the listeners or at least not damage the ethos you already have; and (3) assist the listeners in beginning to think about the topic you're going to develop in this particular speech?

An important objective of the introduction is to attract the listeners' attention. When you arrive at the lectern, you're not faced with a group of automatons whose attention you obtain by punching a button. Many members of the audience will be engaged in other activities as you begin your speech. Some will be daydreaming; some will be worrying about problems; some will be musing over recent or anticipated experiences; some will be actively engaged in conversations with their neighbors. These activities don't end abruptly when you begin to talk. Those listeners engaged in other thought processes only gradually become aware of the speaker. A member of the audience carrying on a conversation rarely stops in the middle of a sentence. Generally he finishes his sentence and may even complete the thought. Not infrequently, his neighbor replies before they both settle down to listen to the speaker. Obviously, then, you need to do something that will attract the attention of all listeners, something that will make your listeners consider it more important to listen to you than to do other things. Whatever you do must be something that is not vital to the development of the specific purpose of the speech, because some of the hearers are going to miss at least part of it. This is the reason you shouldn't normally begin with the purpose sentence. Only when the audience's attention is already fixed on you or on the subject can the speech be opened with the purpose; in such situations the speech needs no introduction.

The introduction should maintain or enhance your ethos. If you bring high ethos to the occasion, avoid doing anything in the introduction that will decrease it. Statements that sound rash or unwise will offend the listeners or cause them to think you can't provide valid information and advice. If your ethos is low or neutral, avoid doing anything that will further damage your image. Instead, do something that will enhance your ethos.

We have seen in chapter 6 that five major sources of ethos are competence, trustworthiness, similarity, attraction, and sincerity. So if you want to increase your ethos, attempt to establish one or more of these qualities for yourself. You can call attention to your qualifications, your concern for the best interests of the listeners, your lack of self-interest, attributes you hold in common with the listeners, personal characteristics that will make you attractive to the listeners, or your sincerity.

Finally, the introduction should cause listeners to think about the topic you're going to develop in the speech. This places some limitations on what you can do to attract the attention of the listeners or what you can do to enhance your ethos. You may have a humorous anecdote that is a proven attention-getter, but if it's irrelevant to the topic, you can't use it. Whatever you do to achieve the other purposes of the introduction must enable the listener to make a smooth transition to the purpose sentence and then to the body of the speech.

The length of an introduction will depend on several factors. Normally an introduction constitutes only about 10 percent of the total speech; in some instances it might be as little as 1 percent and in others as much as 38 percent.[1] If your ethos is low and the topic is an unfamiliar one, you might have to spend nearly a third of the speech on the introduction. In some cases, you might develop background material before you get to your main purpose; necessitating spending a longer time on the introduction. On the other hand, if you have high ethos and the topic is important to the listeners, you might lose the attention of the audience by spending too much time in the introduction. A few brief statements may suffice to get to your purpose sentence. In some rare instances, an introduction might even be detrimental. If the preceding speakers have discussed the topic of your speech, and the listeners are deeply involved in that discussion, you may want to begin immediately with your purpose sentence; to do otherwise may cause the listeners' attention to decline.

Generally any apology should be avoided in the introduction. Don't tell the listeners that you "didn't have time" to make adequate preparation unless that is a clearly legitimate reason for not having prepared properly; that not only insults the hearers by indicating that you didn't esteem them highly, but also damages your ethos. Don't apologize for your ability as a speaker. Let the audience evaluate your efforts without prejudice. They might decide you're skilled and well prepared.

Don't prepare the introduction until you have phrased the purpose sentence and developed the body of the speech. Only then can you know exactly what you want to introduce and what method will best achieve it. If the introduction is prepared before the purpose is clearly formulated and the body developed, the result may be a speech that lacks purpose and significance because the body was suited to the introduction rather than vice versa. When the body of the speech has been completed, you know approximately what you're going to say and can choose an introduction that best prepares the listeners for your remarks.

A number of different types of introductions are available. In the following discussion, the different introductions will be organized by type instead of by purpose, since a good introduction may accomplish the three purposes of attracting your listeners' attention, improving or at least not damaging your ethos, and helping your listeners start to think about your speech topic.

Begin with Reference to the Audience

You may find that a reference to the listeners and their interests will be an effective way to achieve your purpose. Observe how Thomas K. Hearn, Jr., president of Wake Forest University, attempted to make football coaches aware of their responsibilities and risks.

> Your profession—college football coaching—is at risk. Paradoxically, the risk arises from the very success and influence of college football. Successful people in your profession are being given generous doses of the three most dangerous and addictive drugs known: fame, wealth and power. Big time sports has made football coaches into entertainment celebrities. The question is whether the pursuit of the rewards of victory will destroy the comfortable houses your game has made for you. "Impossible" you say? You are one scandal away.[2]

Begin with Reference to the Subject

On some occasions the subject of your speech may be so vital and immediate to the listeners that you'll want to develop the introduction around a reference to that topic. Beginning with a reference to a subject should be used as an introduction only when your listeners have a strong interest in the topic. Fully aware of his listeners' concern for his topic, Lewis K. Uhler, President, National Tax Limitation Committee, moved quickly to his subject in a speech to the Heritage Foundation.

> We have reached a milestone in Federal fiscal irresponsibility: the cash debt of the United States now exceeds the total of the shares traded on U.S. stock exchanges. Think about that—if we were to sell all U.S. stock market traded stocks, which *Forbes* has calculated to have a current value of about $2.2 trillion, it wouldn't be enough to pay off the national debt. Other ways to put the national debt in perspective are these:
> —A family of four's share of the national debt is equal to a mortgage of nearly $40,000.
> —Interest *only* on that mortgage for a family of four amounts to *$60 per week!*
> And that's just the cash debt—unfunded liabilities are huge but impossible to calculate.[3]

In beginning his speech to the Kent State University faculty and students, Alton W. Whitehouse, Jr., chairman of the board of the Standard Oil Company of Ohio, referred to the occasion.

Begin with Reference to the Occasion

> Thank you for this chance to keynote Kent State's honors week events. We gather this week to recognize academic achievement. Oddly, the theme of these proceedings is the approach of 1984, the year George Orwell made a metaphor for totalitarianism. I say "oddly" because the central feature of Orwell's 1984 was the mass mind—whole populations thinking in state-imposed uniformity. Such uniformity strikes me as the antithesis of the individual intellectual excellence that we gather to honor this week, the excellence that René Descartes celebrated in saying, "I think, therefore I am."[4]

If you have qualifications that enhance your expertise, have had experiences that equip you to discuss the topic, or have had previous association with the audience or the topic, you may use a personal reference to introduce the speech. This particular introduction can be especially effective in building your ethos. Listen to this speaker:

Begin with Personal Reference

> It is a long way from the backwoods of Georgia, where I was born, to a speaker's platform on this beautiful campus. Since the invitation arrived nearly a year ago to speak here, I have looked forward with pleasure to giving

your Quinquennial chemistry celebration address . . . and to speak on the subject, "The Letter C No Longer Stands for Courage in Chemistry" . . . and as an old professor of mine loved to say, "There is a special hot place in hell reserved for those chemists who lack courage."

That place is not being held for the courageous Dr. John Shroyer, the distinguished chemist who was chairman of the Bradley Chemistry Department from 1940 to 1967, nor for Dr. Bhagat Singh who has been a profound teacher, administrator and helper of chemistry students at this university for over 40 years. There will be a special place in heaven for them . . . for they are chemists worthy of the title; they knew their task was to ascertain and teach the truth . . . minus any of the public relations nonsense that is so much a part of today's chemist jargon . . . and they did just that.[5]

Begin with a Startling Statement or Startling Analysis

A speech begun with a startling statement will often jerk the listeners to attention. For this reason it can be very effective. Unfortunately, after the use of a particularly startling statement, the rest of the speech may seem anticlimactic, never quite rising to the heights of the beginning. The listener then goes away feeling let down by a speech that would otherwise have seemed effective. The introduction that presents startling information or an unusual analysis can also be effective in attracting the attention of the listeners and has the advantage of being less stark in contrast with the rest of the speech.

There is one major finding that I wish to present in my remarks today: *our schools are producing a nation of economic illiterates!* Now if you don't believe me, then just go out and ask high school students some questions on basic economics and see how they respond. That's the type of study that I conducted with Dr. John Soper of John Carroll University. My conclusion is based on that research and related work.[6]

Begin with Examples

You can use examples to direct the listeners' attention to a principle or principles you plan to develop. The advantage of the example at the beginning is that it makes your idea more concrete and specific for your hearers.

Right now—as we meet in this Keynote Session of the National Urban League's Annual Conference—there's a ten-year-old child selling crack on Rosa Parks Boulevard here in Detroit.

Right now—there's a ten-year-old black child crawling into a makeshift bed in a shelter for the homeless in New York.

Right now—there are ten-year-old black kids going without dinner in Watts, on Chicago's South Side, in ghettos across the country.

Those kids are the reason for our existence. The Urban League Movement is here to provide advocacy, services and hope for America's poor and dispossessed.[7]

Begin with Humor

If you can cause listeners to laugh at the outset of your speech, it does much to develop rapport between you and the audience, especially if you can avoid "canned" humor. But even canned humor can be effective if it is presented effectively and is fresh to the listeners. Examine this speaker's humor:

Thank you very much. I'm reminded of a story from an early American Congress. General Smythe of Virginia and Henry Clay were members.

Smythe was a studious man, but was also a very long-winded speaker who annoyed his colleagues in the House with his prolonged speeches.

One day in particular he was being very tedious, and turning to Mr. Clay, said: "You, sir, speak for the present generation, but I speak for posterity." Clay, without smiling, retorted: "Yes, and you seem resolved to speak until the arrival of your audience."[8]

A speech begun with a quotation can attract attention because of the pleasing quality of the wording of the quotation itself, because of the reputation of its author, because of the timeliness or relevancy of the quotation, because of the humor of the quotation, or because of all or several of these.

U.S. Representative Richard A. Gephardt began his speech to The City Club of Cleveland with an anecdote that included a quotation that was humorous.

> Recently, I heard a story about George Bush being in a coma for three years and waking to find Dan Quayle standing at his bedside. Upon seeing the Vice-President, the President begins to ask a few questions.
>
> After asking how long he has been asleep he inquires about the state of the U.S. economy. To his surprise, Quayle tells him that the budget and trade deficits have been reduced to zero. Then, President Bush asks about inflation, which he figures must be at an all time high. Again, to his surprise, Quayle says that inflation is not a problem. Having his doubts, the President asks for specifics. "How much," he asks "does a first class stamp cost?" "Very reasonable," Quayle responds—"only 30 Yen."[9]

Providing at the outset of your speech a clear definition of the main idea of your speech can ensure that listeners understand what you are trying to say and don't quit listening because they fail to understand what you are trying to do.

Rafael D. Pagan, Jr., President, Pagan International, attempts to indicate the problems involved in trying to identify issues and challenges of the future.

> I am happy to be here once again this year with my colleagues and friends of the Public Affairs Council to discuss a subject to which I have given a great deal of thought—and upon which I have acted—over the years: the globalization of activism and its consequences for corporations.
>
> I would like to recall for you the story of Cassandra, daughter of the king of Troy. Cassandra was given the gift of prophecy by the god Apollo. Later, in a fit of anger, Apollo added a curse: people would disbelieve her when she prophesied coming events. When Cassandra happened to foresee the fall of Troy in a dream, no one believed her. Consequently her name has become synonomous with that of any person whose prescience is disbelieved. For obvious reasons Cassandra is the leading candidate for patron saint of issue managers.[10]

An effective type of introduction for both an experienced and an inexperienced speaker is to open with a justification for the speech. The justification may take several forms. It may explain (1) why you have elected to speak on this

Begin with a Quotation

Begin with a Definition

Begin with a Justification of the Speech

topic, (2) why you are qualified to speak on this topic, or (3) why the topic is important to the listeners.

Credibility is created more easily by this type of introduction because listeners are more interested in information that seems to touch them personally. Moreover, they more readily believe statements from a speaker qualified to speak on the topic. A word of warning, however—your qualifications must be presented in such a way that you don't appear to be bragging. The qualifications must appear to be an integral part of the total narrative, included to clarify other points. For example, a speaker who is going to discuss three basic first aid techniques that any person might use could begin his speech in the following manner:

> Last summer while working with the Henderson Rescue Squad, we were called to an accident on Interstate 85. In my five years of working with the Rescue Squad, I have never seen an accident as bad as that one. Four people were killed and three were seriously injured. Turning our attention to the injured, we were able, in a few minutes, to stop the severe bleeding of one victim, treat another for shock, and place a splint on the broken leg of another. Because of those measures, the victims were in better condition when they arrived at the hospital. The basic first aid techniques that we used are simple ones and can be used by anyone who understands them.

Notice how the information—five years of working with the Rescue Squad—which establishes the qualifications of the speaker on this topic is introduced indirectly and seems to be a natural part of the narrative.

Obviously, then, there are many effective methods to introduce a speech. It is clear also that not all introductions achieve equally well all three purposes of the introduction. Some will attract the attention of the listeners more effectively, some will enhance your ethos to a greater extent, some will start the listener thinking about the subject matter more easily. As a matter of fact, you won't always want these purposes achieved equally; it will frequently be more important to attain one more than the others.

Once the preparation of the introduction is completed, you can begin to think about how to conclude the speech. Whenever possible, you should return in the conclusion to a theme initiated in the introduction.

Conclusions

The primary purpose of the conclusion is to direct the attention of the listeners for the last time to the main purpose of the speech. Focus on your central idea by restating the purpose sentence, summarizing the main ideas, appealing for action or behavior consistent with the main purpose, presenting a quotation that expresses the main purpose eloquently or vividly, giving an illustration that exemplifies the central purpose, issuing a challenge to the listeners to think about or accept the main thought, or stating your intention to follow the ideas developed in the speech. If the conclusion is successful, listeners leave with the main purpose of the speech firmly fixed in their minds.

Second, leave the listeners with a favorable image of you. In most instances, you begin with high ethos, the speech either increases the ethos or does nothing to decrease it, so the conclusion simply has to avoid arousing any negative reactions. On other occasions, however, you may be forced to present ideas that will decrease your ethos with the audience. When this occurs, you must make a special effort in the conclusion to reestablish a favorable image in the minds of the listeners. Otherwise, your ideas may be rejected.

Third, give a sense of completeness to the speech, to avoid an abrupt ending that leaves listeners wondering if they heard all the speech. If you quit on your last main idea, you run a risk of leaving the listeners frustrated and dissatisfied by a feeling that the task was not completed. A conclusion gives the impression that there are no loose ends remaining; everything has been tied up in a nice neat bundle. You can often enhance this impression by returning in the conclusion to a theme or a reference developed in the introduction. In fact, one of the best ways to achieve this is to restate your purpose sentence and summarize your main ideas. The speech then appears to have come full circle. The listener leaves with a sense of completeness; the speech had a beginning, a middle, and an end.

Ordinarily the conclusion should be brief, generally no more than 5 percent of the total speaking time, and frequently even less than that.[11] Once you have finished the discussion of your ideas, move quickly through the conclusion.

A number of different methods of ending a speech are available. Some of the most frequently used ones will be discussed.

End with a Quotation

If you can find an effective statement of your main purpose authored by someone else, especially someone the listeners know and respect, you not only focus the minds of the listeners on the main theme, you add weight to it as well.

> And because what we do affects the lives of others . . . We may choose our own ethical course, but we cannot isolate the consequences of our choice.
> That's what the late, great American journalist, Walter Lippmann, was getting at when he described honorable conduct as "the hygiene of the spirit by which the good life becomes possible."
> In his inaugural address 36 years ago, Dwight D. Eisenhower said:
> "A people that values its privileges above its principles soon loses both."
> As you and I look toward the 1990s, is the needle of our moral compass fixed on principles . . . or privileges?
> How we set our compass determines whether we'll continue to wander in the wilderness, or find our way.[12]

End with a Challenge

One of the most frequently used conclusions is that which attempts to challenge the listeners in some way. The challenge differs from an appeal. Whereas the appeal asks the listeners for a behavioral commitment, the challenge attempts to stimulate listeners to a mental or spiritual commitment.

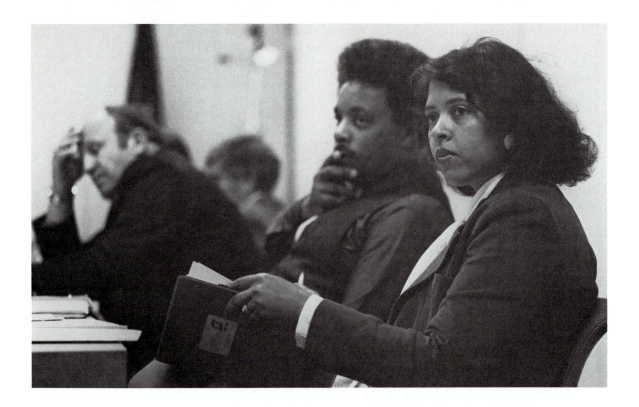

Regardless of your position on the issue—whether it's "too soon for policy" or "we can't afford to wait"—I think it's clear the greenhouse debate will force us to rethink our energy policies and options as we approach the 21st Century.

Mark Twain once said that everybody always talks about the weather—but nobody *does* anything about it.

The challenge we face in the years ahead is to use our collective knowledge to gain more understanding of the workings of our planet. Maybe then, and only then, will we actually be able to do something about climate change.

Virginia Power, and the entire electric utility industry, has a big stake in the outcome of any policy decisions that are made. For that reason, we intend to remain at the center of scientific understanding.

I urge you to stay tuned, stay alert and stay informed. Global warming will undoubtedly be one of the "hottest" issues around for some time to come.[13]

End with an Appeal   When you want the listeners to take some specific action, an effective conclusion is to specifically ask them to do whatever is desired. If the speech has been effectively organized, supported, and presented, they should be ready to act in the desired manner. Thomas K. Hearn, President of Wake Forest University, made a direct appeal to the members of the College Football Association.

It will be easy to disregard the remarks of this president as soft-headed, impractical and idealistic. After all, Wake Forest is a small, private school and hardly a football power—yet. To disregard this message, whoever the messenger, will be an error. Something of the spirit of rectitude in sport I have described underlies the broad public support which the game of football enjoys. Failure to see that spirit embodied in coaches, players and teams will result in the loss of that public support.

Though it is not an apt comparison, consider the fate of professional tennis. The decline in its popularity, I am sure, is related directly to the outrageous behavior of the players, especially Americans, which contradicts a conception of the game central to its appeal. If football or basketball become scenes of violence—on or off the field—if sports deprive young men of the education they are promised by your recruitment—if you humiliate or destroy the self-respect of those you are charged to improve by your example and wisdom, those scattered voices calling for the abolition of big time athletics from universities will be joined by others, including many university trustees, presidents and powerful national organizations which control the distribution of federal funds.

If football belongs in the university where young minds and character are being formed, and if being called "coach" is a title of honor among all coaches, football can lead the movement of reform, beginning today with all of us.[14]

End with Startling Information

Like the introduction that provides startling information, the conclusion that does so vividly grabs the listeners' attention. Coming as it does, in the final moments of the speech, it sends the listeners away with a graphic impression of the speaker's main thoughts.

In her address to a College Convocation at Central University, Iowa, Dr. Anita Taylor, Professor of Communication at George Mason University, Virginia, concluded with startling information.

In the final analysis, you are responsible for your own education. Your college years, if they succeed, only help you learn how to learn. In no other way will you be prepared to cope with the future. Half of the "facts" you learn in college will be obsolete within ten years of your graduation. There will be facts to know then that no one has even dreamed of yet.

Your education must prepare you to keep learning, and if it is a quality education, it will hone your ability to think, write, talk and listen. In short, real education teaches you how to solve problems. Learn that, and you will not be one of the terrified of whom Toffler speaks. You will not succumb to future shock nor futureshlock, and you will not engage in a desperate, futile flight into the past. You will, instead, ride the crest of the Third Wave into the future.[15]

End with a Summary

One of the easiest and most effective methods of concluding a speech is to summarize the main points. Not only is the repetition effective in helping listeners summarize the main points, but if any listeners happened to miss a point during the body of the speech, this gives them an opportunity to hear it.

In summary, it should be clear that the private sector can play a big role in combatting substance abuse. We can support innovative educational efforts like Liberation Programs. And we can offer in-house substance abuse prevention programs that are built on the pillars of education, rehabilitation and tough enforcement. These are the same tools that are vital in the public sector as well.

If we are truly allowed to employ these tools in an effective manner, we will be able to cut deeply into substance abuse. True, we might never see the day when we can proclaim America drug-free, but we can measure our progress in lives saved and lives redeemed. If you don't think that amounts to much, ask the families and friends of people like Everne Johnson, Shawn Clemens and Mary Boucher-Javery.[16]

End with an Example

A particularly interesting, unusual, or vivid example that demonstrates clearly the main theme of the speech can be used effectively as a conclusion. It has the virtue of piquing the attention of the listeners at a crucial moment and calling attention to the central purpose of the speech in an indirect, interesting way.

James E. Davis, President, American Medical Association, attempts in his speech to get everyone involved in medical care. At the same time, however, he argues that, despite the many medical advances, a special relationship between doctor and patient must be maintained.

We *cannot* return to a bygone era. And we certainly would not want to give up modern medical advances, even though we might sometimes wish for a simpler world.

Yet we *must* preserve the special doctor-patient bond, that special trust and faith, that binds each of you to your doctors, in a very special and human way.

We *must* connect doctors and patients in a way that is just as close, just as natural, just as sacred, as the one Norman Rockwell depicted just a few decades ago.

For though the days portrayed by Norman Rockwell may be gone forever, the bond our great illustrator conveyed so well, lives on, the bond that draws America's physicians, and the people we serve, together in a truly unique relationship.

A few days before I left North Carolina for my Inauguration, an elderly patient of mine said to me, "Doctor Davis, I am glad that you are going to lead the AMA. You'll travel the country. You'll travel the world! But always let your office here know where you are, for there may be something I'll want to ask you!"

So this afternoon, I ask *you—let's work together*—so quality health care will not only *continue* in America, but will *continue* to *improve*.[17]

End with Humor

A humorous ending may be used to focus your listeners' attention on the main theme in an easy, painless way. Moreover, the humor will generally leave them in a good frame of mind, thus enhancing your ethos and encouraging acceptance of your ideas. Roskens uses humor to focus on his main theme in the conclusion of his speech.

What happened to John Tower may not have been fair, but it was an event whose time had come. We know that it is time to pay more than lip service attention to the principles by which we would live. In the end, the quality of our civilization and the heritage we leave for our young people, will depend upon it.

Joe Garagiola tells the story of a fight after a Pittsburgh Pirate baseball game. One Pirate player had one of his legs and another one had the other leg. He became alarmed when he heard somebody say "Make a wish. . . ." The tug and pull of moral waffling is like that. What we would rather leave our children is that particularly potent unity of purpose called integrity.

And when we look for meaning, integrity is where we will find it.[18]

No matter what type of conclusion you use, avoid making false stops. Nothing is more irritating to the listener than to hear the speaker reach a logical place to stop and then continue on. Some speakers seem to be unwilling to quit and even continue past several good stopping places.

A final word on conclusions: Try to end your speech on an accented, strong vowel. Language authority James J. Kilpatrick advises writers "to end a piece of writing on an accented syllable. If you can work it with a long vowel or a diphthong, so much the better." Kilpatrick offers some examples: "*The Wall Street Journal* had a piece on Ohio's bank holiday. The final paragraph poses a series of rhetorical questions. This is the last word: 'Will we have . . . a full explanation of what went wrong?' "

Kilpatrick gives another example: "*The Washington Post* comments that industrial democracies need to keep their economies safely and prosperously dull: 'That's never so easy as it looks.' "[19]

If this prosodic device is effective in writing, it should be even more so in speaking where the strong, accented vowel will make its full impact on the ear.

Summary

Introductions and conclusions are important because they provide the initial and final impression that you make on your listeners. Although not always required parts of a speech, they become necessary under certain circumstances in order for a speech to have its maximum impact on the listeners.

An introduction is necessary when you must get the attention of some or all of your hearers, when you need to enhance your ethos with these particular listeners, and when you want to get them started thinking about the topic of your speech.

Many different methods may be used to introduce a speech. Ten of the most commonly used ones were discussed: (1) begin with a reference to the audience, (2) begin with a reference to the subject, (3) begin with a reference to the occasion, (4) begin with a personal reference, (5) begin with a startling statement or startling information, (6) begin with an example, (7) begin with humor, (8) begin with a quotation, (9) begin with a definition, and (10) begin with a justification of the speech.

A conclusion is used to focus the listeners' attention on the central idea of the speech, to leave those listeners with a favorable image of you, and to give a sense of completeness to the speech.

Among the many types of conclusions that might be used, the seven following were discussed: (1) end with a quotation, (2) end with a challenge, (3) end with an appeal, (4) end with a startling statement or startling information, (5) end with a summary, (6) end with an example, and (7) end with humor.

Exercises

1. Prepare three introductions for your next speech. Choose one that you will actually use and explain why you made that decision.
2. Analyze the introduction of one of your classmates' speeches. Which of the purposes of an introduction were achieved? How? Which purposes were not achieved? Why not?
3. Choose a topic toward which your classmates are hostile. For a speech opposing their attitudes, prepare an introduction that would overcome hostility and gain you a favorable hearing from your listeners.
4. Analyze the conclusion of one of your classmates' speeches. What was the speaker trying to do? Did the speaker achieve his or her purpose? How? If not, why not?
5. For your next speech, prepare the following conclusions: (1) one that will challenge your listeners, (2) one that appeals for some action on the part of your listeners, (3) one that leaves them well disposed toward you.

Notes

1. E. Miller, "Speech Introductions and Conclusions," *Quarterly Journal of Speech* 32 (1946):181–83. This study analyzed fifty speeches from *Vital Speeches of the Day* over a three-month period in 1943.
2. Thomas K. Hearn, Jr., "Sports and Ethics," *Vital Speeches of the Day* 55 (1988):20. Used by permission.
3. Lewis K. Uhler, "Taming the Federal Spending Monster," *Vital Speeches of the Day* 54 (1988):716. Used by permission.
4. Alton W. Whitehouse, Jr., "The Misinformation Society," *Vital Speeches of the Day* 47(1981):506. Used by permission.
5. Benjamin H. Alexander, "The Letter C No Longer Stands for Courage in Chemistry," *Vital Speeches of the Day* 55 (1988):155. Used by permission.
6. William B. Walstad, "Economic Literacy in the Schools," *Vital Speeches of the Day* 55 (1989):327. Used by permission.
7. John E. Jacob, "Racial Equality," *Vital Speeches of the Day* 54 (1988):710. Used by permission.
8. Michael J. Davies, "Keeping Newspapers Healthy," *Vital Speeches of the Day* 55 (1988):109. Used by permission.
9. Richard A. Gephardt, "U.S.-Japanese Trade Relations," *Vital Speeches of the Day* 55 (1989):450. Used by permission.
10. Rafael D. Pagan, Jr., "Framing the Public Agenda," *Vital Speeches of the Day* 55 (1989):177. Used by permission.
11. Miller, "Speech Introductions and Conclusions," pp. 181–83. Miller found that the length of conclusions in the fifty speeches studied ranged from 1 to 15 percent of the total length of the speech, with the mean length being approximately 5 percent.

12. C. J. Silas, "A Question of Scruples," *Vital Speeches of the Day* 55 (1989):476. Used by permission.
13. John A. Ahladas, "Global Warming," *Vital Speeches of the Day* 55 (1989):384.
14. Thomas K. Hearn, Jr., "Sports and Ethics," *Vital Speeches of the Day* 55 (1988):22. Used by permission.
15. Anita Taylor, "Talk, Future Shock, and Futureshlock," *Vital Speeches of the Day* 51 (1985):683. © City News Publishing Company. Used by permission.
16. John W. Johnstone, Jr., "The War on Drugs: Saying 'Yes' to Getting Involved," *Vital Speeches of the Day* 55 (1989):327. Used by permission.
17. James E. Davis, "What You Can Do About Your Health Care," *Vital Speeches of the Day* 55 (1988):72–73. Used by permission.
18. Ronald W. Roskens, "Integrity," *Vital Speeches of the Day* 55 (1989):512. Used by permission.
19. James J. Kilpatrick, "The Writer's Art," *The Birmingham News,* May 26, 1985, p. D-3. Used by permission.

CHAPTER 15

Communicating Nonverbally

In an international weightlifting tournament in Manila in 1975, the Russians had been complaining about the slippery surface of the floor. When the Russian came out to attempt the lift that would give him the championship, he kicked rosin away as he reached for the weights. The announcer observed that this was probably his silent way of criticizing the conditions. This illustrates how meaning can be communicated through nonverbal behavior.

The importance of nonverbal communication was demonstrated by asking subjects to infer communicator *attitudes* from words presented with positive, neutral, and negative vocal attitude and from photographs of models with positive, neutral, and negative facial expressions. The researchers concluded that "simultaneous verbal, vocal, and facial *attitude* communications" account for 7 percent, 38 percent, and 55 percent, respectively, of the total communication.[1] Although this study demonstrates the importance of vocal and facial cues in communicating attitudes, we shouldn't draw the erroneous conclusion that these cues communicate information. In fact, the use of single words in the experiment held the communication of information to a minimum. If we could communicate 93 percent of information and attitudes with vocal and facial cues, it would be wasteful to spend time learning a language. What we must remember is that "natural speech content conveys information primarily through the combination of words and sentences rather than through the communication of single isolated words."[2] Nevertheless, the study clearly demonstrates that we can't ignore the effect of nonverbal stimuli on a communicative effort. Observation and experimental research indicate that skillful use of vocal and physical behavior helps develop meaning and credibility.

Skillful Use of Nonverbal Forms of Presentation

In the last few decades empirical research has verified what we have been teaching for thousands of years: nonverbal forms of communication—physical and vocal behavior—contribute to the effectiveness of a speech. They help to make the speaker's idea more credible. As a matter of fact, if they contradict the verbal message, hearers tend to place more credence in the nonverbal communicators.

In an early study 256 students were asked to give speeches on the best and poorest speaker they had heard. After analyzing these speeches 54 additional students gave speeches on the best and poorest speakers they had heard and ranked nine categories of characteristics revealed by analysis of the previous speeches. The best speaker was generally identified "as one who *spoke without notes* and in an optimistic mood with good speech material, *good delivery, a good voice,* and a good personality." The poorest speaker, on the other hand, was usually recalled "as the one who spoke with notes or reading his speech in a factual or pessimistic mood with poor material, poor delivery, a poor voice, and a poor personality."[3]

Beighley investigated the effect of organization and vocal skills on the comprehension of "hard" and "easy" material. He concluded that vocally skilled speakers "helped the audience achieve higher comprehension test scores than did the vocally unskilled ones" when the material was hard or disorganized.[4] Vocal skills made the "hard" material more understandable and thereby more credible.

Vohs presented a well-delivered or a poorly delivered (referring to use of voice) speech to four groups of subjects. Following the speech, each group completed a test of fifty multiple-choice questions. Those who heard a well-delivered speech retained more information than those who heard a poorly presented one.[5]

Bettinghaus presented four persuasive speeches on different topics—two positive and two negative—by different speakers to four different groups. Each speaker gave the speech in the following forms: (1) effective delivery with strong content, (2) effective delivery with weak content, (3) ineffective delivery with strong content, (4) ineffective delivery with weak content. Following each speech the subjects indicated their evaluation of the speaker, the topic, the delivery, and the development of the speech. After analyzing the results, Bettinghaus concluded that "the speaker with better delivery is more persuasive than the speaker with poorer delivery."[6]

McCroskey found that good delivery made a speech with evidence significantly more effective in changing the attitudes of listeners than a speech with evidence and poor delivery, one with good delivery and no evidence, or one with poor delivery and no evidence.[7]

A series of experiments found that facial expression, speech rate, volume, and intonation were significantly related to intended and perceived persuasiveness.[8]

Effective delivery is important in developing credibility for your ideas, enabling them to have their maximum impact. Effective delivery by itself will not change attitudes, but it is necessary for the effective rhetorical message to exert its potential influence upon a receiver. Become familiar with principles of physical and vocal behavior, and skilled in their use.

Physical Behavior

Anything that interferes with communication must be eliminated. Physical behavior can play either a beneficial or a detrimental role. Physical behavior resulting from an outgrowth of your urge to communicate and suited to your purpose, personality, and physical vitality will be most effective with your listeners.

Speakers are frequently advised to *be natural* in their physical behavior. Unfortunately, many people don't use effective bodily action naturally. We are all familiar with people who are naturally awkward, who can't make a movement that has any grace or communicates effectively. For these persons to be natural in a speaking situation simply means they are going to appear awkward in front of an audience. Telling most beginning speakers to be natural is tantamount to telling them to use ineffective physical action. As a general rule, effective physical behavior for the specific skill must be learned and practiced. The polished grace of the skilled ballet dancer is admired by those watching who may forget it has replaced the lumbering movements of a novice only after long hours of hard and dedicated practice. It is important that effective physical behavior be practiced until it *is* natural.

An understanding, then, of the types of physical behavior that may be used is necessary. You need to understand and use effective principles of posture, platform movement, eye contact, facial expression, and gestures.

Posture

Posture influences the listeners' reaction because it reflects your alertness and poise. Don't slump in a chair on the platform; sit comfortably erect. While speaking, avoid collapsing on the lectern, shifting your weight from foot to foot, swaying from side to side, or rocking back and forth. Don't stand in a militarily stilted position or become so relaxed that you appear to be unconcerned.

Distribute your weight equally on both feet, stand poised on the balls of your feet, and give the impression of a person vibrantly aware of the circumstances and able to move immediately to react to any contingency. If your weight is on your heels you aren't fully alert; you aren't capable of reacting swiftly and you show it. Notice, for example, how alert infielders on a baseball team gets poised on the balls of their feet just before the pitcher throws the ball to the batter. It is obvious they are alert to the situation and are ready to respond quickly. Infielders standing with their weight on their heels cannot react as quickly and this lack of alertness is apparent to the spectators. In the same way listeners can detect your alertness by the way your weight is distributed on your feet. Listeners may not be consciously aware of how your weight is distributed, but the muscular tone of your body reflects it. As a result, nonverbal stimuli from your muscular tone influences their impression of you.

Find the most effective posture. Let it convey an appearance of relaxed alertness. Make it appropriate to the situation. In a more formal setting your posture must have a certain rigidity to it. In an informal situation you can appropriately assume a more relaxed posture.

Avoid standing at arm's length from the lectern with elbows unbent and hands on the lectern. If you're going to place your hands on the lectern, stand close enough so your elbows can bend. This looks more relaxed and makes listeners feel more comfortable.

Beginning speakers often worry about what to do with their hands. You can do a number of things with your hands, but whatever you do should seem comfortable and be effective. Some speakers let their hands hang easily at their sides. So long as the hands aren't moved about randomly, this is an acceptable position. Other speakers like to rest their hands lightly on the lectern. So long as they aren't moved about unpurposefully, this too is an acceptable position. Still others find it comfortable to put one hand in a pocket and let the other hand hang easily at the side or rest lightly on the lectern. So long as the hand isn't put in and taken out frequently and isn't used to jingle keys or coins in the pocket, this is an acceptable position if it doesn't interfere with the gestures. Most gestures can be anticipated sufficiently to remove the hand in time to use it effectively for gesturing. On rare occasions it may be desirable to put both hands in your pockets. Although this is acceptable if done infrequently, be careful not to let this position interfere with gestures. Some speakers prefer to clasp their hands behind their back. As a general rule, this is less acceptable and should be avoided. It is rarely used except by soldiers standing at parade rest and it gives the appearance of trying to hide your hands.

Remember that those appendages at the ends of your arms don't look as big or as awkward to listeners as they feel to you.

Increasing attention in recent years to *kinesics*—the study of body motion and its role in communication—has intensified awareness that movement is a significant form of nonverbal communication. **Movement**

Your movement begins to influence the listeners' reaction to you even before you arrive at the podium. Your approach communicates nonverbally your attitude toward the situation. Approaching the lectern in an alertly relaxed manner gives the impression that you have something to say, know you can say it, and want to say it to this particular audience. As a result, your credibility is enhanced.

Movement on the podium is important for a number of reasons. It is effective in getting and holding attention. A proved psychological principle is that, other things being equal, a moving stimulus attracts attention away from a nonmoving stimulus. If you stand immobile in one position you provide an opportunity for other stimuli in the situation to become stronger and attract the attention of the listeners. Animation may be used at the beginning of a speech to capture attention. Movement can also be used to recapture attention.

To gain and hold attention effectively, however, movement has to be meaningful. Unpurposeful movements attract attention but are detrimental because they distract attention from what you're saying or doing in a purposeful way. Shifting your weight from foot to foot is an unpurposeful movement and distracts attention from your purpose. Swaying from side to side or rocking back and forth distracts because it is unmeaningful. Buttoning and unbuttoning your coat, pulling an ear, scratching your forehead, rubbing your chin, tapping the fingers on the lectern, running your hands around the edges of the lectern, playing with note cards, continually putting hands into and taking them out of your pockets, rubbing your hands together, straightening your tie, fingering a bracelet, brooch, or watch—all of these, and similar actions are distracting and detrimental. Because of the movement they attract attention, but because they are unpurposeful, they distract from your main purpose and interfere with effective communication.

Concentration

These irrelevant movements are also indications that you're not concentrating on the act of communication. Observe a golfer preparing to hit a shot or putt. Every muscle is focused on the task at hand; there are no irrelevant movements and the golfer is unaware of events around her. If the golfer feels an itch, she knows she has not concentrated sufficiently. In the same way, if you're concentrating on the act of communication every muscle in your body will be focused on the task. If you feel an itch, then you have failed to concentrate sufficiently on the act of communication. Of course there are times when you're unable to concentrate because of some mental or physical problem. If you have a case of hives, the intense itching may prevent concentration on anything. Under ordinary conditions, however, if you're concentrating, you'll be unaware of minor irritations.

Use movement to emphasize transition from one point to another. At the conclusion of a point you may pause and move to another position on the platform before beginning the next point. This movement serves figuratively as a bridge between the two points and emphasizes to the listeners that you have moved to a new idea.

Use movement as a means of physical relief for listeners. The muscles in the human body can't stay in one position too long; they become fatigued if they do. One set of muscles normally will tense for a while, then relax while another set tenses. This is a constant action of the muscles in the body. Recent studies indicate this occurs even while we're sleeping. As a matter of fact, at least one set of muscles is moving at some place in the body all the time we sleep. In an audience where people are crowded close together and the space between rows of seats is limited, there is restricted opportunity for listeners to move their body for relaxation.

Empathy

The primary means by which listeners can achieve needed muscular change is through *empathy*—the feeling of being a part of what we are observing. The empathic response is natural to all people, more to some than others. We watch on television as the marshall stalks the outlaw in the inevitable gunfight. As the two men approach one another the muscles in our bodies tense. When they grab for their guns, the muscles in our arms twitch and jerk involuntarily as we are pulled into the action we are watching. When you move in front of an audience, listeners are able to flex their muscles through empathy, thus avoiding the restlessness resulting from unused muscles.

Avoid so much movement that you physically exhaust listeners. If you constantly pace back and forth, you fatigue your listeners since their muscles never get a chance to relax. Strive for the proper balance by using neither too much nor too little physical movement.

Use empathy to help get desired audience reactions. Listeners tend to feel the emotions and attitudes being displayed. If you display anger, listeners tend to feel anger; if you display sadness, listeners tend to feel sad.

In all movements strive to appear relaxed, comfortable, confident. Only then can listeners feel relaxed and comfortable. If you appear to be ill at ease, listeners, through empathy, feel ill at ease. It is difficult to get people to listen carefully if they feel uncomfortable.

Eye Contact

Build rapport with listeners by communicating directly with them; make direct eye contact, just as you would in a small face-to-face conversation. Eye contact in a speech should be similar to that which you have when you are deeply involved in a conversation with a group of friends. Eye contact is an important nonverbal means of obtaining a favorable response from hearers. Researchers found "that the same verbal communication" was interpreted as "being more favorable" by a listener when it was accompanied by "more eye contact than when it was presented with less eye contact."[9]

Direct eye contact with the audience significantly increases credibility. Comparing the effect of three levels of eye contact—none, moderate, and high—Beebe found that high eye contact created significantly higher credibility for the speaker's competence and trustworthiness than no eye contact.[10]

You can't look at all members of the audience simultaneously; look at one person at a time, letting your eyes move easily around the room from one person to another. Eye contact should never become mechanical as it does when speakers sweep alternately from one side of the room to the other. Don't be reluctant to look at some of the listeners more than others; in fact, in a large audience you'll be unable to look at every listener. Some hearers will respond more actively and more overtly to what you are saying. Their favorable response can be highly stimulating. It is perfectly all right to talk to these people more than you do to the others, but don't let the speech develop into a private conversation between you and the few who are responding favorably.

Avoid looking at distractions that occur outside the speaking area unless the distraction is so great you can't possibly ignore it. Remember, movement of your eyes to an object outside the speaking area serves to focus the eyes and attention of the hearers on that object. Most extraneous noises go unnoticed unless you call attention to them.

Eye contact permits perception of the interaction of listeners. You can't communicate directly with listeners if you're unaware of and fail to respond to their behavior and reactions. Frowns, smiles, nodding of heads, shaking of heads, applause, hisses, and whispering are all overt responses that tell something of what the listener is thinking. Learn to respond to these reactions in desirable ways.

Facial Expression

Reveal your communicative attitude through facial expression. When you look at listeners with an alert, expressive face and an occasional smile, you tell them nonverbally you are happy to be there talking to them. A frown at the mention of something unpleasant reinforces the words in a way that nothing else can. A contemporary of Tom Corwin, stump orator and senator from Ohio in the 1840s, claimed that "his wonderful effect upon an audience depended more upon his marvelous facial expression than upon anything he said."[11] A number of reporters have claimed that one of the prime reasons for Arnold Palmer's enormous popularity with golf fans is his wonderfully mobile facial expression, which reflects visibly the nuances of his successes and struggles while golfing.

Facial expression is an important determinant of the impact of a message on a listener. Mehrabian found that the nonverbal message conveyed by facial expressions accounted for more than 50 percent of the impact of the total message when the verbal and nonverbal messages were inconsistent.[12]

Experimenters have found a high degree of reliability in interpreting facial expressions of emotional tendencies and attitudes.[13] The deadpan speaker not only loses this valuable nonverbal assistance in communication but also gives the impression of being uninterested in talking to these people and of being a "cold fish," one who is insensitive to what goes on about him. Most of us are unwilling to place our confidence in and submit our decisions to a person unable or unwilling to sympathize with us and our problems.

There are some facial expressions that are detrimental. Avoid grimacing when you make a mistake, it just calls greater attention to the error. Especially detrimental are facial expressions not coordinated with what you're saying.

Gestures are those movements of the head, shoulders, hands, and arms used to assist in communicating ideas. They may serve one or more of three purposes: (1) to clarify or describe, (2) to reinforce or emphasize, (3) to get and hold attention.

The most effective gestures seem to be an integral part of communication. They don't appear to be made for the sake of making a gesture. Each has a definite communicative purpose. Even when they're purposeful, however, they need to appear to be integrated with what you're saying. To achieve this, gestures ought to be made in the listeners' focal area of vision. In most small audience situations, gestures are more effective if made above the waist, somewhere in the area of the chest, and fairly close to the body.

Gestures distract when made below the waist, a peripheral area of the listeners' vision. Listeners are often not consciously aware of these gestures even though they are subconsciously distracting. Once listeners become aware of them, their vision shifts from your face to the gestures. This is distracting because the gestures now seem unrelated to your words; they seem to be an irrelevant part of the total communicative effort. If gestures are made in the line of vision, listeners can see them without shifting their line of vision, since they appear to be integrated with what you are saying. Generally, listeners perceive gestures and respond to them without thinking of them as isolated actions.

The larger the place in which the speech is given and the farther the listeners are from you, the more you are included in the focal area of vision. Thus you can expand the area in which you gesture, since there is less likelihood of the gestures occurring outside the line of vision.

Timing Gestures

Gestures timed to correspond with what you are saying assist the communication of ideas. If you say, "My first point this morning, . . ." and raise your hand with the index finger extended on *this,* the lack of coordination between action and words will minimize the effect of the gesture. To be coordinated the action of the gesture begins before the word it accompanies so the gesture will reach its climax precisely at the moment the word is spoken. The upward movement of the hand in this example should begin slightly before the beginning of the word *my,* then the hand with the extended forefinger should reach the top of the stroke just as the word *first* is said. However, you can't expect to achieve perfect results on the first try; you may not get perfection on the tenth effort. Remember that athletes spend hours practicing development of fine coordination. Don't expect to develop coordination with little practice. The important thing is to start practicing and using gestures in speaking. In time the coordination will develop. The classroom is your laboratory; this is the place to experiment with gestures in front of an audience. Your instructor won't criticize you adversely for lack of coordination; she'll be pleased you're making the effort.

You should strive to use only acceptable pronunciations of standard speech, that used by the majority of cultivated speakers in a community.

A final word of caution: Strive to develop the most effective voice possible, but never adopt a voice that is not yours. Develop your own style with as much flexibility as you can achieve, but leave the imitations for those who make fake diamonds.

Exercises

1. Attend a lecture on campus. Describe the physical behavior of the speaker. What aspects of this person's nonverbal communication contributed to the credibility of his or her ideas? What aspects detracted from the credibility of these ideas?
2. Observe a classmate practicing his or her next speech. Write an analysis of what this student can do to improve his or her physical behavior so that greater credibility is achieved.
3. Listen to a speaker on the radio. Write a description of that person and explain why you developed the particular image that you did.
4. Go to an open area with several friends. Practice your next speech with one person approximately five yards in front of you, another approximately fifteen yards away, and another approximately thirty yards away. Describe your reactions to this experience.
5. Prepare an experience to relate to your class. Without using language, pantomime your message to communicate with your classmates.
6. Define the conversational mode. Describe what some member of your class does that makes you feel the conversational mode is being used. What does that student do that makes you feel it isn't being used?
7. Analyze your own platform behavior in your last speech. What were its strengths? its weaknesses? What can you do to eliminate or minimize these weaknesses? What can you do to capitalize on the strengths? Which of these aid in establishing the credibility of your ideas?
8. Each member of the class should write on a slip of paper the name of a feeling and the part of the body to be used to express the emotion. After exchanging slips, each student should try to express with his or her body the emotion on this paper. The other students should try to guess what feeling was being expressed.
9. A class member is asked to stand in front of and express his or her feelings toward another class member in a nonverbal manner and with exaggeration, as in mime.

Notes

1. A. Mehrabian and S. R. Ferris, "Inference of Attitudes from Nonverbal Communication in Two Channels," *Journal of Consulting Psychology* 31 (1967):248–52. Italics added.

The Speech

2. R. J. Hart and B. L. Brown, "Interpersonal Information Conveyed by the Content and Vocal Aspects of Speech," *Speech Monographs* 41 (1974):372.

3. E. H. Henrikson, "An Analysis of the Characteristics of Some 'Good' and 'Poor' Speakers," *Speech Monographs* 11 (1944):120–24. Italics added.

4. K. C. Beighley, "An Experimental Study of the Effect of Four Speech Variables on Listener Comprehension," *Speech Monographs* 19 (1952):249–58.

5. J. L. Vohs, "An Empirical Approach to the Concept of Attention," *Speech Monographs* 31 (1964):355–60.

6. E. P. Bettinghaus, "The Operation of Congruity in an Oral Communication Situation," *Speech Monographs* 28 (1961):131–42.

7. J. C. McCroskey, *Studies of the Effects of Evidence in Persuasive Communication,* Speech Communication Research Laboratory Report SCRL 4–67, Department of Speech (E. Lansing, Mich.: Michigan State University, 1967), p. 36.

8. A. Mehrabian and M. Williams, "Nonverbal Concomitants of Perceived and Intended Persuasiveness," *Journal of Personality and Social Psychology* 13 (1969):37–58.

9. R. V. Exline and C. Eldridge, "Effects of Two Patterns of a Speaker's Visual Behavior upon the Perception of the Authenticity of His Verbal Message" (paper presented at the meeting of the Eastern Psychological Association, Boston, April 1967). Reported in A. Mehrabian, "Significance of Posture and Position in the Communication of Attitude and Status Relationships," *Psychological Bulletin* 71 (1969):359–72.

10. S. A. Beebe, "Eye Contact: A Nonverbal Determinant of Speaker Credibility," *Speech Teacher* 23 (1974):23–24.

11. J. J. Auer, "Tom Corwin: 'King of the Stump,' " *Quarterly Journal of Speech* 30 (1944):53.

12. A. Mehrabian, *Silent Messages* (Belmont, Calif.: Wadsworth Publishing Co., 1971), p. 43.

13. D. Dusenbury and F. H. Knower, "Experimental Studies of the Symbolism of Action and Voice—1: A Study of the Specificity of Meaning in Facial Expression," *Quarterly Journal of Speech* 24 (1938):436.

14. A. Mehrabian and M. Wiener, "Decoding of Inconsistent Communications," *Journal of Personality and Social Psychology* 6 (1967):109–14.

15. L. S. Harms, "Listener Judgments of Status Cues in Speech," *Quarterly Journal of Speech* 47 (1961):164–72.

16. G. Fairbanks and W. Pronovost, "An Experimental Study of the Pitch Characteristics of the Voice during the Expression of Emotion," *Speech Monographs* 6 (1939):87–104.

17. D. Lewis and J. Tiffin, "A Psychophysical Study of Individual Differences in Speaking Ability." *Archives of Speech* 1 (1934):43–60.

18. C. H. Ernest, "Listening Comprehension as a Function of Type of Material and Rate of Presentation," *Speech Monographs* 35 (1968):154–58.

19. D. W. Addington, "The Relationship of Selected Vocal Characteristics to Personality Perception," *Speech Monographs* 35 (1968):492–503.

20. J. Tiffin and M. D. Steer, "An Experimental Analysis of Emphasis," *Speech Monographs* 4 (1937):69–74.

21. P. B. Gove, ed., *Webster's Third New International Dictionary* (Springfield, Mass.: G. & C. Merriam Co. 1967), p. 40a.

22. Ibid., pp. 6–7a.

CHAPTER 16

Communicating Verbally

Meaning is what communication is all about. You have a certain meaning you want others to understand, appreciate, or accept, so you attempt to communicate that meaning to them. Unfortunately, accurate communication of meaning is extremely difficult. It is probably never achieved perfectly, frequently not even approximately. Credibility of ideas is difficult to achieve if your meaning is unclear.

Three primary factors work to prevent even a reasonable communication of meaning: (1) The meaning as known and interpreted by the speaker does not accurately reflect the realities of the situation. For example, your roommate may be extremely sick one night before you go to bed. The next morning when you get up to go to class, you find that your roommate is still sleeping, so you leave him undisturbed. After class, you stop by and tell the professor the reason your roommate was absent is that he is sick. When you return to your room, you find your roommate awake, well, and angry because you didn't wake him so he could go to class. Your meaning in that message to the professor simply didn't reflect the reality of the situation. (2) The language used doesn't clearly symbolize the meaning that exists in the mind of the communicator. A number of factors can cause this problem. The communicator may lack the necessary vocabulary. The communicator may attempt to conceal the meaning and may use language that is offensive or embarrassing to the receivers. The speaker's ambiguous language may result from imprecise thought processes. (3) The verbal symbols used by the speaker to represent meaning don't evoke identical meanings in the mind of the receiver. This was vividly illustrated when a teenage girl, who had decided she needed to go on a diet even though she was definitely not fat, was trying on pants in a clothing store. When she came out in one pair, her father and mother both said, "Those are too tight." To their puzzlement, she stalked back into the dressing room, changed into her own clothes, and refused to try on more pants. Later she confided to her grandmother that it was embarrassing to have her parents say in front of the salesperson that she was too fat. When her parents said the pants were too tight, they meant *the pants were too small*. But to the daughter the words meant *she was too fat*. Verbal symbols don't necessarily evoke the same meaning in your listener's mind that they do in yours.

Definition of Meaning

Meaning refers to the understanding a specific person has of anything in his or her environment; meaning exists within the person. From the day we are born we begin to attach meanings to things around us. For one baby, "mother" comes to mean the thing that cheerfully feeds it when it's hungry, replaces a wet diaper with a dry one, rocks and coos to it when it's sleepy. For another baby, "mother" comes to mean the thing that unhappily gives it a bottle of cold milk when it's hungry, ignores it when it cries with a wet diaper, and makes loud noises when it wants to go to sleep. Obviously, the meaning attached to the female in its environment will be vastly different for each of these babies. And when each learns that the verbal symbol used to refer to that object is "mother," there will be a drastic difference in the meaning that verbal symbol has for each of them.

Not only do we develop meaning as a result of sensory experiences, we also develop meanings about things that can't be experienced in a sensory way. These meanings we learn through information given by verbal symbols. For example, one father, in answer to his child's query about ghosts, says, "A ghost is the spirit of a dead person. Its presence is sometimes signified by the flickering shadow on the wall, and sometimes by the rustling of the leaves on the trees." Another father, in answer to the same query, says, "There is no such thing as a ghost. It's just the figment of someone's fertile imagination." Neither of these children has sensorily experienced a ghost, but each has a definite meaning for "ghost" that is vastly different from the other's. Because of that meaning, one child goes through life fearful of shadows and rustling leaves while the other perceives shadows and rustling leaves more neutrally.

Not only are meanings *developed* in us, they are not the same for everybody; meaning varies from person to person and from situation to situation.

Relationship of Words and Thought

We use language to communicate values, ideas, and feelings. Communication is dependent upon the ability of the language used to evoke in the mind of the listener the meaning that exists in the mind of the speaker. Meaning has been clearly communicated when the meaning you intended agrees with the meaning your hearer receives.[1] If you are to be effective, the listener must understand your meaning. As Quintilian, the great Roman speech teacher, advised, it is not enough to strive to make statements understandable; you must strive to make them so clear that it will be impossible for a hearer to misunderstand them. Two political journalists report that this was one of the strengths of former President Reagan. They quote a "Democratic state chairman from blue-collar Toledo" who said before the 1984 presidential election: "If we can get the blue collars to think about issues, we can win. But they like Reagan. He makes them feel good about the country. There's the macho thing, and *I've never heard him use a word I didn't understand* (italics added), and working people like that."[2]

Thought and language are intertwined; it's difficult to determine which comes first. Do we have a thought because we have a word that makes it possible, or do we create a word because we have a thought? An oft-cited fact is that the Eskimos have a number of words for snow, whereas we have only one. Because snow is such an all-pervasive and important part of their lives, Eskimos need to distinguish among the various kinds of snow, and their language must communicate unmistakably the difference that exists.

To ask whether thought or word comes first is like asking which comes first, the chicken or the egg. There are times when our thoughts and actions cause us to seek language in order to express them. There was no need for the word "sputnik" until the Russians blasted one into space. Sometimes we are limited in our thoughts by the paucity of our language. On other occasions our language causes us to think in a certain way.

To use language precisely, you must have precise thoughts; to think clearly, you must possess a language that will permit you to do so.

Relationship of Words and Referents

In order to discern clearly the difficulties of communicating meaning to others, we must first understand the relationship between words and their objects. Words are symbols that stand for our conception of or response to some real thing or concept. An individual has a toothache, an experience that is real and painful. But no one else can see it, feel it, hear it, smell it, or taste it. There can be no sensory perception of that toothache by any other person. Even the dentist with all her equipment can't perceive the toothache. In some instances she may find certain signs that lead her to believe that a particular tooth could be causing pain, but the dentist cannot actually perceive the pain. The individual then uses words, symbols, that stand for the response to the pain. In this way he communicates the existence of the pain to others. He presents these symbols to the dentist, who then probes, takes X-rays, and locates the problem inside the tooth that is causing the pain. Without language, the victim of the toothache would have a difficult, maybe impossible, task in letting the dentist know that the pain exists. There is no direct relationship between an object and the symbol used to represent it. That relationship is created in the mind of the speaker. Ogden and Richards demonstrated this fact graphically with their triangle of meaning, shown in figure 16.1.

The dotted line between the referent, or object, and the symbol, or word, indicates there is no direct connection between the two. The connection is made in the mind of the perceiver. If I see a certain four-legged animal and say "cat," and you speak English and agree with my perception, you nod in agreement. But if I have applied the wrong symbol, you would shake your head and say, "No, dog." The fact that I had applied the wrong symbol would in no way change the nature of the animal. Nor would its nature be in any way affected, if the two of us decided that we would no longer refer to it as "dog" or "cat," but would hereafter use as its symbol the word "glip." The symbol has no relationship to the object, except that created in the mind of the user.

You are probably thinking by now, "So what? I already knew that. What difference does it make?" True, so long as we are talking about concrete objects, it really makes little difference. Because whether we use "cat" or "glip" or some other symbol to stand for the animal, we can observe the concrete object itself and know what the symbol represents.

When we begin to talk about abstractions, however, we find no concrete referent to which we can go. The referent exists in the mind of the speaker. When the psychologist talks about the id, there is no referent to which she or he can point. When the politician talks about liberalism, there is no referent to which he or she can point. When the minister talks about heaven, there is no referent to which he or she can point.

Figure 16.1
The triangle of meaning.
Adapted by permission from C. K. Ogden and I. A. Richards, The Meaning of Meaning *(New York: Harcourt, Brace, & World, 1923), p. 11.*

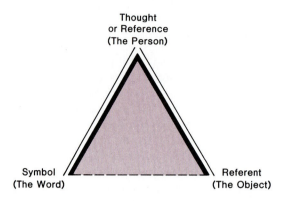

When we make evaluative statements, the referent exists only in our mind. In other words, symbols that communicate abstractions and value judgments are really telling us about the person speaking, not the objects to which the symbols are applied. If two of us stand looking at a picture and I say, "That is a beautiful picture." I am telling you more about myself than about the picture. What that sentence communicates is my reaction to that picture. You may have just been thinking to yourself, "That is a horrible painting." If so, it's obvious that neither of us is talking about the painting; instead we are describing our reactions to the painting. Yet how often do we get into an argument with someone over whether a movie "is" funny, or a book "is" boring or a certain person "is" interesting? If we remember that there is no relationship between the object and the words we use, except the connection we make in our minds, we can avoid such arguments.

Although words are not the things they symbolize, we frequently respond to them as though they were. Some people wince when called a "conservative"; others get upset when called a "liberal." The old saying "sticks and stones may break my bones, but names will never hurt me" should be true, but it isn't. To identify a person as a "ditchdigger" is to place a certain stigma on him or her in our society; to identify one as a "doctor" infuses him or her with an aura of prestige. S. I. Hayakawa, an authority on meaning and semantics, has called attention to the efficacy of words in influencing our behavior.

The word *black* has evil connotations in our culture. For a long, long time we avoided saying "black people." We said "Negroes," because the word black had connotations of dark, black, evil, satanic, sinister, and so on. White had connotations of purity, loveliness, elegance, truth, brightness, clarity, and so on. When people call themselves Black Nationalists, Black Panthers, they, like everybody else, are victims of the English language. So they wear black berets, black sweaters, black trousers, black shoes, and black sunglasses, and they role-play being black, suggesting dark, evil, sinister, satanic.

The policemen of Oakland, California also speak the English language, and they have a semantic reaction to all this Black Panther business. They act as if there were evil, satanic, ferocious, predatory black forces at loose in the world. The Oakland Police Department arms itself, and prepares for all kinds of trouble. So the black people and the white policemen are all role-playing around the words *black-white, black-white*—both of them trapped by the English language.

What would happen if the Black Panthers had called themselves, instead, the Soul Brothers Mutual Assistance Society? It's a beautiful name. Soul Brothers. That's fine. Mutual Assistance. That's fine. And the cops wouldn't have to organize themselves in this ferocious way against the Panthers.[3]

When you use words, constantly be aware that there is no relationship between the symbols you use and the objects they represent except that which exists in your own mind. You should further recognize that evaluative language reveals more about the person using the language than about the object the language represents. Despite the validity of these statements, realize that people do, in fact, frequently respond to language as though it were the object itself.

Relating Meaning to Reality

If you're to communicate precisely with language, if you're to develop credibility for your ideas, you must free your thoughts of error. If your thoughts are unclear or imprecise, there is no way your language can be clear and precise. The application of the following principles will help you clarify your thinking and, consequently, your use of language.

With the explosion of knowledge that has occurred in the last few decades, it is now impossible for anyone to know everything about anything. Even experts who spend a lifetime studying one small facet of a subject never reach the point where they know everything about it.

It Is Impossible to Know Everything

But we who aren't experts must remember that we can possess only a fraction of the available knowledge pertaining to even those events that we ourselves witness firsthand. No one can perceive all facets of a situation, and what one does perceive may be influenced by one or more of many factors.

Interest may determine perceptions: one person standing on a street corner may focus her attention on the people passing by, to the exclusion of all else, because she is interested in psychology and is an observer of human behavior. *Attitudes* may determine perceptions: if one has an unfavorable attitude toward those who are on welfare, he may be very sensitive to the line of people waiting at the welfare office for their weekly check; another person who doesn't have an unfavorable attitude toward welfare recipients may be oblivious to the welfare office line. *Experience* may determine perceptions; if

Figure 16.2
Continuum of the concepts intelligent *and* unintelligent.

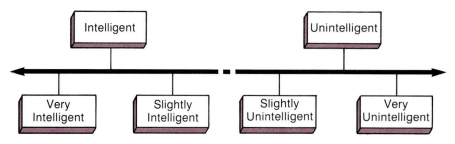

a person has just been bitten by a dog, he will probably be extremely wary when dogs come into his presence; another person who had had no unpleasant experience with dogs may be unaware of their presence. We perceive only a small amount of what occurs about us.

Moreover, what we do perceive we may perceive inaccurately. In a football game on TV a few years ago, a friend and I saw an offensive player go downfield for a pass. Just before the ball arrived, a defensive back ran over and jumped with his arm directly in front of the offensive player's face. The offensive player dropped the ball, but the referee didn't call a face-guarding penalty. My friend and I were bemoaning the fact that the official had blown the play when suddenly the play was shown again on instant replay. But the instant replay camera, from a different angle, showed quite clearly that the defensive back was a full five yards in front of the pass receiver. Many of us have a distorted angle when we perceive the events about us. Unfortunately, we have no instant replay to reveal our distorted perceptions.

Things Are Seldom as Clear-cut as They Seem

Most of us have a tendency to think in "either-or" terms, and in some ways our language encourages this kind of thinking, because it has a tendency to make us think in terms of opposites. We talk about someone being beautiful or ugly, good or bad, intelligent or unintelligent, efficient or inefficient, fast or slow, patient or impatient, sane or insane. Rarely, however, is anyone ever 100 percent any of these things. All sane people have some moments of at least mild insanity, and most insane persons have at least some moments of sanity. A good person is occasionally bad, and a bad person has some moments of goodness. We tend to forget this fact, however, and use language that encourages either-or thinking.

If we remember that most evaluations can be put on a continuum, then it will encourage more precise thinking, which will result in more precise language. In figure 16.2, the concepts *intelligent* and *unintelligent* are on a continuum. There are varying degrees of intelligence, and even the labels we have applied, such as "slightly intelligent," are labels that apply to several points on the continuum. Although most of us know that concepts come in varying degrees, we still have a tendency to use words that communicate finality and certainty.

If pressed, most of us admit that our language reflects only our own view of the world. Yet in actual practice most of us blithely use language with little or no awareness of this fact. Someone says: "Did you see the movie at the Varsity?" The answer comes back: "Yes, that's a good movie." The statement seems to invest the movie with the attribute of goodness, but what the respondent is really saying is "I enjoyed that movie." Had he or she said it in this precise fashion, the "goodness" would have resided within the person talking rather than the movie. The first person could next say, "I didn't enjoy that movie." Each could then explain why he or she did or didn't enjoy the movie, and the chances are good they would now be talking about the movie rather than about themselves. They might discuss the plot, the characterizations, the acting, or the photography; and the language would begin to resemble reality, so long as they didn't merely indulge in value judgments about those items.

Identify value judgments with such labels as, "it seems to me," "I believe," "in my opinion," "I think." A few years ago, a controversy developed in Pittsburgh about what to do with Forbes Field, former baseball home of the Pittsburgh Pirates. Notice the difference in the following statements made by opposing forces in the controversy. A citizen's group opposing demolition of the field issued this statement:

> Forbes Field, in addition to being a beautiful work of architecture, comparable in quality to other monumental turn-of-the-century steel and glass buildings such as Les Halles and the Eiffel Tower in Paris and the Crystal Palace in London, can readily accommodate a variety of uses.

That statement sounds as though the characteristics attributed to Forbes Field inhere within the structure itself, doesn't it? There is no suggestion that the beauty is in the eyes of the beholder. Consider, however, the statement of the chancellor of the University of Pittsburgh: "Forbes Field, in my own personal opinion, is ugly, obsolete and unsafe. . . ."[4] The chancellor's statement makes it quite clear that the attributes he attached to Forbes Field exist within him rather than in the structure itself. It should also be noted that the word *unsafe* is one for which factual data could be amassed, thus removing it from the category of a personal evaluation.

Most of us tend to generalize (on the basis of one or more instance) about our various experiences. Seeing a car fail to stop at a stop sign and go crashing into another car, we conclude that it's dangerous to fail to stop at stop signs. Learning that a couple of friends have had accidents while driving their cars under the influence of alcohol, we generalize that people who have been drinking shouldn't drive. There are many other instances where valid generalizations are drawn daily from a small number of specific instances. But there are also many instances where generalizing causes one of two problems: (1) either an overgeneralization occurs or (2) a previously drawn generalization prevents a valid response to the immediate instance.

In his book *Body Language,* Julius Fast overgeneralizes when he writes "the southern white sees the black as a nonperson, an object not worth concerning himself about."[5] That overgeneralization lumps Ralph McGill and Terry Sanford, and thousands of southern whites like them, with the Grand Dragon of the Ku Klux Klan and the presidents of the various White Citizens Councils, and thousands like them. In Fast's eyes, apparently, *all* southern whites are alike. On the other hand, some southerners overgeneralize when they say, "Northerners have a double standard on the race issue," failing to recognize that many northerners are fully aware of and reject the double standard used by some northerners in discussing racial problems of the two sections. The list of cases in which overgeneralizing occurs is endless.

On other occasions, we permit a previously drawn generalization to obscure the actual features of the immediate instance. Mark Twain gives a wonderful example:

> People who claim to know say that I smoke the worst cigars in the world. They bring their own cigars when they come to my house. They betray an unmanly terror when I offer them a cigar; they tell lies and hurry away to meet engagements which they have not made when they are threatened with the hospitalities of my box. Now then, observe what superstition, assisted by a man's reputation, can do.
>
> I was to have twelve personal friends to supper one night. One of them was as notorious for costly and elegant cigars as I was for cheap and devilish ones. I called at his house and when no one was looking borrowed a double handful of his very choicest; cigars which cost him forty cents apiece and bore red-and-gold labels in sign of their nobility. I removed the labels and put the cigars into a box with my favorite brand on it—a brand which those people all knew, and which cowed them as men are cowed by an epidemic.
>
> They took these cigars when offered at the end of the supper, and lit them and sternly struggled with them—in dreary silence, for hilarity died when the fell brand came into view and started around—but their fortitude held for a short time only; then they made excuses and filed out, treading on one another's heels with indecent eagerness; and in the morning when I went out to observe results the cigars lay all between the front door and the gate. All except one—that one lay in the plate of the man from whom I had cabbaged the lot. One or two whiffs was all he could stand. He told me afterward that some day I would get shot for giving people that kind of cigars to smoke.[6]

In other words, these friends of Mark Twain were unable to respond to the realities of the situation because they allowed a generalization to control their reactions—even to the point of denying a sensory experience.

Remember that each member of a class is a separate entity, even though it possesses many characteristics in common with other members of that class. There has been a tendency for some of the news media to talk about "college students" as though all college students possess the same characteristics. But college students and professors know that almost every campus has students who can be classified as reactionaries, conservatives, moderates, liberals, and radicals, with all the shadings and nuances found within each of those labels.

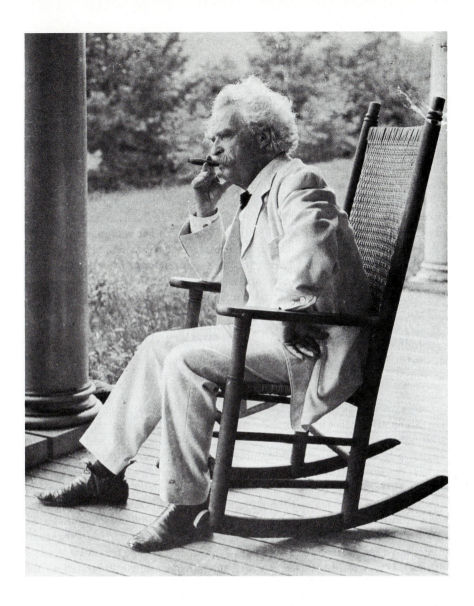

To avoid the error of overgeneralizing or of failing to respond validly to the immediate instance, general semanticists suggest that we index members of any class of objects. Remember that New Yorker[1] is not New Yorker[2] is not New Yorker[3] . . . is not New Yorker[99]. Remember that each individual has particular attributes. We must await specific information about the individual before we can draw any conclusions.

Of course, there are times when one reacts legitimately to the specific situation on the basis of a generalization. If you live in an area where poisonous snakes abound and you see a snake in your yard, you must behave as though it is a poisonous one until you have definite evidence it is not.

Things Change with Time

Some people talk and act as though we live in a static, unchanging world. They expect events and objects to remain constant, and people to behave consistently. There are in this country nearly 1 million women who have had mastectomies. One surgeon who performed some of them recently told columnist Ellen Goodman "I don't do mastectomies anymore." After surveying research that questioned radical mastectomies, he quit doing them. Then he examined research that challenged simple mastectomies and quit doing them. He said to Goodman "I don't . . . believe in mastectomies anymore."[7] Some, especially former patients, will criticize the doctor for behaving inconsistently. But he was undoubtedly doing what the current research suggested when he performed mastectomies, and he is doing today what the current research suggests. To expect a doctor or any person to behave the same way over a period of years is to imply a desire for a foolish consistency that Emerson called "the hobgoblin of little minds."

During the late 1960s and early 1970s, Joan Baez was an ardent foe of the Vietnam War. She made many negative statements about the U.S. government and positive statements about the North Vietnamese government. In 1979, however, she made negative statements about the Vietnamese government's treatment of the Cambodians. In fact, she traveled to Southeast Asia to help the Cambodians and to call attention to the atrocities being committed by the Vietnamese. Some of her antiwar cohorts were critical of her statements and her actions. But Joan Baez recognized what her former allies did not: things had changed; 1979 was not 1969.

There are those who picture the South as a region of economic deprivation, but they are thinking of the South that in the 1930s Franklin D. Roosevelt called the "nation's number one economic problem." Even as late as 1965, the South ranked last among the four major regions in the country in the number of families with incomes of fifteen thousand dollars and above. In 1978, however, the South ranked second among the regions in this important economic indicator.

If you are to communicate meaning that coincides with the reality that the language signifies, you must consider the phenomena you're discussing in the context in which they occurred.

Things Change with the Situation

A person who exhibited the same personality in response to every situation would win an award for being an oddity. The happy, carefree, witty conversationalist would be totally out of place at a funeral. Yet because an individual behaves in a certain way in one place, we attach a label to him or her as though that describes him or her in all places.

Students are frequently amazed when they meet one of their professors in a social situation and find him or her different from what she or he is in the classroom. Some think it is hypocritical for a person to behave differently in one situation than in another; but it is simply an adaptation to changing conditions. A black robe on a minister in the pulpit on Sunday morning is appropriate; that same robe worn to the grocery store would be ludicrous. To argue that adaptations of this sort are hypocritical is to demand a simplicity of behavior that ignores the complexities of one's environment. In arriving at any meaning, therefore, you can establish a more realistic relationship between your meaning and the event itself if you first ascertain the situation in which the phenomenon occurred.

Your language communicates precise meaning only if your thoughts have developed valid meanings. If you're unwilling to apply the necessary principles to produce clear and precise thinking, your language can't be clear and precise. And if listeners recognize your language is unclear and imprecise, you'll have a difficult time establishing credibility.

Style

Once you have assured yourself that your meanings are closely related to reality, turn your attention to the rhetorical process of selecting and arranging the precise language to communicate that meaning to listeners. The result of this process will be the *style* of your speech. Style results from language freely chosen and freely arranged. Grammar involves language chosen and arranged because of prescribed rules.

The style of a speech is important because it can contribute significantly to a speaker's credibility.[8] Five factors affect the style of a speech: clarity, appropriateness, economy, originality, and vitality.

Clarity is the use of words that evoke your intended meaning in the mind of your listeners. If you are to be effective in communicating, each listener must understand your meaning.

Clarity

Exactness in word choice is one way of achieving clarity of meaning. If the words chosen don't mean what you intend, it is difficult for the intended meaning to be evoked in the mind of the listener. During the telecast of a football game recently, the commentator, a former football coach, said "Anytime you have a big receiver—6'4", 200 pounds—it's *apropos* to throw to him." The commentator could have used the word *appropriate* (which he undoubtedly meant), or *correct, proper, legitimate,* but not *apropos.* On the other hand, a minister invited people in his radio audience to come to his church for the morning service, promising them they would not be *impersonated.* He probably meant *intimidated,* but listeners could only guess!

One of the difficulties in selecting the right word stems from the fact that words generate two levels of meaning: extensional and intensional. *Extensional* meaning "is something that *cannot be expressed in words,* because it is that which words stand for. An easy way to remember this is to put your hand over your mouth and point whenever you are asked to give an extensional meaning." On the other hand, the *intensional* meaning of a word is that meaning which exists in a person's head.[9] A word must have intensional meaning or it is just meaningless noise signifying nothing. But a word may not have extensional meaning. The word "ghosts," for example, has no extensional meaning because we can't put our hand over our mouth and point to one.

Extensional and Intensional Levels

The intensional meaning of a word will vary from person to person, then, depending on the experiences the individual has had. This is why communication is most precarious in those situations in which the people trying to communicate are most different from one another. And, "it is partly a matter of vocabulary." The reason is that "each of us, out of his own linguistic history, has built up a very special vocabulary, and the further apart we are in education, social class, occupational specialty, and the rest, the less in common our stocks of words will have."[10]

To help overcome this problem, seek similarities between yourself and your listeners and try to select words that commonly occur in those areas. In a recent study experimenters selected pairs of subjects who were most alike and pairs of subjects who were least alike. The subjects then participated in a modified form of the game "password." Only semantic clues were accepted; no nonsemantic clues such as rhyming, proper names, and other forms of the password were permitted. The results revealed that the communication of meaning between the two subjects was positively related to the similarity of their past experiences.[11]

Ambiguous Words and Phrases

Ambiguous words are an obstacle to clarity. Some words are ambiguous because they are too technical for the particular listener. A student who goes home for vacation and begins to talk to younger brothers or sisters about pragmatism won't communicate clearly because of the unfamiliar word. Some words are ambiguous because they are too abstract. Terms like "Protestant ethic" and "middle class values" have too many different meanings to communicate precisely. Some words are ambiguous because they are euphemisms—a substitution of a mild, indirect, or vague expression for a harsh or blunt one. In the 1988 presidential election, Democrats avoided use of the word "abortion" and spoke of "the fundamental right of reproductive choice."[12]

Some euphemisms are harmless. To say "vehicle appearance specialists" instead of car washers,[13] or "grain-consuming animal units" instead of cows, pigs, and chickens, or "fourth-quarter equity retreat" instead of the 1987 stock market crash, harms no one. But when doctors at a Philadelphia hospital "described one patient's death as a 'diagnostic misadventure of a high magnitude,'" the head of the Doublespeak committee of the National Council of Teachers of English interpreted: "They killed the guy. . . . They perforated his colon and he died."[14]

Gobbledygook interferes with clarity. For example, an exit is defined by the Occupational Safety and Health Administration rulebook as "that portion of a means of egress which is separated from all other spaces of the building or structure by construction or equipment as required in this subpart to provide a protected way of travel to the exit discharge." To avoid confusion, the rulebook defines "means of egress" as "a continuous and unobstructed way of exit travel from any point in a building or structure to a public way and consists of three separate and distinct parts: the way of exit access, the exit, and the way of exit discharge."[15] Gibberish such as this does nothing to aid communication.

If you present your meaning in an ambiguous form, hearers tend to distort the meaning to accord with their own attitudes. One encouraging finding is that there is little distortion of meaning when the communication is well structured. Despite the imprecision of language, it does a remarkable job of communicating when used correctly. On the other hand, when the message is ambiguous, there is a consistent, systematic correlation between the assigned meaning and the person's attitude.[16] Undoubtedly, some take advantage of this tendency, but for those who are interested in accurate communication of meaning, ambiguity must be avoided.

One of the ways to avoid ambiguity is to define unclear words or concepts. Definition offers listeners a precise meaning for whatever you are talking about. In discussing types of workers, one speaker used definition to make his meaning clearer:

> So we have the emergence of what have been called *autonomous individuals*. I first came across this very descriptive expression in a speech by John Panabaker, chairman of Mutual Life Assurance Company of Canada.
>
> Autonomous individuals are confident that personal disaster will not befall them, that they will live a long life and that financial hardship is not a major risk. So they look at the workplace in a much different way. They do not fear their company or fear for the jobs. They are mobile and aggressive. Their social and work relationships are not viewed as permanent or even long-lived. They do want to contribute and to achieve, but the driving force is not economic survival. That doesn't mean that they're less moral or ethical. In fact, they may be more honest and straightforward than the pre-1960 generation."[17]

Any effort exerted to create unambiguous messages will be worthwhile. Carbone found that messages attributed to high-credibility sources had fewer ambiguous sentences than those messages attributed to low-credibility sources.[18]

Appropriateness

Language must be appropriate—to yourself, to your listeners, to the subject, and to the occasion.

If the speaker is an educated person, his or her language must be that of an educated person. This doesn't mean it can't be informal, but it does mean that it must be informal *educated* language. If the president of a university said, "I ain't gonna go," it would seem inappropriate.

Language must also be appropriate to the listeners. The vocabulary used in talking to a group of high school students should be different from the vocabulary used in talking to a group of Ph.D.s. The technical language appropriate to a speech professor discussing ethos with a group of speech professors would not be appropriate if the same professor were discussing ethos with a group of high school or college students. If accurate meaning is to be communicated, use language that is appropriate to the listeners you are addressing.

The occasion will also determine what kind of language is appropriate. If you were talking to a small group in a very informal situation, you would certainly have difficulty in creating credibility with any semblance of formality in your language. To a large group in a less informal situation, you could be more formal in the use of language. In a very formal situation, you might use no informal language; you would certainly use very little. Long ago, classical rhetoricians identified three levels of style—low, middle, and sublime—as being appropriate for different occasions. Today we encourage speakers to use, in most situations, the conversational mode, an informal style that is oral rather than written.

Analysis of extemporaneous speeches and essays prepared by the same students on the same topic showed that (1) oral language was significantly more readable than the written language; (2) average sentence length was significantly shorter in oral language than in written language; (3) the vocabulary of oral language was less varied; (4) oral language used significantly more personal words than written language; and (5) oral language used significantly fewer syllables per one hundred words than written language.[19] Another study found that messages attributed to high-credibility sources used a more diverse vocabulary, more unfamiliar words, and a style that was more oral than written.[20]

DeVito compared random samples of the writings of ten university professors with random samples of their oral comments given in response to questions made up by the experimenter from the professors' writings. The results indicated that (1) there were significantly more self-reference words (I, me, our, we, us) in oral than in written style; (2) written style had more quantifying terms, but not significantly so; (3) oral style had significantly more pseudoquantifying terms (much, many, a lot) than written style; (4) there were significantly more allness terms (none, all, every, always, never) in oral than in written style; (5) oral style had significantly more qualification terms (if, however, but) than written style; and (6) terms indicative of consciousness of projection (apparently, seems, appears, to me) occurred significantly more in oral than in written style.[21]

At first glance it appears that a greater use of pseudoquantifying terms and allness terms in oral language indicates that imprecise communication is taking place. Happily, evidence exists that there may be more precision in these terms than appears. Simpson first presented twenty such terms (*always, never, often, generally, occasionally, frequently*) to students in 1942 and asked them to assign a numerical percentage to each.[22] Some twenty years later he again presented the same twenty terms, plus five additional ones, to "students drawn from all sections of the United States but predominantly from the Midwest." The results for the two groups of students, twenty years apart, were "strikingly" similar. "For only one word, *sometimes,* was the difference greater than five percentage points (20 vs. 27), and in over one-third of the terms the percentages are identical."[23]

In summary, informal oral style is distinguished from written style by the following characteristics:

1. The average sentence length is shorter.
2. The vocabulary consists of fewer different words.
3. The vocabulary includes a larger number of short words.
4. More self-reference words are used (I, me, our, us, we).
5. More pseudoquantifying terms are used (much, many, a lot).
6. More allness terms are used (none, all, every, always).
7. More terms indicative of consciousness of projection occur.
8. Fewer quantifying terms (precise numerical terms) are used.
9. More informal language, such as contractions and colloquial words, is used.
10. More qualifying terms are used.

For your informal speeches, use language described by these ten characteristics. Most people speak and hear it on a daily basis. It is familiar language to them. When you use this language, you'll be relatively sure your listeners will understand what you're saying.

Economy

Economy shouldn't be confused with brevity or conciseness. It means expressing one's meaning in the most effective way, regardless of the number of words used. Just as an individual buys an expensive pair of shoes because it's more economical than purchasing a cheap pair that wears out much quicker, so the speaker is more concerned with the effectiveness of the words used than with the number of words. Striving to attain economy in language doesn't mean eliminating all redundancy, for some is vital to effective oral communication. But it does mean elimination of excess words, which not only fail to add helpful redundancy but also obscure meaning in a forest of words.

Sometimes economy is achieved through the use of fewer words. An excellent example of both wordiness and conciseness was reported by the Washington Post–Los Angeles Times News Service. Robert H. Finch, then HEW Secretary, asked his executive secretary, L. Patrick Gray III, to circulate a message urging his staff to send him shorter briefing memoranda. Unfortunately, Mr. Gray's message itself lacked conciseness, so some unknown recipient revised it to show that the meaning could be communicated more effectively in significantly fewer words.

For example, Gray's opener was:
"As a general rule, and certainly not applicable in all situations, the briefing memoranda forwarded to the secretary have been loaded with an excessive amount of verbiage."
The translation read: "Most of the briefing memoranda forwarded to the secretary have been too wordy."
Gary's memorandum continued:
"In the future, the briefing memoranda should highlight the issue, set forth alternative courses of action or approaches to resolve the issue, and finally, a

recommendation regarding the action to be taken by the secretary should be made with reasons therefor."

Translation: "Briefing memoranda should highlight the issue, state alternatives to resolve the issue, and suggest the action to be taken by the secretary."

Gray said: "it is envisioned that this sort of writing will not require more than a page and half to two pages at the most."

Translation: "No more than two pages should be required."

An equally terse translation—"supporting data may be appended" was offered for Gray's statement that "additional supporting data, information, comments and supporting documentation may be included beneath the writing referred to above, as deemed necessary."

Gray concluded with:

"The secretary does not, in any way, intend that the free flow of information to him be restricted or limited; however, he does desire that the central issue be highlighted and acted upon in the manner set forth in this memorandum."

Translation: "The secretary does not want the flow of information to him restricted. He does insist that the central issue be highlighted and presented as described above."[24]

On other occasions, economy is attained by using a larger number of words. A paragraph from Martin Luther King, Jr.'s "I Have a Dream" illustrates this:

It is obvious today that America has defaulted on this promissory note insofar as her citizens of color are concerned. Instead of honoring this sacred obligation, America has given the Negro people a bad check; a check which has come back marked "insufficient funds." But we refuse to believe that the bank of justice is bankrupt. We refuse to believe that there are insufficient funds in the great vaults of opportunity of this nation. So we have come to cash this check—a check that will give us upon demand the riches of freedom and the security of justice. We have also come to this hallowed spot to remind America of the fierce urgency of now. This is no time to engage in the luxury of cooling off or to take the tranquilizing drug of gradualism. Now is the time to make real the promises of Democracy. Now is the time to rise from the dark and desolate valley of segregation to the sunlit path of racial justice. Now is the time to open the doors of opportunity to all of God's children. Now is the time to lift our nation from the quicksands of racial injustice to the solid rock of brotherhood.[25]

If King had been concerned only with brevity, he could have expressed those ideas, though not as effectively, in a statement similar to the following:

It is obvious today that America has failed to give blacks the freedom and justice they deserve. We have come to this hallowed spot to remind America of the need for immediate action. There can be no delay. Now is the time to eliminate segregation and racial injustice, and to extend democracy and justice to all citizens.

To be effective, search for fresh ways to express ideas. Of course, there are **Originality** times when a trite expression may communicate meaning more effectively than an original phrasing, but in most instances the original statement will be more attention-getting and more effective.

As you try for originality in language, however, you will be quickly reminded of the relationship between thought and language. Unless you can have an original thought, it will be extremely difficult to achieve originality in language. Until he had the thought, there was no way the late Governor Frank Clement of Tennessee could make the following statement in his keynote address at the 1956 Democratic National Convention: "But [Roosevelt] sat there in his wheelchair taller than his critics could stand." Nor could he have given his description of John Foster Dulles as "the greatest unguided missile in the history of American diplomacy," unless the thought had preceded it.[26]

An important way in which originality can be brought to the language of a speech is to use figurative language, which expresses the thought indirectly rather than directly as it would if literal language were used. There are both advantages and disadvantages to using figurative language. It is advantageous because it (1) helps us to understand a new concept either by comparing it with the old concept or by going from the known to the unknown, (2) saves time by "pictorialization," (3) avoids saying something directly which the audience may accept if it is said indirectly, (4) injects a vivid and new sensation because of the establishment of a new relationship. On the other hand, figurative language can sometimes be disadvantageous because (1) the technique may show, and therefore the intent of the speaker becomes suspect, (2) circumlocution may waste time, and (3) it may lead to faulty thinking, causing a breakdown in communication if the audience doesn't understand the allusions.[27]

Concentrate on achieving correctness, clarity, appropriateness, and economy in the use of language. Avoid figurative language until you have mastered these more important elements of language. There is one form of figurative language that seems to come naturally, however, and that is the metaphorical use of language. One student of language has observed that "Some of our literary professors have misled us about metaphor. It is not an extra beauty stuck on to language—it is language."[28] People in all walks of life use such statements as "The car ate up the miles." "The quarter-miler roared around the track."

Reinsch compared the effectiveness of figurative language with literal language by preparing three forms of a speech: one with only literal language, one in which four metaphors replaced the literal language, and one in which four similes replaced the metaphors. All three forms of the speech caused subjects hearing them to change their attitudes in the desired direction significantly more than subjects who heard no speech. But the speech using metaphors caused the subjects to shift their attitudes significantly more than those who heard the literal speech. Although the speech using similes shifted attitudes more than the literal speech, the change was not significantly greater.[29] Feel free to use metaphors. But develop them carefully. One writer says they "ought to be short—almost epigrammatic—and they have to be kept internally consistent. Metaphors are the mint in our juleps, the brandy in the sauce, the pimiento in the olive."[30]

Another important way of achieving originality in language is to use certain stylistic devices. But don't become so involved with stylistic devices that you seem more concerned with them than with communicating. There are, however, a few such devices which, if used sparingly, can add impact to a message. *Alliteration,* the repetition of a sound in two or more adjacent words, can be used effectively. Notice the impact of these phrases: "candidates of competence and conscience," "party of privilege and pillage," "cunningly conceived to convince," "fantastic, frantic, and fatal policy."[31] *Asyndeton,* the omission of conjunctions between a series of related clauses, may occasionally be used effectively. An example of asyndeton occurs in John F. Kennedy's inaugural address: "we shall pay any price, bear any burden, meet any hardship, support any friend, oppose any foe to assure the survival and the success of liberty."[32] *Parallel structure,* a similar phrasing of parts of a sentence or paragraph of equal importance, is probably the easiest stylistic device for the beginning student to use. In his speech, "I Have a Dream," Martin Luther King, Jr., used parallel structure effectively. Following is one example:

> But *one hundred years later,* we must face the tragic fact that the Negro is still not free. *One hundred years later,* the life of the Negro is still sadly crippled by the manacles of segregation and the chains of discrimination. *One*

hundred years later, the Negro lives on a lonely island of poverty in the midst of a vast ocean of material prosperity. *One hundred years later,* the Negro is still languished in the corners of American society and finds himself an exile in his own land. So we have come here today to dramatize an appalling condition.[33]

Vitality

Vitality, or forcefulness, of style is achieved largely through the characteristics of the sentences employed. Sentences are the grammatical units by which we most commonly express our ideas. They may be active or passive, simple or complex, short or long, loose or periodic. Rhetoricians have traditionally advised the use of active sentences—the boy drove the car—rather than passive sentences—the car was driven by the boy. They believed that active sentences were more forceful and easier to comprehend. Evidence indicates this may be an oversimplification. Active sentences were easier for the subjects to recall when an initial noun phrase was used as a prompt. When active and passive versions of the same passage were analyzed by three readability formulas, however, no significant difference in the readability level was found.[34]

Although you don't want to be reduced to the use of short, simple sentences of the "Ned sees the dog" variety, there is evidence you should be wary of using many long sentences. One expert produced ten sentences each of the following lengths: 3, 5, 7, 9, 11, 13, 15, and 17 words. The sentences were recorded and played back to four groups of subjects. Half of each group heard the recording in a quiet condition; the other half heard them with varying degrees of masking noise. Subjects were asked to write the last three words of each sentence. The results revealed that louder noise or increased length of a sentence made it less likely "that a listener would identify the final three words of the sentence, and the longer the sentence the more disastrous was the effect of noise."[35] In addition, too many long sentences bleed vitality from your style.

Introduce variety and suspense into your style by changing a sentence from the loose to the periodic form. A *periodic* sentence is one in which the thought is not complete until the end of the sentence. Here is a periodic sentence: If inflation is to be curbed, wages and prices must be controlled. A *loose* sentence expresses the same idea as follows: Wages and prices must be controlled if inflation is to be curbed. It is obvious that the periodic sentence prompts the listener to keep listening to find out what must be done, whereas the loose sentence tells the listener quickly what the main thought of the sentence is so he may quit listening to the last part. Too many periodic sentences, however, may impart an artificial flavor to an oral speech style, so use them sparingly.

Another type of sentence that may be used sparingly is that known as a *chiasmus,* a sentence with two parts in which the second "is syntactically balanced against the first but with the parts reversed. . . ."[36] Someone recently used a chiasmus to express changed attitudes toward policemen: "Kids used to look up to the cop on the beat; now kids look to beat up on the cop." A chiasmus has also been used to point up the results of inflation: "We used to go to the stores with money in our pockets and come back with food in our baskets—now we go with money in baskets and come back with food in our pockets." Probably the most widely publicized chiasmus, however, is one used by John F. Kennedy in his inaugural address: "Ask not what your country can do for you—ask what you can do for your country." Obviously, too many of this kind of sentence would destroy the oral quality of a speaker's style. But one or two—rarely more than two—well placed in the speech can do much to enliven the style and invigorate the attention of the listener.

A final type of sentence to be considered is the *rhetorical question,* one asked by the speaker to which a reply is neither required nor expected. The answer may either be implied in the question itself or provided shortly thereafter by the speaker. The following speaker used two rhetorical questions without answering either one:

> But average American viewers are currently watching 7 hours and 34 minutes of television every day of their lives. Children between the ages of 6 and 11 are watching an average of 27 hours a week, 1400 hours a year. By the time a youngster graduates from high school, he or she will spend more time in front of the tube than in the classroom—and I ask you, how much of what is available for them to view do you believe can materially raise the level of their taste? How much of it do you believe serves to teach, illuminate, and inspire?[37]

You'll have a difficult time developing credibility if you give the impression you are playing with style, to the exclusion of ideas; but you should, through use of different kinds of sentences, get variety and vitality in your speech.

Summary

Meaning—the understanding a specific person has of anything in his or her environment—exists only in the individual's mind and must be communicated to others by means of language, an imprecise instrument at best. You must always be aware there is no direct connection between the words you use and the objects they represent. The only connection is that made in your own mind.

Thought and language are interdependent. Unless your thoughts, or meaning, accurately reflect reality, language must of necessity distort reality for the listener. Six suggestions are offered to help in relating meaning to reality: (1) recognize that it is impossible to know everything; (2) remember that things are seldom as clear-cut as they sound; (3) remember that language reflects your view of the world; (4) judge each instance on its own merits; (5) understand that things change with time; and (6) understand that things change with the situation.

Once you have ascertained that your meaning is related to reality, you can turn your attention to the rhetorical process of choosing the style of your message. Style is defined as the "selection and arrangement of those linguistic features which are open to choice." Five factors that help to determine style are discussed: (1) clarity, (2) appropriateness, (3) economy, (4) originality, and (5) vitality.

Exercises

1. Prepare a two-minute speech in which you define some abstract word or phrase that is in common use, such as *women's lib, the whole man, New Federalism, affirmative action, flat tax, secular humanism, scientific creationalism.*
2. You have been invited to speak to a high school assembly in your hometown. What qualities of style would you be concerned with in order to create credibility for your ideas? How would this affect your use of language?
3. Analyze the language used by a classmate in a speech. What does the language do to establish credibility? In what ways could the speaker have used language differently to improve his or her credibility?
4. Phrase the main points of your next speech in parallel form.
5. Prepare three periodic sentences to use in your next speech.
6. Select an essay and rewrite it in an oral style.
7. Prepare two chiasmi for use in your next speech.

Notes

1. R. E. Nebergall, "An Experimental Investigation of Rhetorical Clarity," *Speech Monographs* 25 (1958):243.
2. Jack W. Germond and Jules Witcover, "Politics Today," *The Birmingham News,* September 19, 1984, p. 11A. Used by permission.
3. S. I. Hayakawa, "A Search for Relevance," in *Communication: General Semantics Perspectives,* ed. L. Thayer (New York: Spartan Books, 1970), pp. 87–88.
4. AP Dispatch, *Durham Sun,* July 15, 1971.
5. J. Fast, *Body Language* (New York: M. Evans and Co., 1970), p. 70.
6. Mark Twain, "Concerning Tobacco," in *What Is Man* (New York: Harper and Brothers, 1917), pp. 275–76.
7. E. Goodman, "Can You Trust Doctor Who Changes Mind?," *Birmingham Post-Herald,* January 25, 1980. © 1980, The Boston Globe Newspaper Company/ Washington Post Writers Group, reprinted with permission.
8. T. Carbone, "Stylistic Variables as Related to Source Credibility: A Content Analysis Approach," *Speech Monographs* 42 (1975):99–106.
9. S. I. Hayakawa, *Language in Action* (New York: Harcourt, Brace and Co., 1949), p. 47.
10. J. Church, "Cognitive Differences as Impediments to Communication with Some Uneasy Hindthoughts on the Questions What? and Whether?," in *Communication: Theory and Research,* ed. L. Thayer (Springfield, Ill.: Charles C Thomas, Publisher, 1967), pp. 175–76.
11. C. F. Vick and R. V. Wood, "Similarity of Past Experience and the Communication of Meaning," *Speech Monographs* 36 (1969):159–62.

12. "Democrats Turn from Rift, Move on to the Big Battle," *The Wall Street Journal,* July 20, 1988, p. 50.
13. Lloyd Shearer, "Intelligence Report," in *Parade,* April 3, 1988, p. 12.
14. Associated Press, "Year's Worst 'Doublespeak' Recognized," in *The Birmingham News,* November 20, 1988, p. 31A.
15. U.S. Department of Labor, Occupational Safety and Health Administration, *General Industry: OSHA Safety and Health Standards* (29 CFR 1910), OSHA 2206, Revised, November 7, 1978, p. 52.
16. P. G. Zimbardo, "Verbal Ambiguity and Judgmental Distortion," *Psychological Reports* 6 (1960):57–58. Examples of the indeterminate type of ambiguity are "Anyone who has known a scientist personally will know why science is where it is today." "If you have followed recent developments in science, you will know that there can be one solution to the problem."
17. James M. Hay, "The Public Face of the Chemical Industry," *Vital Speeches of the Day* 53 (1987):180. © City News Publishing Company. Used by permission.
18. Carbone, "Stylistic Variables as Related to Source Credibility."
19. J. W. Gibson et al., "A Quantitative Examination of Differences and Similarities in Written and Spoken Messages," *Speech Monographs* 33 (1966):444–51.
20. Carbone, "Stylistic Variables as Related to Source Credibility."
21. J. A. DeVito, "Psychogrammatical Factors in Oral and Written Discourse by Skilled Communicators," *Speech Monographs* 33 (1966):73–76.
22. R. H. Simpson, "The Specific Meanings of Certain Terms Indicating Different Degrees of Frequency," *Quarterly Journal of Speech* 30 (1944):328–30.
23. R. H. Simpson, "Stability in Meanings for Quantitative Terms: A Comparison over 20 Years," *Quarterly Journal of Speech* 49 (1963):146–51.
24. *Durham* (N.C.) *Morning Herald,* March 17, 1969. Copyright, The *Washington Post.* Reprinted with permission Los Angeles Times—Washington Post News Service.
25. D. E. Saunders, ed., *The Day They Marched* (Chicago: Johnson Publishing Co., 1963), pp. 81–82. Copyright 1963 by Martin Luther King, Jr. Permission by Joan Daves.
26. Frank G. Clement, "Keynote Address," *Vital Speeches of the Day* 22 (1956):674–79. Used by permission.
27. P. D. Brandes, "Coding the Communication," unpublished mimeographed manuscript, 1969.
28. H. R. Walpole, *Semantics* (New York: W. W. Norton & Co., 1941), p. 154.
29. N. L. Reinsch, Jr., "An Investigation of the Effects of the Metaphor and Simile in Persuasive Discourse," *Speech Monographs* 38 (1971):142–45.
30. J. J. Kilpatrick, "The Writer's Art," *Birmingham News,* July 4, 1982. Used by permission.
31. Clement, "Keynote Address." For a fuller discussion of Clement's use of style, see B. E. Bradley, "Back to the Red Clay Hills," *Southern Speech Communication Journal* 25 (1960):199–204.
32. *Inaugural Addresses of the Presidents of the United States,* 87th Cong., 1st sess., House Document no. 218 (Washington, D.C.: U.S. Government Printing Office, 1961), pp. 267–70.

33. Saunders, *The Day They Marched,* p. 81. Italics added.

34. J. A. DeVito, "Some Psycholinguistic Aspects of Active and Passive Sentences," *Quarterly Journal of Speech* 55 (1969):401–6.

35. J. W. Black, "Aural Reception of Sentences of Different Lengths," *Quarterly Journal of Speech* 47 (1961):51–53.

36. W. F. Thrall, A. Hibbard, and C. H. Holman, *A Handbook to Literature* (New York: Odyssey Press, 1960), p. 82.

37. Norman Lear, "Does TV Have the Courage to Pioneer a New Commercial Ethic?" in *Representative American Speeches, 1984–1985,* ed. Owen Peterson (New York: H. W. Wilson Company, 1985), pp. 194–95. Used by permission.

CHAPTER 17

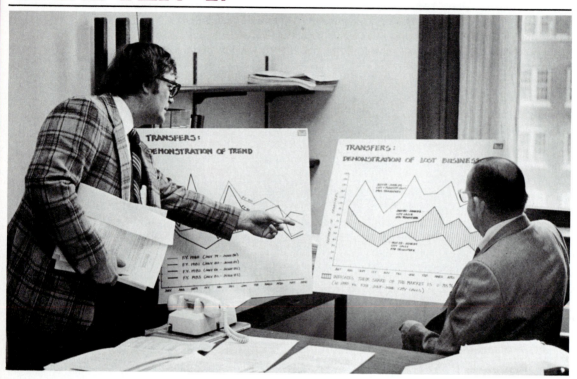

Using Visual Aids

There is an old saying that "Seeing and hearing is believing." That's the value of visual aids in a speech. By seeing pictures or graphs, listeners understand and believe more easily what you're presenting. If you're talking about an object the listeners have never seen, then the reality of the object is provided by a visual aid.

When preparing your speech, identify any objects or concepts unfamiliar to your listeners. If you plan to talk about an unfamiliar object, take it or a replica to the speech so the listeners can see it and thus more fully understand what you're talking about. If you're going to discuss an unfamiliar concept, you can sometimes create better understanding by showing analogous objects or pictures.

Showing a visual aid or a replica to your listeners can help establish a common perception of the object. There will then be less opportunity for listeners to misunderstand what you're talking about.

As soon as you have prepared your speech, decide what, if any, visual aids are desirable or necessary. If visual aids are needed, determine what kind will be best. Then prepare them in the most professional way you can.

Means of Presenting Visual Aids

A number of media are available to aid in presenting your visual aids to the listeners. This unit discusses these media and suggests ways in which they can be used.

The first group of media to be considered is called *demonstration boards*. A *chalkboard*, the same as that on which your teacher writes with chalk, may be used during your speech. If you're giving a classroom speech, you may write on the board in the room. For speeches in other situations, however, you will have to buy or make a chalkboard to carry to the site of your speech. Letters and numbers on a chalkboard should be at least 2 ½ to 3 inches high in order to be easily seen from the back row in a normal size classroom.[1] A significant disadvantage of chalkboards is that many people have poor handwriting, which creates legibility problems.

A *feltboard* or *flannelboard*, as the name implies, is made by attaching felt or flannel cloth to a hardbacking of wood, Celotex, or metal. Give the object to be displayed a backing of felt, flannel, sandpaper, cotton, pipe cleaners, or any substance that will adhere to the surface of the board. Objects shown on the feltboard must be relatively light in weight to keep from falling off.

A *hook 'n loop* board is one that is covered with Velcro. It comes in two forms: a loop type material and a hook type material. When the two are pressed together, they form a tight union and will support rather heavy objects. The loop material is used on the board and the hook material is attached to the back of the objects to be displayed.

A *magnetic board* must obviously be made of metal. Objects to be displayed on this board must have small bar or strip magnets attached to them. Strip magnets are strips of rubber saturated with magnetized steel filings. They can be sewn, glued, or pinned to objects displayed.

A *flip chart,* a pad of large sheets of paper about 27 inches by 33 inches, can be used effectively, especially if you have drawing talent. You can write or draw on the top sheet and when it has been filled, you can flip it over and write or draw on the next one.[2]

Poster board can also be used to present visual material. A disadvantage to guard against is the tendency for listeners to attend to parts of the visual aid you're not discussing. To prevent this, prepare the material so you can leave covered the parts not being discussed. Cover each unit with a strip of paper that can be removed when you're ready to discuss that section. This *strip tease* technique prevents the listeners from moving from the topic you're discussing to the one you plan to discuss next. Only your ingenuity limits what you can do with poster board. You can prepare add-on materials by simply using a loop of fresh masking tape that can be pressed on the back of the object to be displayed and then pressed on the poster board.

The second group of visual aids consists of graphs and charts that make processing of information easier for your listeners.

Graphs are especially helpful if you want to use numerical data to make comparisons. These data can be prepared in different ways to serve different purposes. Bar graphs, pie graphs, line graphs, profile graphs, organizational charts, and pictographs provide various ways to make information clearer and more vivid.[3]

A *bar graph* presents the amount of data by the length of a thick bar. Each bar generally represents one year, although it can also represent a day, a week, or a month. The bars may be perpendicular or horizontal. (See figures 17.1 and 17.2.)

A *pie graph* (figure 17.3 on p. 275) can demonstrate the percentage of the whole amount devoted to a specific item. The visual perception makes clearer the relationship of the various divisions.

A *line graph* can be used to identify visually the changes in amount or numbers over a given period of time. (See figure 17.4 on p. 276.)

A *profile graph* is a line graph with the area under a line filled with colored material to more clearly delineate the area under a specific line. If there is more than one line on the graph, each line's underlying surface is a different color.[4] (See figure 17.5 on p. 277.)

An *organizational chart* identifies the positions and the lines of authority in an organization. It establishes the areas of responsibility for each member of the organization. The organizational chart in figure 17.6 on p. 278 establishes the areas of responsibility for a university library.

The *pictograph* is a variation on the bar chart using a series of small identifying symbols to present the data. The figures are usually arranged horizontally, but may be arranged vertically. Each symbol may represent a single

Figure 17.1
Sample bar graph.
Source: 1989 Agricultural Chartbook. *U.S. Department of Agriculture, Agriculture Handbook No. 684.*

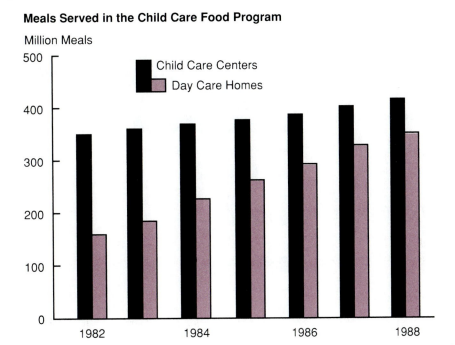

Meals Served in the Child Care Food Program

1988 estimated. Fiscal years.

person or a particular unit. Generally, a symbol will represent a fixed number of persons or units. The number of items is determined by the variable being graphed, which in turn determines the length of the bar. Figure 17.7 on p. 279 illustrates a pictograph with a single person being represented by a symbol.

The third group of media consists of electrical equipment that can present information to an audience. The *overhead projector* flashes information from a transparency onto a screen. The ease of operation—the speaker only has to lay the transparency on top of the overhead projector—makes this an ideal visual aid for a speaker if the information can be put on a transparency. You can increase the effectiveness of a transparency by constructing the basic idea and then using overlay units to add other features that you want to discuss.[5] Many transparencies are developed by commercial firms. In addition, the Learning Resources Center in your institution can easily produce them, generally for only a small fee. Research has indicated that letters on transparencies must be at least ³⁄₁₆, and preferably ¼, inch high in order to be readable at a distance of twenty to forty feet.[6]

Figure 17.2
Sample bar graph.
Source: U.S. Department of Commerce, Bureau of Economic Analysis.

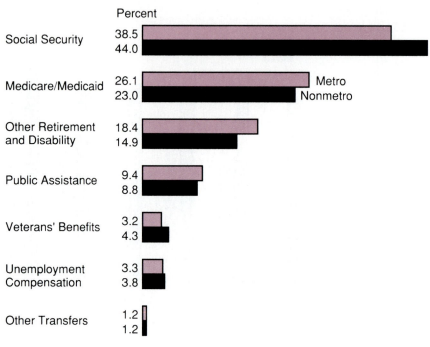

Government Transfer Payments to Individuals

A *slide projector* is one of the easiest electrical media to use and is also one of the most popular. A revolving tray sitting on top of the projector holds the slides. An important and advantageous feature is that, with the projector in the rear, the speaker can stand in front of the audience with a remote control unit and operate the projector. The slides are made when the film is developed. Certain guidelines should be observed in using slide projectors: (1) A day or two before the speech, check to make sure there is an electrical outlet for the projector and that the cord is long enough to reach it. If the slides constitute a significant part of the speech, prudence dictates a backup projector. (2) Be certain the screen on which the slides will be shown is large enough to be seen easily by all members of the audience. (3) Be sure the tray has a cover preventing the slides from falling out. You don't want to have to replace them in proper order just before or during your speech.

Figure 17.3
Sample pie graph.
Source: 1989 Agricultural Chartbook, *U.S. Department of Agriculture, Agriculture Handbook No. 684.*

Number of U.S. Catfish Producers and Total Sales by State

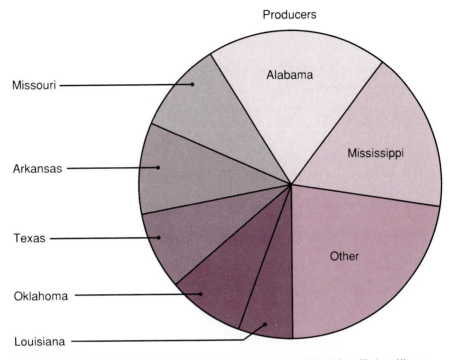

Other Includes California, Florida, Georgia, Kentucky, South Carolina, Tennessee, Idaho, Indiana, Illinois, and Kansas.

A *filmstrip projector* pulls a strip of 35mm film past the lens by a series of sprocket holes. There is no feed or take-up reel. A large number of commercial and free filmstrips are available. Since most filmstrips are very short, they are ideal for demonstrating brief segments in a speech.

All of these projectors require a screen large enough for the images to be seen easily. For most rooms, the screen should be 60″ × 60″. It should be 70″ × 70″ for a large room. The square shape is required for vertical slides and transparencies.[7]

Three other pieces of audio electrical equipment that can be used in the public speaking situation are the *audio tape recorder,* the *motion picture projector,* and the *video tape recorder.* This equipment is less appropriate for most public speaking situations; nevertheless, there are times when one of these pieces of equipment will be helpful and you'll want to use it. You may want

Figure 17.4
Sample line graph.
Source: 1989 Agricultural Chartbook, *U.S. Department of Agriculture, Agriculture Handbook No. 684.*

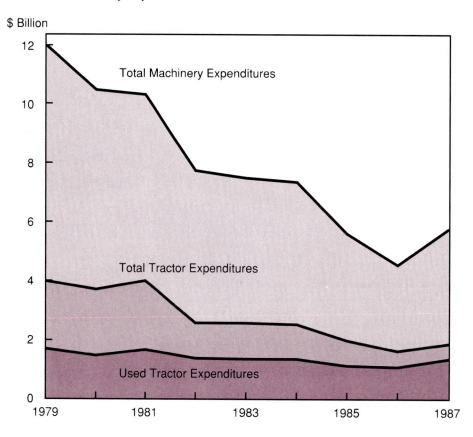

U.S. Farm Machinery Expenditures

to let your listeners hear some sound or some speaker on the audio tape recorder, show a short segment of a movie, or show some action scenes on a television screen.

Preparation of Visual Aids

Some general principles should be applied to all visual aids. First, plain letters work better than fancy ones. Plain ones project a simplicity that is appealing, whereas fancy ones can be difficult to read quickly. Second, the spacing of letters is important. Each letter should not be given the same amount of space, but it should appear that the letters are evenly spaced. For example, if the letter A is given the same amount of space as other letters, it will appear that the A has been given more space than the others. When the A is given a little less space than the others, however, the impression is given that the letters are

Figure 17.5
Sample profile graph.
Source: 1989 Agricultural Chartbook, *U.S. Department of Agriculture, Agriculture Handbook No. 684.*

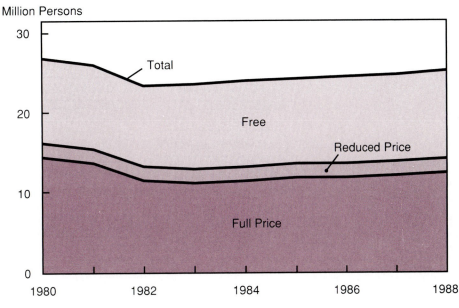

Children in the National School Lunch Program

1988 estimated. Fiscal years.

evenly spaced. Third, visual aids should appear uncluttered. Put only the necessary information on your visual aids. Fourth, colors should be used wisely. A few harmonious colors are better than a large number. Experts recommend that you create a strong contrast among the colors. On a dark background, yellow, orange, red, green, blue, and violet have the greatest carrying power. On a light background, black, red, orange, green, blue, violet, and yellow have the greatest carrying power.[8] Attention to these principles will ensure that your visual aids are attractive and will be easily interpreted.

Principles for Using Visual Aids

Prepare Visual Aids in Advance

There are several reasons for preparing a visual aid before the speech. If you wait to prepare it until the moment in the speech when it's to be used, you generally find yourself unable to create the visual aid and continue talking. Periods of silence thus occur, permitting and encouraging the listeners to focus their attention on other stimuli. You then have a difficult task of regaining their attention; that of some of the listeners will never be regained. Moreover, a visual aid prepared in advance can be attractively constructed: lines straight, circles round, angles precise, colors added to give emphasis and variety to the various parts.

Figure 17.6
Sample organizational chart (the Auburn University Library).

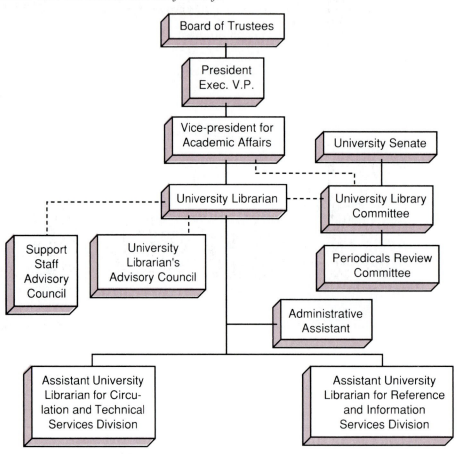

Keep the Visual Aid Covered When Not in Use

If a visual aid is placed uncovered in front of an audience, the listeners begin to scrutinize it and attempt to decipher it. Whatever you say during this time generally goes unheard because few people can attend to two different stimuli simultaneously. Objects themselves should be placed out of sight: in a recess in the lectern, in a box on a nearby table. If the visual aid is on something like poster board, it can be placed on an easel with its blank side to the audience or another blank poster board in front of it. Once you're finished with the visual aid, you should re-cover it or remove it from the listeners' view. If left in view, it can be just as distracting during subsequent parts of the message as during prior parts. A word of warning: don't expose the visual aid too briefly. That only frustrates the listeners. Show it and explain it sufficiently for it to be understood.

Figure 17.7
Sample pictograph.
Source: **Descriptive Statistics,** *00–1834. U.S. Department of Health and Human Services/Public Health Service, Centers for Disease Control, Atlanta, GA 30333. Reprinted January, 1986, p. 17.*

Vaccination Status of Smallpox Cases: United Kingdom—1962, and Sweden—1963

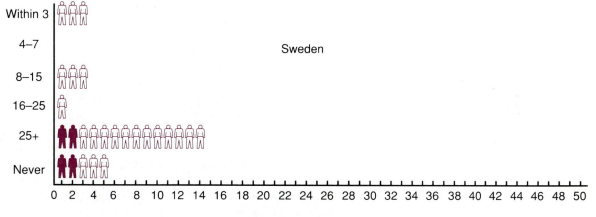

Number of Cases

Remember that you're there to communicate with human beings, not with a visual aid. Talking to the visual aid has a bad psychological impact on listeners; it conveys a lack of interest in talking to them. Furthermore, it prevents you from receiving feedback from the listeners. If some indicate a lack of understanding while you are looking at the visual aid, you'll probably miss that feedback and go blithely on to other ideas, leaving bewildered and confused listeners whose attention you'll probably lose permanently.

Avoid Talking to the Visual Aid

Use Hand Nearer the Visual Aid for Pointing

Using the hand that is away from the visual aid causes you to turn your body toward it, leaving your back toward the listeners. This eliminates direct communication between you and the listeners and discourages close attention by the listeners. It also encourages you to look at the visual aid instead of the listeners. The human body likes to follow the path of least resistance—for the head that means looking straight forward. When the body is turned toward the visual aid, it's only natural for the head to turn that way. Even if you make a special effort to maintain eye contact, your natural impulse is to resume looking toward the visual aid. If you use the hand nearer the visual aid, however, your body remains turned toward the listeners; communication is direct and, following the path of least resistance, eye contact is easily and naturally maintained with the listeners. When you look at the visual aid to find the spot to which you want to point, you naturally look back to the listeners.

Keep Visual Aids Out of Listeners' Hands

A visual aid handed to listeners to be passed around creates a constantly distracting ripple through the audience. At least three persons are more involved with the aid than with what you're saying: the person who just had it, the one who has it, and the one who is expecting to receive it. And this doesn't mention the ones who are never able to understand your ideas once they resume attending to you. Many of these give up in frustration. Even if you have a visual aid for every member of the audience, don't put it in their hands during the speech. It becomes too easy for listeners to attend to different parts of the visual aid. If you want each person to have a copy to examine, announce that ushers will have copies at each exit or they will be available at the conclusion of the speech.

Make the Visual Aid Large Enough

A visual aid should be seen by all members of the audience. There is nothing more irritating than to sit in an audience and be unable to see a visual aid. The size of the aid is determined by the size of the audience, not by the size of the room. If the speech will be given in a room that is thirty feet long, the visual aid can be made large enough to be seen at the rear of the room and it doesn't matter how many people will be present. If the speech is to be given in a room a hundred feet long, but there will be no more than fifty people present, the visual aid needs to be large enough to be seen far enough back to accommodate fifty people. They can be asked to seat themselves close to the speaker. In some large auditoriums, it is simply not practicable to make a visual aid large enough to be seen by all members of the audience. In such situations, it is better to avoid using a visual aid than to irritate and frustrate some because they are unable to see it.

Keep the Visual Aid Simple and Attractive

Remember that a visual aid should be exactly that—an *aid,* not the complete source of information. A visual aid is used because you need some assistance in communicating your ideas. If the visual aid tells the whole story, you don't need to discuss it. Moreover, the less complex the visual aid is, the less the

Figure 17.8
Sample visual aid: the Laffer curve. From Jude Wanniski, The Way the World Works: How Economics Fail—and Succeed. *(New York: Basic Books, Inc., 1978), p. 97. © Basic Books, Inc. Used by permission.*

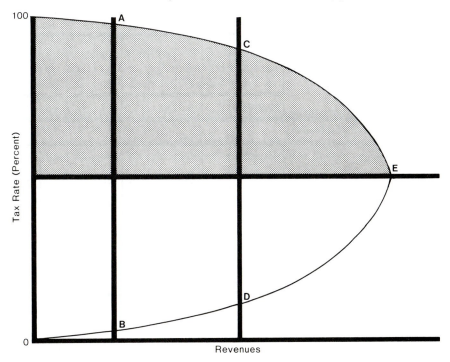

listeners will be distracted by it. The simpler the aid, the easier it will be for you to focus the listeners' attention on the important details. Examine the visual aid in figure 17.8. Note its attractive simplicity, and yet it can't be understood without an oral or written explanation.

Now examine the table in figure 17.9. In this visual aid, the mass of data would be distracting to listeners. They would be shifting attention from one idea to another and from one number to another. In addition, the information is understandable without any explanation. So a listener could stop listening to you and focus full attention on the visual aid.

Finally, remember that visual aids aren't the main part of your speech. They are accessories enabling listeners to process the information you're presenting. Visual aids should never become the focal point of your speech; they should help your listeners identify and understand your main ideas.

Don't expect your visual aid to be effective if it looks amateurish and appears to have been thrown together with little thought and effort. If you prepare it with care and concern, however, your listeners will appreciate your efforts and generally won't develop negative attitudes toward your visual aid.

PART 4

FORMS OF
COMMUNICATION

CHAPTER 18

Informative Speaking

Despite many instances in which people are given insufficient information, speaking to inform is a frequent and important type of communication. Lectures to provide information are presented daily in schools and colleges and to the general public. After installing a new television set, the technician instructs the owner about proper operating procedures. When a car is taken to the repair shop, the owner explains to the service manager what has been happening, when the problem started, under what conditions it recurs, and all other seemingly relevant data that will help the service manager more easily diagnose what is wrong. The President's press secretary informs the media about the President's itinerary on a planned tour of Europe and what the President hopes to accomplish.

Innumerable times each day, all of us either request or give information. Not infrequently, we're led astray or lead others astray by information that is poorly presented or misunderstood. Attention to the principles of informative speaking may improve our communication with others.

In a speech to inform, you want the listener to understand the ideas presented, not for the purpose of persuasion, but simply to have the hearer comprehend. The knowledge of the listener must be expanded; if not, the informative speech can't be considered an effective one. The informative speech is focused more on adding new cognitive elements than on influencing the listener's belief or behavior. A more knowledgeable listener is the goal of the informative speaker.

The following pages discuss the objectives of informative speeches, informative methods to use, and the organization of informative speeches.

Objectives of Informative Speeches

There are several obvious similarities between informative and persuasive speeches. Both need to gain the attention and hold the interest of the listeners. No one can be informed if stimuli other than the speaker are distracting the hearer's attention. Informative speeches are also similar to persuasive speeches in the types of supporting material appropriate for them. Testimony, statistics, and factual data may be used to develop the content of either type of speech. The same sources of information should be consulted, subject to the same tests of credibility, and visual aids can be used to make the content more interesting and more understandable.

Nevertheless, three objectives distinguish informative from persuasive speaking: clarity, balanced development, and retention of material.

Clarity

First, *clarity* is indispensable to the informative speaker. The speaker's meaning must be singularly clear. Audience comprehension is hindered if there is vagueness of meaning. Some persuasive speakers may use ambiguity as a stratagem, even though it frequently backfires. Using such imprecise words as *patriotism, free speech,* and *welfare cheaters,* politicians allow their listeners to attach whatever meaning they desire to these terms.

Clarity begins in the speaker's mind. Comprehension must necessarily precede clarity of thought. Until you understand the subject thoroughly, you can't possibly explain it clearly to someone else. The more you study your subject and understand it, therefore, the easier it will be to achieve clarity of expression.

Clarity can be achieved if you use precise and familiar language, construct sentences in easy-to-follow syntax, select supporting materials that obviously support the reasoning, organize the ideas into a coherent and unified whole, avoid nonverbal forms of communication that contradict the verbal message, and adapt all these elements or factors to the particular listeners.

Balanced Development

Second, the informative speech seeks to provide a *balanced* or *impartial development* of the topic. As a persuasive speaker you can present arguments and evidence supporting your position and ignore opposing positions or information. But biased or overly selective treatment of material is inappropriate for informative speaking. Using materials in informative speaking that deliberately distort or present a misleading perspective is indefensible. As an informative speaker present all facets of the topic and strive to develop a full understanding of the subject. Without a thorough analysis of the topic and a thorough development of the available information, you can't achieve an unbiased, impartial treatment of a topic. Don't be misled into thinking, however, that a thorough treatment must include every detail about a subject; that would only confuse and bore the listeners. Thorough treatment means including an in-depth discussion of important aspects of the subject.

A seeming lack of objectivity can stem from several sources. The audience may suspect bias when pertinent data are ignored. For example, you might discuss the merits of two alternative routes for a highway by considering three topics: (1) cost, (2) engineering problems, and (3) traffic flow. If, however, one route would have a greater impact on residential areas than the other, listeners who live in those areas may assume you're unobjective unless you also discuss that consideration.

You may also appear unobjective if you insert your own value judgments into the presentation. If, after discussing two proposed routes for a highway, you conclude, "So you can see the northern route is bad because it diverts traffic away from our downtown motel district," that is a value judgment and indicates a desire to influence the listeners. In an informative speech, you should present the information and allow the listeners to draw their own conclusions. In this case, the audience may not share the value judgment that it would be bad to divert traffic away from downtown, especially if there is a congestion problem.

On some occasions, the sources of information cited may make the speech appear to be unobjective. Factual information from a source listeners regard as neutral seems more objective than the same factual information from a source perceived as biased. To be an effective informative speaker, choose the particular sources of information with great care.

A third objective of an informative speech is to present material in a way that facilitates *retention of the material*. Most psychologists now agree there are three types of memory—immediate, short-term, and long-term. Immediate memory lasts for only a second or so and then is lost. Information in the short-term memory is available for recall for about thirty seconds and then either goes into the long-term memory or is lost. To get information beyond the listener's short-term memory and into the long-term memory, you must make it possible for memory traces to be strengthened. A memory trace is "a fragile, highly perishable neural response" resulting from a sensory experience. If this memory trace is strengthened, however, "it becomes an actual *change* in the nervous system" instead of a fleeting response.[1] This process is analogous to strolling across a plot of grass between two sidewalks; the slight trace left there is quickly obliterated by rain, wind, snow, or mowing. If you walk that way every day, however, a clear path emerges. As an informative speaker, therefore, you must create paths or "mental sets" for your information in the minds of your listeners.

A number of methods can be used to improve retention of your material.

State your purpose, preview the main points, develop each point separately, and then focus on the purpose and summarize the main points at the end. This repetition should begin to create some pathways. Baird found, for example, that the use of a preview or a summary "significantly increased comprehension."[2] Two types of restatement can be used: repetition and paraphrase. Testimony from other sources to support your ideas can utilize either method to reinforce your ideas in the listeners' minds.

"It is easier to learn and remember something if you understand its overall meaning and can relate it to material you already know."[3] When you use an interesting example that the listener recalls later, you have established an association. For example, I remember only one point made in a speech by a leading educator many years ago: that an educational institution must tailor its programs to the needs of its students and its region. I remember that point because of a story the speaker used to emphasize the importance of considering needs. According to the story, a Southern evangelist went on a speaking tour of New England during the Reconstruction period. Near the end of the tour, he spoke in Boston. After the speech, during a question and answer period, one member of the audience stood and said, "Sir, I'd like to know what you Southerners are most interested in." Without hesitation, the evangelist replied, "Money." Seeing that the questioner was disturbed by his answer, the evangelist said to the Bostonian, "Now let me ask you what is it you Bostonians are most interested in?" Drawing himself a little more erect and speaking with pride in his voice, the Bostonian answered, "Education, culture, and religion." Looking him directly in the eye, the evangelist said, "That's good. Each of us is interested in the things we need the most!"

Retention of Material

Use Repetition

Establish an Association between Your Ideas and Knowledge Familiar to the Listener

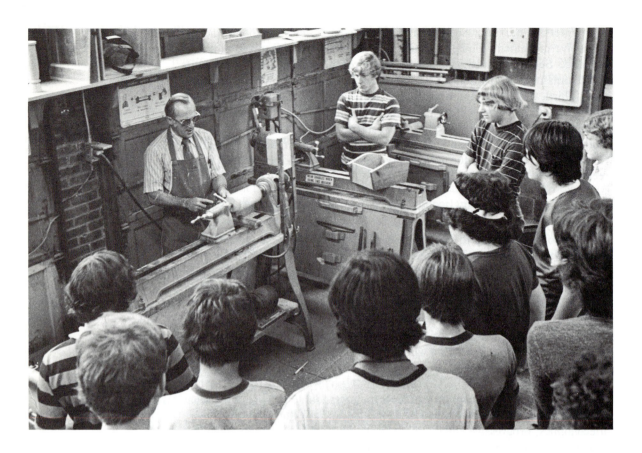

Keep in mind that not all people define things in the same way. Thus, your definition doesn't have to be the same as another person's definition of the same term or concept. Unless the audience understands your definition clearly, however, you won't successfully communicate with them. To be credible, a definition must be a reasonable one. Definitions can be constructed with the aid of dictionaries, books and articles by knowledgeable people, and observation of current practices.

The definition should identify the primary characteristics of the object or concept, be expressed in language easily understandable to the hearers, and be precise. Six types of definition are available.

1. Classify, by likenesses or differences, with other members possessing similar characteristics. Note how one speaker defined a *concentration ratio:* "It's a figure, a percentage, that shows what fraction of an entire industry's production and sales is attained by a limited number of companies."[6] In this definition, a concentration ratio is classified as a percentage and then differentiated from other percentages.
2. Trace the etymology of the term. This method was used in the following application: "Intelligence is derived from two words—'inter'

Forms of Communication

and 'legere' meaning 'to choose' and 'between.' An intelligent person is one who has learned to choose between good and evil, who knows that trust is better than fear, love than hate, gentleness than cruelty, forbearance than intolerance, humility than arrogance, truth than falsehood."[7]

3. Tell what a thing is not, that is, define by negation. In explaining "pursuit of happiness," one speaker used this method:

> . . . we have come to believe that the pursuit of happiness is reducible to the pursuit of pleasure. . . .
>
> Our age has developed the ultimate defense of pleasure as a guide to the moral life. Four years ago, a young Californian explained to an audience how she knew that certain of her actions had been right. She said, "I knew it was right because it felt good when I was doing it." She was not explaining her justification for taking some new drug or for performing a new sexual act. Her name was Susan Atkins, a member of the Manson family, and she was describing her horrible justification for the savage murder of seven people. The criterion of pleasure does not differentiate between higher and lower pleasures or between good and bad pleasures. Once it is agreed that the criterion is pleasure, pleasure becomes its own justification.[8]

4. Give an operational definition—tell what it does. For example, one can use an operational definition to identify a voltmeter as a device used to measure the voltage between two points of an electrical current.
5. Present examples of the item. Listeners may not know the meaning of "pachyderm," for example, but if they're told that it's a large animal with a thick skin such as the rhinoceros, hippopotamus, and elephant, they'll probably understand the term.
6. Compare and contrast the item with others that are familiar to the listeners. For example, propaganda may be defined in this way: "Propaganda, like persuasion, attempts to change the attitudes and behavior of others. Unlike persuasion, propaganda places no restrictions on the use of invalid reasoning, untrue evidence, or unethical procedures."

Therefore, you can define by classification, etymology, negation, operational definition, example, or comparison and contrast.

Although definition may be used in all types of speaking, there is frequently insufficient time to develop a definition in detail. It is sometimes advantageous, therefore, to devote an entire speech to defining a term or concept in order to be able to examine that definition in depth.

Analysis identifies the major divisions or constituent parts of a topic, such as the causes and effects of an event or the essential characteristics of an object. You may analyze the causes and effects of inflation, the essential characteristics of a successful writer, or the qualities of a good stock to purchase. The most important question for you to ask is: What are the logical divisions of the subject?

Analyze

Valid analysis must be logical. It must use a consistent principle to divide a topic into its parts, the parts must be mutually exclusive, and the division of the parts must be exhaustive. For example, one way to analyze highways is to examine the basis of access to them. Thus, we have two types: those with limited access, and those with unlimited access. This analysis conforms with the three requirements above: It uses the same principle, the parts are mutually exclusive, and the division is exhaustive. On the other hand, if highways were analyzed on the basis of three divisions—limited access roads, unlimited access roads, and farm roads—then the three divisions would not be mutually exclusive.

Describe

Description explains how something appears—its spatial appearance, shape, or dimensions. The speaker may describe Bourbon Street in New Orleans, an automobile assembly line, the painting of Andrew Wyeth, the Rocky Mountains, the outer banks of North Carolina, or the Alamo.

Some suggested questions to ask in preparing an effective description are: How long is it? What shape is it? How deep is it? How wide is it? What color is it? What is its texture? What is its temperature? As these questions clearly indicate, description relies heavily upon sensory data. The purpose of description is to stimulate sensory images in the minds of listeners. Consequently, concreteness and specificity are obviously important characteristics of description.

Focus on the items relevant to the purpose of the speech. A description of highways, for example, may focus on safety features, construction materials, scenic aspects, or topographical adaptations. Unless you have determined the purpose of the speech, there will be no principle or criterion for selecting descriptive information. Unfocused descriptive data will only confuse listeners.

One of the pitfalls of description is "information overload," or crowding too many bits of data together so that the listener has little opportunity to digest them. One way to avoid this is to present data that create sensory images for only one of the senses at a time.

Exemplify

This method of informing attempts to create understanding by presenting one or more examples of the ideas, to make clear the meaning. In discussing our criminal justice system, one speaker stated a generalization and then used an example to develop it.

> Some prisons are almost like acting schools that teach convicts jargon the Parole Board wants to hear.
> There was one sad case of a convict in one of our maximum security institutions who willingly applied himself to rehabilitation. But he just couldn't find a way to please the Parole Board.
> One year they told him he needed to learn a trade—so he became a shoemaker. The next year they told him he needed an education—so he got his high school diploma.

The next year they said group therapy was the key to release—so he joined a therapy group. The next year they said he needed to do more time.

This man is only one of thousands of offenders who resent our system. And they have every reason to resent it.[9]

Two methods of informing by example may be used: (1) a specific instance, which is an undetailed example, or (2) an illustration, which is a detailed example. Specific instances are useful to demonstrate typicality, but illustrations may be more "powerful" because they involve the listener more. Examples, whether detailed or undetailed, may be either factual or hypothetical.

Keep examples relevant to your point. If the point of the story has to be labored, the relationship of the example is probably not clear enough for it to be included. Let the introduction of the example establish the connection between it and the point you want to make.

Use interesting examples. Listeners generally find interesting those examples that include a delicate balance of familiar and unfamiliar information; they get bored if a speaker presents only familiar information. Specific and concrete data make examples interesting. Listeners get involved with examples that evoke a sensory response. Examples are more interesting if they concern people, especially if the listener knows them personally or recognizes the names. Examples from your own personal experiences are particularly interesting because they provide information about you as well as the topic.

Adapt examples to the particular listeners: their age, sex, occupation, region of residence, political affiliation. If you're talking to a group of southern farmers about ways to conserve energy, you shouldn't cite examples from urban residents or even from midwestern farmers. The best examples would involve southern farmers.

Compare

A comparison or analogy examines the points of similarity between two things. Unfamiliar objects or concepts can be made more comprehensible if you get the listeners to perceive a relationship between them and something they already understand. A comparison may be literal or figurative. It is literal if the comparison involves two members of the same class. For example, if George Bush were compared to Thomas Jefferson as a president, that would be a literal comparison. A figurative comparison involves members of different classes; for example, our football team uses tactics similar to those of the U.S. Army under General Grant in the Civil War.

Contrast

The speaker uses contrast in exploring points of dissimilarity between two objects or concepts. The use of opposites can clarify meaning for listeners by defining more clearly and more vividly the characteristics of an unfamiliar object or concept. You might make more understandable the nature of a community college by contrasting it with a university in these ways: (1) The community college doesn't have students in residence as a university does.

CHAPTER 19

Persuasive Speaking

Coercion is frequently used to influence the attitudes and behavior of others. In South Africa coercion has been used to maintain separation of the black and white races. Sometime during the term you're taking this course, an airplane may be hijacked. Then will come news the passengers are being held as hostages until some demand of the hijackers has been met. Or the evening television news will show crowds of demonstrators in a place like Seabrook, Maine, trying to develop support for a nuclear freeze. In China, students protesting the absence of freedom will be sent to prison. In varying degrees, all these are coercive means of affecting behavior and attitudes of others.

Most of us, at some time, have wished we had the means of coercing someone to our point of view, but we generally recognize that coercion has its disadvantages. First, if we can coerce someone, then someone else can coerce us. So we protect others from ourselves in order ultimately to protect ourselves. Second, someone who is coerced to a position may not be committed to it. That person may revert to the original, preferred behavior at the first opportunity. There are examples of approved coercion, such as a parent coercing a child to study. Coercion can create behavior to which the coerced person becomes committed. In most cases, however, the coercion of adults is a method that is both resented and ethically questionable.

Persuasion, on the other hand, offers a legitimate, effective way to affect others' attitudes and behavior. First, it permits the intended receiver to decide personally the position to be adopted. Second, it results in stronger commitment to the new position. Although the commitment is made in varying degrees and is subject to reversal by another persuader, the important feature is that the individual makes the decision voluntarily. Third, it is a nonviolent method for settling controversies and making changes in our society.

What exactly is persuasion? It is the process whereby an attempt is made to induce changes in attitudes and behavior through involvement of a person's cognitive and affective processes. As pointed out earlier, it is possible to alter attitudes without affecting behavior. And some may change behavior without modifying their attitudes. Be reluctant, therefore, to infer a relationship between attitudes and behavior. Nevertheless, the objective of the persuasive speech is to cause a change in both attitudes and behavior.

Obstacles to Changing Attitudes

No matter how skilled or clever the persuader, forming and changing attitudes aren't easy tasks. In some instances, the task is so enormous as to be hopeless. A Moslem trying to persuade a group of Methodist bishops to give up their Christian faith and become Moslems is confronted by firmly held attitudes and deep-seated convictions. On the other hand, it isn't very difficult to persuade someone to do what he or she desires to do. In fact, some observers of human behavior have concluded that this is the only time persuasion is truly effective. Aldous Huxley has observed: "Social and political [persuasion] . . .

is effective as a rule, only upon those whom circumstances have partly or completely convinced of its truth."[1] Yet surveys of voters in the presidential political campaigns of 1940, 1948, 1960, and 1964 revealed that 8 to 20 percent changed parties during the campaign.[2] Furthermore, behavioral scientists and communication scholars have accumulated many experimental studies showing that attitudes can be changed if the appropriate methods are used. Nevertheless, a number of factors operate to hinder or prevent attitude formation or change.

Selective Perception

Our various senses are bombarded constantly with innumerable stimuli. These sensations are carried to the brain, whose function is to give some order to them so that a meaningful pattern can be detected. Perception is the process of creating that meaningful pattern. Some discuss selective perception and selective attention as separate processes, but there is no difference in them. All perception is selective, and there can be no perception without attention.

We selectively perceive stimuli because of our interests, training, prejudices, assumptions, values, cultural differences, personality differences, and physical limitations. A hard-of-hearing person, for example, doesn't perceive all sounds in the environment. If an automobile accident were witnessed by a doctor, a lawyer, a minister, and an auto mechanic, each would perceive different aspects of the event. The doctor would perceive the physical injuries of the people involved. The lawyer would tend to perceive where the vehicles were as they collided and who had violated the traffic laws. The minister would most likely perceive the mental and physical suffering of the victims. The auto mechanic would probably perceive the damage to the two vehicles and estimate the cost of their repair.

The situation can affect our perceptions. Two researchers did a study in which one subject was the buyer and the other subject the seller. In one situation there was a broad overlapping of the range in which each could make a good bargain; in the second situation, the good bargain range for each was very limited. After the subjects had completed their bargaining efforts in each situation, the experimenters asked the subjects for their reactions. In the wide bargaining range, the subjects were pleased with the results and observed that real businesspeople ought to conduct their business in similar fashion. In the narrow bargaining range, however, the subjects were unhappy with the results and disliked one another, and each observed that the other was a skinflint.[3]

Our assumptions affect our perceptions. For years we assumed that women were physically weaker than men, more gentle, less ambitious, and the like. Consequently, our society decreed that they couldn't perform many of the jobs men could. In recent years, however, the women's movement has attacked and destroyed these assumptions. Now women are perceived as possessing all the different qualities of men, and in as many varying degrees as men.

Since selective perception can cause listeners to ignore threatening information, attempt to relate important information to the interests, assumptions, cultural differences, and experiences of the listeners. In this way, they may perceive and respond to data that might otherwise go unnoticed.

Although many of the stimuli that impinge upon us daily never make it past our short-term memory, a lot of data become a part of the long-term memory. Most psychologists now believe that data making it into the long-term memory are there relatively permanently. This doesn't mean that we can actively recall all these data; the ability to store information is apparently much greater than the ability to retrieve it. Some can apparently be remembered only when certain parts of the brain are stimulated electronically. Some of the data are repressed or suppressed as a defense mechanism. Humans have a strong tendency to drop from their conscious memory their unpleasant experiences, while remembering the pleasant ones. Most of us look back on our childhood and think what a wonderful time that was. Only rarely do we recall an unpleasant experience from that period of our lives. The nostalgic mood of the 1970s was based on selective recall, retaining in the conscious memory only the pleasant features of previous years. Movies such as *American Graffiti* and television shows such as *Happy Days* and *The Waltons* gained their popularity by focusing on the pleasant aspects of earlier times. This selective remembering reflects a desire, caused by the harsh and bitter struggles of the late sixties and seventies, to return to what is remembered as a simpler and happier way of life. Many recall the "happy" days of the Great Depression. Not a few even remember the exciting and adventurous days of World War II as happy ones, not consciously remembering the loneliness and grief that accompanied the separation of families and the death of friends and kin.

Don't assume that listeners will recall information to which they have been exposed. If the material is important to your purpose, present it afresh in the speech.

Further complicating the persuader's task is the selective exposure of many individuals to communications. In other words some tend to listen only to those who reinforce or support their current attitudes. Females who favored "a firm stand in Vietnam were more likely to expose themselves to a communication in which it was evident that such a policy would be defended. Those female subjects who were only lukewarm in their support of such a policy were less inclined to attend either directly or indirectly to the president's talk."[4]

Not all persons avoid communications that oppose their beliefs. The evidence implies that those who have confidence in their ability to refute opposing messages are willing to expose themselves to differing communications. Women were asked to discuss articles about religion with an unknown partner. They were told the partner agreed with them on the issue, but the amount of knowledge on religion the partner was alleged to have varied from much to medium to little. A control group had no partner. The subjects were then given the choice of discussing an article that favored or opposed their beliefs. The more knowledgeable the woman thought her partner was, the more likely she was to choose material opposing her religious beliefs.[5]

The same hypothesis was tested by preparing four brochures containing political statements that were extremely difficult or extremely easy to refute. The brochures apparently were circulated by organizations supporting one of the two candidates in the 1964 presidential campaign. Half identified the candidate as Barry Goldwater, half as Lyndon Johnson. The brochure offered to send additional free materials upon request. The booklets were then sent to Democratic clubs, Republican clubs, and supporters of both Johnson and Goldwater. Results supported the hypothesis. Those receiving a pamphlet with strong arguments agreeing with their position were more likely to request additional information than either those who received a pamphlet with weak arguments agreeing with their position or one with strong arguments disagreeing with their position. On the other hand, those receiving a pamphlet with weak arguments disagreeing with their position were more likely to request additional information than either those receiving a pamphlet with strong arguments disagreeing with their position or one with weak arguments agreeing with their position.[6]

We can conclude, then, that selective exposure to communications is a more complicated process than has been recognized. How it operates depends on the confidence we have in the validity of our own opinions or our ability to cope with opposing communications. We are apparently willing to expose ourselves to arguments either strongly in favor of our position or weakly opposed to it, and we avoid arguments either weakly in favor of our position or strongly opposed to it.

The strongest possible arguments must always be developed and presented, even when listeners already favor the position being advocated.

| **Degree of Commitment** | The degree of commitment to a position is another barrier to changing a person's attitudes. An ego-involving issue is one that is relevant, significant, or meaningful to an individual. The person's stand or commitment on the issue reveals the extent of ego-involvement. Apparently, the greater the ego-involvement of the individual, the more difficult it will be to effect a change in the person's position.[7] |

After varying source and communication in a number of ways in an experiment, Tannenbaum concluded that "susceptibility to change is . . . [related] to the intensity of initial attitude": the more intense the attitude initially, the more difficult it is to change; the less intense the attitude initially, the easier it is to change.[8] Strong commitment to a group has the same effect. Questionnaires obtained from members of twelve Boy Scout troops revealed their attitudes toward such activities as woodcraft skills, forest lore, and camping activities. A week later an outside speaker criticized these activities and suggested that scouts would profit more from learning about their cities and engaging in activities available in town. An attitude scale completed after the speech revealed that those boys who placed a low valuation on membership in the Boy Scouts tended to change in the direction suggested by that communication. Among those who placed a high valuation on membership in the Scouts, however, the communication had a negative, or boomerang, effect.[9]

To change an individual's attitudes from those of the group to which he or she is committed, you must first weaken that person's allegiance to the group.

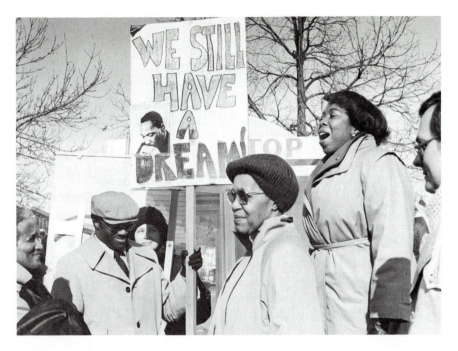

Not only is the degree of commitment of an individual to a concept or thing important, but the type of commitment is important. A commitment may be privately or publicly held.

Public Commitment

If people have publicly committed themselves to a proposal, it is more difficult to change their attitudes. As long as an individual's commitment is known only to him or her, he or she is apparently more willing to change if presented with reasons for doing so. Once the person has revealed that commitment to others, however, there is apparently an ego-involvement that makes that person reluctant to change his or her mind. Messages were presented to subjects either favoring or opposing lowering the voting age to eighteen. Following the message, subjects in each group were asked to write a paragraph stating their attitude. To determine the impact of public commitment on the flexibility of attitudes, half of the subjects were told that their written opinions would be published; they were asked to sign their names. All subjects then received the message presenting the opposite side, and a final opinion was obtained from each subject. The results showed that those subjects who signed their names to the original opinion were more reluctant to change than those whose original opinion had been given anonymously.[10]

To be effective eliminate the effect of public commitments that oppose your intent. Acknowledge these commitments, but show that conditions have changed since the commitments were made, and present your interpretation of the changed conditions. Since most people agree that changed conditions demand new decisions, this will permit most to change their attitude without feeling that it reflects a weakness of character.

Persuasive Speaking   307

Figure 19.1
Continuum of audience attitude.

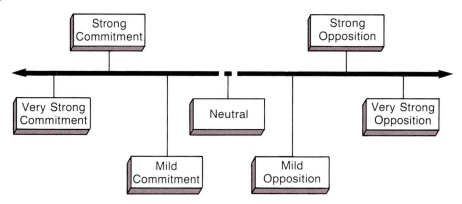

Discrepancy between Listeners' Attitudes and Speaker's Position

The amount of discrepancy between your position and that of your listeners may vary within an audience and from audience to audience. Some audiences will be extremely homogeneous in attitude; others will be extremely heterogeneous. Even the homogeneous audiences may vary in their degree of variance from your position. If we use a continuum to show different degrees of audience attitude, we may locate at least seven different positions, as shown in figure 19.1.

Obviously, the smaller the discrepancy between your position and that of your listeners, the smaller will be the change caused by the message. If you're mildly in favor of a position and are talking to an audience that is neutral on the issue, you have little chance of moving listeners very far along the continuum. On the other hand, if you advocate a position of strong commitment to an audience occupying the position of strong opposition, you have the opportunity to move listeners four points on the continuum. Two investigators found that a large discrepancy between the communicator and the receiver caused a greater shift in attitude than a small discrepancy.[11]

This may not mean, however, that you should attempt to create the greatest discrepancy possible between your position and the attitudes of your listeners. Sherif and colleagues maintain that the important factor is the *latitude of acceptance* on the part of the hearer; in other words, how many positions on the continuum the hearer will find acceptable. They argue that an important element in determining the effect upon attitude change of a persuasive communication is the amount of discrepancy between the position advocated in the message and the hearer's attitude. Their reasoning is that if there is little discrepancy between the message and the hearer's attitude, the hearer will perceive the discrepancy as actually being less than it is and will respond favorably. But if there is much discrepancy, the listener will perceive it as being greater than it is and react unfavorably to the message by making a minimal favorable response, no response, or a negative response. The factor that will determine whether the discrepancy is too great to assimilate is the

Figure 19.2

Continuum of audience position on an issue.

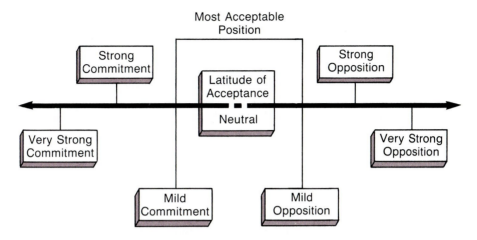

latitude of acceptance, which "is the position on an issue (or toward an object) that is most acceptable, plus other acceptable positions."[12] As shown in figure 19.2, a person whose most acceptable position was at the mild opposition point, but whose latitude of acceptance didn't include the strong commitment point, might assimilate any position from mild opposition to mild commitment. That listener would respond unfavorably, however, to any message calling for a position of strong or very strong commitment. In support of this, Freedman[13] and Whittaker[14] found that subjects who were highly involved in the issues changed attitudes more following more moderate requests for change, whereas subjects having low involvement in the issues changed attitudes more with increasing discrepancy.

Further complicating the problem of message and receiver attitude discrepancy is evidence that the initial prestige of the source affects the impact of discrepancy. A high-prestige source can cause attitude change with a greater discrepancy between his or her position and the listener's than a low- or moderate-prestige source. Subjects were given opinions about poetry that were slightly, moderately, or greatly at variance with the subjects' opinions. When T. S. Eliot was given as the source of the discrepant opinion, maximum attitude change occurred with the highest discrepancy. When another student was given as the author of the discrepant statement, maximum change took place with the moderately discrepant opinion.[15]

After reviewing a number of studies concerned with message discrepancy, Insko concluded that for most uninvolving topics the influence of a moderately credible communicator increases as the amount of disagreement between the speaker and listeners increases.[16]

Until further research proves otherwise, emphasize your similarities to your audience. Attempt to minimize discrepancy between yourself and those listeners who are *involved* in the issues.

Group Pressure

The effect of group pressure as an obstacle to persuasion has been felt by almost everyone. Who hasn't been reluctant to adopt a new clothes style or a new hairstyle because none of their peer group has accepted it? A generation ago, few students would have dared to wear blue jeans to a college classroom for fear of being considered underdressed. In the last several years, few college students would dare not to wear blue jeans to a college classroom for fear of being considered overdressed.

Experiments have even shown that group pressure will cause people to perceive a stationary light as moving and to judge some lines to be longer than others when in fact they are rather obviously shorter or the same length. An important explanation of these results, undoubtedly, is that we doubt our own abilities when confronted with group perceptions that differ.[17]

On the other hand, we succumb to group pressure because we value membership in the group. One of the reasons country club members rake the sand traps and repair ball marks on the golf greens more than people playing on a public course is that the members of a country club constitute a group with a relatively fixed membership who meet in many situations. For fear of being ostracized, no member wants to be known as one who doesn't behave properly on the golf course. On a public course, however, a golfer may rarely, if ever, see again the people playing there. Consequently, there is no group from which to be excluded because of abnormal behavior.

When advocating a position counter to that held by a peer group of the listeners, you may show that new information has changed the situation, that some members of the group have begun to doubt the group's position, or that your position is more consistent with a larger purpose of the group.

In summary, there are at least eight potential obstacles to changing attitudes: (1) selective perception of the communication, (2) selective recall of the message, (3) selective exposure to the communication on the part of at least some listeners, (4) the degree of commitment of the individual to a position, (5) any public commitment to a position, (6) the amount of discrepancy between the listener's and the speaker's positions when the listener is involved in the issue under consideration, and (7) group pressure on the listener not to change.

These obstacles to changing attitudes make the persuader's task difficult, but not impossible. Psychological literature is full of experimental studies in which subjects' attitudes have been changed significantly. Admittedly, many of the experimental situations are artificial and the subjects are more sophisticated in some ways and less sophisticated in others than the general population. But these experimental studies coupled with the many instances of attitude change in various phases of national life indicate that attitudes can be changed.

Speakers should avoid the error of thinking that attitudes can be changed with one persuasive message. An understanding of the role of attitudes in a person's life and an acquaintance with history convince us that persuasion is a slow process that must be continued over a period of time if meaningful attitude changes are to occur and persist. The campaign to abolish slavery in this country went on for almost thirty years before a president could be elected who would say that slavery was evil. Moreover, he was elected as a minority president, and even then he promised not to interfere with slavery where it currently existed. The movement to eliminate child labor from our industrial society took over fifty years. Labor union leaders and advocates had been working for approximately seventy-five years before federal legislation gave full recognition to unions.

An incumbent politician who hasn't incurred the wrath of constituents generally has an advantage over an opponent: he or she has had longer to change the voters' attitudes. Most politicians who have defeated an incumbent did so by attacking him or her. For a challenging politician to run solely on a positive program leaves the long-term persuasion of the incumbent unharmed. To have a chance, the out-candidate must indict the incumbent's programs or credibility, or that of the incumbent's associates.

In order to be optimally successful in changing attitudes, commit yourself to a long-term persuasive effort.

Methods of Forming and Changing Attitudes

Following their review of "the literature on attitude persistence," Petty and Cacioppo concluded that multiple research results and theories could justifiably be considered as supporting "just two relatively distinct routes to persuasion." They identified these as the *central* route and the *peripheral* route. The *central* involves "careful and thoughtful consideration of the true merits of the information presented in support of an advocacy." The *peripheral* involves "some simple cue in the persuasion context (e.g., an attractive source) that induced change without necessitating scrutiny of the true merits of the information presented." Their Elaboration Likelihood Model of persuasion is predicated on these two routes. They define *elaboration* as "the extent to which a person thinks about the issue-relevant arguments contained in a message."[18]

In the following pages, we look at the various issue-relevant and non-issue-relevant ways in which attitudes are formed and changed.

To meet your responsibility as an ethical speaker, develop a position based on a set of arguments supported by valid evidence and logical reasoning. Don't attempt persuasion without first accomplishing this objective. As a realistic persuasive communicator, however, realize that you must do something with the evidence and reasoning you present: interpret it, present it so the listener will perceive it, make it acceptable and credible to the listener, and make it meaningful to the listener. This section explains how attitudes can be formed and changed.

Attitude changes may result from rational deliberation about issue-relevant data and the unification of "that information into an overall position," or they may result from peripheral (nonissue-relevant) cues, such as source expertise, attractiveness, mere number of arguments, pleasant music, source likability, etc. Sometimes, however, a source feature, such as expertise, "may

Build a Case with Evidence and Reasoning

itself serve as a persuasive argument" providing source information (biased or unbiased) that helps the listener evaluate "the true merits of any given argument."[19]

Attitudes changed by issue-relevant information are "more internally consistent, accessible, enduring, and resistant than" when they are based on the peripheral cues listed above.[20]

Research also indicates that attitude changes caused by issue-relevant arguments are better predictors of behavior than changes initiated by cues that are not issue-relevant.[21]

The strength and number of your arguments are important. When a message had high relevance, three strong arguments were more persuasive than three weak ones and were just as persuasive as a combination of the three strong and three weak arguments. When a message had low relevance for listeners, however, three strong arguments were no more persuasive than three weak arguments. But a combination of the three strong and three weak arguments were more persuasive than either of the three argument messages.[22]

There is an interaction between the number and strength of the arguments and the likability of the speaker. When a message with low relevance was presented by a likable source using one strong argument, it was significantly more persuasive than a message using five strong arguments presented by an unlikable source. When the message had high relevance, however, the unlikable source using five strong arguments was significantly more persuasive than the likable source using one strong argument.[23]

The personal relevance of an issue affects listeners' reactions to arguments. When the personal relevance of an issue is ambiguous for listeners, an increase in the number of sources presenting strong arguments strengthens persuasion, but an increase in the number of sources presenting weak arguments lessens the persuasive impact.[24]

The repetition of strong arguments has a positive effect on their acceptance. When a persuasive message using strong arguments was repeated to listeners three times, hearers developed more favorable thoughts and revealed more attitude change, whereas those hearing the message using weak arguments conceived more unfavorable thoughts and showed less attitude change.[25]

To maximize the impact of your case, therefore, do the following: (1) Make clear the importance and personal relevance of your message in order to increase its persuasiveness. (2) When your topic has high relevance for your hearers, use the strongest possible arguments to support your position. When your topic has low relevance for your listeners, use all the arguments you can find. Remember, one person's weak argument is another person's strong argument. (3) Repeat your arguments at least three times.

Involve the Hearers' Emotions

The use of emotion is a legitimate means of persuading others to support or oppose existing or proposed new programs. Used properly the arousing of emotions in favor of programs can stimulate citizens to provide willing and effective support for needed programs. People's emotions are naturally aroused when they feel a project is worthwhile. However, it is unethical for a speaker to arouse listeners' emotions to the extent that they cease to think clearly.

People are frequently reluctant to support a project until they perceive emotional benefits stemming from it. Some oppose a project, such as building a costly new airport, until they're reminded that it will be larger than the one in a rival city. Their city pride (an emotion) then causes them to actively support a new airport because their city will then be "better" than the other.

As a speaker, you can ethically stimulate emotions to create support for valid and worthwhile programs, so long as your projects will improve the quality of life for members of the community and won't create negative or adverse consequences.

Observe how the editor of the *Indianapolis News* attempted to create the emotion of indignation when speaking to the Central State (Newspaper) Circulation Managers' Association.

> There is an eighth grade teacher in Indianapolis who has been giving the same kind of test to his students for 16 years, in order, he says, to try to measure how "large" the student's world is. His most recent testing involved 154 students.
>
> Two of the 154 could not name the current president of the United States. Ninety-five could not name the vice president. Thirty-nine could not name the country in which we live. The name of our nation's capital was missed by 49 students. Nineteen could not name the state in which they live. Twenty-nine did not know Indianapolis was the state capital. Forty could not identify Marion County as their place of residence. (Remember, these are eighth graders.)
>
> Who are the two senators from Indiana? Would you believe that 133 out of 154 did not know. Sixty could not name the mayor of Indianapolis. Seventy-eight did not know that the Atlantic Ocean separates North America from Europe. It is incredible that 111 of the 154 did not know that Mexico is the country along our southern border.
>
> What country did we become independent from in the Revolutionary War? Credit was given for either England or Great Britain, but 112 could not name either. Ten of the 154 eighth graders did not know how many months are in a year. Fifty-two did not know how many states are in our union.
>
> These shocking statistics—and they represent a downward trend for 16 years—were gathered in one of our city's above-average schools. I suspect you might be equally shocked by the answers obtained in your schools.[26]

When Hitler used anti-Semitism as a means of arousing the emotions of the Germans, the results were Buchenwald, Belsen, and Dachau, where many Jewish people died or were scarred for life. Obviously, the speech quoted above wouldn't arouse the listeners' emotions anywhere near that extent. But the speech is developed so hearers will experience low levels of emotion and become concerned and indignant about the educational program discussed. That is the purpose of emotions, to energize listeners to take appropriate action to solve problems in their community: city, county, state, and nation. So long as the speaker doesn't take the listeners past "the threshold of frustration tolerance," (they become so emotional they can no longer behave in a rational manner), then emotions should serve as constructive motivators of behavior to eliminate or correct problems.

Use the Foot-in-the-Door Technique

This peripheral route procedure involves asking someone to do you a favor, and then later requesting that person to do you a larger favor. Freedman and Fraser first confirmed that this process worked.[27] Seligman, Bush, and Kirsch demonstrated that the first request shouldn't be too small, however. They varied the size of the first request and discovered that "the greatest compliance" with the second request resulted from "the largest sized first requests."[28] The reasoning is that once a person has done you a small favor, he or she has made a commitment that causes him or her to feel obligated to respond favorably to the second request, provided it isn't too small or too large. Suppose, for example, you want to ask a neighbor to contribute to The United Way, for which you are soliciting. You might ask the neighbor to do a small sixty-minute typing job as a contribution to The United Way. After the typing job has been completed, you go back and explain that The United Way still has unmet needs because of a lack of money. Then you ask him or her to give a $100 contribution to The United Way. The chances are very good that because of the small commitment of sixty minutes to do the typing job, the person will feel obligated to comply with the larger request and give the hundred dollars.

Forms of Communication

How can you use this in a speech? Let's say you're going to ask the members of the PTA at your local school to contribute funds to pay for off-duty police to direct traffic at key intersections for an hour before school starts in the morning and an hour after school ends in the afternoon. Very early in your speech, you ask for a show of hands of those who feel there aren't sufficient safeguards for schoolchildren at key traffic intersections and would be willing to sign a petition expressing that concern. Then at the end of your speech, you tell the people that you have petitions for them to sign, but you think more needs to be done. You then ask them to contribute $100 each to help pay for the off-duty police who must be hired to serve as traffic guards. There should be a tendency for those raising their hands at the beginning to comply with this larger request for funds.

Burgoon and Bettinghaus suggest the following message strategies when using the foot-in-the-door method of obtaining compliance:

1. The initial request must obtain compliance and must be clearly smaller than later requests.
2. The initial request must be "of sufficient magnitude to trigger self-perceptions that commit the person to future compliance."
3. Another person can make the second request and sometimes be more successful in obtaining compliance than the person making the first request.[29]

This technique must be used with care. Your credibility can be destroyed if listeners get the impression you're trying to manipulate them.

Use the Door-in-the-Face Technique

This peripheral method of gaining compliance works in the opposite way from the foot-in-the-door procedure. Cialdini and colleagues conceived the idea of making the first request so extreme that the recipient would reject it. Following rejection, a more moderate request is presented. It is imperative, however, that the person making the first request also make the second request because the recipient must perceive concession by the requester. This is crucial "in producing compliance with the smaller request." If the receiver perceives concession on the part of the requester, then compliance by the receiver will occur.[30]

Using the example of traffic guards for schoolchildren, we can see that the door-in-the-face procedure works in the opposite way. Instead of asking the parents to sign a petition at the beginning, the speaker would ask them to give $1,000 each to pay for the intersection guards. After discussing the advantages of having the guards and explaining how they would operate, the speaker would say: "It isn't fair of me to ask you to give $1,000 each. I think $100 per family would be fairer. We'll just have to get the rest of the money to pay for this project from other sources." This concession should provoke reciprocal concessions from the listeners.

Burgoon and Bettinghaus suggest the following strategies for the door-in-the-face procedure:

1. The initial request must be sufficiently large that the receivers don't perceive its rejection "as a reflection of their attitudes." Moreover, "the request must not be so large as to make rejection reasonable."
2. The first request must be rejected and the second request must be "unambiguously smaller" than the first one.
3. The first request "must not be so large and absurd as to evoke hostility," or there will be no compliance.
4. The speaker must be perceived as offering concessions or there will be no compliance. Because concessions are required, the same speaker must make both requests.
5. "The second requests do not have to be small or trivial, but must be perceived as smaller than the first request."[31]

Using the door-in-the-face technique can destroy your credibility if your listeners perceive that you're trying to manipulate them.

Show That Desired Behavior Is Approved by Esteemed Person or Group

Adopting behavior derived from another person or group because the behavior is associated with a satisfying self-defining relationship to the person or group has been labeled "identification."[32] Use of this peripheral cue begins at an early age. Children adopt the behavior and attitudes of their parents because of their affection for them. But the practice doesn't end with childhood; it continues throughout our lives. Freshmen on a college campus learn very quickly what behavior and attitudes are in vogue at the moment and quickly acquire them for their own. The peer group can be even more influential for college students than an expert in a given field. One study found, for example, that "college students' judgments of language usage were not affected as much by standards attributed to an expert in language as by those attributed to other students."[33]

A recorded speech challenging the validity of modern teaching methods was presented to different groups of students at a teachers' college. The recording included applause at seven important places in the speech. One group of students was informed the speech had been recorded earlier at their school, thus implying that the applause, indicating a favorable response, had come from members of their own college faculty and community. The other group was told the hearers applauding were not members of their own college community. The speech caused attitude change in the desired direction for both groups, but the change was greater where students thought the applause came from "prestigeful" members of their own college community.[34]

Show That Your Proposal Is Consistent or Inconsistent with a Value Premise

If you can demonstrate your proposal is consistent with a value premise held by your listeners, that will act as a peripheral cue and enhance the possibility of their accepting that proposal. Thus, because most Americans value freedom, you may claim a new governmental program enhances freedom. On the other hand, because most Americans dislike the absence of freedom, you may argue that a proposed program interferes with freedom.

The importance of a value premise to an attitude was shown when researchers attempted to change the attitudes of a group of students toward teaching as a career. Choosing as the value premise the students' need for achievement, they presented to one group a communication arguing that teaching would facilitate satisfaction of the need for achievement, to a second group a communication arguing that teaching wouldn't facilitate satisfaction of the need for achievement, and to a third group a communication on the topic "Going to College." The positive and negative messages on the ability of teaching to satisfy the need for achievement caused corresponding changes in the students' appraisal of teaching as a means of facilitating achievement. Although the support wasn't sufficient "to be considered conclusive," a questionnaire indicated parallel changes of attitude toward a teaching career.[35]

Observe how George A. Stinson, chairman of the board of National Steel Corporation, stressed value premises held by his listeners at the Mountain State Forest Festival, Elkins, West Virginia:

> I said earlier that I wanted to call this talk, "Take me Home, Country Road," because I believe that in the sixties and seventies the nation sometimes strayed away from some fundamental concepts that have made our country strong from its beginnings. There is no doubt in my mind that the most fundamental factor which has made America great has been its commitment to high moral and ethical principles and values. Democracy has worked because we believe in our Bill of Rights which strikes one central theme and that is individual freedom.
>
> But individual freedom doesn't work unless it is supported by economic freedom—freedom to hold a job, to start a business, to save our money, and generally to participate in a sound economic system. This lies at the heart of our superb standard of living, our strength as a nation to be the leader of the worldwide family of nations, and the general sense of well-being which our citizens have always enjoyed.[36]

Whatever value premise you use, be sure it's one held by your particular group of listeners. One of the causes of communication difficulties between older and younger generations is that each bases its proposals on values they cherish rather than on values the other group cherishes.

Appeal to an Alternative Value Premise

This may serve as an issue-relevant argument or as a peripheral cue. It is an issue-relevant argument if you attempt to show that a currently held value premise isn't adequate to cope with contemporary conditions, that new times demand new values. Ecologists in recent years have argued that the esteem of a community for industrial growth is not a realistic value premise for the future. Consequently, they suggest we replace that value premise with one that has respect and concern for conserving the environment. Many educators have long held the opinion that knowledge for its own sake was an adequate value premise on which to base our educational system. Today young people argue that a more meaningful value premise on which to base educational processes is preparation for a career.

In the following excerpt, the speaker attempts to create support for international trade by linking it with peace and civilization:

> If I had to limit myself to one single issue, one single cause to which we in purchasing are most ideally positioned to contribute, there is no doubt in my mind that the cause would be that of peace. The one common goal of ours, of business and industry in general, of all mankind, is world peace.
>
> Peace and trade are preconditions of one another. The nations of the world are all in the same business of buying and selling. Since World War II the volume of world exports has increased by about 800 percent. It is a common fact that international trade increases the standard of living for all countries and that all industries are stimulated by trade. There is no country in the world today that is entirely self-sufficient. Nor is there any nation lacking in resources, goods, or services needed by other nations.
>
> Trade, my friends, is a mutually beneficial enterprise and one of the oldest forms of international communication. It has been said that trade "is the great civilizer. We exchange ideas when we exchange fabrics." Trade is certainly one of the most persuasive reasons for nations to find political accommodation.[37]

It is a peripheral cue if you simply claim that an alternative value premise should be adopted.

Arouse Fear in Listeners

Every individual has had fear used on him or her as a peripheral cue at some time in his or her life. What child hasn't been told: "If you're not good, Santa Claus won't come to see you"? Fear is an issue-relevant argument, however, when we buy traveler's checks because we fear the consequences of carrying a large sum of money and losing it.

John C. Lawn, Drug Enforcement Administrator, alerted his listeners to the fearful consequences of drug use:

> Another drug phenomenon we see is what the media has termed, "designer drugs." I don't like that name because in our society the term "designer" has a positive connotation, and these drugs are so potent, so dangerous, the last thing we need to do is make them sound more glamorous.
>
> These synthetic analogs of controlled substances kill and cripple for life. To help you understand how potent they can be, imagine that a heroin dose would be about the size of an aspirin tablet. To get the equivalent dosage of the heroin analog, fentanyl, one would need much less than one grain of salt. Fentanyl can be between 150 to 1,000 times stronger than heroin. These controlled substance analogs have killed several hundred people, mostly in California, and have left countless others permanently disabled with symptoms that resemble Parkinson's disease.
>
> The continuing bad news is cocaine. We have an epidemic enveloping our country today. Last year, consumption rose 11 percent. Cocaine-related hospital emergencies increased 51 percent in one year. Deaths caused by cocaine abuse have increased by 325 percent since 1980.

. . . And there is also the correlation between cocaine abuse, chronic depression and, ultimately, suicide. Overall, 37 percent of those calling into the hotline believed that their only salvation to their cocaine addiction was suicide, and 9 percent had actually tried to kill themselves. In our country life expectancy has increased substantially for all age groups. That is, except for one—teenagers. Illicit drugs and alcohol are, in great part, responsible.[38]

Fear influences our attitudes and behavior. On the basis of experimental work done so far, the primary question seems to be: How much fear can a persuader safely induce in listeners? The first study in this area unpredictably showed strong fear arousal to be less effective than moderate or low fear arousal.[39]

Because of this study, for many years persuaders were advised to avoid strong fear arousal. In recent years, a number of studies have produced contradictory results. The original study didn't depend on observation of actual behavior, but instead relied on verbal reports. A second study presented persuasive messages—with strong, moderate, and weak fear appeals—to college students asking them to get tetanus shots. University records were used to discover how many actually got inoculated in the next month. Almost twice as many of those hearing the strong fear message got the shot as did those hearing the moderate fear communication. And nearly four times as many of the strong fear recipients got the shot as did those in the control group.[40]

A number of recent experiments have found the high fear arousal message to be more effective than a low fear message.[41] One researcher has concluded that when attitude change doesn't result from a high fear message, it is frequently because the subject feels incapable of coping with the danger.[42]

The most recent evidence indicates that you need have no concern about the amount of fear you arouse in listeners, provided you offer a practical means of removing the cause of fear.

There is disagreement on how much reward is most effective for changing attitudes. Those who favor the reinforcement theory for attitude change predict that attitude change will be positively correlated with the magnitude of the reinforcement.[43] On the other hand, Festinger and his followers claim (on the basis of their experimentation with the theory of cognitive dissonance) that the more reward a person is given for performing an undesirable act, the less he or she will change his or her attitudes. They demonstrated this when they had undergraduates perform repetitive, unpleasant laboratory tasks. Some of the students were then hired as assistants and paid $1 to tell a fellow student that the tasks were enjoyable and interesting. Other students were paid $20 to do the same thing. The authors postulated that the subjects receiving $1 would experience a great deal of dissonance because they had lied for such a small reward. To remove the dissonance, the subject would change his or her attitude toward the tasks. On the other hand, the subjects receiving $20 would experience little dissonance because they would feel amply repaid for lying. The results confirmed these predictions.[44]

Offer a Reward or Incentive

On the other hand, Rosenberg devised an experiment in which subjects were paid either 50 cents, $1, or $5 to write counterattitudinal essays. The results showed that the subjects receiving $5 shifted their opinion significantly more than those receiving 50 cents.[45]

You can offer rewards to your listeners in various ways: show that the proposal will benefit the community; point out that it will positively affect loved ones of the listeners; explain that it will give an economic advantage to the listener.

William R. Miller, Vice Chairman, Bristol-Myers Company, pointed out to his audience the rewards coming to the elderly as a result of developments in pharmaceuticals:

> Very soon now—long before we reach the twenty-first century—this tide of progress will spread beyond the scientific and medical communities where it began, to engage and affect the rest of us. For no one will this be more important . . . more rewarding . . . than the elderly. In fact, the medical and technological breakthroughs that lie ahead offer the only hope of materially alleviating the disabilities of arthritis, senility, cancer and mental disorder that, for so many, make living longer not a blessing but a bane—and an ever-heavier burden for their families and our society.
>
> Along with enabling elderly people to *live*—in some full meaning of that word—rather than just exist, the new therapeutics should in the next century succeed in making a significant dent in the cost of their health care.[46]

Appeal to Motivating Factors

As both issue-relevant arguments and as peripheral cues, motives are to humans what spurs are to horses. They arouse and urge us to increasing levels of activity. They energize us to respond more readily and to adopt motive-related attitudes and behavior. In chapter 7 we considered Maslow's hierarchy of needs as factors to be considered in selecting a subject. Although Maslow's organization of needs is not wholly defensible, it is a helpful way of considering our motives. It is indisputable that those same needs serve as affective agents motivating people to adopt specific attitudes and behavior. To encourage support for your proposal, establish an affective relationship between it and as many of your listeners' needs as possible. Keep in mind, however, that not all people are motivated alike. Fortunately, you don't have to identify the many motivations. Remember that motives are internal; consequently, they have to be inferred by others. Identify unifying agents and use those. For example, people belong to organizations for varying reasons. Look at the different reasons people join a conservation group: some because of an altruistic desire to see conservation principles applied; some because it provides them an opportunity for leadership; some because it provides an opportunity to associate with people; some because they see the movement as providing protection and security for their family; some because it will advance their political aspirations; some for other reasons. You don't need to identify each of these motives in order to relate your proposal to a specific one, however. That would probably present an impossible task. You can relate to all these motivations by establishing a relationship between your proposal and conservation.

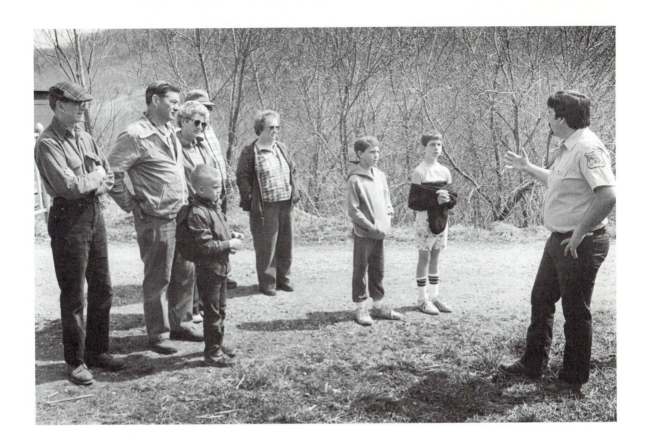

There may be times, nevertheless, when a single motivating factor must be identified and used. Following is a list of motivating factors. As you will notice if you try to organize them into Maslow's hierarchy of needs, most of them can be assigned to as many as four of the levels. One person may want wealth to satisfy safety needs, another to provide for the family he or she loves, another for the esteem it yields, and another because being wealthy is a self-actualizing need.

Persuasive Motives

Success	Strength	Competition	Love of family
Wisdom	Idealism	Cooperation	Social approval
Security	Curiosity	Conformity	Self-realization
Health	Pleasure	Adventure	Respect for diety
Status	Wealth	Recognition	Achievement
Fear	Pride	Acquisition	Superiority
Economy	Affection	Fellowship	Protection

This list is not intended to be exhaustive, but you can start with it to find motives that will move your particular group of hearers.

Provide Explicit Instructions on the Action Advocated

People are frequently persuaded that a particular action is desirable or necessary, but they fail to perform the act. Evidence indicates that the peripheral cue of giving specific instructions on when, where, or how the action can be completed increases the likelihood that it will be done. Researchers attempted to create fear of tetanus in subjects to get them to obtain shots. One group heard a high fear message, the other heard a moderate fear message. Half of each group was given specific instructions on when, where, and how they could obtain tetanus shots. The other half of each group was simply asked to get the shots. The experimenters found that significantly more of those receiving specific instructions obtained the shots, regardless of the fear level of the message.[47]

If you want a receiver or group of receivers to perform an action, therefore, explain specifically how it can be done.

One-Sidedness versus Two-Sidedness

After you decide on the position you're going to advocate in a particular speech and select the main ideas to develop that position, decide whether you want to use a one-sided or a two-sided speech. A two-sided persuasive speech is not one in which you are neutral. It isn't an objective presentation of arguments on both sides of an issue, with the listeners permitted to make up their minds which side to choose. In a two-sided speech, you present a series of arguments (pro) supporting the position you advocate. In addition, however, you present some major opposing arguments (con) and offer refutation of their validity. The one-sided speech discusses only those arguments supporting your position. Evidence indicates the one-sided approach is more advantageous on some occasions, and the two-sided approach is preferable on other occasions.

One-Sided Approach

Experimental studies have indicated that there are four conditions under which the one-sided approach is more effective.

1. When members of the audience are already favorably disposed toward the communicator's position. Toward the end of World War II, researchers prepared two speeches; each of them argued the war with Japan would be a long one, but one also included consideration of opposing arguments. Each was presented to a different group, with a third group serving as a control. Analysis revealed that for those who initially believed the war with Japan would be long, the one-sided speech was far more effective in changing their position.[48]
2. When members of the audience are poorly educated. The researchers discovered the poorly educated members of the two experimental groups were more prone to shift opinion in the direction advocated by the speaker after hearing the one-sided speech than after the two-sided speech.[49] One writer cautions we probably should not conclude the one-sided presentation would be more effective with an uneducated audience. He points out that listeners "weren't allowed to talk to one

another after" receiving the message "and before giving their own opinions nor did they get to hear someone argue that the message was wrong." In a normal situation members of an audience have a chance to talk to other members and hear the opinions of the educated and opposed.[50]

3. When members of the audience are required to commit themselves publicly after being exposed to a persuasive communication. Researchers developed two speeches (one favoring and one opposing) on giving eighteen-year-olds the right to vote. Each speech was given in the first sequence to one audience and in the reversed sequence to another audience. In each case before the hearers heard the second speech they were asked to write an essay "presenting their frank opinions on the issue after the first communication." The subjects were told these essays would be bound and circulated among their teachers and classmates. They were asked to sign their name exactly as they wished it to appear in the pamphlet. Each speech was also given in the first and second situation to two other audiences. Again, subjects were asked to write an essay, but this time they were told the papers would be anonymous, and they were explicitly told not to sign their names. Results revealed that the subjects who thought they were publicly committing themselves responded less to the second communication than those who thought their commitment remained anonymous.[51]

4. When comprehension of the speaker's conclusion is important. One group of investigators obtained comprehension scores from subjects after they had heard either a one-sided or two-sided speech. The results showed the "one-sided presentations tended to produce greater comprehension of the speaker's conclusion."[52]

Two-Sided Approach

The two-sided presentation is sometimes more effective than the one-sided in changing attitudes. Students heard a summary of the prosecution and defense arguments from a fictitious trial. Each position was presented as a one-sided case and as part of a two-sided case. In the two-sided version each position was presented in both the first and second sequence. The results showed that those students hearing the two-sided presentation, regardless of which side was presented first, changed their attitudes more than those hearing the one-sided presentation.[53] Specifically, the two-sided presentation is more effective in three situations.

1. When the audience is well educated. The more highly educated person, when coupled with the two-sided speech, overrides the disadvantage of the listener's initial position. The two-sided communication is "more effective among the better educated regardless of initial position."[54]

2. When the audience initially disagrees with the speaker's position. In this situation, the two-sided presentation is more effective in changing the listeners' opinions.[55]

3. When the audience will be exposed later to counterpersuasion. Researchers presented to groups of college students one-sided and two-sided versions of an alleged radio program claiming that the Soviet Union would not soon be able to produce atomic arms in quantity. Both versions produced a net change in the desired direction in excess of 60 percent. When all subjects were then exposed to a communication expressing the opposite point of view, an interesting thing happened. The net change dropped to 2 percent among those originally hearing the one-sided speech, whereas the net change remained above 60 percent for those who initially heard the two-sided speech.[56]

The two-sided speech has an immunizing effect; it inoculates the listener against subsequent counterpersuasion.

Organization of a Persuasive Speech

Persuasive speeches, like informative speeches, generally have an introduction, purpose sentence, body, and conclusion. Nevertheless, there are some important differences in organizing a persuasive speech.

Introduction

Any of the types of introductions discussed in chapter 14 are appropriate for a persuasive speech. Probably the most important purpose of the introduction, however, is to ensure that the speaker has maximum ethos with the listeners. Too many studies have demonstrated that persuasion is dependent on the speaker's ethos for this vital purpose to be slighted. This isn't to imply, however, that the other purposes of the introduction—to get the listeners' attention and to lead them into the subject—are unimportant or should be ignored. And in cases where the speaker's ethos is no problem, one of the other purposes may assume the greatest importance.

Purpose

In most cases you should state your purpose explicitly in the speech: "This morning I want to persuade you that. . . ." "My purpose tonight is to get you to agree with me that. . . ."

On other occasions, because of strong hostility of the listeners, you may use what is called the *implicative* method. The purpose is never stated. In some cases even the main points are left unstated. The theory is that the evidence and supporting materials will lead the listener to infer your purpose. Unfortunately, research has indicated that without clear statement of the purpose, the listener frequently fails to draw the conclusion desired.

If hostility from the listeners is indeed a severe problem, a *deferred purpose* method may be used. In this case, the explicit statement of the purpose isn't made until after all the arguments and supporting materials have been presented. Then the speaker says explicitly, "My purpose tonight has been to persuade you that. . . ." "After hearing these arguments, I hope you will agree with me that. . . ."

The *deferred purpose* method is preferable to the *implicative* method on both practical and ethical bases. It ensures both that the listeners won't draw a "wrong" conclusion from the speech and that there will be no doubt about where you stand.

Body

The body of a persuasive speech may be organized in almost any of the ways discussed in chapter 13. Some patterns of organization, however, are more appropriate for persuasive speeches, including the motivated sequence, the problem-solution, and the causal patterns. Two other methods especially suited to persuasive speaking need to be considered.

Organizing a One-Sided Speech

In many persuasive speeches, there is a series of arguments for or against a position. Your decision then is whether to put the strongest argument first, last, or in the middle. No study has found any order of arguments in a one-sided speech more effective than any other in changing listeners' attitudes.[57]

Organizing a Two-Sided Speech

After you decide to use the two-sided approach, determine the order of the pro and con arguments. Research has shown that exposure to the pro arguments first caused listeners to accept the conclusions significantly more than those exposed to the con arguments first.[58]

Your credibility is also important. When a two-sided speech is attributed to a high-credibility source, the pro-con sequence is more effective in shifting opinion. When the same speech is attributed to a low-credibility source, a con-pro sequence was more effective. When the pro-con sequence was attributed to a low-credibility source, a boomerang effect tended to occur, causing more listeners to reject the speech's ideas.[59]

Conclusion

Although any of the types of conclusions discussed in chapter 14 are appropriate for a persuasive speech, some are used more frequently than others. Especially apt are conclusions that summarize, make an appeal for action, or present a challenge that stimulates the listeners. Obviously, you must focus on the main purpose of your speech in the conclusion, but it is equally important to leave your ethos high with the listeners.

Summary

Coercion is an undesirable alternative to persuasion because, first, its success is dependent on force or power, and, second, the person may not be committed to the position to which he or she is coerced.

Persuasion, on the other hand, permits an individual voluntarily to adopt a position, results in a stronger commitment to that position, and provides a nonviolent method for influencing others.

Persuasion may be defined as the process whereby an attempt is made to induce changes in attitudes and behavior through involvement of a person's cognitive and affective processes.

Changing the attitudes of listeners is not easy; it is made more difficult by a number of potential obstacles that may deter or weaken attitude change. Accumulated evidence indicates that (1) selective perception can sometimes operate to the detriment of attitude change, (2) selective recall of the message can interfere with change, (3) selective exposure to the communication can deter change, (4) the degree to which a person is committed to an attitude determines resistance to change, (5) public commitment increases the likelihood of resistance to change, (6) the amount of discrepancy between the speaker and listener affects resistance to change, and (7) group pressure on the listener may prevent change.

Despite existing obstacles, much evidence has been accumulated from observation and empirical studies to show that attitude change does occur. At least eight methods are available: (1) build a case with evidence and reasoning; (2) show that the desired behavior is approved by an esteemed person or by the reference group; (3) show that the proposal is consistent or inconsistent with a value premise of the hearer; (4) appeal to an alternative value premise; (5) arouse fear in the listeners; (6) offer reward or incentive to the hearers; (7) appeal to motivating factors; and (8) provide explicit instructions on action advocated.

Research indicates the one-sided approach is more effective when members of the audience are already favorably disposed toward your position, poorly educated, required to commit themselves publicly following the speech, and comprehension of the conclusion is important. The two-sided development is more effective when the audience is well educated, initially disagrees with your position, or will later be exposed to counterpersuasion.

Persuasive speeches, like informative ones, generally have an introduction, purpose statement, body, and conclusion. Sometimes you should either leave the purpose unstated or defer it to the end of the speech.

Exercises

1. Prepare a six-minute persuasive speech in which you use fear arousal as your primary method of attempting to change the attitudes of your listeners. Explain in a brief paragraph specifically how you plan to remove the cause of the fear.
2. Read a persuasive speech in the current issue of *Vital Speeches*. Identify the methods the speaker uses to attempt to change the listeners' attitudes. Evaluate the speaker's use of those methods. How would you have handled them differently?
3. Attend a persuasive speech in the community. Identify the obstacles to changing attitudes with which the speaker had to cope. Describe the method by which he or she successfully dealt with them. If the speakers were unsuccessful in coping with any, explain why. Explain how you would have done it differently.

4. Think of a value held by the people in your community. Explain how you could use that value to attempt to change their attitude toward a social problem on which you have a different attitude.

5. Select one method of changing attitudes that you'll use in your next speech. Explain in detail, including specific supporting material, how you'll use that method.

Notes

1. A. Huxley, "Notes on Propaganda," *Harper's,* December 1936, p. 36.

2. P. F. Lazarsfeld, B. Berelson, and H. Gaudet, *The People's Choice* (New York: Columbia University Press, 1968), pp. xxiii, 65–66; B. Berelson, P. F. Lazarsfeld, and W. N. McPhee, *Voting: A Study of Opinion Formation in a Presidential Election* (Chicago: University of Chicago Press, 1954), p. 23; T. W. Benham, "Polling for a Presidential Candidate: Some Observations of the 1964 Campaign," *Public Opinion Quarterly* 29 (1965):185–99.

3. H. H. Kelley, "Attribution Theory in Social Psychology," in *Nebraska Symposium on Motivation,* ed. D. Levine (Lincoln, Neb.: University of Nebraska Press, 1967).

4. E. McGinnies and L. Rosenbaum, "A Test of the Selective-Exposure Hypothesis in Persuasion," *Journal of Psychology* 61 (1965):237–40.

5. J. Mills, *Experimental Social Psychology* (London: Macmillan & Co., 1969), p. 138.

6. A. Lowin, "Approach and Avoidance: Alternative Modes of Selective Exposure to Information," *Journal of Personality and Social Psychology* 6 (1967):1–9.

7. C. W. Sherif and M. Sherif, *Attitude, Ego-Involvement and Change* (New York: John Wiley & Sons, 1967), pp. 134–35; C. W. Sherif, M. Sherif, and R. E. Nebergall, *Attitude and Attitude Change* (Philadelphia: W. B. Saunders Co., 1965), pp. 168–97.

8. P. Tannenbaum, "Initial Attitude toward Source and Concept as Factors in Attitude Change through Communication," *Public Opinion Quarterly* 20 (1956):425.

9. H. H. Kelley and E. H. Volkart, "The Resistance to Change of Group-Anchored Attitude Change through Communication," *Public Opinion Quarterly* 20 (1956):425.

10. C. I. Hovland, E. H. Campbell, and T. Brock, "The Effects of 'Commitment' on Opinion Change Following Communication," in *Order of Presentation in Persuasion,* ed. C. I. Hovland (New Haven: Yale University Press, 1957), pp. 23–32.

11. C. I. Hovland and H. Pritzker, "Extent of Opinion Change as a Function of Amount of Change Advocated," *Journal of Abnormal and Social Psychology* 54 (1957):257–61.

12. Sherif et al., *Attitude and Attitude Change,* p. 24.

13. J. Freedman, "Involvement, Discrepancy, and Change," *Journal of Abnormal and Social Psychology* 69 (1964):290–95.

14. J. Whittaker, "Attitude Change and Communication-Attitude Discrepancy," *Journal of Social Psychology* 65 (1965):141–47.

15. E. Aronson, J. Turner, and J. M. Carlsmith, "Communicator Credibility and Communication Discrepancy as Determinants of Opinion Change," *Journal of Abnormal and Social Psychology* 67 (1963):31–36.

16. C. A. Insko, *Theories of Attitude Change* (New York: Appleton-Century-Crofts, 1967), p. 348.

17. S. E. Asch, *Social Psychology* (New York: Prentice-Hall, 1952), pp. 450–501.

18. Richard E. Petty and John T. Cacioppo, "The Elaboration Likelihood Model of Persuasion," *Advances in Experimental Social Psychology,* Vol. 19 (New York: Academic Press, 1986), p. 128. Used by permission. Hereafter referred to as Petty and Cacioppo, 1986.

19. Petty and Cacioppo, 1986, pp. 175, 186–87. See also J. Crocker, S. T. Fiske, and S. E. Taylor, "Schematic Bases of Belief Change," in *Attitudinal Judgment,* ed. R. Eiser (New York: Springer-Verlag, 1984). W. J. McGuire, "The Probabilogical Model of Cognitive Structure and Attitude Change," in *Cognitive Responses in Persuasion,* eds. R. E. Petty, T. M. Ostrom, and T. C. Brock (Hillsdale, New Jersey: Erlbaum, 1981).

20. Petty and Cacioppo, 1986, p. 176.

21. Ibid, p. 179.

22. R. E. Petty and J. T. Cacioppo, "The Effects of Involvement on Responses to Argument Quantity and Quality: Central and Peripheral Routes to Persuasion," *Journal of Personality and Social Psychology* 46 (1984):69–81. See also, William L. Benoit, "Argumentation and Credibility Appeals in Persuasion," *The Southern Speech Communication Journal* 52 (1987):181–97.

23. S. Chaiken, "Heuristic Versus Systematic Information Processing and the Use of Source Versus Message Cues in Persuasion," *Journal of Personality and Social Psychology* 39 (1980):752–56. See also R. Rhine and L. Severance, "Ego-Involvement, Discrepancy, Source Credibility, and Attitude Change," *Journal of Personality and Social Psychology,* 16 (1970):175–90.

24. S. G. Harkins and R. E. Petty, "The Effects of Source Magnification of Cognitive Effort on Attitudes: An Information Processing View," *Journal of Personality and Social Psychology* 40 (1981):401–13. See also Petty and Cacioppo, 1986, p. 189.

25. J. T. Cacioppo and R. E. Petty, "Central and Peripheral Routes to Persuasion: The Role of Message Repetition," in *Psychological Processes and Advertising Effects,* eds., A. Mitchell and L. Alwitt (Hillsdale, N.J.: Erlbaum, 1985). See also Petty and Cacioppo, 1986, pp. 143–44.

26. Harvey C. Jacobs, "Readers: An Endangered Species?" in *Representative American Speeches, 1985–1986,* ed. Owen Peterson (New York: H. W. Wilson Company, 1986), pp. 152–153.

27. J. L. Freedman and S. C. Fraser, "Compliance Without Pressure: The Foot-in-the-Door Technique," *Journal of Personality and Social Psychology* 33 (1976):520.

28. C. Seligman, M. Bush, and K. Kirsch, "Relationship between Compliance in the Foot-in-the-Door Paradigm and Size of First Request," *Journal of Personality and Social Psychology* 33 (1976):517–20. Used by permission.

29. M. Burgoon and E. P. Bettinghaus, "Persuasive Message Strategies," pp. 155–59 in *Persuasion: New Directions in Theory and Research,* edited by M. E. Roloff and G. R. Miller (Beverly Hills, Calif.: Sage Publications, Inc., 1980). Copyright © 1980. Reprinted by permission of Sage Publications, Inc.

30. R. B. Cialdini, J. E. Vincent, S. K. Lewis, J. Catalan, D. Wheeler, and B. L. Darby, "Reciprocal Concessions Procedure for Inducing Compliance: The Door-in-the-Face Technique," *Journal of Personality and Social Psychology* 31 (1975):206–15. Used by permission.

31. Burgoon and Bettinghaus, op. cit., pp. 157–59.

32. H. C. Kelman, "Compliance, Identification, and Internalization: Three Processes of Attitude Change," *Journal of Conflict Resolution* 2 (1958):51–60.

33. M. Sherif and C. I. Hovland, *Social Judgment* (New Haven: Yale University Press, 1961), pp. 89–90.

34. H. H. Kelley and C. Woodruff, "Members' Reactions to Apparent Group Approval of a Counter-Norm Communication," *Journal of Abnormal and Social Psychology* 52 (1956):67–74.

35. F. J. DiVesta and J. C. Merwin, "The Effects of Need-Oriented Communications on Attitude Change," *Journal of Abnormal and Social Psychology* 60 (1960):80–85.

36. G. A. Stinson, "What's Right with America," *Vital Speeches of the Day* 46 (1979):88.

37. A. E. Jones, "World Peace through World Purchasing," *Vital Speeches of the Day* 46 (1979):91.

38. J. C. Lawn, "Drugs in America," *Vital Speeches of the Day* 52 (1986):323. Used by permission.

39. I. L. Janis and S. Feshbach, "Effects of Fear-Arousing Communications," *Journal of Abnormal and Social Psychology* 48 (1953):78–92.

40. J. M. Dabbs, Jr., and H. Leventhal, "Effects of Varying the Recommendations in a Fear-Arousing Communication," *Journal of Personality and Social Psychology* 4 (1966):525–31.

41. F. A. Powell, "The Effect of Anxiety-Arousing Messages When Related to Personal, Familial, and Impersonal Referents," *Speech Monographs* 32 (1965):102–6; P. Niles, "The Relationship of Susceptibility and Anxiety to Acceptance of Fear-Arousing Communications," Ph.D. diss., Yale University, 1964, as cited in Mills, *Experimental Social Psychology,* p. 189; H. Leventhal and R. Singer, "Affect Arousal and Positioning of Recommendations in Persuasive Communication," *Journal of Personality and Social Psychology* 4 (1966):137–46; H. Leventhal, R. Singer, and S. Jones, "Effects of Fear and Specificity of Recommendation upon Attitudes and Behavior," *Journal of Personality and Social Psychology* 2 (1965):20–29. H. Leventhal, S. Jones, and G. Trembley, "Sex Differences in Attitude and Behavior Change under Conditions of Fear and Specific Instructions," *Journal of Experimental Social Psychology* 2 (1966):387–99; H. Leventhal, J. C. Watts, and F. Pagano, "Effects of Fear and Instructions on How to Cope with Danger," *Journal of Personality and Social Psychology* 6 (1967):313–21.

42. H. Leventhal, "Findings and Theory in the Study of Fear Communications," in *Advances in Experimental Social Psychology,* ed. L. Berkowitz, vol. 5. (New York: Academic Press, 1970), p. 120.

43. Mills, *Experimental Social Psychology,* p. 213.

44. L. Festinger and J. M. Carlsmith, "Cognitive Consequences of Forced Compliance," *Journal of Abnormal and Social Psychology* 58 (1959):203–10.

45. M. Rosenberg, "When Dissonance Fails: On Eliminating Evaluation Apprehension from Attitude Measurement," *Journal of Personality and Social Psychology* 1 (1965):28–42.

46. W. R. Miller, "Pharmaceuticals for the Elderly, *Vital Speeches of the Day* 52 (1986):397–98. Used by permission.

47. H. Leventhal, R. Singer, and S. Jones, "Effects of Fear and Specificity of Recommendation upon Attitudes and Behavior," *Journal of Personality and Social Psychology* 2 (1965):20–29.

48. C. I. Hovland, A. A. Lumsdaine, and F. D. Sheffield, *Experiments on Mass Communication* (Princeton, N.J.: Princeton University Press, 1949), pp. 201–27. See also C. I. Hovland, I. L. Janis, and H. H. Kelley, *Communication and Persuasion* (New Haven: Yale University Press, 1968), pp. 105–8.

49. Hovland et al., *Communication and Persuasion,* pp. 105–8; Hovland et al., *Experiments on Mass Communication.*

50. Mills, *Experimental Social Psychology,* pp. 166–67.

51. Hovland et al., *The Order of Presentation in Persuasion,* pp. 23–32.

52. D. L. Thistlethwaite, J. Kemenetzky, and H. Schmidt, "Factors Influencing Attitude Change through Refutative Communications," *Speech Monographs* 23 (1956):20.

53. C. A. Insko, "One-Sided versus Two-Sided Communications and Counter Communications," *Journal of Abnormal and Social Psychology* 65 (1962): 203–6.

54. Hovland et al., *Communication and Persuasion,* p. 108.

55. Ibid.

56. A. A. Lumsdaine and I. L. Janis, "Resistance to 'Counter-propaganda' Produced by One-Sided and Two-Sided 'Propaganda' Presentations," *Public Opinion Quarterly* 17 (1953):311–18.

57. H. Sponberg, "The Relative Effectiveness of Climax and Anti-Climax Order in an Argumentative Speech," *Speech Monographs* 13 (1946):35–44; H. Gilkinson et al., "Effects of Order and Authority in an Argumentative Speech," *Quarterly Journal of Speech* 40 (1954):183–92; Berlo and Gulley, "Some Determinants of the Effect of Oral Communication"; Culton, "Effects of Speech Structure."

58. I. L. Janis and R. L. Feieraband, "Effects of Alternative Ways of Ordering Pro and Con Arguments in Persuasive Communications," in *Order of Presentation in Persuasion,* pp. 115–28.

59. R. G. Rea, "An Experimental Study of Source Credibility and Order of Presentation in Persuasion," M.A. thesis, University of Arkansas, 1961.

CHAPTER 20

Evocative Speaking

Evocative speeches are given for special events and specific audiences. They are generally rather brief, only rarely more than five to ten minutes in length. They have many of the characteristics of other speeches, and they should possess the following specific attributes:

1. Organize your ideas to reveal their unity.
2. Develop the ideas thoroughly, with various types of appropriate supporting material.
3. Use words as though there were a limited supply available. Cut excess words ruthlessly.
4. Keep these speeches brief.
5. Keep the language clear. In the short time available, every word must count and be easily understood.
6. Use interesting and attention-getting supporting material to develop the ideas.
7. Make your delivery effective and attention-holding.

Speech to Stimulate

The speech to stimulate attempts to arouse feelings of pride and emotion. Its objective is to praise what should be done, what will be done, or what has been done. It is appropriate for public relations speeches, dedicatory speeches, memorializing speeches, commencement addresses, and motivational presentations. These speeches are designed to create mild emotional reactions within the listeners: sadness for the person memorialized, happiness for the concept or object being dedicated, pride for the accomplishment of the person being graduated, or incentive to perform an important task that is needed.

Contrary to the thoughts of many, emotions are legitimate instigators of human behavior. They are instrumental in helping select a spouse, save money for a child's education, choose the house we will buy, or select the college we will attend. It is emotion that causes a mother to run into a burning home to save an infant child. As human beings we can't ignore our feelings.

Purpose

The purpose of speeches to stimulate is to create enthusiasm, to arouse emotions, or to inspire listeners. These reactions are appropriate when the occasion is to recognize an important achievement of a town; to create an emotional response, such as anger, because of a heinous crime; or to inspire listeners because of the completion of a beautiful building to house a new library. Most of us are reluctant to get involved in new ventures until our emotions tell us the project is worthwhile.

The speech to stimulate should focus on the unifying factors that will strengthen the group's harmony and reduce the conflict and hostility that is often so prevalent today.

In earlier years common goals bound many Americans together. Today it seems that every group has developed different objectives. The speech to stimulate can provide harmonizing factors that will draw together the diverse members of society and create a more harmonious effort to establish unifying incentives. Special occasion speeches, such as the Fourth of July orations that once dominated celebration of the founding of our nation, can be used again to establish solidarity for our people. The stimulating speech can be used to fuse the common loyalties of a group.

There are many situations in which speeches to stimulate are appropriate. Each requires a different set of themes and emotions. Fourth of July and Memorial Day speeches, for example, require patriotic themes. The speaker wants the audience to become emotionally involved. The listeners should experience such feelings as loyalty, patriotism, pride, respect, and devotion. Labor Day speeches, on the other hand, require themes that praise the efforts of the working people of our nation. Especially to be praised are those who create the goods in our factories, who produce the food on our farms, and who see that our transportation and communication needs are realized.

Appropriate Situations

A funeral sermon may be a speech to stimulate when the speaker praises the deceased and comforts the bereaved relatives and friends with descriptions of the decedent's virtues.

To enhance these various responses, the speaker should "utilize the old: old customs, old stereotypes, old heroes, old loyalties, cherished memories. . . . But he must also utilize the new; that is, he must express his ideas in fresh form, he must give new interpretations to the old and represent its influence in new relationships."[1] The speaker wants the listeners to perceive the old in different and unusual ways.

Probably the most famous speech to stimulate ever given was Lincoln's Gettysburg Address. Even today, with the speech totally out of context, the speech still moves readers and listeners. Ostensibly, Lincoln's purpose was to pay tribute to the soldiers who had died in battle. Wiley says, however, that Lincoln's "intent at Gettysburg was to say something to stimulate his countrymen to preserve a government boasting the ideal that *'all men are created equal.'* "[2]

In his Inaugural Address, President John F. Kennedy stimulated his audience to approve and support his objectives to create a better world for humankind. Listen to his words:

> Now the trumpet summons us again—not as a call to bear arms, though arms we need—not as a call to battle, though embattled we are—but a call to bear the burden of a long twilight struggle year in and year out, 'rejoicing in hope, patient in tribulation'—a struggle against the common enemies of man: tyranny, poverty, disease, and war itself.
>
> Can we forge against these enemies a grand and global alliance, north and south, east and west, that can assure a more fruitful life for all mankind? Will you join in that historic effort?
>
> In the long history of the world, only a few generations have been granted the role of defending freedom in its hour of maximum danger. I do not shrink from this responsibility—I welcome it. I do not believe that any of us would

exchange places with any other people or any other generation. The energy, the faith, the devotion which we bring to this endeavor will light our country and all who serve it—and the glow from that fire can truly light the world.

And so, my fellow Americans: ask not what your country can do for you—ask what you can do for your country.[3]

Winston Churchill stimulated the English people to maintain their resolve in World War II when he declared:

Even though large tracts of Europe and many old and famous States have fallen or may fall into the grip of the Gestapo and all the odious apparatus of Nazi rule, we shall not flag or fail. We shall go on to the end; we shall fight in France; we shall fight on the seas and oceans; we shall fight with growing confidence and growing strength in the air; we shall defend our Island, whatever the cost may be; we shall fight on the beaches; we shall fight on the landing grounds; we shall fight in the fields and in the streets; we shall fight in the hills. We shall never surrender, and even if, which I do not for a moment believe, this Island or a large part of it were subjugated and starving, then our Empire beyond the seas, armed and guarded by the British Fleet, would carry on the struggle, until, in God's good time, the New World, with all its power and might, steps forth to the rescue and the liberation of the old.[4]

It was words like these that enabled Churchill to motivate the English people to maintain their spirit while the Germans were saturating their country with bombs. It was words like these that enabled the people to go about their daily labors despite the loss of sleep caused by the dreadful nights with their fearful and numerous bombs.

When the war was over, however, Churchill was no longer able to find the appropriate ways of stimulating the English people. Unable to articulate the means of coping with the post-war problems, his leadership was rejected by the people. Churchill's problem was one that all speakers attempting to stimulate must confront. Unless the rationale for stimulation is clearly identified and effectively enunciated, listeners will ignore the speaker's efforts.

Supporting Materials

Strong motivating appeals should be provided to stimulate support for your programs and objectives. They should be phrased to make them appealing and desirable for your listeners. Political parties at their conventions use banners, bunting, and balloons to put the delegates in a patriotic and friendly mood to create a stronger urge to compromise their differences and support their various candidates.

But, more substantive content should be provided to develop your ideas. Don't be misled into believing that a speech to stimulate is nothing more than catchy phrases and emotion. As one writer noted:

> In a given situation, with a given audience, some kinds of utterance are more likely to induce heightened emotional response than other kinds. But it is perfectly clear that a speaker's utterance may be highly emotive in a given situation and also highly demonstrative of the effective use of evidence and reasoning. It is simply not the case that speeches which are informative and well reasoned are thereby necessarily lacking in emotive power, or vice versa. Accordingly, giving value to reasoned discourse does not imply censure for highly emotive discourse.[5]

Wit and humor can add to the effectiveness of almost every speech, unless you are speaking on a sad or solemn occasion.

Language

The language of a speech to stimulate should be precise, commanding, lofty, striking, and unusual. It should encourage the hearers to join whatever effort you're proposing. To establish an inspiring mood, slang should be avoided. Use concreteness and specificity to create mental images in the minds of the listeners through the use of visual, auditory, gustatory, olfactory, and tactual experiences. The language should involve comparison and contrast. You can use repetition and refrain to make the language more striking and effective. The language should be sufficiently eloquent to involve the listeners' emotions and to lift their spirits in support of the speaker's ideas.

Organization

The organization of the stimulating speech should be inconspicuous. The introduction should strike an emotional chord with the listeners. The purpose of the speech should be implied rather than stated specifically, but it may involve the listeners' emotions. The body of the speech will frequently consist of only one main point. In some instances, it may have more than one main point, but generally not more than two or three. Whatever the number of main points, they shouldn't be numbered; in fact, their existence should be so subtle that they won't be identified by most listeners as main divisions. But their flow should provide a sense of movement. The conclusion should focus on the main theme or themes and cause the listeners to re-experience the emotional responses aroused in other parts of the speech.

Content

The speech to stimulate shouldn't ask the listeners to take some action; that is the purpose of a persuasive speech. That only creates frustration. If you're advocating an action they can't complete, then ask them to make whatever contribution they can to accomplish the desired objective, such as give money, write letters, or petition others. These actions provide a feeling of accomplishment and prevent feelings of frustration because they can't contribute to completion of the task.

Humor can be used effectively to relieve a rhetorical effort to stimulate. It can help to break tension; it can be used to laugh at an opposing position; it can be used to polarize an audience toward the speaker's theme.

An important way of developing effective content is to reinforce the beliefs and feelings of your hearers. Focus on themes and experiences that are approved and sanctioned by members of the audience. If your listeners have demonstrated their high regard for education by building well-designed schools that foster and encourage sound educational practices, then praise them for their efforts. Your words will undoubtedly encourage them to seek the best teachers in the future and to stress to their young people even more the value of acquiring a strong and appropriate education.

Delivery

Eye contact is crucial. Speak directly to the listeners. You must not give the impression that you can't look them directly in the eyes. Establish rapport with your listeners by developing and maintaining strong eye contact with them. You can't give the impression that you must read the speech from a manuscript. Your voice should be strong and forceful, with appropriate pitch inflections. Use measured and forceful gestures and effective physical action to create an impression of strength and forcefulness. Delivery should not only help to hold the attention of the listeners, it should also help to heighten the listeners' feelings.

A Sample Outline of a Speech to Stimulate

A. Introduction

The availability of education in the latter half of this century has been the miracle of our nation. Never before have our young people been able to go as far in education as their abilities permitted, regardless of the lack of wealth. No other nation approaches our ability and willingness to educate so many for so long. No longer does wealth prevent an (ambitious, willing) student from earning high school and college diplomas. Our people and our leaders have clearly proclaimed: let us educate every person to his or her potential.

B. Purpose Sentence: Important advantages are provided to those who are exposed to educational opportunities.

C. Body of the Speech

1. Education enhances a person's intellectual talents.
    a. It improves a person's mind.
    b. It frees people and society to achieve the best possible for the good life.
    c. It enables people to free themselves from narrow-mindedness.
2. Education develops a moral framework for behavior.
    a. It defines the environment in which moral learning and development are shaped.
    b. It prepares students to carry on their lives as responsible members of the community.
    c. It exposes students to the informal codes of conduct that are characteristic of virtuous citizens.
3. Education creates economic value.
    a. It discovers human talent and enhances it.
    b. It enables persons to make occupational adjustments to changes in economic needs.
    c. It adjusts to provide people with the high skills and knowledge needed.

D. Conclusion

Education is no longer a luxury; our people have declared it a necessity. We can no longer permit a single person to be deprived of education because of a lack of wealth. We can no longer permit a lack of education to prevent a single citizen from reaching full potential as a citizen. It not only hurts that person; it hurts the whole nation.

Speech of Introduction

The most common use of the speech of introduction is to present a person making a speech. But it's also used to present a newcomer to a community, a church, a social group, or any other organization. Specifically, your purpose is to create acceptance of the person being introduced and to give his or her

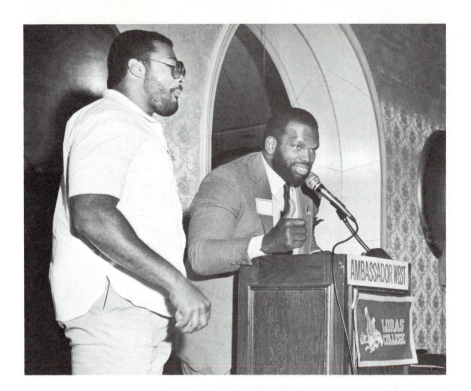

name and identity. Your most important objective is to establish the credibility of the person you are presenting. If you do your job properly, the listeners will want to know the speaker's name and to hear what he or she has to say.

Main Ideas

Discuss relevant personal characteristics of the person being introduced, such as education, experience, objectivity, goodwill, intelligence, and knowledge of subject. If you're introducing a speaker, point out the importance or significance of the subject of the speech.

Clarify the purpose of the meeting if that is relevant or important. If the subject or the occasion of the speech is significant, acknowledge that fact and discuss briefly their special significance. If the choice of the speaker was determined by the specific subject or occasion, you'll probably want to note that fact and explain why to the audience. If the speaker has specific qualifications—position, special capabilities—to talk on the subject, you may call that to the attention of the listeners.

If the size of the audience is unexpectedly large, you may call attention to that fact by congratulating the planners of the event or the members of the audience themselves. But never apologize for or criticize the smallness of the group.

Call attention to the fact this is a special occasion, if that is the case. This may be the first time the speaker has been back to this community since he or she graduated from high school twenty-five years ago. Or he or she may have just been selected as president of his or her company two weeks ago. Or perhaps this is the last time your group will meet at this location.

Don't apologize because the speaker is a substitute for a previously announced one. Announce that the expected speaker was unable to come and this speaker was gracious enough to substitute. Don't compare the two.

Supporting Materials

Supporting material should consist primarily of factual data, including such information as educational background, work experience, accomplishments, honors and awards, and personal achievements.

Various sources can be used to obtain information about the person you are introducing: newspaper articles, friends, and associates. In cases where the person has achieved a level of renown, you may consult biographical works, such as *Directory of American Scholars, Who's Who in America, Current Biography, Who's Who in Education, Who's Who Among Black Americans, Who's Who of American Women.* In some notable cases you may be able to consult a biography or an autobiography. If none of these sources is available, ask the speaker to provide information. You should also ask the speaker if there is anything special he or she wants mentioned.

Be sure the information you collect is accurate. Nothing is more embarrassing to both of you than for the speaker to have to correct something you have said. Give all the important information, but don't exaggerate or build the speaker up too much. That only creates an embarrassing situation for both of you. Don't say anything you don't mean sincerely.

Style

Your language should be suited to the status of the speaker. In most cases, a plain style will be appropriate. This is language that is suitable for most daily communication. In some instances, the person you are introducing may be a dignitary or some accomplished individual. Then you'll want to use a more formal and dignified style. In any case, use language that is clear and understandable to the listeners. Most importantly, when talking about the person being introduced, avoid superlatives; generally they only embarrass both the person and the listeners. Avoid any semblance of insincerity.

Organization

One of two methods of organizing a speech is appropriate for a speech of introduction. You may organize the information in a chronological pattern (the high school years, the college years, the family years) or a topical pattern (accomplishments as a parent, contributions as a private citizen, services as a politician). Because it is important information, put the name of the person and the subject of the speech at the end of the introduction. Then stop!

Delivery

The delivery of the speech should be appropriate to the mood of the occasion. For an informal situation, the speech may be delivered more casually. For a formal event, the speech may be delivered from a manuscript or from memory, although it's preferable for you to deliver it extemporaneously. If you do use a manuscript, be sufficiently familiar with the material to be able to maintain much eye contact with the listeners. If your speech is memorized, be careful to maintain a conversational tone as you deliver your speech. It is imperative that the information in your speech be provided, so get it to the listeners in whatever way is appropriate. Don't forget to announce the title of the speech and the name of the speaker at the end of your introduction. Be especially careful to pronounce the speaker's name correctly!

Speech of Presentation

The purpose of the speech of presentation is to give an award or a gift to a person who is retiring, has completed a project of merit, is moving away, has earned an athletic letter, has performed some distinguished service, or for some reason deserves recognition. The award tells the recipient that he or she has earned the esteem of the givers, and that those giving the award or gift want to express their appreciation for the recipient's efforts.

Main Ideas

Your speech should focus on the good qualities of the person receiving the gift or recognition, or explain the reasons for the person's recognition. Describe the award that is being given, and identify any symbolic values it might have. If it has certain intrinsic or extrinsic values, explain what they are. If a retiring colleague is being given a golf bag and a set of clubs, you might note that the gift has the extrinsic values of preventing boredom, providing enjoyment, enhancing physical well-being, and gently reminding the recipient of the genuine esteem colleagues have for him or her.

If the award is from an organization, then mention it and explain why it's appropriate for that organization to give an award or recognition to this particular person. Tell why the presentation is being made. Try to summarize the sentiments of the organization or group that is giving the award. Make the recipient aware of the esteem that the group or organization has for him or her.

Praise for the person receiving the gift or recognition should be genuine, without becoming overly emotional. Some light humor can help to prevent the occasion from becoming maudlin. Overpraise, especially that which sounds insincere, can embarrass the recipient and the listeners.

If the award is one that has been given to others, you'll probably want to remind your listeners of that fact. If the quality of former recipients will magnify the value of the award, you'll probably want to recall their names and cite some of their deeds, especially if the listeners' silent comparison of the deeds will be favorable to the current recipient.

If the award has been won in competition with others and a few finalists were named, you should recognize them and congratulate them on their quality efforts. Keep the focus, however, on the person and the occasion. Don't overstress the award or its value. The award is a symbol and its true value lies in the reason for bestowing it.

Specific examples demonstrating worthy qualities of the person receiving the award or gift should be highlighted. This information can be obtained from friends, competitors, neighbors, newspapers, and in some cases from books, periodical articles, and speeches.

Supporting Materials

Your language should be suited to the mood of the occasion, informal for a casual situation, formal for a ceremonial event. Your language should reflect the esteem and appreciation the organization has for the recipient's achievements and contributions. Figures of speech are appropriate for a formal occasion. Your words should be put together in a more rhythmical arrangement. You might read Lincoln's three formal occasional speeches—the First and Second Inaugurals and the Gettysburg Address—to understand the definite rhythm he develops. Understand, however, you're not doing this to emulate Lincoln's style, but to understand better the importance of rhythm in language. Your speech can be delivered extemporaneously, written and read from a manuscript, or presented from memory. If you deliver it other than extemporaneously, however, be sure you maintain adequate eye contact with the listeners. Dignity, simplicity, and sincerity should be the characteristics of your language.

Style

The most appropriate pattern of organization will usually be a topical one, identifying as the main topics the qualities of the person or persons being recognized. In some instances, a causal pattern might be used, with the individual points identifying the causes that produced the effect, the award or recognition being presented.

Organization

Except for very unusual situations in which the ceremony is formal, the presentation will be delivered extemporaneously in a relaxed, informal manner. For a formal occasion, the speech may either be read from a manuscript or given from memory. If it is read, be sure that you know it well enough to give fairly long segments without looking at the manuscript. Maintain a conversational tone whether reading or giving from memory. The presentation should be easily heard by all listeners.

Delivery

When the recipient comes forward for the gift or award, shake his or her hand first, then hand him or her the gift or award. Don't continue to clutch it after he or she has taken hold.

Speech to Commemorate

The purpose of this type of speech is to observe anniversaries, dedicate new buildings or new projects, to eulogize the memory of a noted or beloved person, to inaugurate new programs or new administrations, or to celebrate a date in history (the end of the Civil War, the end of World War II, the passage of the Civil Rights Act).

Main Ideas

A commemorative speech should deal mainly with factual data. That factual data should be brought to life, however, by recalling specific achievements made possible by particular human efforts, major obstacles that were successfully overcome, and instrumental virtues demonstrated by key participants.

If you're commemorating an individual, avoid exaggerating his or her qualities and achievements. A more effective ploy might be to recall ways in which the person overcame foibles, weaknesses, or deficiencies to achieve a constructive or noble objective. By all means, avoid controversial events, facts, or persons.

Forms of Communication

Sources of information to develop the ideas may be newspapers of the period involved, books, articles in periodicals, speeches of the period, and old-timers who lived in the area at the time the event occurred.

Supporting Materials

Facts should be presented as vividly as possible to create an inspirational mood. Language should be considered important and you should strive to achieve an eloquent style. Appropriate figures of speech should be used wherever possible.

Style

A topical or chronological pattern of organization to develop your main divisions will probably be best to let you focus on whatever main topics you desire. A straightforward chronological account may not be generally desirable, but one that focuses on the past, present, and future may be desirable and appropriate. The introduction should probably be a brief reference to the event being commemorated. The conclusion should focus on some challenging or inspirational feature of the object, person, or event you are remembering.

Organization

The physical presentation of the speech should be in keeping with the formality of the occasion. Physical action should be subdued, and the solemnity of the occasion should be reflected in the voice.

Delivery

Speech to Entertain

The primary objective of this speech is to help people enjoy themselves. It frequently occurs after a meal, which explains why it is sometimes called an after-dinner speech. This is a time when people are relaxed and content and not in the mood for a long discussion of serious issues or problems.

This speech can draw its main ideas from almost any topic. Especially appropriate are the following topics: describing unusual experiences, telling a dramatic narrative, giving a travelogue (with or without color slides), recounting startling facts, or depicting a fantasy. Only very serious subjects have to be avoided.

Main Ideas

The speech to entertain should utilize interest and attention by presenting novel, vivid, concrete, surprising, or suspenseful information. Examples can highlight ideas and serve as excellent supporting proofs. The speech rarely draws a moral or states a judgment, although it may imply either. Humor is a frequently used type of supporting material, although it doesn't necessarily have to be, nor is it necessarily the best. If humor is used, it should be in good taste, tactful, and appropriate to the listeners and the occasion. It should not be barbed or malicious. The primary characteristics of humor should be exaggeration and the unexpected ending. You can also use understatement and satire for humorous effect. Humor doesn't even have to be funny in the sense that it is laugh-provoking. It can be the quiet kind of humor that causes a person to smile inside.

Supporting Materials

A series of unrelated jokes strung together do not constitute an entertaining speech. A comedian may be able to get away with that, but an entertaining speaker must have a theme and main points, which at times can be developed in humorous or interesting ways.

Style

Language should be the kind that highlights comparisons and contrasts. It should be colorful and specifically descriptive, using words that exaggerate comparisons and contrasts.

Organization

Any pattern of organization can be used in an entertaining speech.

Delivery

The entertaining speech should be delivered extemporaneously. Nothing spoils its effect more than seeing the speaker reading from a manuscript. Notes shouldn't be used. If it's a humorous speech, it can be delivered with a deadpan expression or in a way that reveals the speaker's enjoyment with the material. If you're going to react to the humorous material, you must follow, not precede laughter of the listeners. Then be ready to resume your speech as soon as the listeners are ready. The speech should be brief.

Speech of Nomination

This is a speech of praise that provides the reasons and justification for naming and supporting a particular candidate for a specific position. It is in reality a persuasive speech, because it attempts to convince the listeners that the object of the speech has the requisite qualities to perform ably the duties required of the position to be filled.

Main Ideas

The first thing you should do is discover and define the needs of the office. This may help you to ascertain, for example, that the holder of the position must deal with various types of people, must make a number of economic decisions, and must speak regularly to different groups. Then you can match the nominee's qualifications with those needs. You should make no comparisons, however, with other nominees.

Supporting Materials

The qualifications, experience, and achievements of the nominee will supply the supporting materials for your speech.

Sources of information will be newspapers, friends, teachers, employers, and family members of the nominee, and various biographical sources: *Directory of American Scholars, Who's Who in America, Current Biography, Who's Who in Education, Who's Who Among Black Americans, Who's Who of American Women.* You'll probably also want to consult with the nominee.

Style

The language of the speech should be energetic, colorful, descriptive, positive, and familiar.

The topical pattern of organization allows you to focus on the demands of the position and the qualifications and the attributes of your nominee. You can also use a problem-solution pattern of organization, identifying the problems that have been unsolved in the past, then arguing that the solution is to elect your candidate whose qualifications would ensure that those problems would be solved successfully.

Organization

To be most effective, your speech should be delivered extemporaneously. Obviously, however, you would have to be sufficiently familiar with the nominee's background and qualifications to be able to speak with few notes. In this situation, a speech read from manuscript would be far less effective.

Delivery

Exercises

1. Prepare a five-minute speech to stimulate the members of a group to which you belong. You may give a speech stimulating your fellow members to attend meetings more regularly, to encourage them to seek new members, or to participate in the group's activities more enthusiastically.
2. Find a speech to stimulate in a current issue of *Vital Speeches*. Identify the methods the speaker used to stimulate his or her listeners. Did you consider them effective? Why or why not?

3. Attend an event that involves a speech to stimulate. Identify the methods used by the speaker. Were they effective? Why or why not?
4. Using the outline of the speech to stimulate in this chapter, write a complete speech, including the introduction and conclusion. Write the speech as eloquently as you can.
5. Develop a 3 to 5 minute entertaining speech on one of the following topics: (a) the funniest professor I have had, (b) the most humorous date I have experienced, (c) the most exciting movie I have seen, or (d) the most interesting book I have read.
6. Prepare a 3 to 5 minute speech introducing a classmate to the rest of the class. Using factual information, describe the background and achievements of the person.
7. Develop a 3 to 5 minute speech nominating a friend for an elective office in some campus organization, such as a fraternity or sorority, student government, or honor society.
8. Prepare a 3 to 5 minute speech presenting an award to a member of your class or to someone outside the class. Describe the good qualities of the person and explain the symbolic value of the award.

Notes

1. G. W. Gray and W. W. Braden, *Public Speaking: Principles and Practice,* Second edition (New York: Harper & Row, Publishers, 1963), p. 391.
2. Earl W. Wiley, "Abraham Lincoln: His Emergence as the Voice of the People," in *A History and Criticism of American Public Address,* Vol. II, W. N. Brigance (Ed.) (McGraw-Hill Book Company, Inc., New York, 1943), p. 869.
3. *Inaugural Addresses of the Presidents of the United States,* 87th Cong., 1st sess., House Document no. 218 (Washington, D.C.: U.S. Government Printing Office, 1961), pp. 267–70.
4. *Blood, Sweat, and Tears,* Winston S. Churchill (G. P. Putnam's Sons, N.Y., 1941), p. 297.
5. Donald K. Smith, *Man Speaking: A Rhetoric of Public Speech* (Dodd, Mead & Co., New York, 1969), p. 237.

Appendix A
The Criticism of Speeches

The statement "Speech finely framed delighteth the ears"[1] certainly epitomizes the result of a good speech and indicates that all hearers of a speech engage in speech criticism, whether they realize it or not.

The primary focus in this book is on the principles of oral communication to help you become a more effective oral communicator; throughout the speech course you are taking you'll have a number of opportunities to use those principles in communicating with your classmates. Since the nature of the academic situation demands that you receive at the end of the term a grade that reflects the quality of your efforts, your professor will evaluate most of your speeches—generally in both written and oral forms. In many instances he or she will supplement those evaluations with those of student comments offered during oral critique sessions at the end of a group of speeches. Not uncommonly students will also furnish written criticisms. In other instances the professor won't evaluate the speeches, but will instead substitute ratings by the class members. These are known as "peer group" ratings and are increasingly being used on speech assignments. Because you'll be involved in some form of speech criticism during the course, it is imperative you learn how to criticize speeches in a meaningful way.

This section has five objectives: (1) to consider the reasons for learning to criticize speeches, (2) to examine the bases for criticizing a speech, (3) to establish the criteria by which we judge a speech, (4) to present a model speech for consideration, and (5) to compare the model speech with the criteria.

347

Reasons for Learning to Criticize

A first reason for learning to criticize oral communication is to develop an appreciation of and respect for speech making. Many people don't understand the work, the skills, and the art that are involved. Their attitude is like that of the educator who asked, "Why do we need speech courses in schools? People have been talking since they were small children." After you have listened critically to speeches, identified the communicative principles being used, and recognized some of the problems resulting from failure to use certain precepts, you should have an understanding of the vast difference between "just talking" and "talking with a purpose." Aristotle maintained that truth, skillfully presented, would win against falsehood; but falsehood would win if it were skillfully presented while truth was not. As a speech critic you'll quickly perceive the accuracy of Aristotle's analysis.

Second, learning to criticize speeches helps you improve as a speaker. The critical comments of professor and classmates help you identify your strengths and weaknesses. You then know what things to continue doing and what areas you need to work on. Self-analysis is an important and practical means of improving speaking; but it is also true that you frequently fail to perceive yourself the way others do. And speaking requires such a concentrated commitment to the purpose of communication that it is often impossible to describe what you did at a particular moment. Not only does criticism help you identify strengths and weaknesses, it also provides suggestions of specific methods for improvement. When a critic says, "I didn't know when you moved into your second main point," you have a specific task to work on for the next speech. You know you need to work on transitions from one point to the next and to use attention-getting signposts to identify main points. When a critic says, "I was bothered because you never looked at me," you know you need to work specifically on eye contact in the next speech. For this reason many who speak regularly have someone—an assistant, spouse, adviser, close personal friend—attend their speeches and offer criticism. Experienced speakers know that no matter how effective they are, they have to be constantly on guard against the unconscious development of habits and idiosyncracies that interfere with precise communication. Even if no bad habits have been acquired, there is always room for improvement. Finally, criticism motivates you to improve. Unless you are totally indifferent to your peers, which is highly unusual, you don't like to know that something you're doing falls below their standards. So you're motivated to correct it. Or when you hear their favorable comments and realize that with just a little more effort you can obtain an even more favorable response, you're motivated to work a little harder.

A third reason for learning to criticize speeches is that criticism establishes standards for evaluating speeches in nonacademic situations. You can't listen critically to speeches in the classroom without carrying that behavior into other situations. Students frequently report, "I never paid any attention to the speeches I heard until I had a speech course. Now I hear all the things they're doing wrong." Of course, critics should hear the good points as well as the bad, but the point here is that the individual is now listening to speeches from a critical point of view. Unfortunately, too many people listen to the speakers in their community in an uncritical way. That's one reason irresponsible, demagogic speakers can achieve influential positions on significant issues confronting the people. As your ability to criticize speeches improves, you'll become a more enlightened "consumer" of persuasive speaking efforts. Your defense against illogical and unethical methods should be strengthened. Hence, you make decisions on more valid bases.

The fourth reason for learning to criticize speeches is closely related to the third: speech criticism helps to ensure the existence of high-quality speaking in the general community. When standards are consciously applied to any activity, practitioners begin to measure their efforts by those criteria. In effect, each of you in this course becomes a teacher of communication principles when you go back into your community and apply them in criticizing the speeches you hear there. It is no accident that ancient Greece had more than its share of effective speakers. Rhetoric stood at the core of the academic curriculum and high standards were abroad in the land. Prospective speakers knew they were going to be measured against those criteria and so prepared their communicative efforts with those standards in mind.

Bases for Criticizing Speeches

There are five bases from which speeches may be criticized: (1) whether the speech achieves its desired results; (2) whether it attains certain artistic standards; (3) whether the ideas are sound; (4) whether the speaker is responsible or ethical; and (5) whether it measures up eclectically to these four criteria. There are advantages and disadvantages to applying any of these standards.

Results In basing criticism on the results of the speech, ask: What was the speaker attempting to accomplish? Until this question can be answered with some certainty, there is no way to evaluate the speech on the basis of this criterion. Even if you can prove beyond doubt that specific events definitely occurred because of the speech, you can't praise the speech for causing them until you have established that the speaker's objective was to initiate those events. Examine the speech to discover whether the speaker stated explicitly the purpose of the speech. If not, ascertain whether the speaker implied clearly what the purpose was. Realize there is a large amount of guesswork and speculation in your answer.

Once you arrive at your analysis of what the speaker was trying to accomplish, ask a second question: Did the speaker accomplish the purpose? If the speaker asked the audience to make a total contribution of $100 to give to the Red Cross, you need only find out how much money was actually given. If a student speaker tries to persuade your class that the legislature should reduce tuition to the university and then asks you to sign a petition to the legislature, you'll only need to observe how many listeners actually sign the petition. Even here, however, you may be forced to make a value judgment.

Suppose twelve out of twenty-five students sign the petition. Has the speech accomplished its purpose? Suppose fifteen out of twenty-five sign it? It is clear you have problems even when the speaker is seeking a behavioral response, but those problems are compounded when something other than a behavioral response is sought. If the speaker was trying to change an attitude held by listeners, there may be no measurable way of determining whether a change occurred. You may look for behavioral responses that reflect attitude change. Since we know, however, that attitude change doesn't necessarily produce behavioral change, you still can't conclude that there is no attitude change simply because there is no behavioral change.

Then ask another question: Can a direct causal relationship be established between the speech and the audience response? Suppose you see on the evening TV news the report of devastating damage by a flood to a large area in an adjacent state, and the announcer says the Red Cross is sending in supplies but needs additional funds badly. On the spot you pledge to contribute on the following day. But before you can get to the Red Cross office, which is several miles from campus, you arrive at your speech class to hear another student give a speech asking for donations to the Red Cross. He has made arrangements to take the contributions to the Red Cross office immediately after class; to save yourself that long trip, you give him your money even though you thought the speech was a poor one. But an observer would see only that you gave as the speaker requested. This could lead the observer to the erroneous conclusion that the speech was effective because it achieved its purpose. As a critic, be extremely cautious about assuming a causal relationship between a communicative effort and a later occurrence.

As a perceptive critic, ask the question: Which is more important, the immediate or the long-range response? The audience at Gettysburg, Pennsylvania, on November 19, 1863, is reported to have reacted negatively or neutrally to Lincoln's speech. Apparently it wasn't until later that people decided it was a classic, and today it is one of the most heralded rhetorical efforts ever made. Why did that immediate audience react in the way that it did? Were they right or wrong? Are we wrong today in our evaluation of that speech? These are questions you must ask. Of course, in the classroom you have no opportunity to await long-range results in evaluating speeches, but you still have to be aware of overweighing the immediate result.

Finally, there is a question vital to your task: Do the effects of a speech determine its quality? If a speech doesn't achieve its purpose, is it a poor speech? Lincoln made a conscious effort in his first inaugural to placate the South and avert the impending military struggle. Yet the war came. Can we say that the speech was a poor one? Throughout the 1930s Winston Churchill warned England of what would happen if Hitler were appeased as Chamberlain was proposing to do. Yet the people persistently rejected Churchill's ideas for those of Chamberlain. Can we say that Churchill's speeches were poor ones? On the other hand, if a speech does achieve its purpose, is it a good speech? Adolf Hitler's speaking stands as a monumental example of speeches that accomplished their purpose. With their admitted reliance on the "big lie," can we say those speeches were good ones? Recognize there are times when people's attitudes are too crystallized to heed opposing messages, no matter how valid those messages may be. Whether the end results of a speech determine its quality is a particularly pertinent problem for the student critic, because classroom criticism frequently reveals that the reason students like a speech is that they agree with what the speaker has said.

Obviously, evaluating a speech on the basis of its effects is fraught with problems. It is much like trying to cross an open field by moonlight on a cloudy night: just when you come to a difficult spot, the moon goes behind a cloud and you're left in the dark. You'll often be in the dark when you evaluate a speech solely on the basis of its effects.

Artistic Standards

In evaluating a speech on the basis of artistic standards, be unconcerned with what happened as a result of the speech. Ask, instead, whether the speaker utilized appropriate principles of communication.

Examine the topic of the speech to determine whether it is suited (a) to the speaker's interest, knowledge, and experiences, (b) to the audience, and (c) to the occasion. Determine whether the topic was sufficiently narrow to be adequately developed in the time available for the speech.

Evaluate the content of the speech. Investigate unsupported generalizations to determine whether the speaker left them unsupported because of obvious audience acceptance or through failure or inability to obtain corroborating evidence. Scrutinize the evidence for accuracy, relevancy, freshness, specificity, and concreteness. Determine whether needed qualifications of sources have been supplied. Examine the reasoning to detect any weaknesses in the development of claims from evidence and the warrants that establish the relationship between them.

Consider the organization of the speech. Does it have all the parts it should? If a part is missing, is there a rational explanation for its absence? Does the speaker state the purpose clearly and explicitly? If not, why not? Is there a sense of movement in the ideas? Can the main ideas be identified easily, or must the listener labor to uncover them? Is there a sense of unity and coherence to the speech as a result of transitions and summaries that bind the smaller and larger parts together?

Appraise the language used by the speaker. Consider its appropriateness to the speaker, the audience, and the occasion. Examine it to determine whether it clearly communicated the speaker's meaning in an original and economical way. Because a speech is "not an essay on its hind legs," analyze the language to see if there is an oral quality to it. Investigate the sentence structure to ascertain whether it is clear, correct, and varied.

Study the delivery of the speech. Does the speaker impart a sense of sincerity? Does the speaker have a communicative attitude? Does he or she seem to be interested in talking to this particular audience? Is there an awareness of the audience? Does he or she adapt specifically to their reactions? Does he or she use effective and purposeful bodily action? Are gestures dynamic and varied? Does he or she maintain eye contact with listeners? Does he or she permit notes to become a barrier to communication? Does he or she speak loud enough to be heard by all present? Is the rate of speaking varied and neither too fast to be understood nor too slow to hold your attention? Is there variety in the pitch of the voice? Does the speaker use stress and emphasis to make important words stand out from unimportant ones? Are pronunciations sufficiently standard that attention is not called to them because of their strangeness? Does the speaker use pauses for emphasis and to ease the listener's task?

Finally, remember that even though you analyze and evaluate the speaker's use of all of these principles, it's the overall interaction of them that produces the total impact of the speech. Probably more than in any other enterprise, the gestalt approach is important in evaluating a speech. The impact of a speech is not merely a sum of the individual parts; sometimes it is more than the sum, sometimes less.

The major difficulty in judging a speech exclusively on the basis of esthetic standards is that it tends to divorce speech making from its very rationale for being. After all, the purpose of speaking to a specific group is to achieve a purpose, and if that purpose is not accomplished, then it is difficult to see the point of saying, "But the speech was good on the basis of esthetic standards."

Ideas

When you judge on this basis, you're unconcerned about the results achieved or about the esthetic standards employed. What mainly concerns you is whether the speaker was presenting valid ideas, what some critics would refer to as *the truth*. Those who use this criterion argue that, after all, that is what speaking is all about—an effort to discern what the truth is in a given instance. If that truth can be discovered through the speaking of an unskilled advocate, then the objective has been attained even if the people to whom he or she was talking failed to recognize that truth or to be affected by it.

There is no denying the argument that the ultimate end of speaking is the determination of truth, or the determination of which ideas are the most valid at a particular moment. Unfortunately, there is a major problem that confronts the critic: How do you ascertain which speaker has the truth? Most speaking occurs in the area of public affairs; in that area it's most difficult to determine which speaker's ideas are most valid. Unless that determination can be made, you must either make assumptions or turn to other criteria as a basis for judging a speech.

Speaker's Motives and Ethics

Quintilian said an orator is a *good* man speaking well. In using this basis for criticism, determine the speaker's purpose for communicating. Is the speaker interested in the general welfare or is he or she trying to help a select group of friends or to advance his or her own cause? Unfortunately, unless you're a mind reader, there may be some difficulty in uncovering the speaker's motivation. Unless there is clear evidence to indicate the speaker's intentions, you may be influenced by the same tendency that influences most people: to attribute good intentions to those who agree with our ideas and bad intentions to those who disagree. If that is the case, very little merit can be afforded such criticism.

Even after validly concluding that the speaker desires the acceptance of his or her proposal for the general welfare, you're still confronted with the task of deciding whether the speaker has used ethical means of attaining objectives. Has the speaker built a rational case for his or her position or merely appealed to listeners' emotions? Is evidence used that can be verified?

In the final analysis, you may be left with a *good* person, speaking responsibly, whose speaking doesn't meet minimum esthetic standards and fails to achieve the desired results.

When using the eclectic principles basis, don't rely on one of the four previously mentioned bases. Instead, apply all of them in reaching a decision about the merits of a speech. Discover what happened as a result of the speech. If the desired response wasn't obtained because of something beyond the control of the speaker, then he or she can't be blamed. Include that information in your judgement. Determine how well the speaker used the esthetic standards available and appropriate to that effort. If you discover that principles of communication weren't used, or were badly used, conclude that the speech really had very little to do with what happened. If a protest mob is ready to enter a building forcefully, and someone cries, "Charge the police line," just before the mob surges forward, you can attach little significance to those words. As a critic, be interested in the validity of the ideas presented by the speaker, but also determine how skillfully they were presented and what response they brought from the listeners. The speaker's character and ethics are important in your evaluation, but not to the exclusion of the other three criteria. In sum, when basing your evaluation on eclectic principles, attempt to determine the effects of a speech, analyze the esthetic standards employed, try to ascertain the validity of the ideas advanced, describe the ethics involved, and then arrive at a critical estimate of the total communicative effort.

Now that we've examined the reasons for engaging in speech criticism and have discussed the bases on which our judgments may be founded, let's consider the standard for judging a speech.

Eclectic Principles

Artistic Standards for Judging a Speech

The following are the attributes we can expect a good speech to possess.

1. We can expect a good speech to have structure. It should have an introduction, a purpose sentence, a body, and a conclusion. It should also have transitions that help listeners move from one part to another.
2. We can expect a good speech to have substance. It should present main ideas developed by different types of supporting materials: testimony, statistics, and facts.

3. We can expect a good speech to employ sound reasoning.
4. We can expect a good speech to use language that is clear, appropriate, original, vital, and economical.
5. We can also expect a good speech to be well delivered, both verbally and nonverbally. We can make no judgment on this criterion, however, if we only read the text of the speech.

A Model Speech

Next, we're going to consider a model speech. As you read the following speech, look for the first four characteristics described in the previous section.

Who Is Wise?

Ronald W. Roskens   President, University of Nebraska[2]

1 Speaking as "Poor Richard," Benjamin Franklin once asked "Who is
2 wise?" His answer, as usual, was both definitive and provocative:

3   Who is wise?
4   He that learns from everyone.
5   He that governs his passions.
6   He that is content.
7   Nobody.

8   Are we to conclude that in the absence of perfection there is no
9 wisdom? Is wisdom something divine, beyond the reach of mere mortals?
10 Of course not! Wisdom, like integrity, may be elusive and difficult to define.
11 Yet wisdom is present in human affairs when the abstract and the practical
12 merge, impelling us to act, and coloring those actions which we take.
13 Although some wag has said, "some are wise and some are otherwise," the
14 capacity for wisdom resides within all of us.
15   Most of us regard our universities as seats of wisdom. We at the
16 University of Nebraska cannot, of course, lay sole claim to wisdom. Even
17 so, the rigors of our environment are intended to cultivate this latent trait.
18 As John Masefield said a generation ago, "Wherever a University stands, it
19 stands and shines; wherever it exists, the free minds of men, urged on to full
20 fair inquiry, may still bring wisdom into human affairs."
21   The crucial question is, how well have we at the University of
22 Nebraska discharged our responsibility to nurture your wisdom? It is time
23 to conduct *the* final examination. In this instance, however, the tables are
24 turned. Now it is we, the faculty and staff of the University who must
25 render an accounting. And it is you, our distinguished graduates, who will
26 rate us; not only today but as your lives unfold.

27   For the purposes of this examination we will assume that you give us
28 reasonably high marks in those areas we traditionally associate with a
29 university education. So, let us concentrate on wisdom. I invite you to
30 ponder four questions which are extensions of Poor Richard's definition.
31 And bear in mind that your responses—or, more precisely, your future
32 actions—will be the litmus test which determines the extent to which we
33 are entitled to regard ourselves as a "great" university.
34   Question one: if, as Poor Richard says, he is wise who learns from
35 everyone, do *you* sense the need to form your own opinions and draw your
36 own conclusions?
37   The ability to make wise choices—which is the ultimate aim of
38 education—cannot be taken for granted. We are bombarded with
39 information, much of which is speculative rather than factual. Public
40 opinion polls often seem to dictate rather than measure the national pulse.
41 Quick fixes are, however, no substitute for sober contemplation. The
42 individual who refuses to think independently runs the risk of becoming a
43 clone of someone else.
44   Wisdom pervades the character of those who recognize that the rigors
45 of sifting and weighing facts are and must be lifelong habits. And so we
46 ask: even as you listen to others, are you prepared to chart your own
47 course?
48   If not, we have failed you.
49   Question two: if, as Poor Richard says, he is wise that governs his
50 passions, do *you* sense the need to avoid contributing to the "grossness of
51 our national product"?
52   This deliberate play on words acknowledges some disturbing trends
53 which seem to permeate our public conduct. The media bear witness to the
54 childish tantrums and crude behavior of so-called celebrities. Our television
55 screens are filled with images focused upon the "heartbreak of psoriasis"
56 and the fatal impact of "ring around the collar." Crude messages
57 emblazoned on T-shirts and bumper stickers belie any claim that primitive
58 impulses are no longer in vogue.
59   We often act as though the responsibility for these trends lies
60 elsewhere. Acquiescence to them is perhaps the easier route. But vulgarity,
61 incivility, and discourtesy are not the hallmarks of wisdom. As Ovid wrote,
62 "studies culminate in manners."
63   This is a good time for good taste. And so we ask: have our
64 interactions with you helped you fashion a code of conduct characterized by
65 restraint and good taste, particularly when your behavior impacts upon the
66 sensibilities of others?
67   If not, we have failed you.
68   Question three: if, as Poor Richard says, he is wise who is content, do
69 *you* sense the need to pursue the outer limits of your capabilities?
70   Thoreau tells us that "dreams are the touchstones of our characters."
71 As educated individuals we should understand that the impediments to
72 realizing our aspirations often lie within ourselves. If we are content merely

73 to accept what comes to us and to fashion a life which brooks no challenges,
74 mediocrity—or even failure—will be our lot. We will have killed our own
75 dreams, and no matter how much we might have succeeded in the eyes of
76 others our accomplishments will not have approached the potential which
77 lies within us.
78   The wise individual understands that the best steel is forged under the
79 most extreme conditions. And so we ask: do you understand that dreams
80 and fulfillment will go hand in hand only if your talents are fully invested?
81   If not, we have failed you.
82   Question four: if, as Poor Richard says, nobody is truly wise, do *you*
83 sense the need to keep faith with your fellow human beings and with the
84 social institutions we have created?
85   Each of us is human, and the essence of that humanity is that we
86 have, and will inexorably exercise, the capacity to make mistakes, to be less
87 than perfect. Human weaknesses are inevitably magnified when subjected to
88 the harsh glare of public scrutiny. The shortcomings of one public official
89 trigger a disregard for all elements of government. One practitioner fails,
90 and an entire profession falls into disrepute.
91   Wisdom and skepticism must go hand in hand. The wise individual
92 understands, however, that social institutions are the instruments of our will
93 and reflect the strengths or weaknesses of those who create them. And so
94 we ask: will you balance your skepticism with compassion and avoid the
95 dangers of self-fulfilling prophecies?
96   If not, we have failed you.
97   We return to Mr. Franklin's question: who is wise? The Hebrew
98 prayerbook *Ethics of the Father* tells us:

99 There are seven marks of an uncultured, and seven of a wise man. The wise
100 man does not speak before him who is greater than he in wisdom; and does
101 not break in upon the speech of his fellow; he is not hasty to answer; he
102 questions according to the subject matter, and answers to the point; he
103 speaks upon the first thing first, and upon the last last; regarding that which
104 he has not understood he says, I do not understand it, and he acknowledges
105 the truth. The reverse of all this is to be found in an uncultured man.

106   Do you sense the seeds of such wisdom in yourself? If you do, the
107 University has passed this final examination. If you do not, hopefully you
108 will have found at this University the bases for such wisdom, and may take
109 comfort in the fact that "learning never ends."
110   Whatever your answer, you will find that your time at the University
111 has profoundly influenced you. You will for the rest of your lives play out
112 your experiences here, even as we continue to reach out to you through your
113 memories and in your skills.
114   Who is wise? All of us—if we continue to care about learning and to
115 learn about caring. For that is the essence of wisdom.

Before we begin a critical analysis of Roskens's speech, see if you can complete the following assignments.

1. What is the function of the introduction?
2. Identify the purpose sentence.
3. How many main points are there? What are they?
4. Where does the conclusion begin?
5. What type of reasoning is used most frequently?
6. Find the following types of supporting material: (a) explanation, (b) testimony, (c) definition, (d) example.
7. Find two examples of repetition.
8. Find an example of each of the following: (a) parallelism, (b) rhetorical question, (c) alliteration, (d) metaphor.

Evaluation of Model Speech with Artistic Standards

Before we examine together the speech that you've just read and analyzed, we need to identify the type of speech we're considering. Obviously Roskens wants his listeners to be entertained, in the sense of being interested and not bored. But that isn't his main purpose. Clearly, Roskens wants his listeners to receive information, but that isn't the main purpose of his speech. Roskens wants his listeners to accept certain attitudes toward higher education and to reject particular behaviors of society, but his main purpose isn't to persuade his listeners to take an action or to adopt a particular attitude. Roskens's speech is for a special occasion, a commencement, and he wants to create favorable attitudes toward and acceptance of his ideas. In criticizing the speech, therefore, we won't apply the standards appropriate to speeches to entertain, inform, or persuade.

Next, we need to consider the basis on which we are going to criticize Roskens's speech. We'll criticize the speech on the basis of eclectic principles, not on the basis of results. We don't have the data to make such an evaluation. We don't know how many times the audience responded—with laughter, applause, hissing, and so forth. We have no shift-of-opinion forms on which the listeners registered their attitudes toward any of Roskens's ideas. We can't evaluate the results of the speech. We can criticize the speech on the basis of its ideas, Roskens's motives and attitudes, and artistic standards.

On the basis of its ideas, Roskens's speech rates high marks. His main idea, wisdom and its development, is an important and worthy one to consider with college graduates and their families. The four main points that Roskens uses to develop his main idea seem valid.

Roskens's motives and ethics seem praiseworthy. Except for the acclaim that he would receive for a notable speech, there appears to be no personal motive impelling him to make this particular speech. He builds a rational case for his ideas and uses no unethical means to get them accepted. The evidence he uses is verifiable and representative.

Our most searching analysis of Roskens's speech can be made by evaluating it on the basis of artistic standards. We'll do this by comparing his use of communication principles with the criteria for judging a speech that we established earlier.

We said we can expect a speech to have structure. There is an introduction (lines 1–26). Roskens opens his speech with a brief poem. Then he focuses on the main idea of the poem and begins to develop interest in it. By the end of the introduction, Roskens has made it especially relevant to his specific audience. The introduction ably achieves two of the three purposes of an introduction: it gets the attention of the listeners and leads them into the subject of the speech. Since Roskens's position and reputation give him high credibility, there is no need for him to be concerned with that issue. He then states clearly his purpose and gives a preview: "So, let us concentrate on wisdom. I invite you to ponder four questions which are extensions of Poor Richard's definition" (lines 29–30). The body develops the four questions, and these are identified as main points with numbers as signposts (lines 34–96). The conclusion completes the unity of the speech by returning to the question asked in the first line (line 3) of the poem in the introduction and answering it with a selection quoted from a Hebrew prayerbook (lines 99–105). Moving from that quotation to a restatement of the question posed by Poor Richard, Roskens gives his own answer (lines 114–115). Thus, Roskens establishes the unity of his speech by threading his main idea (wisdom) through the introduction, purpose, main points in the body, and conclusion. Effective transitions throughout the speech add to its unity (lines 8–9, 21–22, 45–47, 63–66, 79–81, 93–96, 97, 106–107).

We said we can expect a good speech to have substance. Mr. Roskens's speech does. It has main ideas (lines 34–36, 49–51, 68–69, 82–84). His ideas are supported by different types of supporting materials. Roskens uses explanation (lines 10–14, 37–43, 71–77, 85–90, 107, 111–113), humor (lines 13–14), testimony (lines 1–7, 18–20, 61–62, 70, 99–105, 109), definition (lines 37–38), and examples in the form of specific instances (lines 54–56). Note that the testimony used by Roskens is given by writers well known to educated persons. Thus their credibility is extremely high. The one instance of humor, in the form of a quotation, is simply attributed to "some wag," a clear indication that it is to be interpreted as humorous.

The reasoning of Roskens's speech is not its strength. Neither is it a weak point. Most of the reasoning is in the form of assertions, many of which are unsupported. But his assertions would probably not be challenged by the majority of people, for they are supported by experience and common sense. Some examples are "Public opinion often seems to dictate rather than measure the national pulse" (lines 39–40). "But vulgarity, incivility, and discourtesy are not the hallmarks of wisdom" (lines 60–61). "Wisdom pervades the character of those who recognize that the rigors of sifting and weighing facts are and must be lifelong habits" (lines 44–45). "The wise individual understands, however, that social institutions are the instruments of our will and reflect the strengths or weaknesses of those who create them" (lines 91–93).

Some assertions are supported by testimony, as when Roskens said, "But vulgarity, incivility, and discourtesy are not the hallmarks of wisdom. As Ovid wrote, 'studies culminate in manners' " (lines 60–62). At other times assertions are supported by other assertions: "Human weaknesses are inevitably magnified when subjected to the harsh glare of public scrutiny. The shortcomings of one public official trigger a disregard for all elements of government. One practitioner fails, and an entire profession falls in disrepute" (lines 87–90). By substituting assertions for examples, Roskens probably helped to establish greater dignity for his remarks. On one occasion, Roskens supported his assertion with specific instances: "This deliberate play on words acknowledges some disturbing trends which seem to permeate our public conduct. . . . Our television screens are filled with images focused upon the 'heartbreak of psoriasis' and the fatal impact of 'ring around the collar.' Crude messages emblazoned on T-shirts and bumper stickers belie any claim that primitive impulses are no longer in vogue" (lines 52–58). The strength of Roskens's assertions largely flows from their ready acceptance by the listener rather than from tight, closely reasoned argumentation.

The language of Roskens's speech possesses several virtues. It is exceptionally clear. Every sentence has been carefully crafted so that subject, verb, predicate, clauses, and modifiers are properly placed and can be easily identified. The language is also economical. There are no unnecessary words; every word contributes to the communication of ideas. The language is appropriate. It is the language of an educated person, elegant without being pretentious. The language is original. Parallelism and restatement are used to strengthen the impact of the ideas and to emphasize the unity of the speech. To summarize each of his four main points, Roskens introduces a rhetorical question by the same phrase, "And so we ask" (lines 45–46, 63, 79, 93–94) and followed by the same sentence, "If not, we have failed you" (lines 48, 67, 81, 96). These repetitions add to the impact of each summary. Originality of language is also achieved by the use of alliteration—"intended to cultivate this latent trait" (line 17), "good time for good taste" (line 63), "inexorably exercise" (line 86), "bases for such wisdom" (line 108), "profoundly influence" (line 111)—and metaphor—"your responses . . . will be the litmus test which determines . . ." (lines 31–32), "The individual . . . runs the risk of becoming a clone . . ." (lines 41–43), " . . . dreams and fulfillment will go hand in hand only if your talents are fully invested" (lines 79–80).

Roskens achieves vitality of language through the use of effective sentences. He presents rhetorical questions that require the listeners to answer them in their own mind, and he uses some that he goes on to answer himself. The second paragraph of the introduction begins with two rhetorical questions: "Are we to conclude that in the absence of perfection there is no wisdom? Is wisdom something divine, beyond the reach of mere mortals?" (lines 8–9). After answering these questions, Roskens next uses a rhetorical question— "How well have we at the University of Nebraska discharged our responsibility to nurture your wisdom?" (lines 21–22)—as a transitional device to the statement of his thesis. A rhetorical question, "Do you sense the seeds of such wisdom in yourself?" (line 106), is used in the conclusion to focus the listeners' thoughts on the central idea of the speech. His final rhetorical question, "Who is wise?" is answered with a balanced sentence that takes a clause and repeats it syntactically with the parts reversed: "All of us—if we continue to care about learning and to learn about caring" (lines 114–115).

Clearly, Roskens understands and employs the principles of effective rhetorical communication. As students, you would do well to go and do likewise!

Summary

Students profit from learning how to criticize speeches because it helps to develop an appreciation of and respect for speech making, it aids the individual in becoming a better speaker, it establishes standards for evaluating speeches in nonacademic situations, and it helps to ensure the existence of high-quality speaking in the general community.

Speeches may be criticized on the basis of five different criteria: the results, the artistic standards employed, the validity of the ideas, the speaker's motives and ethics, and the eclectic basis of all the preceding four.

Notes

1. II Macc. 15:39, *The Holy Bible,* Authorized King James Version (New York: Hawthorne Books, Inc., 1956).
2. R. W. Roskens, "Who Is Wise?" *Vital Speeches of the Day* 47 (1981):529–30. Used by permission.

Appendix B
Sample Speeches

Speech of Introduction
Kyle Butler,   Captain, Retired, U.S. Navy
Used by permission.

Mr. President, members of the Auburn Rotary Club. I am especially delighted to present Dr. Bill Walsh as a new member.

Bill is department head and professor in the Department of Textile Engineering in the University's College of Engineering.

Just prior to coming to Auburn University this summer, Bill was Associate Dean and Professor in the Department of Textile Engineering, Chemistry, and Science in the College of Textiles, at North Carolina State University.

Bill was born in Columbus, Ohio, while his father was a graduate student at Ohio State University. Bill grew up in Columbia, South Carolina where his dad served as a professor at the University of South Carolina.

Bill's is a most impressive résumé. He studied at the University of South Carolina. He was awarded a Ph.D. degree in Chemical Engineering by North Carolina State University.

He has held positions in private industry as an engineer. He has been a teacher, a professor. He has been Associate Dean for Research. He has also served as Associate Dean for Graduate Studies at North Carolina State University.

The listing of professional associations is quite long and includes membership in Sigma Zi, a number of other societies and associations of chemists and engineers, plus the Torch Club.

He is listed in *American Men of Science* and *Who's Who in the South and Southwest*.

His research interests are in textiles—particularly adhesive bonding, surfactants, radiation curing, polymers, and clothing comfort.

Major publications to his credit number over fifty. He holds two U.S. patents for treatment of fibers and fabrics.

He has written a dozen or so research reports under government grants.

During the past 13 years he has presented papers to various international groups from Tokyo and Osaka to Israel, from Montreal to New Orleans and Miami.

This is indeed a very, very impressive résumé.

When one considers such a résumé one feels a need to pause and reflect on how our own lives are affected by work such as his.

I hope each of you realizes that before you is a man, or a representative of the man or woman, who is responsible for giving us the chartreuse polyester leisure suit—which now hangs in our closets awaiting patiently its return to glory. I remember there was a time—had we not had the polyester leisure suit, we would have had no outer garments to wear to Sunday School and semi-formal parties.

It is to Bill's kind we owe our gratitude for other accomplishments.

It was the miracle fibers from the chemist's beaker and the advanced technology from the innovative mind of the textile engineer together which freed women from the embarrassment of girdle line and launched Broadway Joe Namath on his commercial career by giving us runproof, stretchable pantyhose with the so-called breathable crotch.

And let's not forget our cotton fruit of the looms—snug but not binding, soft but durable, all in living color.

Thanks Bill.

I was tempted to tell you about Bill's ability to spin an entertaining yarn, or to weave a tall tale. Or about how he is the very fabric of our society.

But I won't.

I can tell you Bill knows fibers.

Bill's Rotary Ann is Josie. She is from eastern North Carolina.

Josie and Bill have a lovely and talented daughter, Genevieve, who is a senior at Auburn High School.

Bill has been a Rotarian since 1980. He was most recently an active member of the Raleigh, N.C., club.

Our club will certainly be a better club for having him.

Please welcome Bill Walsh and his charming wife, Josie.

Omissions Hurt CEO Ethics Rating

John F. Budd, Jr.   Vice Chairman, Carl Byoir & Associates
Vital Speeches of the Day, Vol. LV, May 15, 1989, pp. 478–80.
© City News Publishing Company. Used by permission.

I appreciate the opportunity to speak first more than you may realize. It gives me temporary territorial rights to wisdom. No one with any professional survival instincts would want to *follow* my colleague, Dick Cheney.

The script or chat indicated says that Dick and I are to assess the level of ethical professionalism of the public relations activities around the two major troubling issues of the past few months, namely the Drexel/Milligan affair and the KKR/RJR* matter. We are really the catalysts to what I am sure will be an animated discussion. I've been known to provoke a few comments.

Well, we can do this—and we'll no doubt get into specifics—but personally, I think that any discussion of tactics bypasses the central question of how businessmen allowed themselves to get into positions where their integrity comes into question.

I have some thoughts on this—and they relate to the proper role of those of us in the PR business.

First, let me say right up front that I believe the substantial majority of top business executives *are ethical!* I have worked closely with twelve CEOs and I will vouch for each and every one.

Given a clear choice—a black and white situation—almost all businessmen will make the right decision.

But they have difficulty in gray areas . . . areas that seem to have trade-offs.

They stumble here, in my opinion, because of three underlying failings. These shortcomings—become a self-fulfilling prophecy by the way they feed public skepticism and legitimize criticism. These failings are:

One—An inability to grasp the fact that "perceptions" *are* reality . . . the real facts themselves are often immaterial!

Two—the lack of a developed philosophical base to support their own role and that of their company in the largest public sense.

Three—bad counsel. Advisors that dogmatically contend that candor and straight talk create personal jeopardy and liability.

To which I invoke a statement of a man wiser than I who said 350 years ago: "he is no man's enemy but his own."

Chief Justice Earl Warren actually called for the development of what he characterized as "professional counsellors" in ethics twenty years ago. As he envisioned it, these counsellors could, and should, "offer sophisticated guidance in ethical decision-making for modern businessmen."

An interesting idea—ahead of its time, but relevant.

I hesitate to ascribe such powers to those of us in the PR business. But, in the sense that we regularly deal with such intangibles as corporate credibility . . . with abstract values like ethics . . . reputations, etc., we can make an anticipated contribution.

Let me discuss the three points I made earlier—and see how they relate to our business.

"Perception."

The average CEO today does not begin to understand that reality is second to the "perceptions of reality." What *we think* are the facts in the case—our perceptions—are very real to us no matter how different the true

---

*Kohlerg Kravis Roberts & Co./R. J. Reynolds Nabisco.

facts are. What this means is that a CEO must not rationalize an activity on the basis of its legal acceptability IF it seems wrong. Because it will be WRONG to the public. Case in point: the Defense Department's allowance of certain charges for the motivation of employees. Three days of golf at a plush spa to the tune of several hundreds of thousands of dollars SEEMS wrong and IS WRONG, however legal it may be. It creates the perception of abuse.

Fighting the plant closing notification law as though their very existence was at stake was wrong because it created the perception of cynical disregard for employees' interests and community well-being. And CEOs lined up to do this despite the fact that most of them, on their own initiative, give ample advance notice with no loss of executive prerogative.

The wrong issue . . . and the wrong place to make a stand on principles. Valid arguments notwithstanding, it was a "Catch 22" because it was universally viewed as an abuse of power. No doubt it caused inestimable damage to employee loyalty and corporate credibility in the community. These are not easily repaired values.

Let's look at takeovers.

When a company is put "into play" the common denominator becomes money—dollars. Not people, not employees, not the community— but dollars. CEOs are told—even threatened—by their advisors that they must "maximize shareholder value." So, CEOs sell out, no doubt with some frustration but also a warm feeling of righteousness. They've "maximized shareholder value!"

It is prevailing, traditional wisdom that doesn't stand critical examination very well. Nor has it been scrutinized carefully. For one thing, most CEOs haven't the philosophical reserve to draw upon to challenge the argument. But consider:

A company is chartered by the state in the public's interest. Implicit in this is that it will make a long-term contribution to the community . . . in jobs, goods and services, taxes, etc.

If it is a healthy, viable, enterprise how is the public's interest served by its demise?

There is a moral argument that says that unless a system produces goods and services and produces them continuously and efficiently, it is of no use to society. Management, and boards, of course, are accountable to their owners, but they are also accountable to the public. They have obligations over and above economic performance.

In this context, the primary obligation is *not* to maximize shareholder value but the *successful continuation* of the enterprise in the best interests of *all* its constituencies.

The average CEO, intimidated by his "fiduciary responsibility" (which, he is regularly reminded, carries the potential of personal liability) feels he has no choice but to sell out the company on behalf of the shareholders. He's really comfortable with the decision because it is a quantitative one. He can't cope with such abstracts as is it ethical, or is it moral? When his motives are criticized, he's genuinely hurt.

This very scenario was recently played out in a case I am very familiar with. A large, hugely successful company received an unexpected takeover offer, the first the CEO ever faced. In fifteen working days—a record of sorts—he capitulated, selling out to a somewhat smaller "White Knight," giving shareholders, potentially, almost 100 percent gain. For himself, he stands to gain several millions of dollars and a few consorts, a proportionate amount of "silver." This is a man who has spent his professional life dealing with hard facts, not abstracts. He has an engineering degree. But he has no philosophical antenna. The concept of a higher, moral responsibility never occurred to him. One of his closest business friends said of him, "he is absolutely oriented to his shareholders . . . any personal feelings will be at a very low level compared to the needs of his shareholders."

This CEO will be honestly shocked to learn that his employees— 30,000 of them worldwide—think he is morally corrupt . . . that personal greed, not shareholders' concerns, motivates him . . . that he doesn't really care being three years from retirement!

I sympathize for him. I think I say this because he is in a judgment arena alien to his career path. He doesn't realize that there is a legitimate, ethical higher ground—and he has no one to counsel and guide him, only lawyers, investment bankers and others operating in a strictly quantitative, dehumanized world.

This shortcoming is more widespread than one might imagine.

Because of it, CEOs, time and time again, find their judgment criticized, their wisdom impugned and, ultimately, their ethical standards challenged. It's hard on them, hard on their families, and not as much their fault as it is the fault of the educational system that trained them to ignore anything that can't be measured.

Fortunately, there are exceptions. Proctor and Gamble's chairman CEO John Smale has been waging an almost lone campaign to introduce the business judgment rule so boards can say "No" when, in their opinion, the corporation's future is improperly jeopardized—and to do this without fear of personal liability.

Reggie Jones, retired CEO of GE, had a high reputation for credibility. His successor, Jack Welch, is widely regarded as one of the world's most ruthless managers (Fortune, 3/27). Who do you think would get the public's benefit of the doubt on any controversial decision?

Finally, we come to the loss of plain speak.

The litigiousness nature of our society makes being a CEO a perilous journey. At every turn well-meaning advisors—generally lawyers and investment bankers—counsel against candor. Straight-talk, CEOs are conditioned to believe, leads *straight* to law suits. So, corporate-speak— mushy elocutions that dispense rhetorical conundrums by the page—result.

By denying simple public explanations of their action CEOs unwittingly sabotage their own credibility. Again leading, as it inevitably does, to sharp censure of their moral principles.

Now, let me tie all this together.

I said that, by and large, CEOs are ethical. But the headlines they make say otherwise.

As I've tried to point out, they are really their own worst enemies. Their guilt is one of omission, by and large, not commission!

If we, in the PR business, really do our job of counseling, the real ethical violators—and they *certainly* exist—will be seen more as *exceptions* to the rule rather than yet another example of moral decay and rot common to management overall.

Now, I don't want anyone to leave here and say that John Budd said there was nothing to this problem of executive ethics that a good dose of PR couldn't cure.

I opened this peroration with a quotation. Let me try to put things in perspective with another . . . ; this one from an Aesop fable. It says: "we often give our enemies the means of our destruction!"

Can I assume that puts things in perspective for you? I hope so.

Now a few words of comment on the "handling" of the Drexel case—and the RJR/KKR affair . . .

My colleague is much more tuned into the daily conflict than I have been. Perhaps then, I represent the average reader more than the pro critiquing another's performance.

First, I was turned off by the early statements by Drexel about the massive opinion-molding might they were bringing to the contest. I may be old-fashioned, but opinions are *earned not "bought."*

Second, I was also turned off by the cynical attempt to characterize Michael Milken as a Boy Scout. To me this was an arrogant, unprofessionally conceived campaign that underscored the superficiality of the advisors.

When I read the in-house publications of Drexel I thought I was in a time warp. That sort of corporate "good news" it served up in the face of daily lurid headlines went out with bowling scores.

Let's talk about consistency . . .

First, Drexel Burnham CEO Fred Joseph takes a hard line. Then he gets softer—and softer. Then he counterattacks and tries to buy "credibility" via Howard Baker. Meanwhile their media experts generate publicity for themselves rather than stories extricating their client from its difficulties.

We can go even further back to some basics.

It is elemental to first read what the client CEO has said publicly. Was what he was saying NOW consistent with what he had said earlier?

Well, what had he said? Let me quote! "We—Drexel Burnham, would finance the winners in any contest. When accused of representing two bidders, (we should) dismiss it as irrelevant."

At a seminar on ethics Drexel's CEO further said that DB deliberately hired "excessively aggressive guys because it fit with our (DB's) aggressive image. I did not want to cut off that aggression, I was actually using it, the word 'greedy,' internally. I did not want to cut out excessive greed."

To me, Fred Joseph comes perilously close to impeaching himself.

Insofar as the Kravis, Kohlberg Roberts/RJR matter is concerned, their efforts to portray takeovers and LBOs as the "efficient market" system at work simply do not work for me. Legally, I have no doubt that they do everything according to the rules but, setting all this aside, they are capitalizing on greed and making the end justify the means. Over the long term I have yet to be convinced that there is any economic or social merit to their concepts. Henry Kravis has assumed celebrity status—and his publicity mill appears to feed this. Economic fads change and he, too, will fade.

Now you've heard me . . . now I look forward as you do to the one man who has been in more of these contests than anyone else, Dick Cheney . . . Dick.

And Then Some

Richard L. Weaver II   *Vital Speeches of the Day* 56 (March 15, 1990): 342–44.
© City News Publishing Company. Used by permission.

A prominent salesman friend of mine summed up his success in three simple words: "and then some." He discovered at an early age, he said, that most of the difference between average people and top people could be explained in three words:

"The top people did what was expected of them—*and then some. They were thoughtful of others; they were considerate and kind—and then some.* They met their obligations and responsibilities fairly and squarely—*and then some.* They were good friends to their friends—*and then some.* They could be counted on in an emergency—*and then some.*"

"And then some"—three little words—and those three little words could transform our society as well as your academic and personal life. It *could* become a philosophy of life—a way of living. Let me show you the power in those words.

What I want to do in this speech is show you how this "and then some" philosophy relates first to society, second to your studies and, third, to your personal life. The unique thing about it is that it can be applied to almost everything with which you have contact! We'll apply it to society first.

Before I get into how "and then some" relates to society, however, I have a confession to make; I have a hang-up. Earlier this year I wrote about my hang-up to the *Toledo Blade*. It was published in January, 1989. Here's what I wrote there:

> "As I watch people throw trash and cigarette butts out their windows, dump their ashtrays in parking lots, and leave the places they visit littered with their leftovers, I am reminded of a beautiful statement I once read: 'We live a life luxurious beyond the dreams of millions of the earth's inhabitants. We are lucky. We were born into it. The least we can do with this magnificent heritage is to preserve it and pass it along as rich and as pure as it came to us.' "
>
> "With the beginning of a new year, with the inauguration of a new President, and with goals of renewal and enhancement, let us all resolve, in the paraphrase of an old Greek promise made more than 2,000 years ago, to transmit this country better than it was transmitted to us." (*Toledo Blade,* January 30, 1989, p. 8)

How do we "transmit (a) country better than it was transmitted to us?" The key, I think, is in those three little words: "and then some."

We are the leaders of the next generation. As far as this campus is concerned, we're the leaders of the current generation. If *we* don't take the responsibility, then who will?

The "and then some" philosophy forces us out of our complacent, self-centered, apathetic, lazy, preoccupied, busy *little* worlds and puts us in touch with a bigger reality. It's a message that says if we don't take responsibility for the world, who will? We *can* make a difference!

Now I am not suggesting you have to suddenly become involved in world affairs, American politics, or even student government—although that wouldn't be bad! I'm not even suggesting that you read a daily newspaper, a weekly news magazine, or watch the TV news—"boring stuff" according to *my* teenage daughter! What I *am* suggesting is taking some responsibility for the world *you* touch—the one with which *you* come into contact. What you will begin to notice is that as you start using this "and then some" philosophy in small ways, it will become habitual, and you will start using it in bigger ways. Some of the little ways might include:

> —leaving a room cleaner than the way *you* found it. The other day I asked my son to straighten up the family room before coming upstairs. He quickly looked around the room and said, "None of this is mine!" (If I had thought more quickly, I would have run into the study to get this speech! I missed an opportunity to practice it.)

Leaving a room cleaner than the way *you* found it is one of the little ways we might begin practicing the "and then some" philosophy in the world we touch. Let me list a couple more:

> —not just being a critic but offering a few suggestions
> —closing a door that needs closing, cleaning a table that needs cleaning, putting dishes or things back where they belong
> —not just giving someone directions but drawing a map

—not just speaking to someone else but offering a handshake
—not just listening to others but actually caring
—not just giving others a smile but offering a few words

Let me share with you an example of "not just giving others a smile but offering a few words." This was a letter to Ann Landers, printed October 19, 1989:

"Last Sunday I attended an art exhibit in Michigan. I was wandering around among hundreds of people when a young woman touched my arm and said, 'You are a beautiful lady.' Ann, I was thunderstruck. I am 88 years old and never considered myself anything special to look at. But I'm healthy and happy and grateful to the good Lord for all his blessings. Maybe this is what comes through in my face.

"What a delight to be told that I am beautiful by a stranger. Every day this week I have been cheered by that lovely compliment. It gave my heart a lift.—Mrs. E. C. W., Kalamazoo."

Do you see what we can do to go above and beyond? I'm sure you can come up with many additional ideas of your own.

So you see, even in little ways, the "and then some" philosophy can help us "transmit this country better than it was transmitted to us." But how can it help us academically?

If I were to single out the biggest problem I see with students today—based on almost twenty-five years of teaching experience—it would be that students allow floors to become ceilings. That is, they allow minimal expectations to become their maximum goals. Now, I recognize that one reason why many of you are sitting here today is that you did *not* allow this to happen, but my guess is that with an "and then some" philosophy you could do much better in this area.

As Director of the basic speech-communication course on this campus, let me share with you an often-repeated experience that occurs in my office. Disgruntled students come in with a paper that they had received a "C" or "D" on from their graduate teaching assistant. Not only did they expect a "B" or an "A," but they tell me, "This is the first time I have *ever* received a 'C' or 'D' on a paper." Here is what they say as they continue, "You know," they almost always start with "you know." Dr. Weaver, "I did *everything* asked for on the assignment for the paper; I just can't understand how I could have received this grade." The first thing I ask them is whether or not they have talked to their graduate teaching assistant. In most cases they say they have; if they haven't, I send them back. If they have, then I look over the paper and read the evaluation. In most cases I find that everything they say is true: they filled all of the criteria for the paper, and they received a low grade. But, inevitably, they stopped short of the "and then some" philosophy! *You* don't need anyone else to ask these questions; you can ask them of yourself:

—What makes *my* effort outstanding or exceptional?

—How does *my* effort distinguish itself from all others submitted that also fulfill all of the criteria? . . . and most important of all . . .

—What is it that makes *mine* a genuinely individual contribution? or phrased a bit differently . . .

—Where in this effort do *I* put *my* own unique imprint on it?

Maybe you think this is unreasonable—an unfair request to make of students. But this is precisely what distinguishes the great from the "also ran," the "exceptional" from the "mediocre." Or, as my salesman friend would say, those who "met their obligations and responsibilities fairly and squarely" and those who did that *and then some*.

One of the pleasures I have in working with students is writing recommendations for them, and one of the things I love to be able to say in those recommendations is: "So-and-so was willing to go the extra mile." The Bible states it this way: ". . . and if any one forces you to go one mile, go with him two miles" (Matthew 5:41 R.S.V.).

Let me play teacher for just a second and plead with you right now. Don't just go the distance. You have the gift; you have the talent; you have the capacity. Now, take the responsibility. If it means becoming your own critic, then do it. Go the distance, *and then some*.

Okay, we've seen how the "and then some" philosophy can help our society, and we've seen how it can help us academically; let's see what kind of contribution it can make to us in our personal lives.

My first suggestion ties our personal lives to education. If I could make one suggestion to students today that would, at least could, make a major difference throughout their lives, it would be this: "become a sponge for knowledge." Never allow *any* opportunity to be an educational vacuum! Turned positively it says, get the most you can from *every* experience! There was a great book published a couple of years ago that escaped many people's attention. It was Sheldon Kopp's *Even a Stone Can Be a Teacher: Learning and Growing from the Experiences of Everyday Life*. His point is simply that every personal encounter offers something worth learning. Any experience can be enlightening. When you realize that it is what *you* bring to experiences and opportunities that create meaning, foster learning, and encourage understanding, you'll stop depending on others—especially others—to do all the teaching. You'll stop waiting to be pushed, forced, motivated, or coerced to learn; you'll start transforming your *own* life! People don't lack strength, they lack will.

The teacher we've always expected to lead, motivate, and energize us, is *us*! The teacher is us. Do you realize that that *is* the very goal of education: to instill the teacher in you!—to inspire the desire for learning in students. See, when your mind is set on fire, you *will* find ways to provide the fuel! So if you are going to be uninterested, uninformed, ignorant of what's going on in the world, you have no one to blame but yourselves. When I finally discovered that, the world became my classroom!

There are at least three hurdles (perhaps barriers)—probably many more than three—that prevent us from exercising this "and then some" philosophy—especially in our own lives: 1) our society, 2) other people, and 3) ourselves. Think about it, our society makes it so easy to become complacent and apathetic. Television and the VCR, alcohol and drugs, prepared meals and junk food, and with "the good life" portrayed to us at every turn, the message is "Relax, take it easy, calm down, become a 'couch potato.'" We are being bombarded daily with flashy, materialistic consumerism, and it is hard to resist.

And with the people around us adopting this lackadaisical philosophy of "the least possible effort," it is hard to break out from the pack. Other people actually become a barrier because if no one else cares, why should I? If no one else is doing anything, why should I? If everyone else has accepted the complacent, apathetic, "couch potato" lifestyle, why shouldn't I?

But beyond society and other people, the biggest hurdle is ourselves. What can you do to get yourself motivated? What can you do to stop putting everything off? See, that's where the "and then some" philosophy comes in. How badly do you *want* to be better—better today than yesterday? More knowledgeable, more educated, more prepared. Think how great *you* would feel if you could end *every* day feeling you've made a contribution? You made some progress today!

It takes tremendous self-discipline. It's not easy. That's why more people don't do it. That's why I'm talking to *you* about it. But it's easy to talk about; *not* easy to do. So let me give you some inspiration. We're all success-oriented, that's why we're here. And the "and then some" philosophy is designed to either keep us, or to put us, in front! To become even more successful!

We have to destroy the mind set—the prison—that we lock ourselves in. All our previous behaviors—our habits and routines—bind us, hold us in, keep us secure. Some people have labeled these our "addictions." Our friends, too, want predictable, expected behavior—nothing new. Often, even our parents stereotype us as children and regard us the same year after year. It's enough to make you lose your motivation and *any* incentive to change. It is easy to be discouraged. What is the most normal response when teachers, friends, relationship partners, and parents hold us back or ignore or reject our efforts to shed our old skin and adopt a new philosophy? We sink back into our *old* selves—the prison (or womb) in which we feel so comfortable. Why try?

It's up to us and us alone! How badly do you want it? Do you think it's worth it? Worth the fight? Socrates said, "The unexamined life isn't worth living." We have to want to discover, to explore, to find out, to challenge our self and our life, to confront who we are and who we want to become. If not us, then who?

I like talking to *this* audience because all of you have been designated "peak performers"! It is for you, especially, that this philosophy of "and then some" is so appropriate. As a peak performer, you are one who:

—uses foresight.
—plans strategically.
—"stretches" to attain specific goals.
—has high self-confidence and self-worth.
—shows responsibility and takes control.
—learns from mistakes and from the past.
—fully utilizes your time and capacities.
—knows that hard, creative work and perseverance will pay off.
—is an innovator.
—feels positive about your work and environment.
—believes in your own ability.
—acts decisively when opportunities present themselves.
—anticipates difficulties and opportunities.
—never rests on your laurels; you never stop learning.

Didn't know you were that good did you? Just imagine what this list of credits would look like if "and then some" were already internalized, implanted, and in action?

All of us want the best out of life. We want to be healthy and happy and to have things that can enrich our experience. Yet, though we strive for these things, we can end up dissatisfied. We may have a "good" life. But if we do not tap into this "and then some" philosophy—to push, shove, and even kick us into doing that little bit more, we may never awaken to the joy of being truly informed, the joy of knowing we have *really* come to know ourselves—the joy of being transformed! At that point, we can say, "I know what joy is for I have done good work!" Remember, joy is not in things, it is in us. With *and then some* internalized—part of our everyday behavior— we will give more, we will get more, and we will want more from life! It will be a life *and then some!*

The Most Pressing Issue for Our Times
William J. Byron   President, The Catholic University of America
Vital Speeches of the Day 51 (August 15, 1985): 653–55.
© City News Publishing Company. Used by permission.

You are gracious and generous to permit me to speak to you in my native language. I apologize for not being able to address you in your native tongue.

I would like to pay you the compliment of a relatively brief but serious commencement address. The thoughts I will share with you today began forming in my mind by way of response to a question proposed to me by a small group of honor students at the University of Seattle in the

United States. I was visiting the university for a public lecture on another topic. The students wrote, in advance of my visit, to ask if I would meet with them in a small group to discuss this direct and very probing question, "What is the most pressing issue you see for us in our generation?" I have been giving that question a lot of thought. I would like to explore it today with you.

My reaction to the question began with an acknowledgement that "most pressing" could mean "most immediate" or "quite urgent," but that it should not be taken in so short-term a context as to lose sight of that which is truly significant. Immediacy, urgency and significance are not always the same thing. So I chose to take "most pressing" to mean simply "most important" in a time frame that would be coextensive with the average life expectancy of those college students. This time frame pushes the perspective out by at least fifty or sixty years, assuming that life on the planet can extend its lease that long. In a very real sense, the students were asking for an estimate of just how long their lease on life would be. They are concerned about survival.

I was being asked to identify an issue of deepest significance and greatest importance to be dealt with by this collegiate generation over its allotted span of life. The question is one that can and should be asked in Taipei, as well as Seattle. It can be asked anywhere in the world. Consider the candidates for inclusion on this list of most pressing issues.

Foremost in the minds of the young in most of the world is the question of war—nuclear war with no winners. We will trip over ourselves into war, many fear, if we continue the nuclear weapons buildup in a senseless arms race with other nuclear powers. No one doubts the importance of the issue of war and peace in our time. But is *it* the "most pressing"?

Another candidate for that title is poverty—around the world and around the corner. Poverty is sustained deprivation. We have to ask: Deprived of what? Sustained by what or by whom? We can measure deprivation of food, shelter, employment, education and health care over against the levels of these necessities which basic human dignity requires for every human person. We know poverty when we see it. We do not so readily recognize its causes. Do systems—economic, political, cultural, and social—sustain the poverty we see? Or, is it sustained by persons; persons other than the poor themselves? Or, is poverty sustained by a combination of systems and persons? How do we get at the problem? How do the poor gain necessary participation in the economic system? How do deprived persons get out from under the oppressive restraints on their human potential? Is this complex problem of poverty the "most pressing" one with which our graduating collegians around the world will have to deal in the decades allotted to them?

Perhaps hunger is the most important problem. Surely for millions it is at this moment the most urgent. Hunger is the most urgent form of poverty. Chronic malnutrition and severe deprivation of food spell ultimate physical deprivation and denial of life itself. Will hunger be the "most pressing" issue confronting our world in the next half century? By the very debilitating nature of the hunger problem, it is obvious that those who must rise to the challenge of eliminating hunger are not those who are afflicted by the scourge of hunger. The same can be said of poverty.

Maybe ecological deterioration is the issue most deserving of attention. If we continue to pollute our streams, abuse our soil, poison our air and lose our croplands to erosion on the one hand and urbanization on the other, we will be without the physical base we need to sustain life. Sustainability may be *the* issue for the next half century.

Is population the most pressing problem? How about the problem of economic development, without which problems like overpopulation and undernutrition will never be brought under control?

Should the memory of the Holocaust in Germany serve to remind us that an ever present problem is our capacity to hate, to murder, to disregard and destroy human life and dignity? The contemporary "life" issues offer additional nominations for the top spot on our list of "most pressing" issues.

There are other pressing problems of course. I think of family instability, the breakup of marriages, the loss of a sense of commitment in our lives and relationships. One of the most difficult words for American youth to utter today is "forever." I know this uncertainty about themselves and their future touches youth all over the world.

I see a widespread problem of purposelessness in America's young. The nation offers them no central project; the economy tells many of them they really aren't needed. The nuclear cloud and the survival syndrome contribute ambiguity rather than clarity of purpose to their lives. The young of other nations are also searching for a sense of purpose, for direction in their lives.

Other problems—all pressing, none open to simple solutions—deserve a place on our list. This final set of problems falls into what I like to call the "isms" category. In English, the suffix "ism" throws a noun into boldface or italics. It signifies a bias, an emphasis, and almost always a disproportion. Racism, sexism, militarism, capitalism and communism would be good contemporary examples. Are the problems they connote high or low on the "most pressing" list for our times?

Atheism is surely a pressing and significant problem for this or any age. If the problem of atheism were attended to, would solutions to the other problems more readily fall into place?

Other "isms" will occur to anyone interested in taking inventory of the really important problems in the world in which we live. The list, then, is long. It is not the point of this exercise to collect, but to choose. The original question put to me by serious and appropriately concerned students was: "What is the most pressing issue you see for us in our generation?" My answer to them was, "materialism." This is the "ism" most to be feared. And materialism, I believe, is an international problem. Poor nations are not exempt; the affluent countries are most vulnerable.

It seems to me that the common denominator underlying the candidates for inclusion in any inventory of urgent, pressing, important and significant problems to be dealt with by the generation now coming out of our educational systems into our world social, political, economic and cultural systems is materialism. The word reminds us of the present and constant danger of overemphasizing the material side of our existence to the exclusion of the spiritual. To have becomes more important than to be. To possess is better than to share. To do for self takes precedence over doing for others. Property takes on more importance than people—other people, that is. And things, rather than ideas, assume a controlling influence in the lives of the materialistic majority in a materialistic society.

As the problem becomes all-pervasive, it touches virtually everyone. This, of course, means that virtually anyone can make a direct contribution toward a solution. Anyone can assess the extent to which the material has displaced the spiritual in his or her life, and decide to take corrective action to restore the balance. Anyone can take a self-administered test to estimate the relative importance of things and ideas in his or her life. Anyone can notice neglect of the soul and obsession with the body. Soul and body belong together, but they belong in balance. We are for the most part quite unbalanced. An unbalanced materialism has produced an unbalanced commercialism in many parts of the world. This permeates our recreation—our music and films—and is now stifling our spirit.

We are a people drowning in a sea of materialism, and we are not really aware that something deadly serious is afflicting us. So we bemoan our fate, buy better locks, withdraw from the needy, and escape these suffocating realities by freely permitting ourselves to become addicted to dependency devices of one kind or another, some more harmful physically and psychologically than others, all, however, taking their toll at that pay station which is me—the individual, unique human person of whatever national origin. And it is precisely there, with the person—the unique, free individual who has the power to choose—that the solution must begin.

Materialism is not the answer. We seem to be incapable of recognizing that fact. Materialism is, in fact, the question—the most pressing, significant, urgent and important question with which the present generation has to deal.

I have a suggestion for today's graduate. I suggest that you write a letter to yourself. Write it in response to the question: "What is the most pressing issue you see for yourself in the years ahead—the span of years that will constitute your postgraduation lifetime?" Be honest, of course, in writing to yourself. And be wise in using what you write. Keep that letter in a place where it can be read once a year, on your birthday, say, or on another easy-to-remember date.

Your personal response—for your eyes only—to the "most pressing issue" question will, perhaps, give you the opportunity to ask yourself: do you believe that to live easily is to live happily? Surely, happiness will figure somewhere in that letter you write. You want happiness for yourself and others. Happiness for yourself and others will have something to do with your personal engagement in the most significant issue of your time. But if the issue you select is truly important, it will admit of no easy engagement, no simple solution, no passing commitment of your time and energy. You will not live happily, if you set out now to live easily.

In that letter you write to yourself, make an estimate of the extent to which materialism has a grip on your life. That is the exact extent of the gap between you and true happiness. It also measures the distance between you and the beginning of your personal contribution to a solution to the most pressing issue you see for your time. Materialism has each one of us in its grip to some extent. So no one of us can say, "I don't know where to begin." Begin right there. Get a better balance between matter and spirit in your life. If a sufficient number of others in your generation do the same all over the world, you will notice your world coming into balance too, and that's the balance that peace and justice are made of. This is possible. And it is possible in the future that begins for you today.

The Jungle Revisited
Kimberly Hyden   Ball State University, Indiana
Coached by Kenda Creasy Dean and Kevin W. Dean
Given at the Interstate Oratorical Association, Mankato, Minnesota, Winning Orations, 1985.

> There was never the least attention paid to what was cut up for sausage. . . . Meat that had tumbled out on the floor in the dirt and (the) sawdust. The water would drip over it, and . . . the rats would race about . . . it. The rats were nuisances, (so) the packers would put poisoned bread out for them, they would die, and the rats, bread, and meat would go into the hoppers together. . . .

In 1906, when Upton Sinclair wrote *The Jungle,* conscience was the stockyard's only regulation. If they felt that rat dung would enhance the flavor of meat, then it was added. No questions asked. *The Jungle* led to pure food legislation and helped clean up and control the food processing industry. Unfortunately, today the jungle is a little closer to home, for when this *pure* food leaves the stockyards for use in *restaurants,* pure food *laws* no longer apply.

The Government estimates that we will spend some 300 billion dollars on food this year alone, and nearly half of that will be spent in restaurants. For some of us, restaurant-eating is a way of life, but as *World Health* of October, 1983, points out, restaurants are now "the main culprits" in food contamination. As a result of their carelessness, Dr. Howard Robert reports that in the last twenty-four trips you made to Noble Roman's, Wendy's, Long John Silver's, or the local pub, you have gotten food poisoning severe enough to warrant medical attention, and one in ten trips will get you a mild case of food poisoning that you may have mistaken for indigestion or a bad stomachache. But why is food poisoning so common? According to *Nation* magazine of March, 1984, it is because one in three of the restaurants that we assume to be safe—isn't.

Sometime over the course of this weekend we will all eat in a restaurant (most of us more than once), and we owe it to ourselves to reduce the risks we are taking for due to unsafe sanitation laws and inconsistent inspection policies, eating out has become risky business.

The healthfulness of restaurants urgently needs to be evaluated, but before we can correct the sanitation and inspection dilemma, we must be aware of the constituents of this dilemma.

The last time you took a break at McDonald's chances are it never crossed your mind that the Government had a hand in preparing your cheeseburger. Theoretically, this Governmental influence should guarantee you that your cheese isn't moldy and your pickles aren't limp, but it doesn't. Government regulations are hopelessly outdated and amazingly inaccurate. Ironically, even though food-related research is now costing more than 400 million dollars a year, food safety laws have not been revised since 1960, and those laws governing restaurant sanitation and inspection leave a lot to be desired.

The regulation governing restaurant sanitation, for example, allows "refrigerating facilities (to) be kept at fifty degrees Fahrenheit." But according to the July/August, 1983, *FDA Consumer,* food spoils at fifty degrees. This regulation also states the "food (should) be . . . free from . . . *gross spoilage.*" A closer examination reveals that "gross spoilage" encompasses only "insect infestation" and "rodent contamination." There are at least two problems with this statement. First, how much constitutes gross? Researchers Hinich and Staelin report that regulations allow restaurants to serve prepared mushrooms that contain no more than twenty-one maggots and seventy-five mites per fifteen ounces, and that's not gross. And second, this regulation makes no attempt to ban the use of food that has spoiled due to heat, handling, or aging.

Of course, serving spoiled or contaminated food in restaurants is a well kept secret thanks to the second problem: inconsistent inspection policies. Restaurants *are* inspected for sanitary approval, but the frequency and accuracy of these inspections are questionable at best.

Legally, health officers are required to inspect each food establishment in his or her assigned area twice a year. As the daughter of a restaurant owner, I've seen inspection at its worst. In the thirty-six years since our restaurant opened, it has received only thirty of the seventy-two required inspections with the most recent inspection coming two years ago this month. In a conversation with a health officer I learned it is standard practice to conduct inspections only once a year, and admittedly, some years contain fifteen months or more.

But even frequent examinations do not guarantee a restaurant's healthfulness. According to *U.S. News and World Report* in December of last year, Food and Drug Administration sponsored health officers should "be the consumer's advocate. (They) have got to keep an arm's length from industry and not in anyone's pocket." Unfortunately, *New York* magazine reported in June of 1983, that "inspectors have been charged (in recent years) with accepting bribes from (merchants) who wanted violations overlooked." With this in mind it should be no surprise that in a survey *Nation* found that "products from 32% of the businesses checked . . . didn't meet Federal standards, even though inspectors had given (them) 'satisfactory' ratings."

Under pressure from the FDA, New York health officers took a step in the right direction by conducting a series of unscheduled inspections. *The New York Times* reported that between April 1 and September 9 of last year, 646 area restaurants were cited for "violating (the) health code" and closed until the violations were corrected. These businesses included several Burger Kings and Kentucky Fried Chickens, Luigi's and Mayor Koch's favorite restaurant.

Unfortunately, New York City is not the only place where restaurants pose a health hazard. According to *The New York Times,* on June 3, 1984, at a sports banquet in Hoboken, New Jersey, 169 athletes, cheerleaders, and coaches were hospitalized for food poisoning. The cause? The banquet's main course was refrigerated at just under fifty degrees.

If you have never had a severe case of food poisoning, consider yourself lucky because author Elliot Dewberry points out that the instances of food-borne illnesses has increased more than twentyfold since 1946, and now, one in twenty cases of medically detected food poisoning results in death.

If you find these statistics a little hard to believe, call Hoboken, New Jersey, where seven of the athletes, cheerleaders, and coaches died.

The December 3, 1984, *U.S. News and World Report* stated that the FDA:

> is viewed by industry and the American public (alike) as both a guardian angel and the devil incarnate. (It is) . . . an agency of 7,000 people (who) . . . have the responsibility for monitoring a 450 billion dollar industry that accounts for twenty-five cents of every dollar spent in the country.

This is a responsibility that they seem not to take seriously. According to *Nation,* the FDA sponsors "a total of 359 . . . Federal (food-related) programs." The first step toward establishing new legislation would be to give one of these 359 agencies the exclusive right to set the standards for restaurant sanitation and inspection. Once established, this agency should accept the *Burns Statutes* as law. The *Burns Statutes* are not laws but rather recommendations for restaurant sanitation and inspection that are based on the utmost common sense. The statutes recommend that refrigerating facilities be kept between thirty-two and thirty-six degrees Fahrenheit and nonperishable foods should be kept in airtight storage cases to protect them from "filth . . . insects, (and) vermin," as well as bacterial spoilage. The *Burns Statutes* also recommend that the inspection process be made a checks and balance system with inspectors as well as restaurant management being subject to legal prosecution if the articles are violated. This plan would be achieved by using some of the 400 million dollars in research funds to establish a state level committee whose only duty would be inspecting the inspectors.

The *Burns Statutes* contain many good ideas, and one simple piece of legislation can make them law and stop millions of *us* from being needlessly poisoned. Food poisoning is never pleasant, and it can be deadly. It can also be prevented by executing a simple three point plan every time you eat out. First, upon entering a restaurant, look for a current health permit. This permit is issued following a satisfactory inspection and should be visible to *all* customers. Although the possession of a health permit does not guarantee a restaurant's sanitation, its absence assures contamination. Second, avoid ordering spicy food or foods that have been prepared in advance. *Travel Holiday* of May, 1983, reports that spices are often used to mask food discoloration and odor, and according to *World Health,* the "preparation of food . . . in advance of eating . . . allow(s) (harmful bacteria) to multiply," and third, if something you've ordered tastes at all strange, *stop eating,* and demand an explanation. Consumer awareness—and involvement—will make all the difference.

In 1906, Upton Sinclair told us of "meat that was . . . found (to be) sour, and how they would rub it up with soda to take away the smell, and sell it at the . . . lunch counters." Seventy-nine years later not much has changed. For due to unsafe sanitation laws and inconsistent inspection policies, it's still a jungle out there.

Scoliosis
Susan Jones   Auburn University
Used by permission.

Everyone sit up straight! How many of you have ever been told this, sit or stand up straight? Most of us think that this was just an annoying command our mother liked to give to criticize us about our poor posture. But have you ever thought about how lucky you are to be able to stand up straight? There is a spinal abnormality that develops during adolescence, and if not detected and treated early, can cause severe curvature of the spine. This abnormality is called scoliosis. I am very familiar with scoliosis because my sister has it and has just recently finished treatment.

Today, I would like to talk to you about the problem of scoliosis. First, I will explain what scoliosis is, its treatments, and its effects on a person's health. Second, I will tell you about school screening programs, one solution to this problem.

Scoliosis, as defined in a paper entitled *Scoliosis* published by The Scoliosis Association, Inc., is a lateral or sidewards curvature of the spine. Scoliosis is not a disease and does not result from anything that the parents or child did or did not do. A pamphlet entitled *Brace Yourself for Scoliosis* published by the University Youth Spine Center lists several causes of scoliosis. These include being born with improperly formed vertebrae, having muscle weakness or paralysis, or suffering a severe injury. In most cases, the cause of scoliosis is unknown and is referred to as idiopathic scoliosis. According to *Scoliosis—A Handbook for Patients* published by the Scoliosis Research Society, this type of scoliosis is responsible for approximately 75 to 90 percent of cases treated in most scoliosis centers. Consider this fact: the Scoliosis Association states that 10 percent of the adolescent population has some degree of scoliosis. This means one million children in the United States alone have scoliosis, and approximately one-fourth of these will require medical attention.

The term "medical attention" brings me to my next point: the effects of scoliosis on a person's health. According to an article entitled "Diagnosing and Treating Curvature of the Spine," by Louise Fenner, a writer for the Food and Drug Administration, as a spine with scoliosis grows, it gradually rotates on its own axis. This rotation pulls the rib cage around so that, in the back, one side of the rib cage becomes higher. The ribs on the inward side of the curve are gathered together, while those on the outer edge are spread apart. This distortion of the rib cage can restrict the lungs and result in respiratory problems. Also, heart problems can possibly result. Research has shown that, on the average, adults with advanced forms of scoliosis die younger than those without scoliosis.

These effects, however, do not have to occur. There are three basic treatments for scoliosis which I would like to cover briefly. Discussed in *Brace Yourself for Scoliosis* are observation, bracing, and surgery. Observation is exactly what it says. the patient is watched to make sure the curve does not progress further. Braces are designed to stop the progression of mild or moderate curves. Finally, surgery is employed when no other treatment can prevent the curve from interfering with a healthy life-style. Surgery involves fusing a portion of the spinal column to prevent curve progression.

As is the case for most illnesses, in order for treatment to be successful, diagnosis must be made early. The solution I propose is school screening programs—a way of early detection. Because the onset of scoliosis is gradual and coincides with "growth spurt" years, a program designed to check children between the ages of ten and thirteen could provide detection before scoliosis has time to progress too far. Doris R. Cantrell, a graduate of Auburn University, wrote her master's thesis on the "Reliability of Health and Physical Education Teachers' Screening for Scoliosis After Instruction." Her study involved eight junior high schools and eight health or physical education instructors. These teachers underwent three two-hour training sessions to learn the testing procedure. The test involved two observations—a standing and a forward bending test. In the standing observation the child is observed from the back. The teachers look for obvious curvature and differences in the hip or shoulder levels. These things are again looked for in the forward bending test. Four thousand and nineteen students were examined during the course of her research. During the examination period 85.7% adequate referrals were made. This statistical interpretation indicates that health and physical education teachers, after instruction, can adequately screen students and refer to specialists those thought to have scoliosis. These referrals are early detection and are what could keep scoliosis from progressing too far. Therefore, they are a possible solution to the scoliosis problem.

Today, I hope you have learned about a problem of our society that frequently goes unnoticed. I have explained what scoliosis is, its types of treatment, and its effects on a victim's health. The solution I have proposed is school screening programs. I hope, now, that you understand how the programs would work. Also, by learning of the successful early detections made in Doris Cantrell's study, I believe that you can see that screening programs are one solution to the problem of scoliosis.

1. Brower, Eleanor M. and Nancy H. Hinckley. *Brace Yourself for Scoliosis.* Ohio: The University Youth Spine Center, 1979.
2. Cantrell, Doris R. "Reliability of Health and Physical Education Teachers' Screening for Scoliosis After Instruction." diss. Auburn University, 1982.
3. Fenner, Louis. "Diagnosing and Treating Curvature of the Spine," *Consumers Research,* October, 1984: 24–25.
4. *Scoliosis.* The Scoliosis Association, Inc., 1979.
5. *Scoliosis: A Handbook for Patients.* Scoliosis Research Society.

Smoking

Lori Kennedy   Auburn University
Used by permission.

"It's the puff of glamour, the smile of sin, the grit of pain all rolled into one." This is what William Weis and Bruce Miller think about smoking. More than 500,000 Americans a year die as a result of smoking. Smoking is a very real problem facing our society today. It affects all of us. I know it has directly affected me by causing the death of two members in my immediate family. As a result I became interested in the problem of smoking and did extensive research in the area. If it hasn't already it will probably affect you too in one way or another sometime during your lifetime.

Today, I would like to talk to you about smoking, a serious problem facing us today, and one possible solution to it: quitting. First, I will tell you why people smoke and the effects of it. Second, I will offer one solution to the problem, quitting, and how it can be achieved.

Dr. Dee Burton and Gary Wohl in their book, *The Joy of Quitting,* offer a couple of initial reasons people start to smoke. First is the influence of others: "all my friends do," "it's the cool thing to do," or "because my parents do." All of these are influences of others. A second reason people start to smoke is media hype. Burton and Wohl found that, in 1975 alone, 275 million dollars were spent on cigarette advertising in the United States. This advertising was done in magazines, newspapers, billboards and such. There were no television commercials because they have been outlawed. These ads suggest to women that it's the liberated thing to do. It's sexy, sophisticated, and glamorous. These ads also promote the idea that these cigarettes are safer because they're low in tar and nicotine, which is a chemical found in tobacco, but there's no evidence to support this. According to Morton Arkava, author of *Kick the Smoking Habit,* there are a few other reasons people smoke. They like the taste of tobacco, it helps them relax, or they think it prevents weight gain, which is false. You're smoking rather than eating, and chewing gum would work just as well as a cigarette.

All of these are reasons people begin smoking. Why do they continue to smoke? They become addicted: it's habit forming, or it's a way for them to relieve stress. I've discussed why people smoke: the influence of others, media hype, the taste of tobacco, helps them relax, and they think it prevents weight gain. They continue to smoke because it's addictive, habit forming, and a way to relieve stress.

Now let's look at the effects of smoking. There are several bad effects of cigarette smoking. According to the Surgeon General in a report entitled the *Health Consequences of Smoking,* smoking can cause several bad health effects. The first of these is lung disease. Approximately 70 percent of chronic obstructive lung disease deaths are attributed to cigarette smoking. Eighty-five percent of lung cancer is directly attributable to smoking.

Emphysema is another lung disease caused from cigarette smoking. Emphysema causes a shortness of breath, making it difficult to breathe. My grandfather had emphysema and he just ran out of breath and died.

Another effect of smoking is to pregnant women. It can harm the fetus. The average birthweight of a child born to a smoker is less than that of a child born to a nonsmoker. Smoking can cause spontaneous abortion. In addition, the children of smokers show a greater susceptibility to respiratory diseases.

Heart disease is another effect of smoking. Cigarette smoking is one of the major risk factors contributing to the development of chronic heart disease. Dr. Alton Ochsner in his book *Smoking and Your Life* states that cigarette smoking causes an increase in heart beat and blood pressure. This puts a strain on your heart and can be especially dangerous in people who are already suffering from a heart condition. Dr. Ochsner also says that according to the Surgeon General's report the death rate among smokers from coronary disease is 70 percent higher than among nonsmokers. Cigarette smoking causes a weakening of the heart and reduces your life.

So far I have discussed with you the problem of smoking: why people smoke and the effects, such as lung disease, harm to the fetus of a pregnant woman, and heart disease. I would now like to offer the only true safe solution to smoking: quitting. The book *Smoke-Free Workplace,* by William Weis and Bruce Miller, points out that no matter the length of time you've smoked it's always beneficial to stop. Within the first few days after you quit, your body starts to repair the damage caused to your heart and lungs.

But how do you quit? In his book, Dr. Alton Ochsner offers a program to stop smoking. First, stop: abruptly, completely, and permanently. Just go cold turkey. Second, build up your resolution. Say, "I'm going to stop. I'm going to break this habit." Next, burn the bridges to the habit. Throw away any cigarettes, cigarette holders, ashtrays—anything that might tempt you to pick up a cigarette. Time your break. Do it at a time when you're not in a totally smoking environment. Deny the withdrawal symptoms which consist of nervousness, irritability, and craving for a cigarette. This is half the battle. Adopt a substitute habit: chew gum, drink a glass of water, or something like this when you want a cigarette. Finally, think of the benefits. You're probably prolonging your life.

Remember, it's never too late to stop. Do it abruptly, completely, and permanently. Build up your resolution. Burn the bridges to the habit. Time your break. Deny the withdrawal symptoms. Adopt a substitute habit. Finally, think of the benefits.

I hope today I've given you some insight into the problem of smoking. First, we looked at why people smoke and the effects. Next, we looked at the one safe solution to the problem: quitting. I hope now you can see just how serious the problem of smoking is and now know how to beat this dangerous habit.

1. Arkava, Morton L. *Kick the Smoking Habit.* Saratoga, California: R & E Publishers, 1984.
2. Burton, Dee and Gary Wohl. *The Joy of Quitting.* New York: Macmillan Publishing Company, Inc., 1979.
3. *Health Consequences of Smoking: The Changing Cigarette.* Washington, D.C.: U.S. Department of Health and Human Services, 1981.
4. Ochsner, Alton. *Smoking and Your Life.* New York: Julian Messner, 1965.
5. Weis, William L. and Bruce W. Miller. *The Smoke-Free Workplace.* New York: Prometheus Books, 1985.

Glossary

A

active listening Listening that involves all four aspects of the listening process: creating mental images, empathizing with the speaker's emotions, capitalizing on the difference between the speaking and thinking rate, and responding to the speaker's communication.

actuative claim An assertion or conclusion that deals with questions of policy, whether or not a thing should be done.

affective component One of three components of an attitude. It consists of the feelings that a person has about an object, concept, or person.

alliteration The repetition of a sound in two or more words in the same sentence.

analogy A method of reasoning concluding that when two particulars are alike in a number of known respects, they will be alike in an unknown respect.

> **analogy, figurative** One in which the comparison involves members of two different classes.

> **analogy, literal** One in which the comparison is of two members of the same class.

analyze To identify the major divisions or constituent parts of a topic.

articulation The creation of sounds by interfering with the outward flow of air through the mouth and nose to create the various sounds of a language.

assimilation The acceptable running together of sounds in normal speech. Too little assimilation results in overly precise speech. Too much assimilation results in unintelligible speech. A proper amount creates speech that is intelligible and easy to listen to.

asyndeton The omission of conjunctions between a series of related clauses.

attention The focusing of perception on specific stimuli in the environment and the processing of those stimuli.

attentive listening Involves maintaining eye contact with the speaker, avoiding distracting projects, avoiding daydreaming and distracting behavior.

attitude A judgment, evaluation, or feeling about a person, object, or concept.

attraction One of the five sources of ethos. It is created by developing a positive orientation with people.

audience analysis The identification of listeners' characteristics that affect the way they will probably respond to a communication.

B

backing for the warrant Evidence and reasoning used to make the warrant credible and acceptable to listeners.

barriers Anything that interferes with communication, causing an incorrect meaning or no meaning to be communicated.

behavioral component One of three components of an attitude. It involves the actions that a person takes toward an object, concept, or person as a result of one or more attitudes.

boomerang A change of attitude by listeners opposite from that desired by a speaker.

385

C

causal pattern   A method of organizing the main points in a speech according to their cause-effect relationship.

causal reasoning   An attempt to explain why something has happened or will happen.

centrality   A characteristic of an attitude. It refers to its importance or role in the whole attitude system.

channel   The means by which communicative stimuli are transmitted from a source to a receiver.

chiasmus   A sentence of two parts in which the second is syntactically balanced against the first but with the parts reversed.

chronological pattern   A method of organizing the main ideas in a speech according to their relationship in time.

claim   An assertion or conclusion made on the basis of evidence and a warrant.

cognitive component   One of three components of an attitude. It refers to the perceptions, thoughts, and beliefs a person has about an object, concept, or person.

cognitive consistency   Refers to the effort on the cognitive level to restore balance to our attitudinal system when two or more attitudes become imbalanced.

communication   The way in which human beings develop and share meaning.

competence   One of the five sources of ethos. It is established by expertise or an indication that the speaker is a source of valid information.

conclusion   The final part of a speech designed to focus the listeners' thoughts on the subject of the speech, leave a favorable image of the speaker in the listeners' minds, and give a sense of completeness to the speech.

constructive listening   Involves keeping an open mind, looking for points of agreement, identifying the central idea and organizational pattern of the speech, and deciding whether to listen for general ideas or specific details.

content   All information used in supporting the speaker's statement of purpose.

conversational mode   A manner of delivering a speech that gives an impression that the speaker is conversing with the listeners.

credibility-centered ethics   A form of ethics recognizing that a speaker's credibility will be dependent on the ethics he or she embraces.

credulity, primitive   The belief that those things we experience are real, i.e., that our senses cannot mislead us.

D

definitive claim   Concerned with questions of definition, what a thing is.

demographic analysis   Identification of potential listeners' important and salient characteristics in order to make inferences about their attitudes.

designative claim   Concerned with questions of fact, whether a thing is true.

direction   A characteristic of an attitude. It identifies whether the attitude is positive or negative, favorable or unfavorable.

door-in-the-face technique   To make of another person an extreme request that will be refused, then to present a more moderate request that will generally be granted.

E

economy   The use of no more words than necessary to communicate a particular meaning.

empathy   The feeling by listeners or spectators that they are a part of whatever they are observing. It is what makes us recoil when we see someone else about to get hit.

ends and means ethics   A type of ethics claiming that desirable ends justify any means of attaining them.

enthusiastic listening   Desire to hear what the speaker has to say, and to focus on positive features of the communicative situation.

ethos   The impression the speaker makes with his or her communication. The credibility of a speaker stemming from competence, trustworthiness, similarity, attraction, and sincerity.

euphemism   The substitution of a word that is inoffensive for one that would offend listeners.

evaluative claim   Concerned with questions of value, what the merit of a thing is.

evidence   Something that gives reason for believing. It is something that shows or proves.

exemplify   To present examples to make meaning clear.

extemporaneous   A well-prepared speech that has not been written or memorized. The exact choices of words and construction of sentences are made during delivery of the speech.

eye contact   To look directly into the eyes of the people with whom we communicate.

F

facial expression   To reflect in your face the emotions and feelings that you experience as you communicate with others.

factual information   Evidence that is verifiable by objective measurements, sensory perception, or historical investigation.

fallacy   A process of reasoning that is faulty or in error.

fallacy, special   Tricky or specious devices—use of language, source materials, and audience attitudes and values—used to prevent others from perceiving the nonlogical basis of a person's statement or conclusion.

   appeal to tradition   The argument that a current practice should be continued because that is the way it has always been done.

   appeal to ignorance   The argument that because others cannot prove that a proposal will not work, it should be adopted even though its advocate cannot prove that it will work.

   appeal to authority   The argument that a proposal should be adopted because some authority—a governor, a professor, a minister—says we should.

   attack on a person   The argument that a proposal should not be adopted because the person advocating that position is not a desirable person.

   appeal to emotions   The argument that a person should take a certain action because it is something he or she would enjoy or it is something that would be detrimental to someone he or she dislikes.

   appeal to popular approval   The argument that a proposal should be adopted because it is desired by a majority of the people.

feedback   The reactions and responses of listeners that are perceived by the communicative source.

foot-in-the-door technique   To request a small favor from a person, and when it is granted to request a larger favor.

frame of reference   A perspective from which to evaluate and respond to messages, people, and situations.

G

general purpose   An objective in a speech, the general response you want the listeners to make.

generalization   The making of a conclusion about a class of objects based on the examination of a representative sample.

gestures   Movements of the head, shoulders, hands, and arms used to assist in communicating ideas.

I

identification   To adopt the behavior of another person or group because it is associated with a satisfying, self-defining relationship to a person or a group.

illustration A detailed example.

impromptu speech To give a speech unexpectedly with no prior warning or preparation.

inform To provide data in order that the listeners will become more knowledgeable.

intensity A characteristic of an attitude. It refers to the strength—strong, mild, weak—of an attitude.

interpersonal communication Communication that involves more than one person.

intrapersonal communication Communication that takes place in one person. It involves no one else.

introduction The opening part of a speech designed to get the attention of the listeners, establish the ethos of the speaker, and start the listeners thinking about the subject of the speech.

issue-relevant argument An argument resulting from careful and thoughtful deliberation about the quality of the reasoning and evidence presented to support an argument.

K

kinesics The study of body action and its function in communication.

L

latitude of acceptance The number of attitude positions on a continuum that a person will find acceptable.

listening A communication skill of great complexity that involves four distinct processes: receiving, perceiving, interpreting, and responding.

    receiving One of the four processes of listening that consists of seeing and hearing.

    perceiving One of the four processes of listening that enables a person to focus on specific stimuli in the environment.

    interpreting One of the four processes of listening that involves discerning the intended meaning of a communication.

    responding One of the four processes of listening that involves overt responses and requires active processing of the speaker's ideas.

loose sentence A sentence in which the main idea is revealed in the first part of the sentence.

loudness The psychological interpretation by a listener of the intensity or amplitude of a vibrating object.

M

manuscript speech A speech that has been written and is delivered by reading from the manuscript.

meaning The understanding that a specific person has of anything in his or her environment.

    intensional Meaning that cannot be observed because it exists only in the mind of a person.

    extensional Meaning that can be observed. The person using a word can point to the object. Thus, another person can observe the meaning of a symbol.

    triangle of meaning A triangle that graphically shows the relationship between a symbol and an object.

measure of central tendency A measure that identifies an average measurement of a group.

    mean A measure of central tendency that is computed by summing the values of all items and dividing the sum by the number of items included.

    median A measure of central tendency that is determined by ranking the items from lowest to highest and then identifying the item one-half the distance between the lowest and highest. That item is the median.

    mode A measure of central tendency that identifies the datum or class of data that occurs most frequently.

memorized speech A speech that is completely written out, memorized, and delivered from memory.

motivated sequence A method of developing a persuasive speech originated by Alan H. Monroe. It utilizes five main divisions—*attention, need, satisfaction, visualization, and action*—to present a persuasive speech.

N

narration   To relate a sequence of events or to tell a story.

nonfluencies   Breaks in a speaker's fluency, usually filled by "uh," "and-uh," "you know," etc.

nonverbal   Communication that is achieved by bodily action, facial expression, vocal inflection, and other nonlanguage sounds.

O

objective listening   To listen with an open mind, to avoid selective perception, and to guard against emotional reactions to anything a speaker says.

occasional speeches   Special types of speeches that are adapted to the specific occasion. See also *speech of introduction, speech of nomination, speech of presentation, speech to commemorate, speech to entertain, and speech to stimulate.*

one-sided speech   A persuasive speech that only presents arguments for the position advocated by the speaker.

opinion, expert   Testimony given by a person who is an expert in the field on which he is speaking.

organization   A method of developing not only the major parts of a speech, but also the subordinate divisions within each of those parts.

P

parallel structure   To phrase in a similar way parts of a sentence or paragraph that are of equal importance.

pause   A meaningful moment of silence during speaking.

perceiving   One of the four processes of listening that enables a person to focus on specific stimuli in the environment.

performance apprehension   The normal anxiety that occurs in a person confronted with a situation in which the performance is important and the outcome uncertain.

periodic sentence   A sentence in which the main idea is not presented until the end of the sentence.

peripheral cue   A cause of persuasion that does not involve deliberation about the quality of information presented in a persuasive message. Instead, persuasion results from some quality of the speaker, such as appearance or sincerity.

persuade   To create a new belief or attitude, to change the direction of an existing attitude, to increase the intensity of an existing attitude, or to obtain a behavioral response.

pitch   The psychological interpretation of the sound produced by the frequency of the vibrations of a vibrating object.

preparation outline   An outline used in preparing a speech. It helps to check the logical relationship of ideas and supporting materials. It is not used in giving the speech.

preview   Tells the listeners exactly what the main points of the speech will be. Is an extension of the purpose sentence.

problem-solution pattern   A method of organizing a speech so that there are two main parts of the body: explanation of a problem and description of a solution.

pronunciation   The way in which words are spoken.

public opinion polls   Scientific methods of identifying attitudes and beliefs of various groups of citizens.

purpose sentence (thesis)   The sentence that tells listeners specifically what a speaker is going to talk about in a speech.

purposeful listening   To have a specific objective in mind when one listens to any communication.

purpose-oriented analysis   A method of analyzing an audience which focuses on the potential interaction of a particular speech topic and relevant attitudes of a specific group of listeners.

Photo Credits

Photo research by Mike Hurm.

Table of Contents and Part Openers

Part 1 and 2: © James Shaffer; **Part 3:** © Alan Carey/The Image Works; **Part 4:** © Howard Dratch/The Image Works

Chapter 1
Opener: © Robert Kalman/The Image Works; **p. 7:** © Alan Carey/The Image Works; **p. 11:** © James Shaffer

Chapter 2
Opener: © James Shaffer; **p. 19:** © James Shaffer; **p. 21:** © Theodore Mann

Chapter 3
Opener: © James Shaffer; **p. 28:** AP/Wide World Photos; **3.1:** © James Shaffer; **p. 32:** AP/Wide World Photos; **3.2:** © Theodore Mann

Chapter 4
Opener: © Howard Dratch/The Image Works; **p. 44:** © John Maher/EKM-Nepenthe; **p. 49:** © Patsy Davidson/The Image Works

Chapter 5
Opener: © James Shaffer; **p. 56:** Historical Pictures Service, Inc.; **p. 59:** © James Shaffer

Chapter 6
Opener: © James Shaffer; **p. 66:** Historical Pictures Service, Inc.; **p. 69:** US Army/FPG International; **p. 74:** Historical Pictures Service, Inc.

Chapter 7
Opener: © Ken Olson; **p. 81:** © James Shaffer; **p. 84:** © Robert Eckert/EKM-Nepenthe; **p. 89:** © James Shaffer; **p. 93:** © James Ballard

Chapter 8
Opener: © James Shaffer; **p. 109:** © James Shaffer

Chapter 9
Opener: © James Shaffer; **p. 121:** The Bettmann Archive

Chapter 10
Opener: © James Shaffer; **133:** © James Shaffer

Chapter 11
Opener: © James Shaffer; **pp. 144, 151:** © James Shaffer

Chapter 12
Opener: © Richard Anderson

Chapter 13
Opener: © James Shaffer; **p. 182:** © James Ballard; **p. 190:** © Alan Carey/The Image Works; **p. 195:** © James Shaffer

Chapter 14
Opener: © James Shaffer; **p. 211:** © Robert Kalman/The Image Works; **p. 216:** © Robert Eckert/EKM-Nepenthe; **p. 219:** © Mike Douglas/The Image Works

Chapter 15
Opener: © James Shaffer; **p. 228:** © Robert Eckert/EKM-Nepenthe; **p. 234:** © Robert Kalman/The Image Works

Chapter 16
Opener: © Richard Anderson; **p. 255:** UPI/Bettmann Newsphotos; **p. 263:** © James Ballard

Chapter 17
Opener: © James Shaffer

Chapter 18
Opener: AP/Wide World Photos; **p. 292:** © Mark Antman/The Image Works; **pp. 296, 299:** © James Ballard

Chapter 19
Opener: UPI/Bettmann Newsphotos; **p. 307:** © James Shaffer; **p. 314:** © Mark Antman/The Image Works; **p. 321:** © James Shaffer

Chapter 20
Opener: © James Shaffer; **p. 334:** AP/Wide World Photos; **pp. 338, 342:** © James Shaffer; **p. 345:** AP/Wide World Photos

Name Index

Petty, R. E., 311, 328
Phillips, W., 98
Pirie, M., 177
Pond, J. B., 102
Powell, F. A., 329
Pritzker, H., 327
Pronovost, W., 245

R

Radloff, R., 39
Rajecki, D. W., 102
Rea, R. G., 330
Reagan, R., 27, 58
Reinsch, N. L., Jr., 264, 268
Rhine, R., 328
Richards, I. A., 249, 250
Robinson, E. R., 33, 39
Roosevelt, F. D., 121, 122
Roper, B. W., 147
Rosemier, R., 283
Rosenbaum, L., 327
Rosenberg, M., 329
Roskens, R. W., 218, 219, 222, 354, 357,
    358, 359, 360

S

Saine, T. J., 76
Satterthwaite, L., 283
Saunders, D. E., 268
Schambra, W., 158
Scheier, M. F., 42, 52
Schmidt, H., 206, 330
Schuller, C. F., 283
Schweitzer, D., 76
Sears, D., 206
Secord, P. F., 76
Seligman, C., 314, 328
Severance, L., 328
Shaffer, L. F., 26, 38
Sharp, H., Jr., 206
Shearer, L., 268
Sheets, B. V., 28, 34, 39
Sheffield, F. D., 330
Sherif, C. W., 101, 308, 327
Sherif, M., 101, 308, 327, 329
Siipola, E., 206
Sikkink, D. E., 157, 158
Silas, C. J., 222
Silber, J. R., 301
Simpson, R. H., 268
Singer, R., 329
Sleemer, P., 283
Smith, D. K., 346
Smith, R. G., 77, 206
Spicer, C., 205

Sponberg, H., 330
Starr, P., 158
Steer, M. D., 245
Stetler, C. J., 77
Stevens, W. W., 128
Stinson, G. A., 317, 329
Stockman, D., 153
Stokes, D. E., 102
Stotland, E., 206
Svehla, G., 102

T

Taft, H. W., 128
Tannenbaum, P., 76, 306, 327
Taylor, A., 222
Thistlethwaite, D. L., 206, 330
Thomas, C. K., 242
Thomas, N., 117, 118, 128
Thompson, E., 205
Thonssen, L., 56, 61
Thrall, W. F., 269
Tiffin, J., 245
Toulmin, S., 161, 162, 163, 164, 177
Trembley, G., 329
Truman, H. S., 117
Tubbs, S. L., 206
Tucker, R. K., 158
Turner, J., 327
Turner, J. A., 76
Turner, R. H., 102
Twain, M., 254, 267

U

Uhler, L. K., 221

V

Vernon, M. D., 52
Vick, C. F., 267
Vincent, J. E., 328
Vohs, J. L., 225, 245
Volkhart, E. H., 327

W

Wagner, G. A., 157
Waldhart, E. S., 52
Walker, D., 301
Walpole, H. R., 268
Walstad, W. B., 221
Walster, E., 77
Wanniski, J., 281
Watts, J. C., 329
Weddle, P., 158

Subject Index

fear and, 318–19
foot-in-the-door technique, 314–15
involve hearers' emotions, 312–14
motivating factors, and, 320–21
reward or incentive and, 319–20
show desired behavior approves, 316
Channel, 9–10
Chiasmus, 265
Chronological pattern of organization,
190–91
Claim, 162–63
defined, 162–63
types of, 162
Clarity, 256–59
Cognitive component of attitudes, 80
Cognitive consistency, 85
Cognitive dissonance, 85
Commitment, degree of, 306
Common ground, 71
Communication, 5–14
characteristics of, 4–6
credibility and, 3–4
definition of, 4–6
elements of, 6–14
Communication model, 5
Communication process, 6–14
barriers to communication, 11–12
channel, 9–10
feedback, 12–14
message, 9
receiver, 10–11
situation, 6–8
source, 8
Comparison, 295
Competence, ethos and, 67–69
Comprehension of message, 181
Conclusions, 214–20
length of, 215
purposes of, 214–15
types of, 215–20
Concreteness, 146
Congruency theory, 85
Content, 140–59
consistent with listeners' experiences,
142–43
from a respected or authoritative
source, 143
high-ethos source and, 143–45
knowledge and attitudes of listeners
and, 141–42
sources of, 130–38
specific and credible evidence and,
143–45
types of, 147–56
Contrast, 295–96
Conversational mode, 22–23
Credibility, 3–4, 63–65
Credibility-centered ethics, 58–60
Criticism of speeches, 347–60
artistic standards and, 353–54
bases for, 349–53

eclectic principles and, 353
ideas and, 352
a model speech, 354–57
motives and ethics and, 352–53
reasons for learning, 348–49
results and, 349–51

D

Definition, 213, 291–93
Definition of communication, 4–6
Demographic analysis, 86–91
Demonstration, 291
Demonstration boards, 271–72
Description, 294
Development of speech, 184–97
Dialects, 241–43
Differences between outline and speech,
204
Documents, 132
Door-in-the-face technique, 315–16

E

Eastern dialect, 241
Economy, 261–62
Effective sentence structure, 265–66
Elements of communicative process, 6–14
Empathy, 229
Emphasis, 241
Encyclopedias, 136–37
Ends and means, 55–56
Entertaining, 343–44
Ethical bases of speaking, 55–60
credibility-centered, 58–60
ends and means, 55–56
situation, 57–58
social utility, 56–57
Ethics, freedom of speech and, 54–55
Ethos, 63–77
definition of, 63–65
sources of, 66–75
Euphemism, 258
Evidence, 143–56
definition of, 147
instances in which helpful, 145
Toulmin model and, 163
types of, 147–56
ways should be used, 146
Evocative speaking, 331–46
commemorate, 341–43
entertain, 343–44
introduction, 337–40
nomination, 344–45
presentation, 340–41
stimulate, 332–37
Example, 212, 218
Exemplify, 294–95

M

Manuscript, reading from, 119–23
  advantages of, 120
  comparison with extemporaneous, 122–23
  disadvantages of, 121–22
  principles of, 119–20
Meaning, 247–57
  definition of, 247–48
  language and, 247–57
  reality and, 251–57
  triangle of, 250
Memorized presentation, 123–24
  advantages of, 123
  disadvantages of, 123–24
Message, 9
Metaphors, 264
Methods of forming and changing attitudes, 311–22
  appeal to alternative value premise, 317–18
  appeal to motivating factors, 320–21
  arouse fear in listeners, 318–19
  build case with evidence and reasoning, 311–12
  involve hearers' emotions, 312–14
  offer reward or incentive, 319–20
  show desired behavior approved by esteemed person, 316
  show proposal consistent or inconsistent with value premise, 316–17
  use door-in-face technique, 315–16
  use foot-in-door technique, 314–15
Methods of presentation, 116–28
  extemporaneous, 117–19
  impromptu, 124–27
  manuscript, 119–23
  memory, 123–24
Motion picture projector, 275
Motivated sequence, 195–96
Motive, 79
Movement, 227

N

Narration, 290–91
Noise. *See* Barriers to communication
Nonverbal communication, 224–43
  physical behavior, 225–33
  vocal behavior, 234–43
Note cards, sample, 137–38
Notes, use of, 119

O

Objectives of informative speeches, 287–89
  balanced development, 288
  clarity, 287–88
  retention of material, 289
Obstacles to changing attitudes, 303–11
  degree of commitment, 306
  discrepancy, 308–9
  group pressure, 310–11
  public commitment, 307
  selective exposure, 305–6
  selective perception, 304
  selective recall, 305
Occasion, speech, 107–8
One-sidedness vs. two-sidedness, 322–24
One-sided speech, 325
Opinion, 147–51
Oral style, 260
Organization, 180–206
  attitude change and, 182–83
  ethos of speaker and, 182
  informative speech and, 296–99
  listener's comprehension of message and, 181
  listener's frustration and, 183
  one-sided speech and, 325
  persuasive speech and, 324–25
  two-sided speech and, 325
Originality in language, 263–65
Outline, sample, 199–201
Overhead projector, 273

P

Parallel structure, 264–65
Patterns of organization, 190–96
  causal pattern, 193–94
  chronological pattern, 190–91
  motivated sequence, 195–96
  problem-solution, 194
  spatial pattern, 191–92
  topical pattern, 192–93
Pause, 240–41
Performance apprehension, 25–39
  bodily action and, 36
  concentration and, 36–37
  controlling, 33–38
  harmful, 32–33
  helpful reactions from, 29
  not peculiar to certain people, 27–29
  physiological reactions and, 29–31
  speaking experience and, 34–35
  students and, 27

DATE DUE

DEMCO